China

China

by
Robert Delfs
Thomas D. Gorman
and
Owen D. Nee, Jr

Published by
Euromoney Publications
in association with

The Bank of East Asia

Berenberg Bank

Coudert Brothers

First Interstate Bancorp

Peat, Marwick, Mitchell & Co

Swiss Bank Corporation

Westpac Banking Corporation

Published by
Euromoney Publications Limited
Nestor House, Playhouse Yard
London EC4V 5EX

Copyright © Euromoney Publications 1986

ISBN 0 903121 82 4

Typeset by PW Graphics
Printed in Hong Kong by
Mandarin Offset Ltd

Contents

Euromoney is grateful to The Bank of East Asia Limited, Berenberg Bank, Coudert Brothers, First Interstate Bancorp, Peat, Marwick, Mitchell & Co, Swiss Bank Corporation and Westpac Banking Corporation for their support and assistance in the preparation of this book.

Preface

by Lord Chalfont

China is one of the giants of civilisation. It covers nearly 10 million square kilometres of the earth's surface; and it has a population of over a billion – twice that of the United States and the Soviet Union combined. As Michael Yahuda points out in the historical introduction to this book, China, alone among the great nations of the world, has a continuous history of statehood and culture stretching back into distant antiquity. No western visitor of average sensibility can fail to be overwhelmed by this sense of history, by the traditions and culture of a people whose civilisation has been developing for over 3,000 years. The giant, however, has been sleeping for many centuries. It began to stir in 1949, when Mao Zedong established the People's Republic of China. Now, at last, it has begun to awaken; and its awakening will change, irreversibly, the calculus of power in the world.

With its enormous geographical area and massive population now being developed by a pragmatic and dynamic leadership China is emerging as one of the great powers of the world. It has set itself the task of quadrupling the value of its annual industrial and agricultural output by the end of the 20th century. It is planning to bring about in less than 20 years what it has taken 200 years for the industrial West to achieve. In pursuit of this staggeringly ambitious aim, the Third Plenum of the 12th National Party Congress recently endorsed plans to revitalise Chinese industry and to accelerate the process of modernisation in such areas as industry, agriculture, science and technology.

Recent developments in Chinese government thinking have given rise to a belief in certain sections of the western press that China is 'going capitalist'. This is, to say the very least, something of an oversimplification. It is probably more accurate to say that what is happening in China is that the Chinese are positioning themselves to live on equal terms in the international community with the great capitalist economies of the West.

For this reason alone, it is essential that the West should nourish and develop its relations with the People's Republic. But there is a more specific motivation as well – the imperatives of common interests in the geo-political and strategic sphere. This is not the place to rehearse the familiar and convincing evidence of the global threat to western security. The growing strength of Soviet military power and the persistent readiness of the USSR to use it in pursuit of expansionist foreign policies are now accepted by everyone except the unilateralist, neutralist and anti-American elements in our political and public life.

It is, however, relevant in the context of China's

(Preceding pages) River people at Guilin (Kweilin) in Guangxi Province

strategic position to underline one aspect of Russian military policy, and its growing strength in North-East Asia. The Soviet Union has decided, in common with many western strategists and economists, that the centre of gravity of global power is moving progressively from the European-Atlantic area to the Pacific Basin; and the Russians, who understand as well as anyone the role of military power in foreign policy, have laid their plans accordingly. The Chinese role in this metamorphosis will be crucial. In general the Chinese analysis of Russian global strategy is remarkably similar to the consensus among western strategists. It postulates the ultimate Soviet aim of world supremacy, by way of the progressive separation of Western Europe from the United States, the neutralisation of America, the 'Finlandisation' of Europe and the eventual drive to the East. Yet the Chinese would be the first to admit that their own armed forces have certain limitations. Their equipment is in need of modernisation; their defensive strategy is still based on the concept of the 'People's War', envisaging the swallowing up of invasion forces in the vast areas of the Chinese heartland; and it has a long standing and recently reiterated policy of 'no first use' of nuclear weapons.

The conclusion from this analysis must be that the West has a clear interest in the emergence of a defensively strong China. This is not to suggest anything so simplistic as a military alliance, which, in present circumstances would be unwelcome to the Chinese anyway. There is, however, a strong case for increasing collaboration at the diplomatic and military staff level; and it would certainly make sense for the West to give every assistance to China in building up modern, highly trained defence forces, equipped with the kind of modern weapons and military technology which it needs to deter the Soviet Union from any military adventures in Asia.

It is in this general politico-strategic context that we have to consider future relations between the West and the People's Republic. There is an appropriate point of departure in the agreement recently arrived at between the United Kingdom and China on the future of Hong Kong. It is an agreement which has produced reactions ranging from something approaching euphoria in some quarters, through the equivocal judgement that it is 'the best of a bad job' to the disenchanted assessment that it is an almost unmitigated abdiction of British responsibility.

The agreement provided for the return to the Chinese not only sovereignty of territories ceded to Britain for 99 years in 1898, but of the island of Hong Kong (granted to Britain in perpetuity in 1842 by the Treaty of Nanking) and certain territories on the mainland, also granted in perpetuity by the Convention of Peking in 1860. The People's Republic has never regarded these treaties as just and, after intensive negotiations it was agreed in 1984 that, from 1 July 1997, the Chinese would resume sovereignty over all these territories.

From that date, Hong Kong will become a Special Administrative Region under Article 31 of the Chinese constitution. The Hong Kong SAR will enjoy a high degree of autonomy in its domestic affairs, while foreign policy and defence matters will be the responsibility of China. Hong Kong will be vested with executive, legislative and independent judicial power, including that of jural adjudication. The laws currently in force will remain basically unchanged. The present social and economic system will continue. Rights and freedoms, including those of the person, of speech, of the press, of assembly, of association, of travel, of movement, of correspondence, of academic research and religious belief will be preserved.

Hong Kong is to retain the status of a free port, a separate customs territory and an international financial centre. Foreign exchange, gold, securities and futures markets will continue. The Hong Kong dollar will continue to circulate and remain freely convertible. There will be no exchange controls and free flow of capital will be protected. Hong Kong will manage its own finances; China has undertaken to levy no taxes in the Hong Kong SAR. Furthermore, Hong Kong will be allowed to maintain and develop its own economic and cultural relations and to conclude relevant agreements with other foreign countries and international organisations. There are, of course, many people both in the United Kingdom and in Hong Kong who simply refuse to believe that such an agreement can possibly survive the handover in 1997.

It is beyond doubt that the agreement is the highest form of binding commitment between two sovereign states; and the record of China in honouring its international commitments will bear comparison with that of the rest of the international community. There is a limit to which, in practice as opposed to theory, a government can bind its successors; and there are those who point to a recent history of turbulence and unpredictability in the Chinese political structure; others express doubts about the Chinese ability to manage a capitalist economy, of which few Chinese leaders have much experience; still others fear that after 1997 mainland Chinese will resent the special status of Hong Kong SAR and press for restrictions on its free market economy. For many it is simply impossible to conceive of half a century of viability for a free-wheeling, brash and extravagant capitalist enclave within the collectivist system of the People's Republic.

The resolution of these problems will depend to a large measure on relations between China and the West. It is those relations which will, in the long run, dictate the international power structure of the 21st century. In the present climate, China has no conceivable interest in damaging the prosperity and stability of the West. It must be the aim of western foreign policy to ensure that this state of affairs persists. Britain, together with its allies in the United States and the EEC must collaborate with China in such a way that the People's Republic becomes so involved in the geo-political and strategic concerns of the outside world that it is never again driven, or tempted, back into isolation.

It is equally important to ensure that the pattern of China's commercial and economic relations with the West continues to develop and expand. In 1984 the foreign trade of the People's Republic had grown to a record value of US$50 billion (although this still represents only 1.5 per cent of total world trade). This increased involvement in the world trading system can be traced back to the late 1970s, when, between 1978 and 1981, the dollar value of China's trade doubled, and many experienced observers believe that it could double again by 1990. China is a significant supplier of oil products, textiles, clothing and pharmaceuticals, light manufactured goods (including cameras and watches); and a major purchaser of grain, chemical fertilizer, metals, machinery and equipment. The largest export item is oil, of which the People's Republic is now a net exporter.

China's sales to the industrialised countries represent just over 40 per cent of its total exports, but less than 1 per cent of those countries' imports. Exports to the non oil-producing developing countries have grown considerably in recent years and now account for nearly half the total. By contrast the industrial countries provide more than two-thirds of China's imports. Only 20 per cent come from the non-oil developing countries, and of this more than a third comes from Hong Kong. China's principal trading partners are Japan, Hong Kong and the EEC countries. There has been some recent growth in trade with the Soviet Union, but it was from a very small base, and even now exports to the Soviet bloc account for less than 5 per cent of the total.

Direct foreign investment was reintroduced in 1979 after a ban lasting 30 years. Four areas in the Guangdong and Fujian provinces were designated as Special Economic Zones (SEZs) for the establishment of joint ventures to promote export-orientated industries. In 1984 and 1985, 14 major coastal cities and several other coastal areas were opened up to foreign businessmen and investors, with discretion to offer tax incentives to firms bringing modern technology into China. At the end of 1984, China claimed that planned investment in the country amounted to US$10 billion, with more than half allotted to the SEZs. Potential western investors have, however, been deterred by failures of communication which have led to confusion about the regulations governing the zones.

Meanwhile, in May 1985, China announced an unexpected tax on foreign companies, back-dated to the beginning of the year. It involved a 15 per cent 'enterprise income tax' to be levied on foreign firms earning money from services and consultation and a 5 per cent 'industrial and commercial tax' on other foreign enterprises. These developments have demonstrated once again the somewhat unpredictable nature of Chinese economic policy. Chinese leaders, however, continue to insist that the open-door policy would remain unchanged.

The countries of the West thus have a special role and a special opportunity. If it is to achieve its goal of an economic and industrial revolution in 15 years, China needs the cooperation of the United States, Japan and Western Europe which have special skills and talents to offer. One of the basic engines of the Chinese modernisation programme will be energy supply. China will need to develop its coal and oil resources; to expand its supplies of natural gas; to develop hydro-electric and alternative energy sources; and to engage in an ambitious programme of nuclear energy generation. The United Kingdom is already involved in the construction of a nuclear plant with two 900 megaton pressurised water reactors in Guangdong Province in collaboration with Hong Kong; and this is only one example of the opportunities which will exist in the future for western industry, science and technology.

There is an almost unique opportunity, in the current political and economic climate, for western countries to develop and expand a series of special relationships with China, not only in the industrial field but in the spheres of diplomacy and grand strategy.

It is essential therefore that we should now move into a new phase of relations between China and the West based upon a realisation of the changing geo-political environment in which the global centre of gravity is shifting towards the Pacific; upon a shared appreciation of our common strategic and economic concerns; and upon the foundation of trust and civilised communication typified by the Hong Kong Agreement.

In the commercial context, however, a word of caution might be in order. Too often businessmen and industrialists have bustled off to China, expecting to conclude great deals and finalise mammoth projects in a few weeks or even days. The Chinese are a careful, austere and thrifty people. They are tough negotiators and they have a number of idiosyncracies which western businessmen find unfamiliar. For example, they believe you should not borrow money unless you have a reasonable certainty of paying it back; and the Chinese simply do not understand our obsessive desire to conclude negotiations, however complicated the issue, in a few days of hectic bargaining. They have, after all, an historic time-frame which is somewhat different from our own.

Yet, with patience and imagination on both sides, cooperation and friendship between China and the West can enter a new dimension and exert a substantial influence on the way the world will look in the next century. One of the principal obstacles in the way of that new relationship is the sheer lack of knowledge in the West about China, its economy, its political institutions, its legal systems, its fiscal arrangements and its cultural traditions. The aim of this book is to make a modest but substantial contribution towards remedying that deficiency.

25 November 1985
London

Historical introduction

by Michael B. Yahuda

China alone of the major states has a continuous history of statehood and culture stretching back into distant antiquity. The Chinese civilisation may not be the oldest in the world – those of Egypt and Mesopotamia, for example, precede it by more than 1,500 years – but nowhere else are the lines of continuity from ancient to contemporary times more significant. Despite the impact of the modern world and the Nationalist and Communist revolutions, the legacy of traditional China is still evident in social attitudes, especially in the countryside, in styles of politics, and in culture and the arts.

Contemporary Marxist Chinese historians describe traditional China as feudal. They reject the theory of the Asiatic Mode of Production as inapplicable to China. The preference for feudalism can be seen as a nationalistic desire to place China in the mainstream of historical development as outlined by Marx. If traditional China can be described as feudal, it was of a kind significantly different from that of Western Europe or Japan. Indeed, one of the reasons why China, unlike Japan, was unable to adapt its traditional system and begin a process of modernisation in the latter part of the 19th century was the nature of the difference of the system. As in medieval Europe, rigid social positions prevailed in Japan even though the economic situation of the Samurai warrior caste had been undermined and a more independent mercantile class had emerged in the cities. Thus it became possible for hereditary authority to prevail in the initial stages of the transition to modernity during the Meiji Restoration begun in 1868. In China, by contrast, where social positions were less determined by birth and where authority was more clearly linked to the traditional values, the traditional system proved to be less adaptable, and it took two revolutions in the 20th century to put China on the path to modernity.

The origins of the Chinese traditional system

The beginnings of Chinese civilisation were located deep inland along a tributary of the Huang He (Yellow River). Not much is know about the legendary Xia (Hsia) Dynasty that preceded the Shang (1766–1122 BC). However, the Shang, as ancient rulers elsewhere, claimed divine authority for their rule. The Emperor was the Son of Heaven who received a mandate to rule over all that was below Heaven. When the Shang were overrun by the less civilised Zhou, the latter took over the system of government and culture of the former. The Shang, it was claimed towards the end, proved themselves unworthy of the mandate. The crops failed in the fields while Court behaviour became dissolute, so the Heavenly mandate shifted to the Zhou. The Heavenly preference had been proved by the defeat of the Shang by the Zhou. This set the precedent for the divorce of dynastic succession from strict hereditary principles. In later Chinese historiography dynasties were depicted in cyclical terms. Typically, a new dynasty would begin with capable rulers carrying out vigorous reforms and extending the boundaries of Chinese administration. These would be followed by a golden age of stability, prosperity and cultural achievement. But as patterns became established, corruption and decay would set in and finally the dynasty would fall because of internal rebellion or external invasion, only for a new dynasty to be established and the pattern to repeat itself.

The reverence for the past and the view of history as repetitive cycles no doubt played a part in impressing the Europeans with a view of an eternal and unchanging China. While understandable, the view is highly misleading. Chinese history is in fact marked by considerable change and economic development. As the territorial influence of the early Chinese empire spread eastwards for some 1,500 miles to the sea and southwards for more than a 1,000 miles to the Chang Jiang (Yangtze River), the Zhou administration found its effective power increasingly reduced as regional principalities asserted their independence. The Zhou became emperors in name only as the states fought among themselves for power and influence. This was the period of the early founders of Chinese philosophy: Lao Ze (Lao Tse, b. 604 BC) who shaped Daoist (Taoist) thought, and Confucius (551–478 BC) whose sayings – together with the commentaries on them – were to become the official basis for Chinese government for 2,000 years, have both become widely known throughout the world. But mention should also be made of Zhuangzi (Chuang Tse, 4th century BC) who was the earliest best-known exponent of Daoism, of Mozi (Mo Tzu, 5th to 4th century BC) the proclaimer of universal love for mankind, and of Mencius who developed still further the philosophy of Confucius. Arguably, Xunzi (Hsun Tzu, 3rd century BC) and the Lord of Shang of the previous century were of more immediate influence. The Confucianist Xunzi held, in contrast to Mencius, that human nature was innately bad requiring both correction and education, while the Lord of Shang was the first spokesman of the Legalist School calling for strict laws and their severe implementation.

This was the period known in Chinese history as the 'Warring States' (c. 481–221 BC). Feudal princedoms nominally owing allegiance to the Zhou emperor vied and fought among themselves nominally to re-establish a unified empire. Among their knightly warriors were also strategists and thinkers who sought to advise them not only on warfare but also on the principles of good government. This was the age when the Hundred Flowers of Thought bloomed and the Hundred Schools of

11

The legacy of traditional China

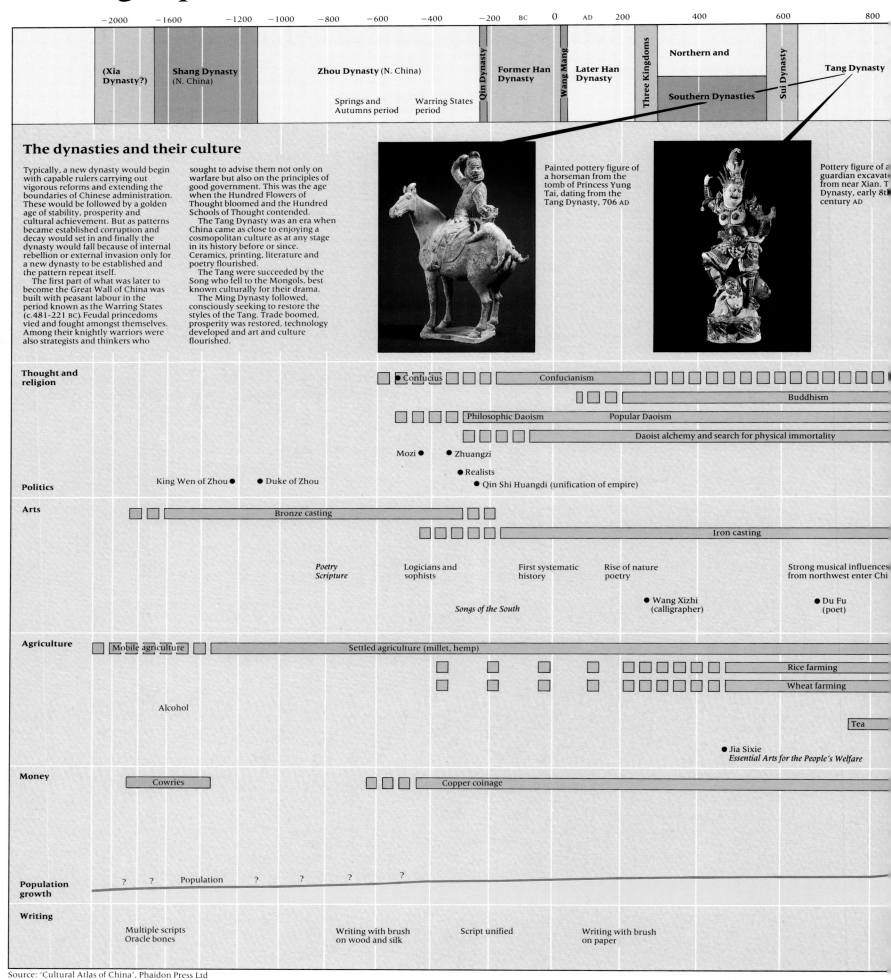

| −2000 | −1600 | −1200 | −1000 | −800 | −600 | −400 | −200 | BC | 0 | AD | 200 | 400 | 600 | 800 |

(Xia Dynasty?)

Shang Dynasty (N. China)

Zhou Dynasty (N. China)
- Springs and Autumns period
- Warring States period

Qin Dynasty

Former Han Dynasty

Wang Mang

Later Han Dynasty

Three Kingdoms

Northern and Southern Dynasties

Sui Dynasty

Tang Dynasty

The dynasties and their culture

Typically, a new dynasty would begin with capable rulers carrying out vigorous reforms and extending the boundaries of Chinese administration. These would be followed by a golden age of stability, prosperity and cultural achievement. But as patterns became established corruption and decay would set in and finally the dynasty would fall because of internal rebellion or external invasion only for a new dynasty to be established and the pattern repeat itself.

The first part of what was later to become the Great Wall of China was built with peasant labour in the period known as the Warring States (c.481-221 BC). Feudal princedoms vied and fought amongst themselves. Among their knightly warriors were also strategists and thinkers who sought to advise them not only on warfare but also on the principles of good government. This was the age when the Hundred Flowers of Thought bloomed and the Hundred Schools of Thought contended.

The Tang Dynasty was an era when China came as close to enjoying a cosmopolitan culture as at any stage in its history before or since. Ceramics, printing, literature and poetry flourished.

The Tang were succeeded by the Song who fell to the Mongols, best known culturally for their drama.

The Ming Dynasty followed, consciously seeking to restore the styles of the Tang. Trade boomed, prosperity was restored, technology developed and art and culture flourished.

Painted pottery figure of a horseman from the tomb of Princess Yung Tai, dating from the Tang Dynasty, 706 AD

Pottery figure of a guardian excavated from near Xian. T... Dynasty, early 8th century AD

Thought and religion
- ● Confucius — Confucianism
- Buddhism
- Philosophic Daoism — Popular Daoism
- Daoist alchemy and search for physical immortality
- Mozi ●
- ● Zhuangzi
- ● Realists

Politics
- King Wen of Zhou ●
- ● Duke of Zhou
- ● Qin Shi Huangdi (unification of empire)

Arts
- Bronze casting
- Iron casting
- *Poetry Scripture*
- Logicians and sophists
- First systematic history
- Rise of nature poetry
- Strong musical influences from northwest enter Chi...
- *Songs of the South*
- ● Wang Xizhi (calligrapher)
- ● Du Fu (poet)

Agriculture
- Mobile agriculture
- Settled agriculture (millet, hemp)
- Rice farming
- Wheat farming
- Alcohol
- Tea
- ● Jia Sixie *Essential Arts for the People's Welfare*

Money
- Cowries
- Copper coinage

Population growth
- ? ? Population ? ? ? ?

Writing
- Multiple scripts Oracle bones
- Writing with brush on wood and silk
- Script unified
- Writing with brush on paper

Source: 'Cultural Atlas of China', Phaidon Press Ltd

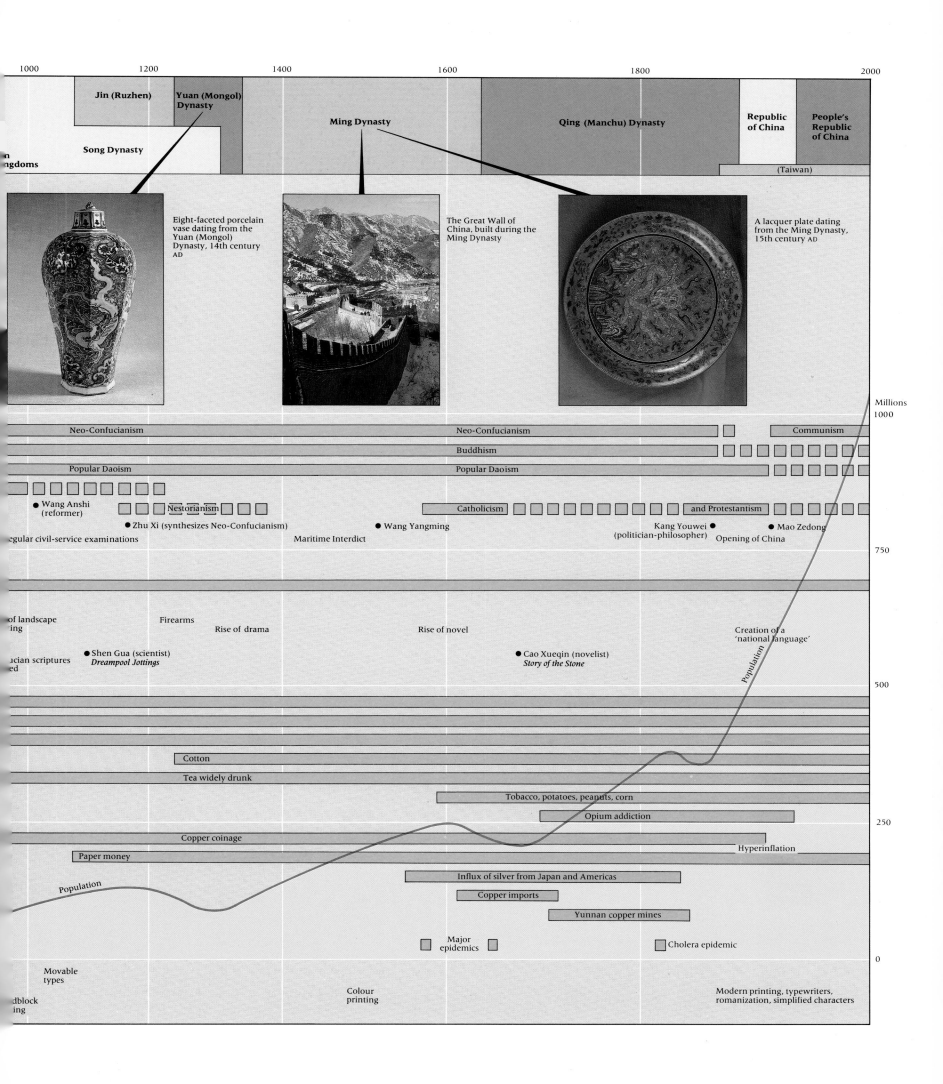

1000	1200	1400	1600	1800	2000

Jin (Ruzhen)

Yuan (Mongol) Dynasty

Ming Dynasty

Qing (Manchu) Dynasty

Republic of China

People's Republic of China

Song Dynasty

...ngdoms

(Taiwan)

Eight-faceted porcelain vase dating from the Yuan (Mongol) Dynasty, 14th century AD

The Great Wall of China, built during the Ming Dynasty

A lacquer plate dating from the Ming Dynasty, 15th century AD

Millions
1000

Neo-Confucianism   Neo-Confucianism   Communism

Buddhism

Popular Daoism   Popular Daoism

● Wang Anshi (reformer)   Nestorianism   Catholicism   and Protestantism

750

● Zhu Xi (synthesizes Neo-Confucianism)   ● Wang Yangming   Kang Youwei ● (politician-philosopher)   Opening of China   ● Mao Zedong

...egular civil-service examinations   Maritime Interdict

...of landscape ...ing   Firearms   Rise of drama   Rise of novel   Creation of a 'national language'

...ucian scriptures ...ed   ● Shen Gua (scientist) *Dreampool Jottings*   ● Cao Xueqin (novelist) *Story of the Stone*

Population

500

Cotton

Tea widely drunk

Tobacco, potatoes, peanuts, corn

Opium addiction

250

Copper coinage   Hyperinflation

Paper money

Influx of silver from Japan and Americas

Population

Copper imports

Yunnan copper mines

Major epidemics   Cholera epidemic

0

Movable types

Colour printing

Modern printing, typewriters, romanization, simplified characters

...dblock ...ing

Thought contended. It was also the period of feudalism in the Western European sense of the term. Greater lords and princes held territory as fiefs of the emperor, and they in turn enfeoffed lesser lords and knights in return for service with their retinue, and peasants in times of war. Parts of what was to become the Great Wall of China were built with forced peasant labour.

This feudal period came to an end as the State of Qin (Ch'in) finally completed the conquest of the other states and unified China to set up the Qin (Ch'in) Dynasty in 221 BC. The first emperor, Shi Huangdi (221–209BC), revolutionised China. He ruthlessly set about destroying the old feudal centres, unified the currency, weights and measures, established new armies and imposed a dictatorship based on harsh laws. He improved transport and irrigation and linked together many of the separate walls built to protect China's cultivated lands from the marauding nomads to the north. He carried out military expeditions against them and achieved widespread renown. The European name for China is derived from his dynasty. However, Shi Huangdi is notorious in Chinese history as the man who 'burnt the books and buried the scholars alive'. In order to enforce his dominion he ordered the destruction of all past heterodox writings and the killing of those who propagated principles of government opposed to his. Interestingly, more than 2,000 years later, towards the end of his life, Mao compared himself to Shi Huangdi as a revolutionary who was also determined to change the system. The grave of the first Qin emperor including the thousands of life-size images of his warriors was recently excavated near the old imperial city of Xian.

Far from lasting for 10,000 years as prophesied by its founder, the Qin Dynasty was overthrown three years after his death. The feudal remnants whose victory it was did not, however, turn back the clock. The leader Liu Bang who was of peasant origins proclaimed himself founder of the Han Dynasty. This was to last for 400 years (206 BC–AD 220) and it set the pattern for the social and political order for China until the breakdown under the European onslaught in the 19th century. Softening some of the harsher aspects of Qin rule, the Han emperors adopted Confucian paternalistic principles for governing their extensive empire. A new administration staffed by educated men recommended by patrons carried out the tasks of government. Free tenure of land led to a landlord and tenant system that persisted until the Communist revolution. The empire expanded southward to Guangzhou (Canton) and into Central Asia as far as the Caspian Sea, making some contact with the Roman empire. The writing of history and the keeping of accurate records reached a high level and set the standard for subsequent dynasties. Paper and ink replaced bamboo strips for writing. So emphatic was the mark of the Han Dynasty that to this day Chinese describe themselves ethnically as Han people.

The 400 years of unity under the Han was followed by an equally long period of confusion and division known as the Six Dynasties. The great popular novel about power and intrigue 'The Three Kindgoms' was written about this period. A brief unity was imposed by the Jin only to lose northern China to Tartar invaders. The south was held by short-lived Chinese dynasties. However, this was no 'Dark Age'. Literature flourished, Buddhism and Buddhist art forms reached China from India and spread widely, but quickly acquired Chinese characteristics. The Tartar invaders were absorbed to become indistinguishable from the majority Chinese.

The high points of empire: the Tang and Song Dynasties

The empire was reunited in 581 by a short-lived vigorous and martial Sui Dynasty, to be replaced in 618 by the Tang Dynasty which lasted until 906. Positions in the administrative bureaucracy became dependent on performance in competitive examinations, based on the Confucian classics and approved commentaries. Apart from the Court, the old administrative military class had virtually ceased to exist, to be replaced by what is loosely called the gentry – mainly well-to-do families with land and highly educated members who had passed at least the lower levels of the imperial examination.

The administration of government was developed to levels that were not to be known elsewhere for several centuries. This was an age of trade and prosperity with the population reaching 60 million as recorded by an accurate census in 754. It was an era in which China came as close to enjoying a cosmopolitan culture as at any stage in its history before or since. The great trade routes through Central Asia flourished, bringing with them extensive cultural influences. The great religions of the Mediterranean world reached China. Nestorian Christians established themselves in the capital; a Jewish community flourished in Kaifeng in Central China that was to last for nearly a thousand years; and Islam gained adherents in the south-west while Turkic peoples converted to Islam settled in the far west. Han Chinese, however, was more influenced by Buddhism. At the popular level this became mixed with traditional animist and Daoist practices.

This period was also the high point of Chinese cultural influence on its East Asian neighbours, due less to Chinese proselytising than to their visits to Chinese seats of learning. The Japanese Court, for example, modelled itself on that of China, and Japanese Buddhists spent lengthy periods of study in Chinese centres of learning. Within China itself ceramics, painting, literature and especially poetry flourished. This was the time of Li Bo (Li Po) and Du Fu (Tu Fu), perhaps the greatest of China's poets.

The Song Dynasty (960–1279), which succeeded the Tang after a brief interlude, lacked the martial and cosmopolitan vigour of the former. The north-eastern territories lost to nomadic invasions at the fall of the Tang were never recovered. In 1127 northern China was lost to Tartar invaders confining the Song to China south of the Chang Jiang (Yangtze River).

Under the Song the civil service administration was refined further. The Buddhist high tide among China's élite receded as officials and scholars developed a more intricate metaphysical and spiritual Confucian doctrine known as neo-Confucianism. As much of the trade through Central Asia declined, trade with the outside world fell more into non-Chinese hands in the south. But this was also a period of considerable cultural vitality. Song painting is among the most highly prized. Technology was of a high order including the further development of printing (invented during the Tang Dynasty) the invention of the magnetic compass, gun powder and the cannon, and advances in silk spinning and porcelain manufacture. Maritime trade extended to Southeast Asia and to areas covered by Arab traders.

The middle and late empires

The remainder of the Song fell to the Mongols who established the Yuan Dynasty (1280–1368). Their conquest was especially destructive in the north, where vast fertile areas were transformed into wilderness and denuded of population. The Mongols sought to rule through their military armies divided into banners and the use of officials drawn from Central Asia. Although hated by the Chinese élite, the Mongols still ruled over a prosperous country with large cities of a sophistication which astounded the Venetian Marco Polo. As for culture, the Mongol period is best known for the development of drama (for example, the celebrated Peking Opera) by unemployed scholars.

In less than 100 years the hated Mongols were overthrown by a peasant revolt leading to the establishment of the Ming Dynasty (1368–1644), which consciously sought to restore the styles of the Tang and Song. Although Ming rule was autocratic it restored stability and prosperity.

The introduction of new crops such as the sweet potato from the Americas led to the beginning of a growth of the population which laid the foundation for the huge population spread that took shape in the 19th, and especially in the 20th century. The restoration of the great canals and irrigation works accompanied by refinement of the existing technology of farming and pre-industrial skills in urban centres also led to a great expansion of internal trade.

One of the great questions of history is why China during the Ming Dynasty did not go on to make a breakthrough into an industrial revolution. Many of the technological inventions thought necessary for this had been made in China; mercantile capital had been accumulated in many huge fortunes. Moreover, it was in the early Ming period (1405–33) that huge naval expeditions were sent to Southeast Asia, India, the Persian Gulf, the Red Sea and even to East Africa. These were stopped abruptly to meet the pressing threat from the north, only a couple of decades before the Portuguese appeared in those waters.

Many theories have been advanced to explain the failure to develop an industrial breakthrough. These include the suggestion that the existing technology in agriculture was so efficient that there were disincentives to moving towards a more capital-intensive technology. A more widely accepted explanation focuses on the absence of a socially independent urban middle class and the operation of an officialdom that both preyed upon and recruited from the richer merchants. Whatever the best explanation, the Ming responded positively to the increased contact with Europeans. Catholic missionaries headed by the famous Matteo Ricci were well received in Beijing where they taught the élite mathematics and astronomy. Their astronomical instruments may still be seen in Beijing. However, their notion of converting the high Chinese élite fell foul of a clash of authority between

the Son of Heaven in Peking and the Vicar of Christ in Rome. The Ming fell in 1644 to an internal rebellion that gave the Manzhou from the north-east (Manchuria) the opportunity to conquer the country.

The Manzhou (Manchu) took the dynastic title of Qing (1644–1911). Although the Manzhou administered the country through the traditional civil service, the imperial troops were primarily Manzhou and the Court imposed its racial superiority by forcing ethnic male Chinese to shave the front of their heads and to wear their hair in a queue (pigtail) at the back. They imposed a strict literary censorship. The most notable scholarly achievements of the period were in philosophy and textual criticism.

Under three highly capable emperors the first 150 years witnessed prosperity and stability in an expanded empire that reached deep into Central Asia. The population continued to grow, reaching approximately 400 million by the year 1800. The growth of trade with Europeans, primarily the British operating by extension from India, was initially very profitable to China, but the Manzhou distrusted the foreign traders and confined them under highly restricted conditions to operating from outside Guangzhou (Canton) in the far south. The pattern changed with the illegal export of opium to China from fields in India. By this stage the dynasty had begun to decay. The Manzhou armies lost their effectiveness and had great difficulty in suppressing peasant rebellions.

The costs of empire were high and official positions could be gained for money rather than through performance in the examinations. Corruption became widespread and effective government declined. This was the China that in the following century collapsed under the impact of the Europeans and the challenge of the modern world they brought with them.

The Western impact

By the 19th century the European traders were no longer content to be confined to the far south, restricted and hampered in a variety of ways. Denied access to what they regarded as a market of 400 million by what they saw as a venal and xenophobic bureaucracy and by a corrupt and alien legal system, the British in particular put pressure on the government in London to open China to free trade. Opium became the *casus belli*. By the 1830s it was being smuggled into China in such vast quantities that it was undermining society in the far south and draining silver from the Chinese economy, thereby undermining the taxation system which was calculated in silver but paid in copper cash. When the Imperial Commissioner Lin Zexu confiscated and burnt huge amounts of opium in 1839 the British government found this intolerable. Lord Palmerston sent a military expedition to 'bring China into the Community of Nations'.

The Chinese were unable to match the British fleet, and following a series of defeats they were forced to sign the Treaty of Nanjing in 1842, by which Hong Kong island was ceded 'in perpetuity' and five ports were opened for Western trade establishing the Treaty Port system. This involved the concession of areas where foreigners exercised the right of extraterritorial jurisdiction. Among these was the fishing village of Shanghai, which soon grew into a major city with an International Settlement protected by its own armed forces drawn from several nations. The Treaty of Nanjing set the precedent for a number of others, all of which were to be described later by the Chinese as 'unequal treaties'. The Chinese Court at first refused to recognise the nature of the Western challenge. Only after Britain and France inflicted another major military defeat in wars between 1858 and 1860, in the course of which they occupied Beijing, did the Court finally accept the diplomatic equality of the Europeans.

Meanwhile the Russians took advantage of the situation to compel the ceding of vast territories in the north. Internally, the dynasty was fatally weakened by the unprecedented Taiping rebellion of the 1850s which was fired by a heady mixture of Christian and nativistic revolutionary precepts. The rebels, who at one point were on the verge of toppling the dynasty, ravaged central China for more than a decade, leading to the death of more than 20 million people. The defeat of the Taipings was engineered by regional armies specially recruited by high-minded provincial governors.

The new breed of governors together with a few like-minded Manzhou princes at Court sought in the 1860s to meet the challenge of the Europeans through a process of self-strengthening. Recognising that the Europeans were qualitatively different from any previous 'barbarian' threat to Chinese history, they aimed at copying the European superior technology in armaments and ships so as to expel the Europeans and re-establish the traditional system and its values. They coined the slogan 'Chinese learning for substance and Western learning for practical utility'. The attempt failed partly because of resistance from the more conservative entrenched officialdom amid continual encroachments from the European powers in a context of xenophobic reactions by a displaced Chinese peasantry, and partly because of the inherent difficulties of the exercise of trying to introduce Western-style armament factories to the unwelcoming and unprepared Chinese environment. The comparison with the contemporary attempt to modernise by drawing on the capitalist West while preserving the Chinese socialist system is instructive. Although the two situations are very different, the 19th-century experience points up some of the great difficulties inherent in the ambitious exercise.

The ultimate failure of the Chinese response was brought home by China's defeat at the hands of the hitherto despised Japanese in 1894-95. It was one thing to lose suzerainty of Indo-China to the French in 1885, but it was altogether different to lose that of Korea and to cede Taiwan to Japan. The defeat spelt the end of China's traditional system. A brief attempt at reform from above was scotched by the redoubtable and reactionary Empress Dowager in 1898. After the failure of the Boxer uprising even she was compelled to recognise the need for change, but by then it was too late.

Republican China

The defeat by Japan swelled the numbers of young Chinese intellectuals who sought a Western education and found inspiration in Western ideas. The first leader of the Republican movement did not come from among these. Sun Yixian (Sun Yat-sen), a native of Guangzhou, had been educated as a youngster in Hawaii and graduated in medicine in Hong Kong. His world was that of the overseas Chinese which was much influenced by the West. Finding radical reform blocked by Chinese officialdom he became a revolutionary republican. After years of tireless activity to raise funds and build an organisation among the overseas Chinese his influence grew among young Chinese studying in America and especially in Japan. His followers also penetrated the new model army being trained in China.

Eventually, when yet another revolutionary plot in China was on the point of failure, the revolutionaries were able to compel the local commander to side with them. Others in the south rallied to their side. The emperor abdicated. This was the 1911 revolution. Sun Yixian was proclaimed the first President of the Republic of China established in 1912, but he soon withdrew in favour of the strongest military leader. The latter overestimated his strength and tried to set up a new dynasty with himself as emperor, only to collapse in ignomy in 1916, leading to a decade of strife which was marked by manoeuvring between rival warlords to gain control of revenues and access to foreign loans and military purchases. The country fell into ever greater chaos, banditry and rural distress. The seeds of revolution were germinating.

Meanwhile, since the fall of the empire a generation of Chinese had grown up many of whom were strongly influenced by Western education and Western political values. Highly nationalistic, they were swayed by the promises of President Wilson for a just international settlement at the end of the First World War. In May 1919, when the news emerged from Versailles that the warlord government had sold out Chinese interests to Japan, the students from the new Western-style University of Peking rioted and unleashed a new intellectual movement, known as the May 4th Movement, with a great following in the cities. The intellectual and social ferment of the time set the political agenda for the remainder of the century. Rejecting the traditional past there was agreement on the need for modernisation and radical social change, but there was disagreement between liberals and socialists, with the tide shifting in favour of the latter.

Influenced by the Bolshevik revolution, which the socialists interpreted in highly nationalist terms, the Chinese Communist Party was formed in 1921. Its two early leaders, Chen Duxiu and Li Dazhao, differed in their emphasis: the former stressing rationality under the slogan of 'Mr. Science and Mr. Democracy', and the latter emphasising a more populist revolutionary approach that called for unleashing the latent energies of the masses. The differences between these strands of Chinese Communism were to become important, especially after 1949.

The Nationalist Party of Sun Yixian languished in Guangzhou, unable to gain the support of any of the Western powers. In 1923 a deal was struck with the Soviet Union which offered arms and advisors. The party was organised along dictatorial Communist lines and a modern army was trained. In 1924 the Nationalists and Communists established a united front and prepared for a northern expedition to defeat the warlord armies; in

The Chinese Dynasties

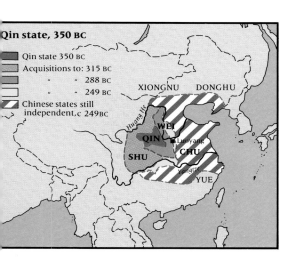

Qin state, 350 BC

- Qin state 350 BC
- Acquisitions to: 315 BC
- " " 288 BC
- " " 249 BC
- Chinese states still independent, c 249 BC

XIONGNU   DONGHU

Huang He

WEI
QIN   Luoyang
SHU   CHU

Yangtze

YUE

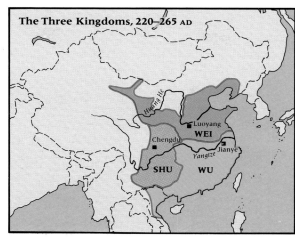

The Three Kingdoms, 220–265 AD

Huang He

Luoyang
WEI

Chengdu
Yangtze   Jianye

SHU   WU

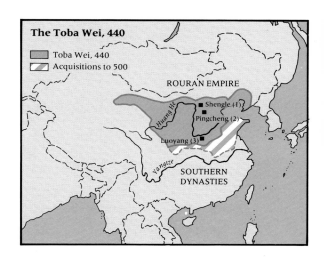

The Toba Wei, 440

- Toba Wei, 440
- Acquisitions to 500

ROURAN EMPIRE

Shengle (1)
Huang He   Pingcheng (2)

Luoyang (3)

Yangtze   SOUTHERN
DYNASTIES

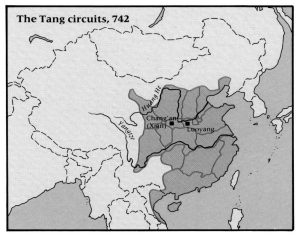

The Tang circuits, 742

Huang He

Yangtze   Chang'an
(Xian)   Luoyang

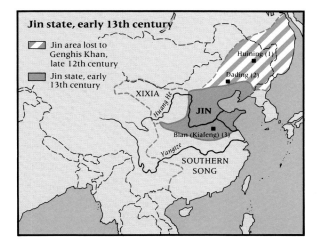

Jin state, early 13th century

- Jin area lost to Genghis Khan, late 12th century
- Jin state, early 13th century

Huining (1)

Dading (2)

XIXIA   Huang He

JIN

Bian (Kiafeng) (3)

Yangtze   SOUTHERN
SONG

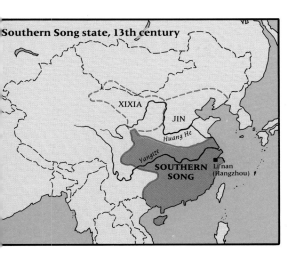

Southern Song state, 13th century

XIXIA

JIN

Huang He

Yangtze
SOUTHERN
SONG   Li'nan
(Hangzhou)

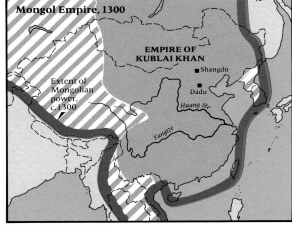

Mongol Empire, 1300

EMPIRE OF
KUBLAI KHAN

Shangdu

Extent of
Mongolian
power,
c. 1300   Dadu

Huang He

Yangtze

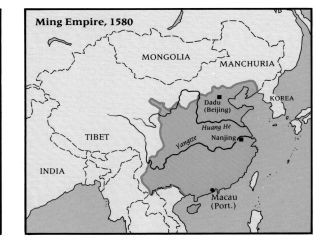

Ming Empire, 1580

MONGOLIA   MANCHURIA

Dadu
(Beijing)   KOREA

TIBET   Huang He

Nanjing
Yangtze

INDIA

Macau
(Port.)

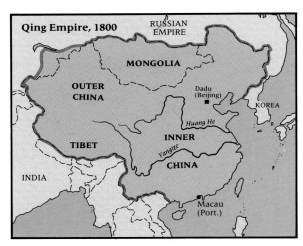

Qing Empire, 1800

RUSSIAN
EMPIRE

MONGOLIA

OUTER
CHINA   Dadu
(Beijing)

KOREA

TIBET   Huang He
INNER
Yangtze   CHINA

INDIA   CHINA

Macau
(Port.)

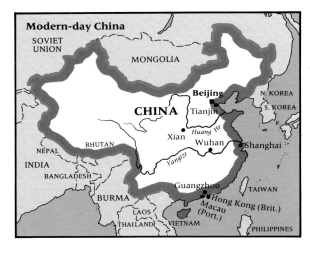

Modern-day China

SOVIET
UNION   MONGOLIA

CHINA   Beijing
Tianjin   N. KOREA
S. KOREA

NEPAL   Xian   Huang He
BHUTAN   Wuhan   Shanghai

INDIA   Yangtze

BANGLADESH   TAIWAN

BURMA   Guangzhou
Hong Kong (Brit.)
Macau (Port.)

LAOS   VIETNAM   PHILIPPINES
THAILAND

1926 it was duly launched with easy successes. On reaching Shanghai in May, Jiang Jieshi (Chiang Kai-shek), the authoritarian military commander who had taken over as leader after Sun Yixian's death, suddenly turned on the Communists, killing them in their hundreds and destroying them as an urban force. Jiang set up a right-wing government which found favour with the Western powers. The Communist remnants in the countryside built up a base area in the hinterland of south-east China, where under Mao's leadership they developed revolutionary guerrilla warfare and carried out land reforms.

The Nationalists achieved considerable success in improving industrial and agricultural output in the late 1920s and early 1930s, but they were constrained by the effects of the crash of the world economy, by the civil war against the Communists and by pressure from Japan who occupied Manchuria in 1931. After a series of military expeditions the Nationalists forced the Communists out of their rural base in south-east China. The latter embarked on their legendary Long March of 6,000 miles which eventually brought a tenth of their number to Yanan in the arid north-west.

The Japanese invasion of China in 1937 doomed the Nationalist government. While their armies languished in idle corruption in Sichuan in south-west China, the Communists were able to expand in the north where they carried out social reform and guerrilla warfare against the Japanese. At the end of the Second World War the more vigorous, better organised and idealistic Communist armies were soon able to defeat the modern and four times as numerous Nationalist forces. Jiang Jieshi (Chiang Kai-shek) and his remnants fled to Taiwan, still claiming to be the legal government of the Republic of China. Amid patriotic euphoria Mao proclaimed the establishment of the People's Republic of China on 1 October 1949, claiming that at last 'the Chinese people have stood up'.

CHAPTER 1

Policies and performance

by Robert Delfs

China in the mid-1980s is mid-course on an ambitious programme of sweeping change. In less than a decade since the death of Mao Zedong (Mao Tsetung), China's leadership has moved to repudiate both the Maoist vision of a highly-collectivised egalitarian communist society and the Soviet model of a centrally-planned and administered economic system. In their place, China is pursuing an alternative model of socialism which incorporates many structural features of a capitalist market economy.

The origins of these changes are exceedingly complex, developing out of decades of struggle within the Communist party, which in part can be seen as an episode in a long-term debate about China's future that began in the 19th century, before the fall of the Qing dynasty.

China is abandoning the Maoist and Soviet models of development simply because they are seen to have failed in terms of the task which three generations of Chinese revolutionary reformers have posed as their ultimate justification and objective: modernising China.

Although China remains formally a planned economy, its leaders now explicitly accept the importance of market forces in determining price levels and channelling investment. Competition, once condemned as the anarchic inefficiency of capitalism, is now embraced as a necessary method of stimulating innovation, efficiency and productivity.

Paralleling the restructuring of China's domestic economic systems is a new openness to foreign investment and recognition of the benefits of exposure to foreign technology and business practices. This is a sharp contrast to China's attitudes of only a decade ago, when China was rigidly committed to self-reliance in economic and technological spheres, and foreign businessmen were regarded as imperialists. After decades of near seclusion, China has become an important factor in regional and world markets, a significant exporter of petroleum and other primary goods, and increasingly important as a supplier of textiles, clothing and other manufactured goods.

The post-Mao reformers' specific goal is that China achieve the economic level of the world's middle-income economies by the year 2000 and catch up with the developed nations by the middle of the 21st century. The implications for the rest of the world of a modernised China will be profound.

Simply because of its size, even slight changes in China's economic situation can be quite significant when aggregated over a population of more than one billion. If China can achieve a per capita gross domestic product

(GDP) of US$850 (in constant US dollars) by the year 2000 — near the current average for lower-middle income countries and an ambitious but quite feasible goal — its total GDP would exceed US$1 trillion, essentially matching the GDP of Japan in 1982.

While the hazards and uncertainties that lie ahead for China's economy are many and large, the reformists' record since 1978 has been surprisingly successful.

Rural reforms have overturned two decades of collectivist policies, returning to China's farmers the use of land and the profits from their labours. This has been the most dramatic and successful of the reforms to date, directly affecting the 80 per cent of China's population who live in rural areas. It has resulted in dramatic expansion in crop production, particularly in staple grains (China became a net exporter of grains in 1985) and cotton. There have been dramatic improvements in rural incomes, which more than doubled between 1978 and 1983, and in the supply of foodstuffs to cities.

Within only a few years, the scope of market forces has steadily expanded. Today, the Chinese economy in transition could perhaps best be described as a dual or two-tier system, in which the state-controlled system of supply and distribution co-exists with a multiplicity of market networks, and where state enterprises increasingly find themselves in competition with collective and even privately-owned enterprises.

Market forces now play a significant and even dominant role in important sectors of the Chinese economy, including the production and supply of such critical commodities as foodstuffs, energy, steel products and machinery. After three decades of tight state control over almost every aspect of economic life, China is moving to replace the direct state administration of production and distribution with the indirect macro-economic controls of monetary, credit and fiscal policy.

In many ways — economically, politically, as a trading nation, as a regional and emerging world power, as the largest and now the fastest growing developing country in the world — China is already a very different society and economy than the China of the late 1970s when the reforms began.

Macro-economic overview

Historical background

An 'informed observer considering the prospects for economic development and modernisation in Asia from the vantage point of 1840', wrote Alexander Eckstein, 'might have picked China, rather than Japan, as the most likely candidate.'[1] But despite China's apparent superiority in terms of resources and internal markets, as well as social and political institutions, it was Japan that successfully modernised. Within approximately 100 years, from 1870 to 1970, Japan achieved an industrial capability and per capita income levels comparable to the most developed nations of the West.

China, during this same period, experienced the collapse of its traditional political institutions and social structure, political fragmentation under regional warlords, invasion by Japan and a communist revolution. There was significant industrial development in China in the first half of the 20th century, but largely limited to the north-east, after Japanese control was established in the 1930s, and the coastal treaty ports, particularly Shanghai, where modern factories producing textiles and other light industrial products developed on a base established by foreign businessmen.

China's economy as a whole, however, remained predominantly agrarian and traditional. Modern manufacturing accounted for only 7 per cent of GDP in 1933 and only 17 per cent in 1952, when the post-war recovery under communist rule was completed.[2]

What industry there was, was concentrated in a few coastal cities and the north-east. With the exception of Wuhan and Chongqing, both on the Chang Jiang (Yangtze River), there was little industry in the hinterland, and the internal transport links were underdeveloped.

In the rural sector itself, farming practices and technology were little changed from a century before, relying primarily on manual or animal labour and with little use of modern inputs such as chemical fertilisers, insecticides or improved varietal strains.

Structural developments 1949–79

In the three decades following the Communist takeover of power, China experienced rapid industrial development based on high rates of investment focused on heavy industry. National income, an index of economic performance used by socialist countries which is analogous to national product, grew on average 6 per cent per year between 1952 and 1979. Industry, which accounted for only 19.5 per cent of national income in 1952, surpassed agriculture for the first time in 1970, and by 1979 represented 46 per cent of national income. (Since 1979, industry's share of national income has declined to 41-42 per cent, largely because of the success of rural reforms in boosting agricultural output.)

Within industry, heavy industry grew extremely rapidly. In the baseline year of 1952, light industry – textiles, clothing and other consumer goods – accounted for about two-thirds of all industrial output. Heavy industry overtook light industry by 1958, and by 1979 accounted for 56.3 per cent of total industrial output.

Industrialisation did not, however, have much affect on rural areas during this period. There was little movement of population to the cities, and rural production levels changed very little in per capita terms before the rural reforms of the early 1980s, despite significant increases in deliveries of chemical fertilisers and some advances in farm mechanisation.

In effect, China followed a Stalinist policy of stressing development of heavy industry, but, unlike the Soviet Union, China did not allow mass migration from the countryside to the cities. Rather, China acted to isolate the rural sector from the urban industrial sector, prohibiting migration to the cities, thus reinforcing a dualism between the traditional rural sector and modernising urban industrial sector that began in the days of the treaty ports.[3]

Structure of industry

Due to concentrated heavy industrial development since 1952, the structure of the Chinese economy is atypical for a developing country. Industry's proportional share of GDP, approximately 45 per cent, is the highest of any low-income economy, and close to the range of advanced industrial market economies. In India, the corresponding figure is 26 per cent and the average for all low-income economies is only 19 per cent.[4] Agriculture's proportional contribution to GDP, 37 per cent, is precisely the average share for low-income developing economies, while industrial market economies typically generate less than 10 per cent of GDP from agriculture.

The most striking structural contrast between China and all other non-socialist economies is the very low share of services, contributing only 18 per cent to GDP. India's service sector generates 38 per cent of GDP and the average for all low-income economies is 29 per cent. The proportional share of services tends to rise in step with higher per capita GDP, exceeding 60 per cent for industrial market economies.

China's undeveloped services sector is partly a consequence of an over-planned economy and the stress on heavy industrial development in past decades. It is even more a result of collectivisation and elimination of the private businesses sector in the mid-1950s, which closed thousands of small private shops, restaurants, transport and service providers, as well as privately-owned factories.

The demise of small businesses and service-providers had predictably negative consequences on general economic efficiency and effectively lowered living standards by forcing the distribution of goods into the narrow channels of state-run stores and marketing services.

One important aspect of the recent economic reforms has been the re-legitimisation of small private businesses. Between 1980 and 1985, the number of private businesses grew from approximately nil to over 10 million, of which 5.8 million are commercial establishments, one million food stalls or restaurants, 790,000 repair shops and 800,000 transport enterprises. Self-employed workers now exceed three million in urban areas and more than 12 million (non-farming self-employed) in rural areas.

The collective sector – enterprises owned and run by collectives such as townships (ex-communes), villages in rural areas or by the operator-employees in urban areas – has expanded even more rapidly in the wake of reforms, accounting for a quarter of all industrial output in 1984 and a steadily growing share of commerce and transport. Collective enterprises accounted for 40 per cent of all retail sales in 1984, which together with the 14 per cent handled by private businesses exceeded the state-owned enterprise share of 45 per cent. Employment in collective enterprises now exceeds 32 million, and private and collective sectors together now employ 29 per cent of the total workforce.

Per capita GDP in China was approximately US$300 in 1984, slightly higher than India and the average for all low-income economies. Personal incomes, however, are much higher in urban than in rural areas. The average per capita expendable income in cities and towns in 1984 was Rmb608 (US$212 at year-end exchange rates), more than two-thirds higher than the average per capita rural income of Rmb355. Rural incomes are gaining faster than urban incomes, however, with average annual increases of more than 16 per cent since 1980. Rural incomes vary significantly by region, with highest incomes in the prosperous river deltas and suburbs of large cities, where farmers can market directly to urban markets and set up rural-based industrial and commerce activities.

Background and overview

Economic recovery and consolidation of power 1949-52

In October 1949, Mao Zedong, chairman of the Chinese Communist Party (CCP), proclaimed the founding of the People's Republic of China in Beijing, bringing to an end more than two decades of armed struggle against Jiang Jieshi's (Chiang Kai-shek) Guomindang.

The immediate tasks facing the regime were to establish its own legitimacy and political authority, build a functioning government, and initiate the process of economic reconstruction in a society shattered by invasion and civil war. These tasks were complicated by the speed of the Guomindang collapse. The CCP was over four million strong in 1949, but it had little or no political presence in many cities, particularly in the south, nor were there sufficient numbers of trained cadres to take over administrative duties in provincial and local government offices.

The People's Liberation Army (PLA) therefore played a key role in rebuilding local government in the early years of Communist rule. Initially, the central government led by Mao Zedong, Marshal Zhu De, Liu Shaoqi and Zhou Enlai, directly controlled only the north Chinese plain and the cities of Beijing and Tianjin. The north-east was governed by a People's government established in 1946 under Gao Gang. The First Field Army, led by Peng Dehuai, took control of the north-western region. The south-west was ruled by the Second Field Army under Liu Bocheng, He Long and Deng Xiaoping. Shanghai and the eastern provinces were under Rao Shushi and Chen Yi of the Third Field Army. The Fourth Field Army, under Lin Biao, Ye Jianjing and Li Xiannian, ruled the central and south-eastern provinces.

The importance of these regional administrations gradually waned through the early 1950s as the central party and governmental apparatus was strengthened and the regional leaders transferred to posts in the central government in Beijing.[5] But the government and regional leaders of this period would continue to play decisive leadership roles in China in subsequent years.

The Chinese economy in 1949 was in shambles. Inflation had soared to incredible levels in the last years of Guomindang rule. Relative to pre-war levels, agricultural output had fallen by a quarter and industrial output by half. The first steps were the introduction of a new currency unit, reducing the volume of currency in circulation, and a rationing scheme for rice, edible oil, wheat flour and cotton cloth.

Land reform began in June 1950. The Agrarian Reform Law divided the rural population into five classifications: landlords (who lived entirely on the labour of others), rich peasants (who both worked their own land and rented land to others or hired labour), middle peasants (who worked their own land without exploiting others), poor peasants (who rented land) and hired farm labour.

Land reform was intended to distribute the land and other property of landlords and rich peasants among poor and landless peasants. While most were independent landowners, working their own small parts, 50 per cent or more of all land was owned by landowners before 1949. Rents were high (typically half of the main crops) and many smallholders were victims of usurious practices by landlords.[6] The Guomindang had failed miserably on Sun Yixian's (Sun Yat-sen) original promise of land to the tiller. The grievances of poor and landless peasants became the primary organisational base of the Communist party.

The campaign was also intended to serve as a means of politically educating the peasants and mobilising support for the CCP. Party cadres were dispatched to the villages to initiate the process of class struggle within the villages. Public trials frequently resulted in torture or execution of landlords and rich peasants. By the conclusion of the campaign in 1952, over 45 million hectares of farmland — more than half the national total — had changed ownership and an estimated five million or more landlords and rich peasants had lost their lives.

China's leaders announced in 1949 their intention of 'leaning to' the side of the Soviet Union in the Cold War and in 1950 signed a treaty of friendship and alliance with the Soviet Union. China received US$300 million in credits and Stalin dispatched thousands of scientists, technicians and military advisors to China. The atmosphere of hostility towards the United States based on US support for Jiang Jieshi during the Civil War was intensified after the Korean War, in which China intervened with a million troops in 1950 after the landing of US forces under the United Nations banner. The United States had also responded to the North Korean invasion of South Korea by sending the US Seventh Fleet to the Formosa Straits, in effect committing the United States to the survival of Jiang Jieshi's regime on Taiwan. Relations with other Western countries atrophied further in the wake of the United Nations trade embargo instituted in 1951.

Foreign enterprises, viewed as imperialist, were discriminated against and their property was confiscated. By 1952, most foreign economic enterprises had been eliminated. The operations of foreign churches, charitable institutions and hospitals were also curtailed and their establishments nationalised. Most Western journalists were expelled.

Steps to eliminate remaining centres of Guomindang resistance escalated in 1951 into mass campaigns to suppress counter-revolutionaries. Chinese sources indicate that the number of deaths in these campaigns, which also extended to investigations and purges within the military and bureaucracy, may have exceeded two million.

By the end of 1952, only three years after the proclamation of military victory, China had secured its borders, isolated the Guomindang forces on Taiwan and re-established Chinese control over Tibet for the first time since 1911. Civil order was restored, but at a considerable cost in lives. Pre-war production levels in industry and agriculture had been recovered and prices stabilised. Western commercial interests had been largely eliminated, and China had demonstrated its ability and willingness to act militarily against Western powers when its national security was at stake.

The period of the first Five Year Plan 1953-57

Economic recovery was completed by 1952 as industrial and agricultural output reached pre-war levels, but food production was still barely at subsistence levels in per capita terms while urban demand grew with the recovery. It was also proving extremely difficult to extract from the rural sector revenues needed to finance industrial development. These problems led to the institution of compulsory delivery quotas for farm produce in 1953 (a measure that was only being rescinded in 1985) and collectivisation of agriculture.

Collectivisation had began experimentally in 1951 with the formation of Agricultural Production Cooperatives (APCs) on the basis of existing mutual aid teams. Tools and machinery were collectively owned in the APC, while land remained privately owned but was collectively cultivated. In late 1953 a mass movement was launched to accelerate the development of APCs. In 1955-56 the cooperatives began to be converted into 'higher-level' cooperatives in which land was pooled and members paid according to their work, retaining ownership of only their houses and private plots. Virtually the entire rural population had been organised into 'fully socialist' higher-level cooperatives by the end of 1957.[7]

The decision to collectivise agriculture was based on the idea that surplus rural labour could be mobilised as a substitute for conventional modern economic inputs. This labour force would make it possible to expand the amount of cultivated land and undertake construction of waterworks, roads and other infrastructural projects without subsidisation. This would raise production levels and facilitate the transfer of capital to China's primitive industrial sector.

Collectivisation also reflected Mao Zedong's growing conviction that it was possible to move the countryside toward socialism without prior development of the 'means of production', i.e. mechanisation. Furthermore, it acted to consolidate party control and blocked the re-emergence of a landlord class in the countryside.

Grain output, which in 1953 increased by 2 per cent over 1952, grew 4.5 per cent in 1954, 8.2 per cent in 1955 and 4.9 per cent in 1956, very rapid growth by historical standards. In terms of mobilising labour power, collectivisation was dramatically successful. There was a net outflow of funds from the rural sector to the state in the 1950s, mostly in the form of taxes on industrial and commercial goods sold in rural areas, and the compulsory delivery of agricultural products at fixed low prices essentially subsidised urban consumers.

However, the efficiency of input use in the rural sector declined and the production increases were achieved at the cost of increasing mismanagement and declining personal incentives, so that much of the benefits of increased inputs were lost.[8] Overall agricultural annual output growth over the five-year period 1953-57 averaged only 4.5 per cent.

A state planning committee to coordinate industrial development was established in 1951 under the leadership of Gao Gang, head of the north-east regional administration. The first Five Year Plan (1953-57) was not actually put into implementation until February 1955 due to delays, revisions and dissension within the leadership. Gao Gang and Rao Shushi were purged at an extraordinary party conference in 1955.

The reasons for the purge are unclear. Among the theories that have been advanced are Gao's close relationship with the Soviet Union, differences within the leadership over industrial policy and agricultural collectivisation, Gao's desire for priority development of the north-eastern region and purely factional issues.[9]

The Five Year Plan called for 694 major industrial projects, of which 141 were to be built with assistance from the Soviet Union. The Soviet assistance was to be immediately paid for in Chinese goods. In 1954 an additional agreement was reached adding 15 additional industrial enterprises and providing for a Soviet credit of US$130 million. This, plus the US$300 million credit extended in 1950, is all the Soviet aid known to be extended until 1957. Additional projects were added in 1956, and in all, 166 industrial projects were completed with Soviet assistance, and several thousand Chinese engineers and technicians received training in the Soviet Union.[10]

Impressive industrial gains occurred in the period, fuelled by high levels of investment. Total capital construction investment more than doubled from 4.4 billion renminbi (Rmb) in 1952 to Rmb9.2 billion the following year and reached Rmb16.1 billion in 1956. More than 90 per cent of investment during this period was financed with state funds.

Gross industrial output value more than doubled between 1952 and 1957, from Rmb34.3 billion to Rmb78.4 billion at 1952 prices.[11] Growth was fastest in heavy industry, where investment was concentrated, and which in 1949 had been almost entirely limited to the north-eastern region, primarily due to earlier Japanese and Russian development.

Parallel to the collectivisation movement in the countryside, the state moved in 1956 to accelerate the transformation of privately-owned industry and commerce into joint state private enterprises and then into wholly state-owned enterprises. By the end of 1956, privately-owned industry had been eliminated; state ownership accounted for two-thirds of all industry and joint state-private enterprises for the rest. Retail shops and restaurants were converted into state-controlled cooperatives or wholly state-owned enterprises. Unlike the rural land reform movement, however, owners were compensated and, if only because their skills were needed, made directors of their former firms.[12]

Mass organisations were forged during this period that embraced huge segments of the population, residential organisations (modelled on security systems of imperial China) were formed and party penetration of work units consolidated. An ideological campaign to impose tighter ideological discipline over intellectuals was launched in 1954 and escalated in 1955. Thousands were arrested and imprisoned and hundreds of thousands were affected by the campaign.

It quickly became apparent, however, that demoralisation of intellectuals was having adverse effects on economic affairs, and much more liberal policies appeared in 1956, reinforced by Khruschev's denunciation of Stalin in the same year.

The eighth party congress in September 1956 was the first congress since 1921 with elected delegates. Dominated by Liu Shaoqi and Deng Xiaoping, the congress established a new leadership organ, the Politburo Standing Committee, composed of Mao, Liu, Zhou Enlai, Marshall Zhu De, economic planner Chen Yun and Deng Xiaoping.

The high point of political liberalisation was the 'Hundred Flowers' movement, launched by Mao's speech 'On the Correct Handling of Contradictions among the People' in February 1957, which called for criticism of the party from outside. Forums for criticism were set up in a number of cities, the most important of which were Beijing, Shanghai and Tianjin. The intellectuals' points were far sharper than the party leaders anticipated, going to the root issue of the leadership role of the CCP in society. There were demands for open elections, and end of one-party rule and the resignation of Mao and other Communist leaders.

As students and workers became involved in the swelling tide of criticism, the party launched a counter-offensive in June 1957. The ensuing campaign quickly developed into a large-scale purge of intellectuals and other critics both within and outside the party. As many as half a million were sent to forced labour camps, although the estimated number of deaths associated with the Anti-Rightist Campaign of 1957-58 was less than 1,000.

The Great Leap Forward and its aftermath

The years 1957-58 marked a critical turning-point for Communist China. The party had embarked on a liberalising course in the belief that the substantial economic achievements of the first Five Year Plan period had been translated into broad popular support. But the unexpectedly critical response to the Hundred Flowers opening, and the apparent depth of that response, stung the leadership and lent indirect support to proponents of more radical political and economic policies.

The expansion of heavy industry had intensified the gap in production levels and living standards between the modernising urban industrial sector and traditional peasant agriculture. This created a certain tension with the CCP's historical commitment to the peasantry and the anti-urban bias of some party members, and priority development of heavy industry had led to a degree of dependence on Soviet technical assistance. But the huge size of China's rural sector precluded any attempt to develop agriculture through capital-intensive methods.

The party leadership found itself strongly divided for the first time since 1949. While economic planners such as vice premier Chen Yun, chairman of the State Planning Commission Lu Fuchun and chairman of the State Economic Commission Bo Yibo supported gradual growth in the context of the Soviet model of a planned economy, Mao opted for a new strategy of accelerated economic growth, simultaneously developing industry and agriculture. As in the initial rural collectivisation movement, mass political movements would be used to mobilise labour to substitute for the shortage of capital and technological inputs.

By mid-1958, Mao and his supporters, including Marshal Lin Biao, had won the support of key provincial and party leaders for the Great Leap Forward. Industrial output targets were raised, and Mao's supporters among the provincial leaders began merging rural cooperatives and mass mobilisation campaigns to develop local industry and irrigation projects.

In August 1958, the Central Committee adopted a resolution calling for establishing rural communes nationwide. The rhetoric of the Maoists had also shifted from an economic to a political frame of reference – by revolutionising the social relations of production, China would leapfrog stages of economic development in the transition to communism.

Within months of the Central Committee's August 1958 Beidaihe Resolution, nearly all of rural China had been organised into vast rural communes. Typically comprising 5,000 households, the commune imposed a quasi-military regimentation on the countryside. Within the commune, families were organised in production brigades (*shengchan dadui*), which in most cases were simply the agricultural production cooperatives established in the earlier phase of collectivisation.

Aided by favourable weather, the 1958 autumn harvest was spectacularly large. But over-inflated early reports misled central planners who issued directives to reduce areas sown to grain and increase plantings of industrial crops. The drive to develop rural industry was also interfering with agricultural labour.

By the time the real results of the 1958 harvest were known, it was too late. Grain output fell from 200-215 million tonnes in 1958 to only 170 million tonnes in 1959. This was the beginning of three years of famine. Per capita food grain consumption did not regain 1957 levels again until 1979.

The industrial phase of the Great Leap Forward proved equally disastrous. Industrial production in 1958 was first reported to have increased by more than 30 per cent, and steel production, swelled by the output of thousands of primitive 'backyard steel furnaces', was reported to have more than doubled. But the quality of this steel was so poor that it was useless. The planning and allocation system established over the period 1951-57 broke down under the pressure of unrealistic targets and wildcat decentralisation.

Resistance to collectivisation mounted. Peasants hoarded grain and slaughtered their pigs rather than turn them over to the commune, and some areas were virtually in a state of insurrection.

Some of theses problems were already apparent in early 1958, and even Mao had criticised the excessive zeal of some party cadres and accused himself of

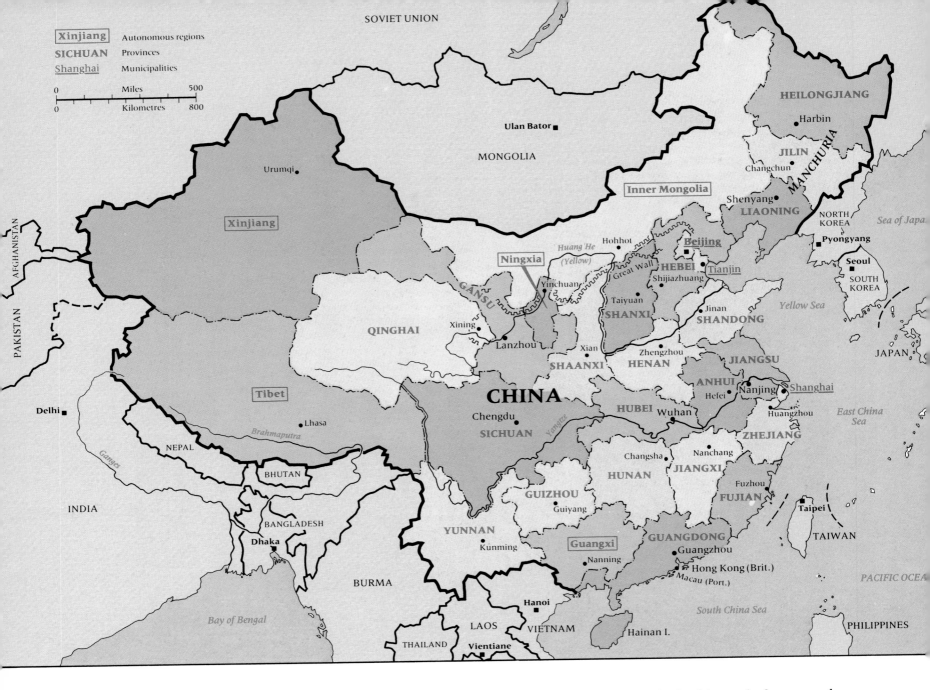

'adventurism'. In the attempt to force rapid socialist transformation without giving due account to the concrete problems of economic development, Mao said, the party has been 'like a child playing with fire, without experience, knowing pain only after getting burned'. But Mao continued to defend the broad goals of the Leap.

In the face of the evident failure of the Leap, a challenge to Mao's leadership was mounted at the Lushan Conference of the Central Committee in July-August of 1959, led by Minister of Defence Peng Dehuai, who had expressed scepticism of the Leap from the beginning. China was not materially ready for an imminent transition to communism, Peng argued, nor could subjective factors of mass enthusiasm or transforming the relations of production through collectivism compensate for China's material shortcomings.

Mao charged that Peng's criticisms were a 'frantic attack against the party' by 'rightist opportunists', and demanded that the Central Committee choose between his leadership and that of his critics. Fearing a crisis of leadership, the Central Committee bowed, condemning the 'anti-Party' clique headed by Peng Dehuai and

reaffirming both Mao's leadership and the general policies of the Leap.

As the true scale of the disaster became clear, the Leap policies were quietly abandoned, and with them Mao's influence with the top party leaders waned. But in the aftermath of Lushan, it had become politically impossible to openly confront the failure of the Leap and its implications for Mao's leadership. The commitment to collectivism, in theory if not in practice, was maintained intact until the post-Mao era.[13]

Despite the disastrous results, however, the objectives of Mao's Great Leap Forward policies can hardly be condemned root and branch. In seeking a balanced development of agriculture and industry as an alternative to the Soviet model of squeezing agriculture to finance heavy industry, Mao's thinking was closer to Deng Xiaoping's rural reforms of the late 1970s than is generally understood, and anticipated modern developmental theory.

Mao's concern that priority development of heavy industry was making China increasingly dependent on the Soviet Union is also quite defensible. The rural

24

commune, although abolished in name, remains as the township the key economic and political entity of rural China. Township industries, many of which were founded as commune and brigade enterprises during the Great Leap Forward, have emerged as one of the most dynamic sectors of China's economy in post-reform China.

The methodology of the Great Leap Forward, however, attempting to force high-speed agricultural growth through massive application of labour, and in particular the collectivisation of rural society and the attempt to displace the family as the locus of economic activity, compounded by the rushed manner in which the changes were implemented, was an unmitigated disaster. Moreover, the factional polarisation within the party that developed in the wake of the Great Leap Forward seriously impaired the party's ability to adjust its policies and set the scene for the internecine struggle of the Cultural Revolution.

Conditions in the countryside deteriorated rapidly as the dislocations of the Leap were compounded by the worst three years of natural disaster in decades. At least 10 million are believed to have perished under famine conditions during 1960-62, and China was forced to import grain from Canada and Australia.

Industrial production also fell, mainly due to the dislocations of the planning and allocation system attributed to the Leap, but also because of food shortages and the breakdown in production of other agricultural products.

With the failure of the 1960 harvest, China reverted to the regional administrative structure of the early 1950s, establishing six regional Politburos. The regional leaders quietly took steps to effectively decentralise the communes, assigning land, tools and farm animals to production teams. These reforms were supported by the party leaders Liu Shaoqi, Deng Xiaoping and Zhou Enlai and were adopted as nationwide policy in 1961.[14] The central-south region under Tao Zhu, assisted by Zhao Ziyang, went further by guaranteeing private plots and free rural markets, and contracting output to households. These steps were widely emulated in 1961-62 and later became the core of the rural reform policy of the late 1970s.[15]

Despite the effective dismantling of the Leap policies in practice, Maoist policies had not been explicitly disavowed. Peng Dehuai's attack on Mao's leadership and policies were revived in the course of the 1960s recovery in the form of veiled criticism in literature and journalism. Most notable of these was the play 'Hai Jui Dismissed from Office' by Wu Han, a brilliant historian of the Ming Dynasty and vice-mayor of Peking. Hai Jui was a 16th-century official of the Censorate whose brave criticism of a possibly mad emperor led to his disgrace and banishment. Wu Han's play was widely understood as an attack on Mao and the dismissal of Peng Dehuai at Lushan.

The Great Leap also came under attack by Marxist economists such as Sun Yefang, who argued that the subjectivist approach of the Leap had undermined the economy and violated objective economic law. The economists argued for decentralising management of industry and investment, restoring free markets and returning to the individual household as the basic economic unit in the countryside, all policies that would

be taken up again in the reforms of the late 1970s and early 1980s.[16]

These arguments were taken up by state chairman Liu Shaoqi, party secretary-general Deng Xiaoping and other party leaders. In response, Mao and his supporters formed an alliance with Lin Biao, who had replaced Peng Dehuai as Minister of Defence, and initiated a programme of political indoctrination in the PLA. By 1962, the leadership was clearly polarised along a left-right axis between the party central leadership headed by Liu on the right and the leftist group centred around Mao. The rightists, however, were divided on the issues of liberalisation and ideology, with Liu and Deng stressing the need to enforce the authority and discipline of the party.[17]

Foreign relations and the Sino-Soviet split

China's regional posture had softened in the mid-1950s as support of revolutionary movements in neighbouring countries was cut back and Zhou Enlai developed the theme of coexistence. China's successful support of Ho Chi Minh at the 1954 Geneva Conference and the statesmanship of the urbane Prime Minister Zhou Enlai won a measure of respect for China. Zhou's performance at the Bandung Conference in 1955, reiterating China's commitment to the principles of peaceful coexistence, confirmed China's new status as a leader of the world's developing nations.

China embarked on a suddenly assertive foreign relations posture in the year of the Great Leap Forward. The shelling of the island of Quemoy, held by Nationalist (Guomindang) forces, in August 1958, successfully neutralised Quemoy and Matsu as bases for Nationalist harassment operations on the Chinese mainland, but it also led to renewed US commitment to Jiang Fieshi's forces on Taiwan.

A tribal uprising in Tibet escalated into open revolt in 1959 when the Dalai Lama, the nominal ruler under Chinese suzerainty, fled to India. The revolt was suppressed by Chinese troops, and what had been a substantial degree of Tibetan autonomy under the Dalai Lama came to an end. The consolidation of Chinese power in Tibet and the discovery that China had constructed a road into Tibet over land claimed by India stirred Sino-Indian tensions, and border clashes between Chinese and Indian troops suggested the limits of the principles of peaceful coexistence.

China was also becoming more assertive within the Soviet bloc. The relationship with the Soviet Union had been problematic since the 1930s, when Mao, advocating an unorthodox peasant-based revolutionary strategy, had wrested control of the Chinese party away from a Moscow-orientated faction. Mao, whose relationship with Khruschev was brittle, scorned the Soviet leader's denunciation of Stalin and the 'cult of personality'.

In the aftermath of the Hungarian uprising of 1956, the widening gap between the two socialist countries became increasingly apparent. Beijing began to attack what it termed 'revisionism' within the Soviet bloc, presenting itself as an alternative centre of Communist leadership. Moscow pointedly distanced itself from Beijing's position in the Quemoy-Matsu crisis and the Sino-Indian border dispute.

Hostility between the two socialist powers intensified into open dispute at the Romanian party congress in 1960, and in July the Soviet Union downgraded relations with China from one of fraternal parties to a state-to-state level and withdrew all Soviet advisors from China. This act had the effect of inflaming Chinese nationalist sentiments, undercutting the position of Soviet-trained scientists and technicians in China and rallying support within the Chinese party leadership behind Mao.[18] It also left China virtually a pariah state in the world, committed to a hostile posture towards both the United States and the Soviet Union. Cut off from any source of technological, military or economic assistance, China fell back on the Maoist doctrine of self-reliance which strongly reinforced the more radical aspects of Maoist economic policy.

The Cultural Revolution 1965-75

The dispute between Mao and the central party leadership came to a head in September 1965, when Mao's demand for a new party rectification campaign to silence his critics, and specifically to condemn Wu Han's play, was refused by the Politburo Standing Committee. Among Wu's defenders, who would later be purged, were Deng Xiaoping and Beijing's mayor Peng Zhen. Mao retreated to the southern city of Hangzhou where he met with his closest allies, including his wife, Jaing Qing, and the head of the eastern China regional administration bureau, Zhang Chunqiao.

The first salvo of the Cultural Revolution was an attack on Wu Han's play, which appeared in November in the Shanghai newspaper *Wen Hui Bao* under the byline of its editor, Yao Wenyuan. The criticism was at first rebuffed in the Beijing papers under party control, but it was reprinted in *Jiefang Ribao* (Liberation Army Daily), which was controlled by Mao's ally Lin Biao. The leftists also won the early support of the All-China Federation of Trade Unions and the central-south regional administration head, Tao Zhu.

The leftists quickly expanded the targets of their attack, issuing a circular in May 1966 charging that capitalist roaders had infiltrated the party, government and army. Peng Zhen was dismissed from his positions in late May, signalling the first of many waves of purges of the party, military and state apparatus. The struggle was extended to universities and colleges in May, and violence erupted between leftists and student groups supporting the party leadership. In August the leftists convened a Central Committee plenum, from which their opponents were excluded, which endorsed the Cultural Revolution policies, made Lin Biao Mao's chief deputy, and demoted Liu Shaoqi, Zhou Enlai, Zhu De and Chen Yun from vice-chairman to ordinary Politburo members.

In October, Red Guard groups supporting the leftists demanded the resignation of Liu and Deng. Peng Zhen, Peng Dehuai and other critics of Mao were arrested, and provincial party organisations began to come under attack. Leftists took over Shanghai's municipal government and newspapers in January 1967, a step that was quickly emulated by leftist groups in other provinces and cities. Party organisations resisted and the confrontations between contending groups escalated into armed struggle. This led to intervention by the military.

Although the central military leadership under Lin Biao was pro-Maoist, the response of regional and local commanders varied. In the provinces of Heilongjiang, Shandong, Shanxi and Guizhou, and in Shanghai and Beijing, the military supported the left. In other provinces, the military either opposed the leftists or were neutral, but invariably the old party leadership and state apparatus was removed, with control passing either to a revolutionary committee (combining leftist party members and representatives of the military and the 'revolutionary mass organisations') or direct military command.[19]

The Maoists then re-focused their attacks on military commanders, and violence between leftists and military forces escalated, culminating in the mutiny of the Wuhan military command in July 1967. Heavy fighting with significant numbers of casualties were reported in Hunan, Guangzhou, Hubei, Sichuan and other provinces. Red Guards in Beijing occupied government ministries, including the Ministry of Foreign Affairs.

In the countryside, peasants were no longer allowed to farm private plots. Grain output declined by 4.2 per cent in 1968. Output levels were restored but only by committing all resources to grain production. Efficiency levels dropped radically and output of other crops — oilseeds, cotton, sugar and market vegetables — declined precipitously.

In this extreme situation, an alliance was formed between the military and those moderates who still survived in the central party leadership, most importantly Zhou Enlai, and a new purge began directed against the most extreme leftists, many of whom were associated with Mao's wife, Jiang Qing. Lin Biao moved to cooperate with Zhou and the regional military leaders in restoring civil order. Young Red Guards were sent down to the countryside to engage in labour and learn from peasants, eliminating what had become an unpredictable and uncontrollable military force. By the end of 1968, the worst of the violence was over and the political challenge of the extreme left had been deflected.[20]

Tentative steps to rehabilitate former cadres were begun and some previously purged leaders began to reappear in positions of responsibility, but the military retained the upper hand in the regions while the leftists around Mao remained in control of Shanghai and most cultural and propaganda organs.

Lin Biao, who had achieved a dominant position in the uneasy balance of power in Beijing, resisted efforts to reduce the role of the military. In 1969-70, Lin launched a renewed campaign to promote leftist economic policies, exacerbating tensions with the civilian party officials who were returning to positions of power and gaining support from regional military commanders. Lin may also have been at odds with Mao and Zhou over foreign policy issues such as rapprochement with the United States.

This conflict culminated, according to official sources, with Lin Biao's death in a plane crash in Outer Mongolia during a foiled attempt to escape to the Soviet Union after an aborted attempt to assassinate Mao and stage a military coup.

The leftists around Mao — Jiang Qing, Wang Hongwen, Zhang Chunqiao and Yao Wenyuan — retained control of the cultural, propaganda and education fields as well as exercising primary influence in Shanghai, but control of government administration and economic policy was now returning to the hands of rehabilitated party officials. Deng Xiaoping was rehabilitated in August 1973 and quickly became a member of the Central Committee Politburo. In 1975, Deng became a vice-chairman of the Politburo Standing Committee and was clearly being presented as the successor to Zhou Enlai, who was ill with cancer. The party also was able to engineer a reassignment of regional military commanders, and the veteran Marshal Ye Jianying filled the post of Minister of Defence, vacant since Lin's death, in 1975.

When Zhou died in January 1976, he was succeeded as premier not by Deng Xiaoping but by the Minister of Public Security, Hua Guofeng, and attacks on Deng as a capitalist roader reappeared in wall posters and the press. A spontaneous memorial service for Zhou Enlai in Tiananmen Square in Beijing on 4 April took on political characteristics with posters criticising Jiang Qing and rioting on 5 April. On 7 April, Deng was dismissed from his posts in the party and government, reportedly at the instigation of Mao.

Mao died on 9 September 1976, a month after a devastating earthquake in Tangshan, near Tianjin – a traditional omen that a dynasty is coming to its end. Hua Guofeng ordered the arrest of the radical Politburo members – Mao's widow Jiang Qing, party vice chairman Wang Hongwen, vice premier Zhang Chunqiao and the ideologist and critic Yao Wenyuan, henceforth called the Gang of Four – on 6 October and was appointed party chairman, succeeding Mao, on the following day.

Beyond reasserting his personal power in the Cultural Revolution, Mao had sought to counter trends toward bureaucratisation and social inequality, and renew the Chinese people's commitment to revolutionary change. In directing a mass campaign against the party itself, however, Mao released forces of fear and resentment which literally devastated the country.

The cultural life of China was destroyed, historical monuments defaced, books and paintings burned. Religion, art and scholarship were brutally suppressed, the educational system dismantled. The CCP was nearly eliminated and split into warring factions. The institutionalisation of class struggle in everyday life at every level of Chinese society brutalised an entire generation and cost many lives.

Post-Mao China and the rise of the reformists 1976-79

Deng Xiaoping was reinstated in his posts in July 1977 and the dismantling of Cultural Revolution policies began. The party leadership adopted a consensus position stressing economic construction and modernisation. However, signs of continuing differences between the hard-line critics of the Cultural Revolution centring around Deng and surviving moderate leftists became increasingly apparent.

The rural reform policies that would eventually extend to all of China began in Sichuan Province under the direction of the first party secretary, Zhao Ziyang, in the second half of 1977. In the following year, experimental industrial reforms were initiated in Sichuan, expanding the decision-making power of enterprises and introducing market factors into economic planning. At the same

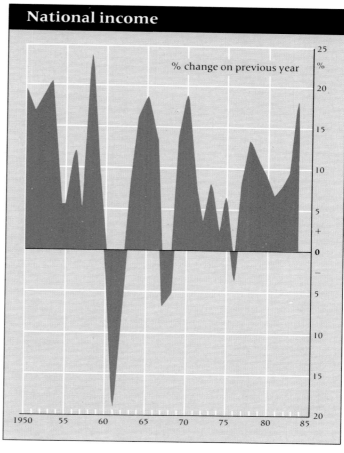

National income

% change on previous year

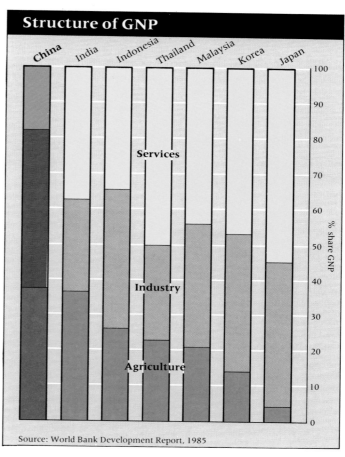

Structure of GNP

Services

Industry

Agriculture

Source: World Bank Development Report, 1985

27

time, Zhao began to adopt a higher public profile and travelled abroad for the first time, visiting Romania, Yugoslavia and Iran with Hua Guofeng. Hu Yaobang, a rehabilitated former head of the Communist Youth League, was made head of the powerful party organisation department in 1977.

The third plenum of the 11th Central Committee in December 1978, a major turning point in the reformists' consolidation of power, adopted a programme of economic reforms based on the experiments in Sichuan and other provinces. Hu Yaobang, economic planner Chen Yun and Deng Yingchao were appointed to the Politburo. Criticism of the Cultural Revolution and remaining leftists heightened in the following year.

Anxiety about concessions to the United States on the issue of Taiwan and concern over mounting domestic criticism of communism and the leadership role of the party checked the pace of liberalisation in 1979. Leading dissidents were arrested and Democracy Wall in Beijing, where critics displayed wall posters, was shut down.

Excessive imports of industrial equipment and overly high levels of investment led to readjustments of policies under the leadership of Chen Yun in 1979 and 1980. The work of economists such as Sun Yefang was revived, and the outlines of a broad programme of economic reform incorporating market forces and heightened autonomy of enterprises began to take shape and underwent experimental implementation in selected cities and provinces.

In September 1980, four key leaders of the remaining Maoists, including Wang Dongxing, formerly Mao's bodyguard who had played an important role in the arrest of the Gang of Four, were removed from their state and party posts. Hua Guofeng, associated with the moderate Maoists, was replaced as premier by Zhao Ziyang. Hua was removed from the chairmanship of the party in June 1981 and was replaced by Hu Yaobang.

Within five years, the anti-leftists led by Deng Xiaoping had largely eliminated the remaining moderate Maoists from the party leadership and set China on a course of radical economic and political reform, repudiating the collectivist and egalitarian theories of Mao and Lin Biao, but also increasingly distant from the orthodox system of centralised state economic planning and control modelled on the Soviet Union.

Recent economic policies and performance

In late 1978, a coalition of Chinese party leaders headed by Deng Xiaoping succeeded in establishing a common front powerful enough to tilt the policies of the CCP decisively in the direction of major economic reform. Since the third plenum of the 11th Central Committee in December 1978, the party has moved to repudiate the Maoist vision of a highly collectivised, egalitarian society and begun a shift toward a mixed economy modelled on the successful mixed-market economies of East Asia and the West. The reformists' economic programme has progressed on three fronts, commonly referred to as rural reform, urban reform and the open door policy.

Rural reform is the decollectivisation of agriculture, returning to the family as the essential economic unit in the countryside, and lifting controls to allow peasants to freely market their surplus production. This was the first thrust of the reforms in the late 1970s and had been extremely successful.

Urban reform is a broad umbrella term encompassing every aspect of industry and commerce. It includes efforts to expand the autonomy of enterprises, provide material incentives to workers and enterprises, loosen planning and price controls, replace state investment with credit finance, encourage small-scale private enterprise and allow market forces to supplant unified state control over the distribution of commodities and materials.

The open door policy refers to opening China to foreign investment and technology and expanding foreign trade. This policy touches and overlaps urban reform in many ways as Chinese enterprises have become involved in export markets, acquired more imported equipment, begun to participate in joint economic ventures or production arrangements, and as imported goods have entered Chinese domestic markets.

China today has essentially completed its rural reform programme and is in mid-course on its programme of urban reform and developing foreign trade and investment.

Rural reforms since 1979

In moving to endorse rural reforms at the third plenum of the Central Committee in late 1978, the CCP — still shaky, unpopular and severely demoralised after a decade of violent internecine struggle — acknowledged the failure of collectivisation policies imposed on the countryside two decades before. The party was also responding to powerful pressures from the rural population.

Decollectivisation was already appearing spontaneously in the countryside. Jinyu (Goldfish) commune in Guanghan County, Sichuan Province, secretly divided the fields among its production teams in 1977, and it was there, the following year, that the practice was first condoned as an experiment by the provincial party first secretary Zhao Ziyang, now China's premier.

Beginning in 1979, the Chinese government moved swiftly toward comprehensive rural reforms, dismantling the communes and returning to the individual farming family as the basic agricultural production unit under what is called the 'production responsibility system'. Accompanying decollectivisation were major adjustments, increasing the base prices paid by the state to peasants for grain by 21 per cent, cotton by 15 per cent, oilseeds by 25 per cent and pigs by 25 per cent. Retail prices paid by urban consumers for these staple foodstuffs were not increased proportionately, however, which has led to a mounting subsidy burden on the central government.

Several variants of the production responsibility system have emerged in the past five years. Under what is now the most common form, *bao gan dao hu* (contracting everything to the household), individual households sign contracts which specify an output quota and allocate certain plots of land to their use. The specified output quota is turned over to the collective and sold to the state at the fixed base price. Above quota production may be sold to the state at a higher negotiated price, or it may be sold directly in rural and urban markets.

Contracts are typically signed for periods of three to five years and longer-term contracts are now becoming more common. The household may purchase and own other means of production, i.e. implements and machinery. The household is required to pay taxes and contribute funds to collective welfare schemes and labour to public construction projects.

Ownership of productive land is retained by the collective; the household's position is perhaps most analogous to that of a leaseholder. Allocation of land among households is determined under a variety of different schemes. The most common system is that each household receives a base allocation of land for each member of a household. The household may then seek to contract for additional land above the base allocation, and competing claims are resolved through bidding.

The plots of land involved are exceedingly small in most cases, even by the standards of highly populous developing countries. There are three farm workers for every hectare of arable land in China, compared to 2.3 in Bangladesh, 1.6 in Indonesia and 1.0 in India. Agriculture in China resembles gardening in much of the rest of the world.[21]

Similar contractual arrangements are made for subsidiary agricultural production such as raising farm animals and poultry, and for specialised agricultural services such as mechanised ploughing, treatment with pesticides, equipment repair, etc.

Beginning in 1985, the remaining coercive aspects of the compulsory quota system for crop delivery, which was introduced along with rationing in the 1950s at a time of widespread food shortages, are to be eliminated and replaced by voluntary supply contracts between peasants and state purchasing agencies. It is as yet unclear how far this step has been implemented.

The rural reforms spread rapidly. There is now almost nowhere in China that does not practice some form of responsibility system – contracting land and production responsibility either to the work team or the individual hopusehold – and in more developed provinces upwards of 90 per cent of peasants practice the household responsibility system.

By any standard, the rural reforms have been an outstanding success. From 1979 to 1984, agricultural output value grew at an average annual rate of 9.2 per cent (the average rate over 1953–78 had been 3.2 per cent). Grain output increased by 22.5 per cent to 407.1 million tonnes in 1984, and China is expected to be a net grain exporter by the end of 1985. Production of cotton, China's most important cash crop, nearly tripled to 6.1 million tonnes, turning China, which had been the world's biggest cotton importer in the late 1970s, into a cotton exporter and the world's biggest cotton producer.

Sugar production has increased by a half over 1979 levels, and meat production by 42 per cent. Although comprehensive statistics for vegetable production are not available, the quantity and variety of vegetables sold in urban markets has improved markedly over the past five years.

The expansion of grain output has been accomplished entirely through increased yields per hectare (the total sown acreage devoted to grains has steadily decreased since 1979). In the case of cotton and other cash crops, sown area has been expanded, but yields have improved even faster, thereby generating dramatic increases in output.

The results of a 1984 survey of 30,427 peasant households in 600 counties astounded even China's leaders. The results indicated that rural incomes more than doubled between 1978 and 1984 in real terms, the first significant improvement in rural living standards since the early 1950s.

Most analysts, including Chinese economists, consider the incentives created by the production responsibility system to be the key element in the success of rural reforms. However, higher state procurement prices for staple food products introduced in 1979 have also played an important role. Another factor has been the loosening of controls of the transport and marketing of agricultural produce by rural collectives and individuals.

Rural traders and transport collectives have provided new links between rural producers and urban markets. The free market in the countryside is a fact. Those peasants who can reasonably transport excess and sideline produce to the cities and towns, do so. Every city and town in China has its free market, and in many areas these markets have burst their original bounds. Peasants and traders line the streets selling vegetables, fruit, rice, cut flowers, spices and medicinal herbs.

Since 1984, producers and traders have been allowed to transport their goods across county and provincial borders, and new regional and even national networks for distributing agricultural produce are beginning to emerge alongside the state distribution system.

Agriculture

Agriculture is the base of the Chinese economy and the most critical sector for its people. It accounts for 37 per cent of China's gross domestic product (GDP), a proportion similar to other low-income economies, e.g. India (36 per cent) and Bangladesh (47 per cent), but far higher than the middle-income countries, where agriculture's share of GDP ranges from 10 to 20 per cent, and the industrial market economies (2-8 per cent).[22]

Considering agriculture as a proportion of GDP actually understates the importance of agriculture in the Chinese economy. Because GDP is calculated on the basis of output value, proportional calculations are very sensitive to relative prices. Agricultural goods are priced very low in China relative to world prices: quota prices for grain are as little as 10 per cent of international levels, and market prices, which vary seasonally, are about one-third of world price levels or less. The price differentials for meat, poultry, fish and cash crops such as cotton and tobacco are even higher.

While primary industrial products, particularly energy, are also priced low compared to world prices, manufactured goods are generally priced at or above world levels. Calculating a hypothetical GDP which evaluated sectoral output at prices comparable to world levels results in a

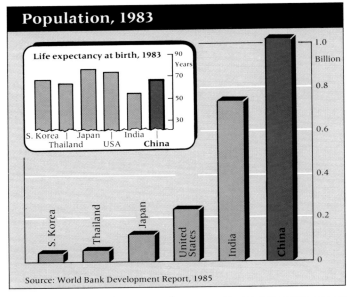

Population, 1983

Life expectancy at birth, 1983

Source: World Bank Development Report, 1985

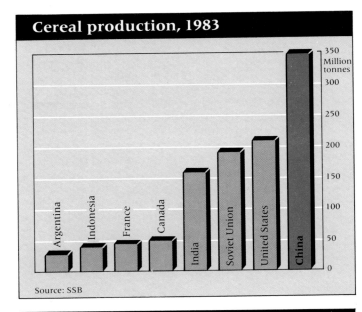

Cereal production, 1983

Source: SSB

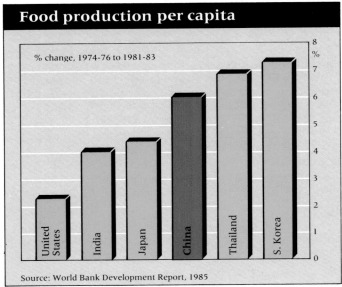

Food production per capita

% change, 1974-76 to 1981-83

Source: World Bank Development Report, 1985

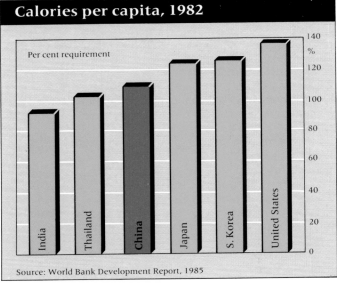

Calories per capita, 1982

Per cent requirement

Source: World Bank Development Report, 1985

higher overall GDP figure in which agriculture would occupy a significantly larger overall share.

Most of China's 800 million rural population owe their livelihood directly or indirectly to farming. Agriculture directly employs 70 per cent of the Chinese workforce, over 300 million people. As much as one-third of agricultural labour is redundant at present levels of agricultural technology. One of the most important questions for the future will be how much of the rural labour force can be successfully absorbed in industry, both urban and rural-based, and services. (See also below: Diversifying the rural economy.)

Growth rates in the agricultural sector have dramatically improved since the rural reforms were instituted in 1979 and the farming household again became the basic producing unit in agriculture. This also reflects large-scale investments in water management and fertiliser production capacity over the past three decades. But beyond expanding irrigation and fertiliser application, the agricultural technology in China has changed little, remaining primarily focused on highly intensive cultivation of small plots with little mechanisation.

Arable land

Arable land in China is very scarce. Official estimates calculate that the total amount of cultivated land is less than 100 million hectares (ha), about 10 per cent of total land area. Although preliminary results from satellite imaging studies suggest that the actual cultivated land area may be considerably larger, perhaps as much as 130 million ha, this would be only 13-14 per cent of the total land area. By comparison, 46 per cent of all land is cultivated in India, 66 per cent in Bangladesh and 25 per cent in Taiwan.

There is a constant tendency for arable land to be lost as it is claimed for use by housing and industry. Official estimates show a decline of about one million ha between 1980 and 1983. Actual losses were larger, but are offset by reclamation of unused land. However, there is a tendency for the most productive land to be lost, as in the fertile but populous delta regions, while newly-reclaimed land may be only marginally productive.

Multiple cropping in the south has increased the effective arable land area by nearly a half, although there has been a slight decrease in multiple cropping since the

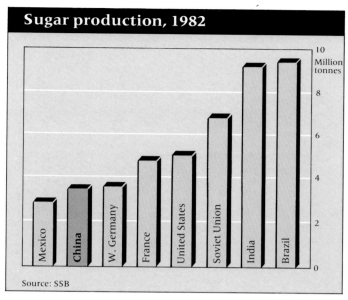

Sugar production, 1982

Source: SSB

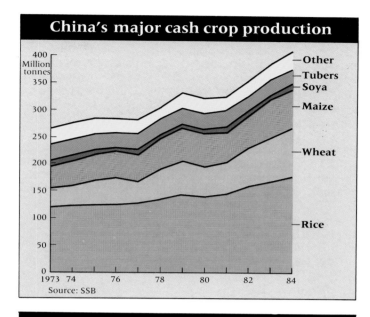

China's major cash crop production

Source: SSB

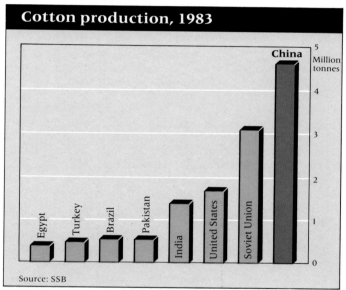

Cotton production, 1983

Source: SSB

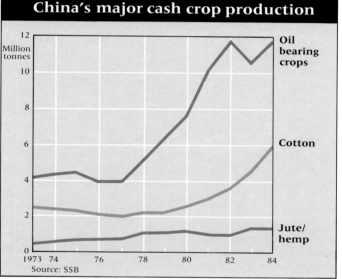

China's major cash crop production

Source: SSB

implementation of rural reforms, probably because the practice had been taken to uneconomic degrees by the late 1970s.

Arable land, and population, is concentrated in the eastern half of China, an area that in ancient times was forested and is roughly bounded by a line drawn between Harbin in Heilongjiang Province and Kunming in south-eastern Yunnan Province. Agricultural production in the predominantly arid western and north-western regions is negligible.

Within the arable region, another line drawn from the Qin Ling mountain range along the course of the Huai River (entering the Yellow Sea in northern Jiangsu Province) divides China into the arid north, where wheat is the staple grain crop, and the predominantly rice-growing south.

Soil

Generally speaking, cultivated soils north of the Huai River are neutral to alkaline brown forest pedocals (containing calcium carbonate, also called *korichnevyi*

soils), with large deposits of loess soils in the north-west and brown podzolic (leached non-calcareous) soils in the north-east. South of the river soils are neutral to acid red podzolic and, in the south-eastern coastal region, yellow and red lateritic.

The fertile soils of the Chang Jiang basin, particularly the delta region, are highly modified as a result of centuries of intensive cultivation, particularly paddy rice growing, and this unique soil is sometimes termed paddy soil. However, almost all soils in China have been affected by extensive human cultivation.

Salinity, due to inadequate drainage and aridity, affects large areas in the north which are now the subject of extensive reclamation projects. Erosion is a serious problem in many areas, exacerbated by the effects of deforestation, both historical and recent, and excessive grazing by sheep and goats in mountain and steppe areas. Cultivated soils tend to be relatively deficient in organic matter, which is attributed to extensive use of crop stalks and waste as fuel or animal feed, or burning of stalks where they are used in the fields.

Fertilisers

The rate of chemical fertiliser application in China is extremely high, exceeding 150 kg per cultivated ha, including multiple-cropped acreage. This is slightly higher than the application rate in the United States and more than three times higher than in India, but lower than in Japan and South Korea. The annual growth in consumption of fertiliser averaged 11 per cent over 1970-80 and has accelerated since the rural reforms and higher agriculture procurement prices were introduced in 1979.

China produces 85 per cent of the chemical fertiliser it consumes. The rapid increase in consumption was made possible by 13 large nitrogen fertiliser plants imported in the mid-1970s, which came on stream in the late 1970s. The rate of consumption growth is likely to slow down over the next few years, as there are no new plants of comparable scale currently under construction, and some local producers whose quality is below standard are likely to close.[23]

The ratio of nutrients in chemical fertilisers is seriously imbalanced, however. Phosphorus (P_2O_5) application represents only 31 per cent of nitrogen (N) content, and potassium (K_2O) only 2 per cent, while the corresponding ratios in the United States are 100:46:54, and in Japan 100:112:83. The shortage of P_2O_5 and K_2O is partly compensated by the use of organic fertilisers, which are rich in phosporus and potassium and account for approximately 40 per cent of total fertiliser application. However, fertiliser imbalance remains the limiting factor in improving fertiliser effectiveness in many areas.

Climate

Rainfall in China is governed by the monsoon cycle. In winter, intense high-pressure zones build up over the cooling landmass which generate steady seaward movement of the very dry and cold polar and Siberian airmasses.

In summer, low pressure develops over the warm landmass and high pressure shifts to the Pacific Ocean. The Siberian airmass retreats as warm, humid and unstable tropical airmasses move inland from the south and south-east. This is the basis of the typical monsoon weather pattern: rainfall concentrated in the summer months, and relatively dry winters. Over 80 per cent of China's rainfall occurs between May and October.

The amount of rainfall decreases as one moves from the humid south-east coastal regions, which may receive 2,000 mm annually, toward the north-west, with rainfall of less than 375 mm along the Huang (Yellow River). In the extreme west, rainfall is negligible or non-existent.

Rainfall in any particular location is extremely variable. In years when the south-eastern summer typhoon is weak, warm humid airmasses may not reach the north China plain but remain bottled over central China. The excess rains can cause extensive flooding in the central region, leaving the north under the influence of the dry Siberian airmass. This is the source of the seemingly paradoxical incidence of simultaneous drought in the north and flooding in the central region and south, as occurred in 1981.

Due to its size, China experiences extreme climatic variation from north to south. In the tropical south-eastern coastal region there is no winter, and summers last from five to eight months, while in north-eastern Heilongjiang Province, and on the Tibetan plateau, there are virtually no summers and extremely long winters. Mean annual temperatures vary from 20°C or higher in the south-east to 15°C in central China and less than 0°C in northern Heilongjiang Province. Most of this variation occurs in the winter months. There is little temperature difference between northern and southern China in the summer; the hottest areas are along the Chang Jiang: mean July temperatures in the 'furnace' city of Wuhan may exceed 30°C.

These factors together mean that the growing season is shortest in the north, where rainfall is slightest and the least dependable. Irrigation is therefore vitally important in the north, but it is also very important in the south, where taking advantage of the warm but usually dry winter months for crop cultivation generally requires irrigation as well.

Irrigation

Official estimates indicate that 45 per cent of China's arable land is irrigated, an extremely high figure, although this may be over-stated as a result of under-estimating total arable land. Total irrigated area has increased by approximately 50 per cent since the mid-1950s, primarily as a result of large-scale water conservation works in the north. This has greatly reduced farmers' vulnerability to the vagaries of the weather.

The threat of drought has not been eliminated, however. Extended drought can easily drain reservoirs and the actual irrigated area in China is less than the irrigable total one year in four. The water table beneath north China is declining precipitously, due to both agricultural and urban demand.

Current plans to expand irrigation would bring the total irrigated area to over 50 million ha by the year 2000, half of which would be added south of the Huai River by improving existing facilities. The most ambitious project now scheduled would divert Chang Jiang water northward and to the west.

Rural organisation

The communes which dominated rural life in China since the late 1950s have not disappeared, but their functions and operations have changed with the advent of rural reforms and the return to family farming.

Renamed *xiang*, or township, the communes remain the most important political unit below the county level in most regions and play a key role in the lives of its members. The *xiang* governments play a particularly important role in developing rural industry. They are responsible for organising large-scale infrastructural projects such as irrigation and roads, and may administer or oversee rural collective welfare schemes. Communes vary considerably in size; the population of a commune in densely-settled areas may range from 15,000 to 40,000 or more.

Below the commune, the village unit which became the brigade, or *dadui*, during the collectivist period is again simply the village, or *cun*. The village has become a less important unit as its managerial powers have been cut back with the responsibility system, which gives individual households a high degree of managerial control. However, the village remains an important social unit, often with strong clan and marriage ties linking its member families. Villages operate their own industrial enterprises, which are still referred to as brigade enterprises in most of the literature on China, and often maintain collective welfare schemes. Typically, a village may consist of 200-500 families, or 800-2,000 people.

The production team, or *shengchandui*, was a basic work unit under the commune system and became the primary unit contracting agricultural production in the early stages of rural reform. Now termed the *cunmin xiaozu*, or villagers' group, it has become much less important with the popularisation of the household responsibility system.

Despite the shift of functions and responsibility and the formal change in names, the terms commune, brigade and team are still widely used, and – reports that the communes are dead notwithstanding – the *xiang* in particular continues to play an important role. The *xiang* is the interface at which the state meets the most numerous segment of the Chinese population, the peasantry.

Because it is close to the people it administers, the *xiang* can be highly responsive to their needs and demands. The speed and apparent ease with which the responsibility systems have been implemented between 1979 and 1984 attests to this, since most observers agree that one effect of the reforms has been to reduce the power of party cadre at the commune level, who might have been expected to resist them.

Investment

Total investment in agriculture, although small compared to urban industry, rose steadily between the late 1960s and 1977. But in the same period there was a serious decline in the efficiency of resource use and in output growth.

The rapid output growth rate of the last five years reflects in part the exploitation of investments made in previous years, including water works, farm machinery and fertiliser production capacity, that have not been maximally utilised. This 'free' boost to agricultural output will not continue indefinitely.

Expanding yields has provided most of the gains under the reform policies since 1979, but yields in China are already high, and the costs of further expanding yields are likely to increase. By the late 1970s, China had already attained average rice yields comparable to Taiwan and South Korea in the mid-1960s and wheat yields close to those in the United States.

Future gains will be progressively more difficult. Foreign analysts have expressed doubt that decollectivisation itself, without expanding new investment in agriculture, can provide the basis for sustained growth in agriculture. This scepticism is increasingly shared by researchers and policy-makers in China.

State funds play a relatively small role in rural investment. Budgetary allocations to agriculture, including forestry, water conservation and meteorology, declined from a high of Rmb16.8 billion in 1979 to Rmb11.3 billion in 1982, and only Rmb9.4 billion in 1985, about 6 per cent of total budgeted spending. Of this, approximately half is absorbed in administrative costs and approximately 20 per cent is devoted to relief funds and subsidies to poor regions and localities affected by natural disaster. Only Rmb3-4 billion is available for basic construction investment.

Most investment is therefore generated by the *xiang* (township) and *cun* (village) collectives and by individuals. According to World Bank estimates, state funds accounted for only 5 per cent of the total Rmb65 billion gross rural capital formation in 1982; collectives generated 20 per cent, and 75 per cent was individual household investment. Two-thirds of the private investment, however, was in housing and accumulation of stock, neither of which constitutes productive investment. Half of the collective investment was devoted to township and village industry, which does not address the investment needs of agriculture.

A problem noted in almost all studies of the reform is that the collective-level organs – the *xiang* and *cun* – now have less income from agriculture, the returns from which now accrue to families, and less power to draft labour for collective projects. Not only have rural households tended to invest most of their higher incomes in housing and savings, but many of the important infrastructure projects which must be undertaken at the local level, such as roads and local irrigation works, are not likely to receive voluntary support from individual households.

The current phase of rapid growth, based mainly on gains in efficiency due to initiative and energies released by the rural reforms, can be maintained until 1987 or 1988, according to Lu Wen, a Senior Research Fellow at the National Research Centre for Rural Development in Peking.[24] Further progress beyond the end of this decade will depend on new materials inputs to agriculture.

The shortfall in agricultural investment, however, is not quite as serious as it first appears, primarily because the funds needed are available in the form of private rural savings. A 1985 World Bank study estimated the average annual fixed investment in agriculture needed to sustain an average 3.6 per cent growth in crop production over the next 20 years at Rmb20 billion (in 1982 prices) per year, starting at Rmb11-12 billion per year and rising to Rmb33 billion by the year 2000. This estimate is lower than some other estimates of investment requirements in agriculture, and very low compared to current rates of gross rural capital formation.

Current agricultural investment levels, assuming approximately Rmb3-4 billion in state funds and Rmb5-6 billion in collective funds, are close to the target levels, and could be increased considerably by mobilising and diverting a relatively small proportion of rural savings currently absorbed in new housing or held in unproductive forms.

Prices and policies

Following the freeing of non-staple food prices and the liberalisation of free markets for agricultural goods, the government moved to dismantle compulsory purchases of grain, cotton and oil crops in 1985. This was a fundamental change affecting the most basic aspect of the state's economic role in China. The system of compulsory delivery quotas for grain and other foodstuffs, also known as the state unified purchase policy, was initiated in the early 1950s in conjunction with market rationing to ensure adequate supplies at fixed low prices.

Ploughing with water buffalo in southern China

Raising procurement prices for agricultural goods in 1979 was successful in creating larger incentives for peasants to expand production, and rationalised the ratio of the costs of agricultural inputs, such as fertiliser, to ex-farm prices. But at the same time, it created an enormous subsidy burden for the state, which was constrained by political considerations to maintain the low fixed prices for staple foodstuffs in urban markets.

The cost of subsidising grain purchases by urban consumers was Rmb12.2 billion in 1981, equivalent to 11 per cent of total state revenues in that year, and was probably much higher in 1984 and 1985 because procurement levels were higher and many peasants managed to get more of their output purchased at higher negotiated price levels. Total subsidies costs, including housing, transport and energy, are estimated to be equivalent to 25 per cent of all government spending, a major reason why China's leaders have decided to make food prices the first item on the price reform agenda.

Another reason is that large surpluses accumulated in several successive years of bumper harvests, including stocks maintained by producers, have made rapid upward price swings unlikely.

The state plans to purchase 75-80 million tonnes of grain, approximately 20 per cent of anticipated total grain production, in 1985 through voluntary contracts at two price levels: 30 per cent is to be purchased at the old base price for state purchases under quota (approximately Rmb52/tonne for paddy rice, Rmb77 for wheat and Rmb117 for soyabeans) and 70 per cent at the old negotiated (above-quota) price (Rmb80/tonne for paddy rice, Rmb115 for wheat and Rmb136 for soyabeans).

The remainder of marketed grain, approximately 5 million tonnes, will be sold at market prices and subject to market price fluctuations, according to an article by premier Zhao Ziyang in the February 1985 issue of the party journal *Red Flag*. If necessary, Zhao wrote, the state will step in and purchase any surplus grain at the base purchase price if market prices fall below state purchasing prices, and the state can also intervene by selling stocks if prices rise too high.

The idea of using government grain stocks as a buffer against violent price swings has a long and distinguished history in China. The legalist political philosopher Guan Zhong in the 7th century BC advised his patron, Duke Huan, the ruler of the state of Qi, 'Collect and accumulate when things are cheap and distribute into circulation when things are expensive'. Attempts to realise price stabilisation by means of 'ever-normal' state granaries have preoccupied Chinese leaders ever since.

The problem is that even the resources of the state are ultimately limited and can be overwhelmed by sharp or prolonged swings in supply and demand. An attempt by the minister Sang Hongyang to implement a buffer stock stabilisation scheme during the Western Han period foundered under the pressure of a longer drought than Sang anticipated, leading a rival and critic to suggest to the emperor that Sang be boiled alive in oil.

China has already experienced some difficulties in the course of dismantling the compulsory procurement system for grain in 1985, as rural rice traders emerged in the Dongting Lake area of Hunan Province to arbitrage between the state buffer stock sale price and the higher local market prices.[25]

There are serious questions, however, whether any feasible state-administered price stabilisation system alone could successfully dampen heavy seasonal price oscillations, or moderate any serious swing in supply and demand. China is the world's biggest rice producer by far and, along with the United States and the Soviet Union, is one of the world's big three wheat growers. The financial resources needed to stabilise grain prices effectively in a completely unregulated environment are impossible to estimate, but would likely be much more than the current grain subsidy cost of Rmb12-14 billion.

In north China, the average costs of cultivation rose 10-15 per cent from 1983 to 1984 while the returns on grain cultivation declined.[26] This tendency is likely to intensify with the end of mandatory grain output quotas, particularly when currently subsidised prices for fuel and chemical fertiliser come within the range of price reforms. Currently prices of chemical fertilisers supplied under the State Plan are between one-half (for ammonium sulphate) and one-ninth (for super phosphate) of average world prices.

If farmers are to be induced to substantially increase investments in agricultural inputs, they will need some means of hedging against price volatility, particularly as the marginal costs of increasing production grow. This would imply the need for a futures market or its functional analogue. Legitimising commodity trading by enterprises and individuals would seem unavoidable, and implicit in the very concept of market regulation. Commodity trading in China, if extremely profitable, is still liable to be condemned as speculation and subject to legal and party sanctions.

China's recent grain surpluses are largely a relative phenomenon, due to the low levels of per capita consumption. While some localities, notably the north-eastern provinces of Liaoning, Jilin and Heilongjiang, experienced difficulties in storing and marketing grain in 1984 and 1985, this was primarily related to local transport and distribution problems or inadequate storage facilities, and did not mean saturation of demand for grain on a national level. In per capita terms, China's bumper grain harvest in 1984 represented 400 kg of grain per person – an enormous achievement for China but only barely adequate by world standards when processing losses and the growing ratio of conversion into meat is taken into account.

While it is relatively easy to purchase rough long-grained non-glutinous rice anywhere in China, superior-quality and glutinous varieties are in very short supply. There is still a shortfall in wheat production which is made up from imports, and there are serious shortages of barley and sorghum, the raw materials for manufacturing beer and the most widely-consumed form of spirit.

According to Ji Yecheng, writing on grain issues in *Liaowang* (Outlook) in January 1985, the apparent grain surplus in 1984 is entirely structural, that is 'caused by the irrational distribution structure and the irrational structure of varieties'. Shifting the product structure toward more desirable varieties and higher quality will inevitably result in higher prices.

Diversifying the rural economy

With staple crop yields near maximum feasible values, raising land unit productivity will require increased specialisation and investment. But the labour-intensity and small scale of family farming in China is a major obstacle to specialisation, and obstructs mobilisation and deployment of investment funds in the countryside.

The only way to achieve the needed degree of specialisation, improvements in labour productivity and release of investment potential, Chinese economists say, will be to move a very large proportion, 60-70 per cent, of China's 300 million rural workers out of agriculture over the next 15-20 years.

According to researchers in rural development, by the year 2000 the percentage of the rural workforce engaged in cultivation, now approximately 85 per cent, is projected to decline to only 30 per cent. The largest share of the rural workforce will be absorbed by rural industry and commerce. Another 20 per cent will be engaged in forestry, animal husbandry and aquaculture will be 20 per cent. The remaining 10 per cent will move to cities, working mainly in services and construction, or remain in the country as mine workers.

The implications of such a transformation within a single generation are staggering, not least because Chinese planners expect it to be accomplished not by state directives and coercion but rather through economic forces already at work in the countryside.

Those who remain on the land as cultivators will be professionals, according to Lu Wen, using better technology and more capital-intensive methods, and farming three times the current average acreage. They will be the survivors who emerge from the current phase of reforms on the basis of their abilities, contracting for larger production on larger areas of land as the less skilled turn to other pursuits.

Such specialised producers, better able to exploit local comparative advantages, are already appearing. Specialised households, including households engaged in rural processing and services, now account for an estimated 14 per cent of China's 180 million rural households. In more developed coastal provinces such as Zhejiang and Jiangsu, the proportion has reached 30 per cent. On average, specialised households market over 70 per cent of their output. The average percentage of marketable produce, or commodity ratio, for all agriculture and by-products is approximately 50 per cent. For grain producers, the average commodity ratio is only 30 per cent.

The crucial factor in diversifying the rural economy will be the development of rural industry and commerce and its capacity to absorb surplus rural labour.

Cereal crops

Overall grain production in China, excluding soyabeans which are normally included in Chinese statistics, was 364.8 million tonnes in 1984, about one-fifth of the world's total cereal production and 352 kg per capita. Cereal output production grew an average annual 4.3 per cent over 1974-84, well above the average world growth rate. Much of this growth occurred over 1981-84, however, when production growth averaged 8.5 per cent per year.

Rice

Rice is China's most important cereal crop, accounting for 50 per cent of the total cereal tonnage (44 per cent using China's broader category of grain). China's rice crop was 38 per cent of the world total in 1984.

Rice yields averaged 5,271 kg/ha in 1984, according to FAO estimates, a very high level. There has been steady improvement in yields, with an average annual increase of 4.6 per cent over the past decade and 6.5 per cent over 1981-84. China's yields are 64 per cent higher than the average for Asian producers, although this figure may be slightly overstated because of under-reporting of actual acreage in production.

Among major producers, only North and South Korea, Japan and Australia have higher yields, and except for Australia all these countries have higher rates of fertiliser application.

Only 20 per cent of the 34 million ha of rice-sown area is planted with hybrids, a figure that is expected to rise significantly over the next two decades. The net yield advantage of hybrid rice over non-hybrid rice is about 20 per cent, according to the World Bank, but Chinese consumers prefer non-hybrid rice which normally sells for 10 per cent less than traditional hybrid varieties.

Wheat

Wheat production has grown even faster than rice, with average growth per year of 7.4 per cent over 1974-84 and 14.2 per cent over 1981-84. Wheat is the second most important grain, and the 1984 crop of 87.68 million tonnes accounted for 24 per cent of China's total cereal output in that year, and 17 per cent of total world wheat production. Wheat yields are well above the world average, and among developing countries second only to North and South Korea, Mexico and Egypt, all of which have high fertiliser application rates and higher levels of irrigation. China's wheat yield is also twice as high as Australian average yields, although again actual sown acreage figures may be misleading.

Wheat is double-cropped with maize in the north and with rice in the Chang Jiang valley and further south.

Maize

The 1984 maize crop in China, 72.7 million tonnes, was a third successive record year, and marked the entrance of China as a grain exporter. China's production represents about 16 per cent of total world production and three-quarters of all maize produced in the Asia-Pacific region.

Maize yields in China are moderately high for a developing country, but well below developed country averages. Yields are improving rapidly, however: an average annual increase of 8.3 per cent over 1981-84. Hybrid maize accounts for 70 per cent of total maize area, but the quality of the seed and soil treatment is variable. Maize is a crop where there remains considerable scope for improvement in yields.

Soyabeans

Soyabean production, 9.7 million tonnes in 1984, was 11 per cent of total world production. Production growth has been relatively modest, an average 3.6 per cent over 1974-84 and only 2.0 per cent per year over 1981-84, with a decline of about 1 per cent in 1984. However, sown acreage declined by nearly 4 per cent over the same 1981-84 period. Yields averaged 1,293 kg/ha in 1984, near the average for developing countries, but well below levels of major producers among developed countries.

Commercial crops

Cotton production, 6.1 million tonnes in 1984, had the fifth consecutive record year since 1980. In terms of raw (seed) cotton, China's 1984 production was 18.2 million tonnes, 34 per cent of total world production. Growth has been extremely rapid, an average 9.3 per cent per year over 1974-84 and a startling 27.2 per cent per year over 1981-84. This is far higher than the increase in sown area, 2.8 per cent and 9.4 per cent per year respectively for the same periods. Yields of seed cotton, 2,642 kg/ha, are extremely high: 77 per cent above the world average.

Cotton has benefited from increasing specialisation, made possible by the rural reforms. In Shandong Province, the most important cotton producer, sown area increased by 150 per cent between 1979 and 1983. China has emerged as a significant cotton exporter.

Rubber

China's natural rubber production is relatively small, 189,000 tonnes in 1984, but growing rapidly, with an average annual increase of 12.9 per cent over 1974-84 and 13.7 per cent over 1981-84. Even so, total production is only a fraction of that of Indonesia and Malaysia, 1.2 million tonnes and 1.5 million tonnes respectively. Yield and acreage data are not available.

Sugar

Sugar cane production, 39.7 million tonnes in 1984 (46.2 million tonnes according to FAO estimates), was 5 per cent of world production. Production growth has averaged 6.6 per cent per year over 1974-84 and 4.7 per cent per year over 1981-84. China is the second largest producer in the Asia-Pacific region after India.

Sugar beet production, 8.3 million tonnes in 1984, has been relatively flat since 1981 after rapid growth in the late 1970s. Yields, about 12.8 tonnes/ha, are very low compared to Japan or India.

Tea

China is the world's second largest tea producer after India. Total production in 1984 was 435,000 tonnes, about 20 per cent of world production. The harvested area is huge, about half the world total, but yields average 328 kg/ha, only a fifth as much as India.

Jute and related fibres

Jute and jute-like fibre production in China, 1.5 million tonnes in 1984, was 36 per cent of the world's total production. Production growth averaged 7.2 per cent per year over 1974-84 and 4.7 per cent per year over 1981-84.

Groundnuts

China is one of the world's major groundnut (peanut) producers. Production was 4.9 million tonnes in 1984, about 24 per cent of world production. Production growth has been rapid over the last decade, averaging annual increases of 9 per cent over 1974-84 and 7.1 per cent over 1981-84. Yields, in excess of 2,000 kg/ha in 1984, are very high: nearly twice the world average and in the Asia-Pacific region second only to Malaysia.

Plots of land are mostly very small

Energy

China is the third largest consumer of energy in the world. Commercial energy consumption was 92 per cent of production in 1983 and approximately 90 per cent in 1984. Per capita consumption, 667 kg of standard coal equivalent (CE) in 1984, is several times the average for other low-income countries (e.g. 260 kg in India), but is low relative to middle-income economies and less than 10 per cent of the average for industrial market economies.

If Chinese energy consumption were to reach even half the United States per capita level of 10,053 kg CE, China's total energy consumption would exceed 10 billion tonnes CE, a figure that far exceeds the world's current total coal and oil production.

Energy consumption per unit of GDP, however, is extremely high. For each dollar of GDP in 1983, China consumed 2.43 kg CE. The average for all low-income economies, in contrast, was 0.9 kg per dollar of GDP, for middle-income economies approximately 0.6 kg and for industrial market economies 0.4 kg.[29]

China is twice as inefficient in the use of commercial energy per unit of GDP as India and four times as inefficient as Japan or West Germany. Even with much higher assumptions for actual GDP, China's efficiency in the use of energy per unit of economic output is at least a third below the standard of low-income economies and only half the middle-income economies' level.

Industry is the largest consumer of commercial energy, accounting for approximately 60 per cent of final commercial energy consumption. China's consumption of energy per unit of industrial output is very high, only slightly less efficient than India but four times as inefficient as most developed industrial economies. This is partly because energy-intensive goods are a large proportion of total industrial output, but other factors are inefficient technology, the prevalence of small-scale plants and low energy prices which do not adequately reward conservation and efficiency.

China's poor performance in terms of these indices is not wholly due to inefficiency in energy utilisation *per se* – the potential savings available through conservation and better utilisation are marginal in comparison to discrepancies of this scale. It also reflects structural factors in the Chinese economy.

Impressive gains in efficiency have been made in recent years, although there is still a long way to go. In the steel industry, energy consumption fell from 73.8 million tonnes of standard coal equivalent (TCE) in 1978 to 69.1 million in 1983 while output grew 26 per cent, a reduction in energy consumption per unit of 25.7 per cent. This was accomplished in part by shutting down or amalgamating inefficient small steel producers.[30]

Consolidated savings due to conservation are estimated to be equivalent to 25 million TCE per year over 1980-84, according to the State Statistical Bureau, which attributed only 40 per cent of the improvement to better production processes and 60 per cent to 'restructuring', i.e. closing inefficient plants.

The implication is that China could theoretically support a much higher GDP at a given energy consumption level, but this will require approaching the middle-income and industrial market economies' pattern of diversifying into and expanding sectors which are not energy-intensive, as well as continued improvements in economic efficiency.

This is one of the key conclusions of a World Bank report completed in 1985, which called for slower industrial growth but more rapid growth of the service sector to ease future strains on energy supply. The bank's high and low projections for average annual growth in energy demand between 1980 and the year 2000 range from 3.4 per cent to 5.5 per cent.

With high (8 per cent) average rates of industrial growth, primary demand would approach 1.4 billion TCE under the most optimistic efficiency assumptions, according to World Bank projections, and in the worst case, demand could climb to 1.8 billion TCE. This is far beyond likely maximum energy production levels. Severe energy shortages would be experienced and growth of national income would slow significantly.

With lower (7 per cent) industrial growth and optimistic assumptions about efficiency improvements, total primary commercial energy demand would reach 1.27 billion TCE in the year 2000, in line with targets.

These projections indicate the need for higher targets for energy production, of the order of 4.5 per cent growth per year. It would be extremely risky to rely on the prospects for increasing oil and gas production above the original targets, since it would depend on replacing the output of existing fields which are becoming depleted with new sources, nor can hydroelectric generation be increased much faster than is already planned. The additional increases in production, therefore, will in all likelihood have to come from coal.

Total primary commercial energy production in 1984 was equivalent to 765.1 million TCE of which 10 per cent was exported in the form of crude oil and coal. In addition, China produces about 220 million TCE of non-commercial energy each year in the form of wood, and agricultural and animal residues.

Coal makes up 72 per cent of the primary commercial energy supply, crude oil, most of which is consumed by industry in the form of fuel oil, 22 per cent, hydroelectricity 4.4 per cent and natural gas 2.2 per cent.

Chinese economists estimate that every rural household requires at least 4,500 kilocalories of heat to cook three meals a day, but only 3,500 kilocalories are available to the average household, and serious fuel shortages affect 40 per cent of all rural households.

Commercial energy is only 25 per cent of total rural energy consumption. Rural industrial development is boosting rural demand for commercial energy, particularly new or marginal rural enterprises. The ratio of energy consumption per unit of output value between Jiangsu and Zhejiang, where rural enterprises are extremely sophisticated and extensive, and less developed areas in the west is as high as 5 to 1.

Total rural demand for commercial energy is estimated at 280 million TCE (250 million tonnes of coal, 400 billion kWh of electric power and 35 million tonnes of petroleum-based fuels), while actual consumption is approximately half, about 140 million TCE in 1983. Demand for non-commercial (biological) energy is estimated at 280 million TCE; supply represents only 220-250 million TCE, and due to the poor efficiency with which biological fuels are burned in traditional stoves, actual heat generated is only 23 million TCE.[31]

Coal

China depends on coal for 70 per cent of its commercial energy supply, and will continue to do so well into the next century. One of the three biggest coal producers in the world, along with the United States and the Soviet Union, China has the world's largest proven coal reserves (the official claim is 781 billion tonnes) and total reserves are estimated to exceed three trillion tonnes. More than half the proven reserves are located in Shanxi Province and the adjacent Inner Mongolia Autonomous Region. Economically recoverable reserves are believed sufficient to meet projected demand for well over a century.

Coal production grew rapidly through the first three decades of Communist rule in China, reaching 635 million tonnes in 1979, but declined in 1980 and 1981 due to neglect of new tunnelling. Output growth resumed in 1982 and quickened in 1983 and 1984, when total production reached 772 million tonnes.

Much of the rapid growth from 1982 to 1984 was due to the expansion of local coal mines, particularly mines operated by rural townships, or communes and villages, or production brigades. Between 1980 and 1984, the number of mines operated by rural collectives and individuals rose to 61,000 and their total output rose 80 per cent to 216 million tonnes, 28 per cent of national production. The output of state-run coal mines increased by 14.8 per cent over the same period. There are over 3,000 collective mines with a capacity of more than 30,000 tonnes per year, and over 10,000 mines run by private individuals.

The growth of small local mines raises certain problems: many are considered inefficient and have relied on subsidies from local government agencies (although subsidy requirements are less as collective coal is now traded at market prices), quality control is uneven and safety conditions, according to one analyst, atrocious. A more serious problem is that some small local mines operate in fields which would be more suitable to low-cost large-scale exploitation.[32]

Nonetheless, the performance of local coal mines over the past five years has impressed both Chinese planners and foreign observers. One factor in the importance they have assumed is that small collective mines, which can exploit small deposits which would be uneconomic for large state operations, have developed a considerable volume of production in the eastern and south-eastern regions where demand is highest, avoiding the transport deadlock that blocks increased shipments from the larger north-eastern mines.

A 1985 World Bank study proposes raising the target for raw coal production in the year 2000 from 1.2 billion tonnes to 1.4 billion tonnes, equivalent to 1 billion TCE. Meeting this target implies average increase of 40 million tonnes per year. Under this scenario, state-owned mines operated by the central government would produce 800 million tonnes, provincial state-owned mines 250 million tonnes, and collective and privately-run mines 350 million tonnes.

Medium-term growth prospects are quite positive. Tunnelling has been expanded, totalling 81,637 metres in the first quarter of 1985, the highest quarterly figure since 1973. Local collective mine operations are still expanding in response to new price incentives.

Shanxi Province, which has China's biggest coal reserves, produced 177 million tonnes in 1984, about 23 per cent of total production. 70 per cent of Shanxi's production is moved by rail to other provinces and regions, mainly north China (Beijing and Tianjin) and the east coast (Shanghai and Jiangsu Province). Coal is also moved by rail to the port of Qinhuangdao for onward shipment by coastal steamer to east China and for export to Japan. (Both the railway and port at Qinhuangdao have been developed with Japanese funding and technical assistance.) Exports to Japan total 500-600,000 tonnes per year.

Long-term development efforts are centred on Shanxi Province and the Inner Mongolian Autonomous Region. Shanxi production is projected to reach 350-400 million tonnes by the year 2000.

As of mid-1985, there were 130 mines under construction or major expansion by the Ministry of Coal Industry, with a combined output capacity of over 131 million tonnes, of which 15 million tonnes was scheduled to go into operation by the end of 1985.

Most of this huge additional capacity consists of seven mammoth open-pit mines in the north-west, several of which are to be developed with foreign assistance. The critical consideration for all these mines, however, will be the development of transport capacity to move coal from the mines to major consuming areas in the east, north-east and south-east coastal regions.

The seven open-pit mines are:
- Antaibao No. 1 at Pingshuo, in Shanxi Province, proven reserves 12.7 billion tonnes, projected annual capacity 15.3 million tonnes. Occidental Petroleum Corporation (US) to participate as joint-venture partner.
- Junggar, Inner Mongolian Autonomous Region, proven reserves 24 billion tonnes, projected annual output 10-25 million tonnes. Likely participation by Bechtel Corporation (US).
- Shenmu, in Shanxi Province, proven reserves 87.7 billion tonnes. Likely participation from Bechtel Corporation and others.
- Yiminhe, Inner Mongolia Autonomous Region, proven reserves 12 billion tonnes, projected annual capacity 1 million tonnes or more. Possible Soviet participation.
- Yuanbaoshan, Inner Mongolia Autonomous Region, projected annual output 8 million tonnes.
- Huolinhe, Inner Mongolian Autonomous Region, projected annual output 15 million tonnes. Possible participation by Fluor Corporation (US).
- Fushun, Liaoning Province, expansion to 6.5 million tonnes annual capacity. Participation by Fluor Corporation.

Other important mines now in the planning or construction stages are:
- Changcun, in Shanxi Province, proven reserves 490 million tonnes, projected annual capacity 4 million tonnes. Assistance from the World Bank and West Germany.
- Guqiao, in Anhui Province, proven reserves 2 billion tonnes, projected annual output 10 million tonnes. Domestic development.
- Xingantai, in Heilongjiang Province, proven reserves 700 million tonnes, annual output capacity to be expanded to 5 million tonnes with assistance from the Soviet Union.

Mining technology in China ranges from state-of-the-art mechanised operations to very primitive small-scale mines relying on picks and shovels. China has imported a considerable number of sets of mechanised tunnelling and shaft-sinking machines from Europe, but most mines are excavated by conventional drilling and blasting methods. Underground mines mainly use the European longwall system, although there is growing interest in US-style room-and-pillar techniques in shallow mines with thin or non-continuous seams.[33]

Coal exports totalled 7 million tonnes in 1984, earning Rmb643 million (US$279 million), according to Chinese Customs Statistics (external estimates place Chinese earnings on exports of coal and coke in 1984 at US$551 million). China is a low-cost producer by international standards, with operating costs approximately Rmb20/tonne and capital costs of mine construction approximately Rmb110/tonne capacity. China's prospects as an exporter, particularly in the Pacific Rim region, are very good.

Only 18-20 per cent of coal production is washed, mainly coking coal used by the steel industry. Industry analysts say that washing capacity must be expanded to meet the future needs of the steel and chemical industries, although high costs and losses may make washing inappropriate for coal destined for other uses.

Doubling coal consumption to 1.4-1.6 billion tonnes per year by the year 2000 (equivalent to 40 per cent of world production in 1978) raises serious environmental threats. Chinese cities already suffer from serious air pollution attributed to coal, much of which is particulate matter due to direct burning by households and small, relatively primitive industrial boilers. Fortunately, the sulphur content of Chinese coal is relatively low. But installation of new centralised combustion equipment for factories and towns to replace boilers that are low in efficiency and highly polluting will be necessary over the next decade, and it will be necessary to replace and control direct burning of coal by households, particularly in major cities.

Petroleum

Onshore fields make up almost all of China's current production, of which nearly half is generated by the giant Daqing field in north-eastern Heilongjiang. China verified 2 billion tonnes of confirmed onshore reserves over 1981-84, bringing the total to approximately 2.5 billion tonnes, though some industry sources would double that figure.

As much as 60 per cent of China's total land area – 4.2 million square kilometres – is sedimentary basin, of which little more than 10 per cent has been intensively explored to date.[34] Total offshore and onshore reserves are estimated at 66 billion tonnes of petroleum and 20-25,000 billion cubic metres of natural gas.

After five years of negligible growth, crude oil production began to move upwards again in 1984, increasing by 8 per cent to 114.53 million tonnes (2.29 million barrels per day). China accounts for 4.3 per cent of total world production, ranking sixth in the world in production, after the Soviet Union, the United States, Saudi Arabia, Mexico and the United Kingdom. Production is estimated to increase by 9 per cent in 1985 to 125 million tonnes, with 150 million tonnes targeted for 1990.

Faced with accelerating domestic demand and a need to free part of the production for exports, China adopted rationing measures and accelerated conversion of boilers and generators from oil to coal, reducing domestic oil consumption from 88.72 million tonnes in 1980 to 80.86 million tonnes in 1982. But consumption surged ahead to 85.2 million tonnes in 1983 and to nearly 90 million tonnes in 1984, boosted in part by new demand from vehicular transport.

China exported 22.01 million tonnes of crude oil in 1984, earning Rmb9.35 billion (US$4.06 billion), plus 5.7 million tonnes of refined petroleum products worth Rmb3.14 billion, representing 21.5 per cent of all export earnings according to official customs statistics.

An oilfield in Taklimakan desert, Xinjiang. China is the world's sixth largest oil producer

Crude oil exports soared in the first half of 1985, reaching 14.27 million tonnes, 46 per cent over the six-month figure for 1984, despite oversupply of crude oil in world markets. Industry figures say that actual sale prices for Chinese crude oil reached as low as US$25.30 a barrel in 1985, well below its official price of US$27.35. Most of China's crude oil sales are to Japan, the Philippines, Singapore and Western Europe. Japan is the biggest purchaser, with estimated purchases of 8.5 million tonnes in 1985.

China's refinery capacity is estimated at 101.2 million tonnes per year, of which nearly 35 per cent is concentrated in the north-east. The utilisation rate is estimated to be about 67 per cent, relatively high compared to other refiners in Asia. Chinese refineries have very little catalytic cracking or other secondary processing equipment.[35]

Fuel oil makes up 41 per of refinery output, diesel fuel 27 per cent, gasoline 16 per cent, kerosene 6 per cent and lubricants 3 per cent. This reflects industry's still heavy reliance on fuel oil. Refining industry sources say quality control in China's refineries is relatively poor, particularly with regard to diesel oil and lubricants, and gasoline octane ratings are very low. Increasing amounts of Chinese crude oil have been processed at Singapore refineries since 1984.

Industry accounts for approximately 70 per cent of all consumption, heavy industry alone consuming more than 60 per cent, mostly burned as fuel oil. Transport and agriculture absorb approximately 10 per cent each and households approximately 5 per cent.[36]

Onshore oil

Foreign oil companies have been involved in onshore exploration and surveys in the western regions and provinces of Xinjiang, Qinghai, Gansu, Ningxia, as well as Shanxi and Sichuan.

In 1985, 10 provinces were opened to onshore development by foreign oil companies: Anhui, Fujian, Guangdong, Guangxi, Guizhou, Jiangsu, Jiangxi, Hunan, Sichuan and Zhejiang. The newly opened area comprises a total of 1.83 million square kilometres and 136 sedimentary basins with oil or gas potential. The most promising areas in the newly opened regions are believed to be the Subei basin in northern Jiangsu, for which bids for joint exploration were solicited in July 1985, the Baise field in Guangxi and the Chuxiong basin in Yunnan.

The state-owned China National Oil Development Corporation (CNODC) approved the first onshore exploitation contract with an Australian consortium in May 1985, covering 2,800 square kilometres on Hainan Island.

China's most important oil field, Daqing in Heilongjiang Province, was opened in 1960 and developed without significant foreign assistance. Production exceeded 50 million tonnes in 1976 and reached 53.56 million tonnes in 1984, 46.8 per cent of China's total output. It is estimated that production in 1985 will exceed 54 million tonnes.

Daqing officials claim that they can maintain output levels of 50 million tonnes or more until 1990, when rising water content of the offtake from water injection and flooding will probably bring about decline. A World Bank project is under way at Daqing to enhance recovery techniques and develop deep oil strata.

The Shengli field in Shangdong Province, first developed in the early 1960s, has shown dramatic increases in the last two years. Crude oil production reached 24.1 million tonnes in 1984 and is likely to exceed 26 million tonnes in 1985. Rmb25 billion are to be invested in the field over 1985-90 to bring production up to 50 million tonnes. A new shallow-sea section discovered in 1984, Gudong, has been developed with foreign participation and imported drilling ships, and is rapidly becoming an important new production area, projected to reach a capacity of 8.1 million tonnes by 1987.

The Huabei field, south of Beijing in Hebei Province, consists of 18 blocks, of which Renqiu is the largest (the entire field is also referred to as Renqiu field in some literature). The field declined from a reported 17 million tonnes in 1979 to 10.15 million tonnes in 1983, and is now expected to remain stable for several years.

Poor permeability of oil-bearing structures has scaled down hopes that the Dagang field in eastern Hebei Province would be another Daqing. Production is believed to have declined from 2.78 million tonnes in 1982. At Liaohe, however, the northern extension of the Bohai basin in southern Liaoning Province, imported technology has helped to overcome geological problems and boosted output to 7.67 million tonnes in 1984, an increase of 21 per cent over 1983.

The most recently developed field in the Bohai basin, Zhongyuan in Shandong Province, is believed to hold 200 million tonnes of crude oil and 20-25 billion cubic metres of gas. World Bank assistance has helped this field meet its 1985 crude oil production target of 5 million tonnes a year early. Gas production in 1984, 700 million cubic metres, was well over the 1985 target. Two new pipelines were completed in 1984-85, linking the field to a refinery at Luoyang and a fertiliser plant in Kaifeng.

The far west is an active region for exploration by Chinese and foreign teams. Current output is relatively low. The Yuman oilfield in Gansu Province, initially developed with Soviet assistance, has been revived with new drilling, and output reached 3.85 million tonnes in 1985. Karamay, another old field in the far western Junggar basin in Xinjiang Province, also produced about 3.8 million tonnes per year. Exploration of new fields in this basin is continuing, and three exploratory wells are yielding significant flows.

Offshore oil

Excitement over China's offshore oil development has paled since the early 1980s. No dramatically large fields have been discovered so far, and weak world prices for crude oil have squeezed the outlook for profits on the secondary structures that have been found. Total offshore offtake by 1987 is now expected to be no higher than 300,000 tonnes per year.

Despite the lack of dramatic strikes, drilling operations are continuing, and in mid-1985, 23 operators were reported participating in a second round of bidding for exploration contracts in the South of China and Yellow Seas. The China National Offshore Oil Corporation (CNOOC) announced that it is dropping the 12.5 per cent royalty requirement for small fields producing less than 1 million tonnes per year in this round.

A total of 92 offshore test wells were drilled in the South China Sea areas from 1980 until mid-1985, of which 34 showed oil or gas flows, but few have been commercially attractive.

The first South China Sea offshore field, Wei 1013 in the Beibuwan basin, is scheduled to begin production in June 1986. A joint venture between France's Total Chine and the CNOOC's Nanhai Western Petroleum Corporation, the field is expected to produce 600-700,000 tonnes of crude oil per year.

Also believed to be marginal are Esso/Shell's Wenchang 19-1-2 strike, the ACT Operators Group (Agic, Chevron and Texaco) strike at Huizhou 33-1-1 and the Phillips/Peacten Xijiang 24-3-1, all in the Pearl River area of the South China Sea.

In the Sino-Japanese exploration zone of the northern Bohai Sea, 27 test wells have been completed and 56 production wells developed in the Bohai Chengbei field near Tianjin. According to Chinese sources, the estimated maximum output for this field, 400,000 tonnes per year, will be reached in 1990, while output from other Bohai wells is expected to reach 1.8 million tonnes per year by 1990.

Natural gas

Natural gas production, 12.4 billion cubic metres in 1984, is below the maximum level reached in 1979, largely due to declines in the Weiyuan basin fields in Sichuan

Province resulting from water encroachment. Sichuan, where the world's first natural gas wells were sunk in 53 BC using bamboo piping, accounts for nearly half of total gas production. Most of the rest of onshore natural gas production is associated with petroleum – Daqing field in Heilongjiang Province produces about half as much as Sichuan.

Recent offshore exploration has found significant natural gas deposits, including one field off Hainan Island classified as a 'super giant field' by world standards, according to a spokesman of Atlantic Richfield Co (US), which is negotiating to develop the find. The field could potentially produce 6 billion cubic metres per year, well above current Sichuan levels.

China has received a World Bank loan of US$21 million to assist in boosting output from the Sichuan fields, and several foreign companies, including Bechtel (US), Société National Elf-Aquitaine (France), Diouel R. Fuseler (US) and Halliburton (US), are assisting in exploration and development of natural gas deposits in Sichuan.

Chinese geologists have suggested that Sichuan production could double to 11-12 billion cubic metres by 1990, but other analysts suspect that production in the province can at best be stabilised at current levels. If so, natural gas production over the medium term is likely to parallel new oil production, with no substantial increases before the end of the decade, but good prospects for substantial growth in the 1990s as new onshore and offshore petroleum fields go into production. The northwest region, particularly the Tarim basin, is considered extremely promising; the current target for natural gas production in the year 2000, 25 billion cubic metres, is considered to be conservative.

The most important use of natural gas is likely to be in the production of petrochemical feedstock, although gas may play an important role in satisfying residential energy needs in areas where transport costs are not prohibitive.

Exploitation of newly discovered deposits will require considerable investment in storage and transport facilities, and possibly liquefaction, particularly for the output of offshore or remote western onshore fields.

Electricity

Total generated electricity, 375 billion kWh in 1984, has more than doubled since 1974 and quadrupled since 1969. China's total generated power ranks about fourth in the world after the United States, the Soviet Union and Japan. However, the supply of electric power is still insufficient to satisfy peak load requirements in many areas, particularly in the eastern and southern coastal regions. Generating capacity is 10,000 MW below the required level, according to official estimates, and generated electricity falls 50 billion kWh short of actual demand.

Chinese economists have estimated that as much as 20 per cent of China's industrial capacity is idle or cut back due to power shortages at any given time; and rationing, including alternative days operation for heavy industrial consumers, is practised in many cities.

Growth in generated output has speeded up since 1980-81, when annual increases were very small, with expansion of the production of generating equipment,

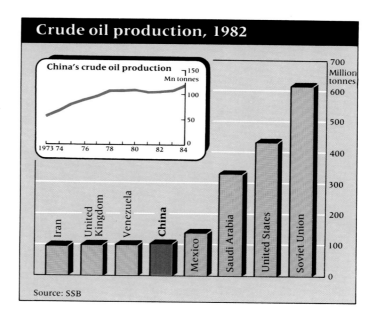

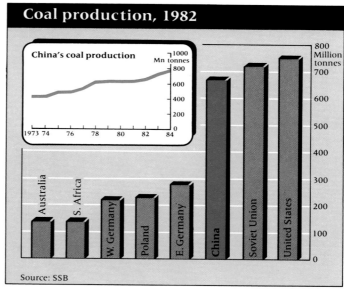

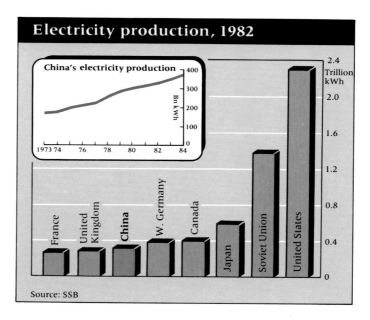

primarily for coal-fired power plants. The generated total in 1984 was 6.6 per cent higher than in 1983 and an 8-9 per cent increase was expected in 1985.

Manufacturing is the single most important consumer of electric power, accounting for approximately 75 per cent of final electricity demand, excluding electricity consumed by the power industry itself.

Industrial demand is projected to increase by a factor of four or more between now and the end of the century. Transport, currently a small consumer, will become a significant consumer as electrification of the rail system expands. Residential and commercial use, currently only 10-12 per cent of total final demand, is expected to increase sharply.

Total demand is expected to reach 900-1,200 billion kWh by the year 2000, depending on the actual rate of industrial growth and progress in improving efficiency of energy use, particularly in the energy-intensive metallurgy and chemical industries, which currently account for 35 per cent or more of industrial consumption. This will require expanding total generating capacity from the

present 80,000 MW to 240,000 MW. Medium-term projections call for an increase of 35,000 MW in installed capacity by 1990 to enable total generated power to reach 570 billion kWh.

In what may prove to be an important step in expanding supply, the State Council rescinded what was essentially a state monopoly on electricity generation and sale in May 1985, allowing local authorities, departments and enterprises, acting either singly or in concert, to build and run power plants and fix their own charges. Decontrolling electricity generation and allowing market pricing may prove to be the key to inducing local investment in what previously had been regarded as a singularly unprofitable area.

Agriculture, which currently accounts for 10 per cent of demand, will probably only show modest growth. Electric power is available at 90 per cent of all rural townships (communes) and about 70 per cent of all rural villages, with the highest levels of electrification in the north-eastern and northern regions, and the lowest in the north-west and south-west.

About 80 per cent of total installed generating capacity and 90 per cent of actual generated power is distributed through six regional power grids and seven important provincial grids.

Hydroelectricity

Generated hydroelectric power, 85.5 billion kWh in 1984, was 22.7 per cent of total generated electricity. This represents utilisation of only about 6 per cent of China's huge theoretical hydroelectric potential, estimated at 38,000 MW. The drawback of hydropower is the extremely high capital cost of development per unit of output capacity compared to fossil fuel exploitation. This is compounded in China by the relatively inaccessible location of most hydropower sites in the south-western and north-western regions. The average cost of building one megawatt of hydrogenerating capacity in China increased from Rmb1 million in the mid-1960s to Rmb1.5 million in 1982, which probably does not include adequate provision for costs of relocation and compensation of affected populations.[37]

The Three Gorges dam proposed for the upper reaches of the Chang Jiang (Yangtze River) in Sichuan Province would be the largest hydroelectric dam in the world, with an installed capacity of 13,000 MW, producing 64.6 billion kWh per year. The dam could also have important flood control value, but the reservoir created would extend as far as 500 km up river, which would inundate 44,000 hectares and at least three towns, and would require relocation of, according to various estimates, between 400,000 and 1,400,000 people. It would also raise the water level in the gorges by 100 m or more, changing forever an important historic and scenic area.

Construction of the Three Gorges dam, which will cost an estimated Rmb10 billion, cannot begin until the Gezhouba dam downstream in Hubei Province nears completion in the late 1980s. Gezhouba, with 2,700 MW installed capacity will be the largest dam built in China to date and is largely the product of Chinese design and engineering technology.

The Three Gorges project has been delayed because of the huge costs and bureaucratic wrangling between the leadership of the old Ministry of Electric Power, which

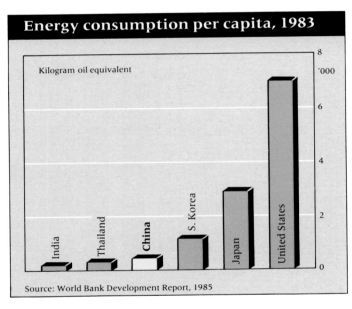

Energy consumption per capita, 1983

Kilogram oil equivalent

Source: World Bank Development Report, 1985

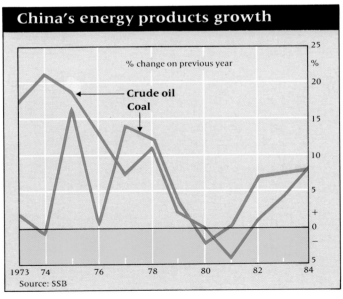

China's energy products growth

% change on previous year

Crude oil
Coal

Source: SSB

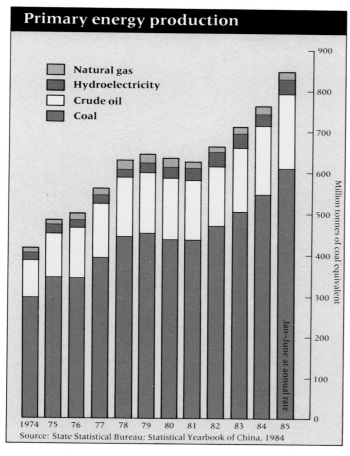

Primary energy production

Natural gas
Hydroelectricity
Crude oil
Coal

Million tonnes of coal equivalent

900
800
700
600
500
400
300
200
100
0

1974 75 76 77 78 79 80 81 82 83 84 85

Jan–June at annual rate

Source: State Statistical Bureau; Statistical Yearbook of China, 1984

favoured this project, and the Ministry of Electric Power, which did not. The wrangling apparently has continued following the merger of the two organs into a super-ministry of Water Resources and Electric Power (MWREP) in 1982, and reflects a general dispute within the ministry over whether priority in planning and operating dams should be given to flood control or power generation.[38]

Current development plans are extremely ambitious. They call for a total 60,000 MW new installed capacity — three times the current level — by the year 2000, mostly through projects on the Chang Jiang and Hongshui.

On the Hongshui river system in Guangxi Province, 10 hydroelectric power stations, with a total installed capacity of 11,000 MW and annual production capacity of 60 billion kWh, are under construction or planned.

The Hongshui system is the most ambitious example of integrated river planning in China to date. The 10 dams are designed to have a cascade effect, with upstream dams moderating seasonal water flows and thereby increasing the generating capacity of dams below. Several US firms and the US Army Corps of Engineers have conducted studies for the Hongshui system projects.

Small hydropower plants, which numbered 78,000 at the end of 1984, have a total installed capacity of 9,000 MW and produced 21.6 billion kWh in 1984, a quarter of total generated hydroelectric power. Small hydro stations make electric power available in many rural areas which have no access to regional electrical grids. However, construction costs of these plants are high in terms of unit capacity, and output is often seasonal due to limited water storage capacity.[39]

Thermal generation

Thermal power generation, 289 billion kWh in 1984, accounted for 77 per cent of all generated power. China has been attempting to move away from using petroleum for generating electricity.

Seven new thermal stations are under construction, with a total installed capacity of 6,900 MW when they are brought on-line, and an additional 5,820 MW of capacity is planned through expansion of existing plants over the next five to 10 years.

Over the longer terms, plans call for adding a total of 110-130,000 MW thermal capacity between 1985 and the year 2000.

Nuclear power

China plans to build over the next 15 years six nuclear power plants with a combined generated capacity of 10,000 MW. Four have been designated as of mid-1985.

The best-known project is the 1,800 MW Daya Bay plant, a joint venture between Guangdong Province and Hong Kong's China Light and Power Co, using imported technology from Framatome (France) and General Electric Company (UK).

Alternative energy

China is the world leader in biogas applications, with an estimated three to five million small and a number of community-sized biomass digesters in operation. Several million additional digesters are believed to have fallen into disuse because of poor initial construction or lack of adequate fuel.

Experimental exploitation of geometrical energy has begun near Beijing, with water from underground hot springs used for residential and industrial heating. Similar projects have also been planned for Tianjin and Tibet.

Industry

The background to reform

China is an economic paradox. It is overpopulated and poor, a low-income developing nation with a per capita gross national product (GNP) only slightly over US$300. It is also one of the world's largest economies, ranking ninth in total gross domestic product (GDP), behind Italy and ahead of Brazil, and is one of the world's most important industrial economies.

Industrial development in China is very high compared to other low-income countries. Industry accounts for a startlingly high 45 per cent of China's GDP, more than twice the average for other low-income economies and higher than most industrial market economies.

While precise comparisons are difficult due to differences in pricing and product structure, China probably ranks fifth or sixth in the world in terms of net value of industrial output, following the United States, the Soviet Union, Japan, West Germany and very close to the United Kingdom.

In addition to being the world's biggest grain and cotton producer, China ranks:
– first in world cotton cloth production;
– second in cement production behind the Soviet Union;
– third in production of coal, chemical fertilisers and

sulphuric acid behind the United States and the Soviet Union;

— fourth in production of pig iron, steel and televison sets behind the Soviet Union, Japan and the United States;

— fifth in production of crude oil, chemical fibres and caustic soda; and

— sixth in total generated electricity and paper and paper products.

Most of China's industrial capacity has been built since the Communist victory in 1949, as is the result of huge sustained investments focused on heavy industry over the past three decades. The proportion of China's available national income devoted to investment (the so-called accumulation rate) averaged about 24 per cent in the early 1950s, and climbed to over 40 per cent in the years of the disastrous Great Leap Forward. Since the mid-1960s, the rate of accumulation as a proportion of national income in China has averaged over 30 per cent, an extremely high level even for a developing country. Industry has consistently absorbed nearly half or more of all construction investment.

The structure of the command economy

The post-1949 industrial system was structurally patterned after the command economy of the Soviet Union. Overall direction of industrial enterprises was centred in state ministries in charge of different industries, and most industrial materials and products were allocated by the state. The state planning apparatus determined output norms or quotas for each enterprise and allocated to the enterprise sufficient materials to fulfil its quota. Each year, the planners had to balance the expected output of goods from every factory with the demands of other factories and enterprises, adjusting quotas and allocations upwards and downwards as necessary.

Capital investment in new plant and equipment was also planned and allocated by the state. The State Plan identified priority areas of investment, and the various ministries competed for their share of investment funds. Exchanges of materials and products between enterprises were compensated, at prices fixed by the state, which theoretically reflected the average costs of production for an industry as a whole, disregarding capital costs. Manpower, both trained and unskilled, was allocated to enterprises in much the same way.

The system resembled the wartime production controls instituted in many market economies such as the United States during World War II. Essentially, both systems were designed to achieve full employment of all resources in maximising the production of key goods. Both systems also employed rationing and allocation of industrial materials and products and some consumer goods to avoid inflation.

China's actual economy has deviated from this system to varying degrees at different times. The nationalisation of private industry first proceeded gradually during the early 1950s, and the industrial sector was then a mixture of state-owned, private and joint state-private firms, although the state increasingly dictated to and circumscribed the operation of the remaining privately-owned enterprises. Conversion of private and joint state-private

China has in the last few years emerged as a significant exporter of cotton

firms to state ownership accelerated at the time of the Great Leap Forward, but there was a simultaneous decentralisation of authority over output and operations to enterprises as the planning system essentially broke down.

Even at the height of state control of the economy in the mid-1960s (by 1965 state-owned enterprises accounted for 90 per cent of all industrial output), the state allocation system only controlled 300 to 400 different types of materials and equipment. Smaller enterprises, including all rural collective industry, operated outside state planning; they acquired the materials they needed and sold their products to the state trading system or in informal markets, which survived in China for various miscellaneous items, and met the needs of state enterprises outside the allocation system. These *sub rosa* markets expanded in the late 1960s and early 1970s as the planning system again broke down and many state enterprises effectively ceased operations under the political stress of the Cultural Revolution.

A number of problems associated with China's pattern of state-run industrial development had become apparent as early as the 1960s. The weighting toward heavy industry was proving extremely costly in demand for energy and raw materials. Output of consumer goods and foodstuffs, and improvements in living standards lagged far behind the overall rate of industrial growth.

Growth in industrial output between the late 1950s and the late 1970s was almost entirely based on new investment – China was not achieving the gains in economic efficiency that market economies experienced at comparable stages of development. While the indices of output of basic industrial products showed steady and rapid growth, the system was proving incapable of translating this capacity into manufacture of final products.

The quality of many industrial products was poor, and China's factories failed to match the improvements in design, technical processes and productivity that market economies saw in the post-war period. Other products were absurdly over-engineered and represented far higher costs in materials and man-hours than comparable products manufactured in Western economies. But China's relative isolation from the rest of the world and its markets during the 1960s and 1970s concealed from the Chinese public and its leaders the extent to which China's industry was falling behind international levels of performance.

The nature of the planned allocation system does not encourage efficiency at the enterprise level, and often even acts as a disincentive. To protect its interests and ensure fulfilling its quotas, each enterprise has a strong interest in minimising its output quota and maximising its allocation of raw materials. Extraordinary gains in output or improvement in resource utilisation efficiency can be damaging to the enterprise because the higher performance levels may be made the norm.

The planning and allocation tends to be clumsy, and slow to identify and react to shortages and other problems. These deficiencies mount as the economy develops toward higher complexity, and the number and variety of raw materials and intermediate products needed multiplies.

It is difficult for the system to identify and react to the demand for new products as planners become more and more pre-occupied with increasing the output of the key commodities they can control. The steel bureaucracy will focus its energies on expanding the plants under its control to produce more and more steel, for example, and may not give adequate attention to the problems of meeting other sectors' actual needs for speciality steels and alloys, or for particular shapes and forms.

The difficulty which manufacturing enterprises experience in trying to obtain high-quality or speciality raw materials and intermediate products through the allocation system induces them to find ways to manufacture or process these products themselves, to integrate both vertically and horizontally without considering actual economies of scale. This contributes to the 'large-and-complete' and 'small-but-complete' syndrome, as each enterprise consolidates as much primary and intermediate processing and manufacturing as possible.

It is not unusual for a relatively small enterprise to undertake basic casting and forging operations which would more efficiently be left to a specialised supplier, or to find that a factory has designed and built some of its own heavy machinery. This results in duplication of under-utilised equipment and capacity and greatly increases production costs.

State enterprises tend to compete for investment resources even when the potential economic returns are low or negative, because expanding fixed assets and production provides more resources for staff and workers' welfare, and enhanced prestige and power. Sectoral claims on investment are not necessarily linked to rational calculations of demand, and the tension between enterprises' attempts to expand investment at any cost and central planners' desire to control overall investment levels produces sharp oscillations in investment levels which may affect all sectors.

The greatest disadvantage of the centrally-planned economy, however, is that it fails to encourage and reward innovation. At a time when the world's market economies were rapidly developiong new products and new technology, with steady improvements in productivity and efficiency, China's factories stagnated.

All these problems were compounded by the politicisation of the workplace in China. The authority and power of the factory manager was eroded and finally eliminated. Able administrators and technicians, including party representatives, were the target of political campaigns, particularly during and after the Cultural Revolution. Bonuses, awards, pay differentials and other forms of material incentives were condemned as capitalist. The educational preparation of new workers and staff deteriorated. Many factories were plagued with chronic absenteeism and loafing.

Urban reforms since 1979

Awareness of the need to change China's industrial system had percolated among certain party economists, administrators and planners since the mid-1960s if not earlier, but the risks of openly advocating change in the highly politicised atmosphere of the 1970s inhibited free discussion of reform. This was particularly true of any measure that appeared to be a return to 'capitalist' methods.

Reform of industry and commerce, frequently termed

urban reform, is far more complex than rural reform. Rural reform was easy: it required no new institutions – Chinese peasants did not need to be taught to farm their own fields or sell their own produce – but only the concept that the ownership of land could be separated from its use, satisfying the political requirement that socialism must not be repudiated while providing a line of defence against resurgence of landlord-tenant relationships.

The urban economy, however, is much more difficult to reform. Most of China's industry has come into being since 1949, securely embraced in a rigid system of state planning, state investment, state subsidies, state prices and state allocation of goods and materials. Managers will not learn overnight to play their enterprise's future in a competitive environment. It is no less difficult to dismantle the bureaucracies which run China's rigid distribution system and bring into being the intricate web of relationships among producers, distributors and consumers that make up a functioning system of market exchange.

There is deep concern and fear among many in the leadership, including people who accept the need for reforms, that abrupt decontrol threatens chaos. Many associate the decentralising effect of the new reforms with the non-market decentralisation promoted with disastrous results by the left during the Great Leap Forward and the Cultural Revolution.

Ending tight state controls of industry and commerce also threatens entrenched bureaucratic interests, and it creates a new world of opportunities for corruption at all levels, while the development of the investigative, auditing and legal systems needed to deal with corruption lags behind.

Price reform is central to the restructuring of both enterprise management and commerce, but abrupt decontrol threatens economic and social chaos. The mechanisms by which markets balance supply and demand do not exist, and there is a fear of inflation among urban residents, many of whom remember the disastrous hyperinflation of the late 1940s.

The first experiments in industrial reform began in 1979, immediately following the historic third plenary session of the 11th Central Committee, which marked the accession of Deng Xiaoping and his allies to a dominant position in the party leadership and the beginning of large-scale rural reform.

Eight state-owned factories were initially selected for experimental reform. These experiments were designed to expand the enterprises' decision-making powers over planning, production, marketing and personnel, and allow them to retain a portion of their profits for reinvestment and distribution as bonuses. The experiment was extended to 4,200 more enterprises at the end of 1979, to 6,600 in 1980 and to 30,000 in 1981.

Replacing the delivery of profits to the state by a system of tax payments was instituted at 450 selected enterprises in 1982. The system is now being extended to all state-owned enterprises.

A compromise framework for planning and price reform emerged in late 1982. Party general secretary Hu Yaobang, in his report to the 12th National Party Congress, called for a tripartite mixed economy which would retain mandatory planning and price controls for certain key commodities, have voluntary guidance planning and floating prices for a wide range of industrial products and consumer goods, and free market sales of non-staple foodstuffs and other items.

Thousands of different products and goods are now produced entirely or partially outside the State Plan and sold at floating or free prices. As of November 1983, the scope of mandatory planning and allocation in industry has been limited to major products such as coal, petroleum, steel and non-ferrous metals, timber, cement, electricity, chemicals, large electrical and mechanical equipment and military products. Even for these products, producers can sell their above-quota production at essentially free floating prices. As of mid-1985, as much as one-half of all steel sales are through the market rather than the allocation system.

The enterprises purchasing these materials on the market do so in order to obtain additional materials above their allocation to enable them to produce beyond their quotas for market sale. Certain enterprises, including the entire rapidly-growing rural industrial sector, obtain nearly all of their raw materials and sell all of their output at market prices.

The October 1984 Decision and the seventh Five Year Plan

The general programme for comprehensive reform of the urban industrial economy was outlined in a remarkable document adopted at the third plenary session of the 12th Central Committee in October 1984, and further detailed in the proposal for the seventh Five Year Plan (1986–90) adopted by a special national party conference in September 1985.

The 'Decision of the Central Committee of the Communist Party of China on Reform of the Economic Structure', (the Decision), adopted in 1984, scathingly criticised excessive centralisation and state control in the economy. It called for accelerated and comprehensive reform of the nation's economic structure and institutions. Embracing a broad range of reforms designed to free enterprises from state and party control, the Decision was a major turning point in the struggle by Deng Xiaoping and other reformists within the party to overthrow the Soviet model of a centralised socialist economy. What emerges in the document is a very flexible concept of socialism, largely decoupled from any specific doctrines or texts. This concept is to be achieved by 'integrating the basic tenets of Marxism with actual conditions in China'.

The reason the socialist system has until now failed to realise its potential in China is 'a rigid economic structure which cannot meet the needs of the growing forces of production', the Decision states. Its major defects are (1) the lack of a distinction between the functions of government and enterprises; (2) bureaucratic and geographical barriers; (3) excessive and rigid state control of enterprises; (4) failure to attach adequate importance to the law of value and the regulatory role of the market; and (5) egalitarianism in distribution which has sapped the initiative and creativity of enterprises and workers.

The present economic structure 'hinders development of the forces of production', and the Decision urges drawing 'upon the world's advanced methods of management, including those of developed capitalist countries, that conform to the laws of modern socialised production'.

In what is put forward as a 'self-improvement and development of the socialist system', the principle of ownership of the means of production by the whole people is to be upheld, but ownership will be 'separated from power of operation' – enterprises will be independent entities, responsible for their own profits and losses, acting as a 'legal person' with specified rights and obligations.

Although the leadership of the Communist Party and state organs will continue to play a role in leading and organising economic construction, that role is to be largely one of formulating strategy, plans, principles and policies – 'government departments at various levels will, in principle, not manage or operate enterprises directly'.

The Chinese economy will remain a planned economy, but planning 'does not necessarily mean the predominance of mandatory planning'. Mandatory planning is to be reduced in favour of guidance planning (using the economic levers of tax, price and credit policies rather than administrative direction to achieve macroeconomic targets) and regulation by free market forces.

The real significance of the Decision is that it formally committed the party to the reform policies and to the vision of a fundamentally different socialist order which the Decision articulates. Although the theoretical and practical issues raised by the reforms have been extensively discussed in the Chinese press, the party's earlier positions on industrial reform had been much more ambiguous, reflecting the lack of a broad consensus on the urban reform programme within the party leadership.

The proposal for China's seventh Five Year Plan (FYP) for 1986–90), approved by the National Party Conference on 23 September 1985, was a further victory for the reformists. Despite signs of economic instability – excessively high levels of investment, industrial growth and imports – in late 1984 and 1985, the plan proposal shows no retreat on reform and little evidence of compromise.

China has actually only implemented two previous FYPs, neither of which was put into effect until well into the plan period. The first FYP (1953–57) was not implemented until early 1955 due to policy differences within the leadership, and the sixth FYP (1981–85) was approved two years late, at the end of 1982. The second FYP (1958–62), outlined in proposal form at the eighth National People's Congress in 1956, was swept aside by the Great Leap Forward, and the intervening third, fourth and fifth FYPs, covering years of intense internal political struggle in China, were merely notional.

Total investment in fixed assets in 1986 and 1987 is to be held to the 1985 level. Actual fixed assets investment has in 1985 skyrocketted, but the effect of holding this figure steady for the following two years would be to gradually reduce investment as a proportion of GNP.

Economic growth in terms of output value is targeted to rise over 1986–90 by an average of 7 per cent per year for industry and 6 per cent for agriculture. The total value of industrial and agricultural output (GVIAO) in 1990 is expected to reach Rmb1.6 trillion, approximately twice the 1980 level in real terms. The proposal, also gave a GNP growth target of 7 per cent per year, with total GNP expected to reach Rmb1.1 trillion in 1990. The proposal

also targets 1990 output levels of electricity generation (550 billion kWh, 46.8 per cent more than in 1984), coal (1 billion tonnes, 30 per cent higher than in 1984) and crude oil (150 million tonnes, 31 per cent over 1984).

The proposal strongly supports the controversial rural industries, which have expanded rapidly in recent years, notably in southern Jiangsu and northern Zhejiang Provinces, and have become the most dynamic sector of the entire Chinese economy. But they have been blamed for contributing to the excessively high growth in industrial output in 1984 and 1985. Conservatives are nervous about rural enterprises because most of them operate entirely outside state planning and controls. The proposal, however, describes township and village enterprises as 'the essential way to revitalise China's rural economy', and the key to 'systematically transferring surplus rural labour from growing crops to other lines of work'.

The proposal envisages a steadily expanding demand for better-quality and more diversified kinds of consumer goods, including food, clothing, housing and consumer durables. These sectors are to retain priority access to credit, foreign exchange, energy and materials. Price differentials between higher-quality and ordinary products are to be increased.

'Centralised construction and allocation of housing in cities and towns, collecting low rents . . . has hampered solution of the housing problem and imposed an increasing financial burden on the state', the proposal states, calling for methods to commercialise housing as soon as possible. This will stimulate the residential construction industry and correct the 'lopsided concentration of urban residents' purchasing power on durable consumer goods'. The World Bank has also recently argued that commercialising housing would simultaneously ease the subsidy burden of the government and soak up urban purchasing power.

Energy prices should be gradually raised, according to the proposal. Freight volume should reach 30 per cent beyond the 1985 level by 1990, and automobile manufacturing should be developed as a key industry. Production of rolled steel is targeted to reach 44 million tonnes by 1990, an increase of 30 per cent over 1984. This is to come about primarily through expansion and renovation of existing steel mills.

The proposal stresses accelerating the development of tertiary industry (service industries including commerce, transport and finance) and expanding the share of services in the national economy. Tertiary industry is 'one of the marks of a modern economy', the proposal status, and the key to launching tertiary industry 'lies in further relaxing restrictions and vigorously developing the collective and individual sectors of the economy', although state investment in tertiary industry is also to be increased.

Expanding, renovating and improving the technological level of existing enterprises as an alternative to building new enterprises is an obvious means of holding down investment costs. However, it also strikes at one of the key weaknesses of the Chinese economy: the extraordinary gaps in relative efficiency and technical sophistication between the most advanced and the general level of enterprises in any particular sector.

'It is China's basic national policy to open to the

The Coca Cola plant in Guangzhou (Canton)

outside world', the proposal affirms, and calls for an increase in total imports and exports of 40–50 per cent between 1985 and 1990. This will require moving the export product mix further from primary to finished products, and continued reform of the foreign trade system, including rational adjustments of the exchange rate in response to price movements in both domestic and world markets, a point which may presage further devaluation of the renminbi.

Foreign commercial borrowing should be increased in developed areas, according to proposal, primarily for projects with high anticipated rates of return or potential for earning foreign exchange, or for projects which can develop import substitutes. Concessionary loans should be concentrated on energy, transport and other infrastructural areas. (The World Bank, in a statement issued on 30 September 1985, also noted that China will need to rely more on commercial borrowing because its access to concessional lending to China over the rest of the decade will be limited to no more than US$600 million a year, mostly from Japan, beyond what is available from the World Bank.)

Only by establishing an integrated network of markets, the proposed states, 'can we enable competitive forces to play their role in selecting the superior and eliminating the inferior, and allow economic levers to perform their regulatory functions. . . .' The plan explicitly endorses opening and expanding domestic markets for funds and technology as well as commodities and materials, and implies further liberalisation in finance, particularly equity financing of domestic enterprises, and greater job mobility for certain categories of workers. As market networks develop, the scope of mandatory planning is to be further reduced in favour of guidance planning, although administrative means will still be required, particularly in 1986, to reinforce indirect macro-economic controls, such as credit and fiscal policies, which remain primitive and largely ineffective.

The key to expanding market forces is price reform. The proposal states that price controls on consumer goods should be systematically relaxed. For machinery and materials, currently distributed under a dual price system, the proportion sold at state-set prices should be gradually reduced and the state prices adjusted to converge with market prices.

The independence and power of the People's Bank of China is to be strengthened so that the central bank can better control money and credit supply, interest rates and foreign exchange. The specialised banks, however, will gradually be transformed from government agencies into enterprises operating independently within the policy guidelines set down by the central bank.

Problems of reform

The fundamental dilemma of economic reforms in China is that, on the one hand, reforms must be gradual to

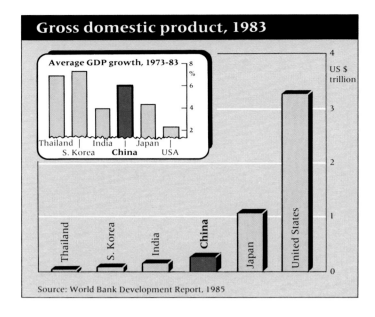

Gross domestic product, 1983

Average GDP growth, 1973-83

Thailand | S. Korea | India | **China** | Japan | USA

US $ trillion

Thailand | S. Korea | India | **China** | Japan | United States

Source: World Bank Development Report, 1985

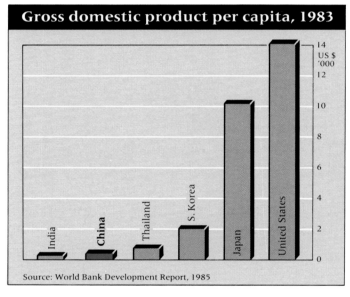

Gross domestic product per capita, 1983

US $ '000

India | **China** | Thailand | S. Korea | Japan | United States

Source: World Bank Development Report, 1985

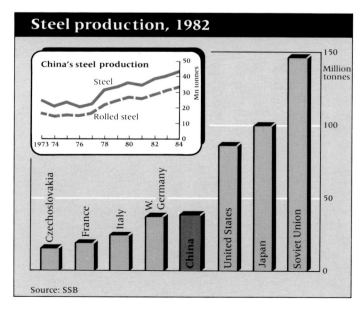

Steel production, 1982

China's steel production

Steel

Rolled steel

Mn tonnes

1973 74 76 78 80 82 84

Million tonnes

Czechoslovakia | France | Italy | W. Germany | **China** | United States | Japan | Soviet Union

Source: SSB

avoid economic instability and dislocation. On the other hand, each aspect of economic reform – price reform, expanding enterprise autonomy and decision-making power, and decontrolling the flows of materials and financial resources – seems to depend on the prior and successful implementation of all the others.

Implementation of the reforms is posing tremendous stresses on the economy and the state organisations. Wrenching power over economic affairs from the hands of cadres is a formidable undertaking. Transforming inefficient state-run enterprises into truly independent entities can hardly be accomplished by mere *fiat*. The realities of true economic competition demand marketing and managerial skills that few Chinese enterprises now possess.

Industrial output jumped an incredible 23.1 per cent (in current prices) in the first half of 1985, following a 14 per cent increase in real terms in 1984. The rapid growth was generated by high levels of investment and reflects extraordinary output gains by the collective sector, particularly rural industrial enterprises in the coastal provinces.

Partial liberalisation of controls over lending and investment has not necessarily led to more rational patterns of investment. Irrationality of prices has led to over-investment in sectors with high state-fixed prices and under-investment in unprofitable sectors such as energy and transport, while occasionally near-absurd bureaucratic tangles in the distribution system create justifications for bewilderingly inappropriate projects.

The unplanned rise in the total volume of investment funds apparently is largely due to increased lending by the newly quasi-independent specialised banks – particularly the Agricultural Bank of China, which operates mainly in rural areas and overseas rural credit cooperatives, and the Industry and Commerce Bank. The specialised banks are now being subjected to tighter controls by the People's Bank of China.

Capital construction investment by state-owned units in 1984, Rmb73.5 billion, was 23.8 per cent higher than in 1983. Despite new tight credit policies, investment levels remained high in the first half of 1985. Most of the new investment was unplanned and financed by loans or enterprises' own funds. Accurate figures for investment by collective enterprises are not available, but bank lending increased by 160 per cent in the first five months of 1985, and self-financed investment by 83 per cent, while investment under the state budget increased by only 1.6 per cent.

Steel consumption for investment by state enterprises from January to April 1985 was 37 per cent higher than the corresponding period in 1984, leading to price increases for steel sold outside the State Plan – market prices for steel in the north-eastern provinces of Liaoning rose from Rmb1400 (US$492) per tonne in March 1985 to as high as Rmb2,000 in July 1985.

The fear that industrial growth may outstrip growth in energy and transport has preoccupied Chinese planners since the beginning of the decade. China's sixth FYP (1981–85), revised in late 1982, envisaged annual growth of industry and agriculture of 4 per cent over 1981–85, with efforts to achieve a higher growth rate of 5 per cent. Since 1981, the actual growth rate of industrial output has averaged 10.7 per cent per year, and agriculture 11.7 per cent, while the average increase in energy supply and generated electricity has been only 6.5 per cent and in freight tonnage 7.7 per cent.

In an attempt to slow down unbudgeted investment, the State Council has approved new regulations requiring all enterprises – state or collective – to deposit any funds intended for construction purposes in the Construction Bank of China (previously used to channel state-budgeted investment) for a period of six months, but it is unclear when the effects of this measure will be apparent.

Import volume surged in the second half of 1984 and the first half of 1985. The rise in imports cut the expected surplus on foreign trade in 1984 to nil (China registered positive trade balances in excess of US$4 billion in 1982 and 1983). Imports over the first seven months of 1985 were 90 per cent of the entire 1984 total, and by August 1985 China had accumulated a trade deficit of US$7.8 billion.

Prominent among the import commodities which showed rapid growth since the fourth quarter of 1984 were television sets, motor vehicles and cassette recorders. However, imports of these three items taken together still only account for a fraction of the trade deficit.

A more important factor was the increase in purchases of equipment and machinery, including computers and office equipment, which by the last quarter of 1984 were already running at 2.5 times the average 1983 level. Other commodities whose import level increased significantly in 1984 were iron, steel, scientific and industrial instruments, synthetic resins and plastics, tobacco and beverages and metal manufactures. New import controls to arrest the haemorrhage in foreign exchange are focused on consumer goods and other non-export generating categories.

Expanding exports to meet the foreign exchange squeeze is proving difficult. Domestic prices for many exportable manufactured products are higher than prevailing international prices, and domestic demand is high, so there is little incentive for enterprises producing higher-priced goods to export.

Opposition to reforms
Differences regarding reforms still exist within the party at high levels. The position of absolute oppositionists, however, has been severely eroded by the general success of the reforms so far, particularly the rural reforms. Most Chinese – both rural and urban – have good reasons to consider themselves better off now than in 1979. Real incomes, purchasing power, and availability of foodstuffs and consumer goods have improved dramatically.

The most serious differences within the Chinese leadership are now centred on the question of how far and how fast the reforms should proceed, not whether there shall be reforms.

The conservatives are led by Chen Yun, a member of the Politburo Standing Committee with an outstanding record as China's foremost economic planner of the early 1950s, and an early and steadfast opponent of Maoism at the time of the Great Leap Forward. Chen is concerned that decentralisation is proceeding too quickly, threatening chaos and disorder.

Chen Yun's arguments have been supported by signs of economic instability arising in late 1984 and 1985, including overheated industrial growth, excessive imports and a rise in corruption. There is no sign as yet, however, of retreat on the fundamental commitment to reform.

The existence of differences within the party, even if those differences appear more a matter of distance and degree rather than fundamental opposition, touches closely on the importance for the reformists of defining the reforms as socialist and justifying their validity in Marxist terms.

There is no question that Deng Xiaoping's reforms are an historic departure from what has conventionally been regarded as Marxist doctrine, and the reformers openly acknowledge that they are seeking to incorporate into the Chinese economy market mechanisms which are fundamental to the capitalist market economies. However, they deny that these steps constitute a rejection of Marxist and socialism or that the reforms are capitalist.

It is easy to forget at times that the reformers are the leaders of a ruling Communist party and derive their legitimacy and power from the party and its monopoly of all political power in China. Within the party at least, there is no open disagreement as to whether or not China shall be socialist or capitalist, but the reformists insist upon the right to reconsider, in the words of Deng Xiaoping, 'what is Marxism, and what is socialism?'

The idea that Marxism can be treated as a flexible methodology rather than a rigid pattern of rules is well established. Lenin, proposing in pre-capitalist Russia a revolution which Marx anticipated in the most advanced

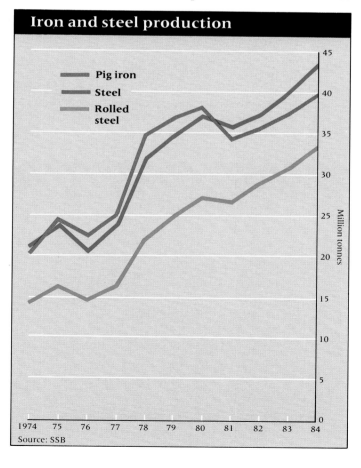

Iron and steel production

Pig iron
Steel
Rolled steel

Million tonnes

1974 75 76 77 78 79 80 81 82 83 84

Source: SSB

53

capitalist societies, wrote in 1894 that Marxists 'borrow from Marx's theory only its invaluable methods, without which an elucidation of social relations is impossible'.

Mao Zedong, in his report to the sixth plenum of the sixth Central Committee in October 1938, called for the party to apply the theory of Marxism-Leninism to the specific circumstances of China 'so that its every manifestation has an indubitably Chinese character'. This statement was made at a time when Mao, opposed by a pro-Moscow faction within the party, was defending both the independence of the CCP from Moscow and the peasant-based military and political doctrines developed under his leadership.

Mao returned to this theme again in the late 1950s to justify policies of rapid collectivisation which were unconventionally leftist in relation to the Soviet model of socialist development. Deng Xiaoping uses the same mode of argument – that Marxism must be developed through practice, citing Mao's dictum that the source of truth is fact, to defend his programme of reforms against more doctrinaire Communists.

The Dengists' key point of departure from doctrinal Marxism is not the idea that Marxism can be developed, but rather the assertion that China, while socialist, remains a commodity economy. This may seem obscure, but it is crucial to Deng's need to justify his reforms in Marxist as well as practical terms.

In 'Capital', Marx analysed in great detail the structure of capitalist society and sketched the outlines of a future communist society into which capitalism, as he maintained, would eventually transform itself. The problem of a socialism transitional to communism in a pre-capitalist society, however, was not considered.

The starting point of capitalism, Marx argued, was the creation of a world-embracing market in which commodities are exchanged for money and money for commodities. Marx considered the profit accruing in the purchase and sale of a commodity to be surplus value derived from the labour expended in producing the commodity. According to Marx, the creation of capital is in the expansion of exchange value occurring in the process of production and exchange of commodities. This concept of commodity economy was opposed to a natural, or barter economy, in which goods having only use-value are exchanged for other goods and the creation of capital does not occur.

Under capitalist conditions, Marx said, both labour and the means of production appear as commodities and are exchanged on the market. But in socialised production, society would distribute labour and the means of production to the different branches of production, eliminating money-capital and ending the appropriation by capitalists of the surplus value produced by labour.

This bare formulation leaves considerable latitude to a society which considers itself in transition to communism but not from the starting point of advanced capitalism. The Dengists' position is that the commodity economy is a natural stage of social development which China, backward and undeveloped, cannot bypass or abolish. Previous attempts to accelerate the transition to communism by prematurely imposing advanced relations of production on China's backward base, as during the Great Leap Forward, were disastrous in practice, Dengists hold, and were the result of ultra-left subjectivism – a failure to take adequate account of China's backwardness and the principle that society develops by stages.

The implications of this are quite profound. If China is a developing commodity economy, it follows that structurally China will resemble a capitalist economy in many respects and that many of the laws which govern capitalist economic development apply to China as well. Commodity exchange, in particular, would be expected to operate similarly in either capitalist or socialist commodity economy. To achieve communism in the future, China must first pass through the commodity economy stage which will require markets, competition and many of the other structural aspects of a capitalist economy.

This is the Marxist justification for jettisoning the Soviet model of a centrally planned and administrated economy and the embrace of market forces. There have been previous cases, notably Lenin's New Economic Policy and Mao's New Democracy, in which communists have accepted a mixed economy as a temporary neces-

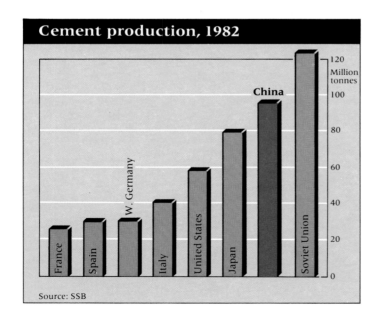

Cement production, 1982

Source: SSB

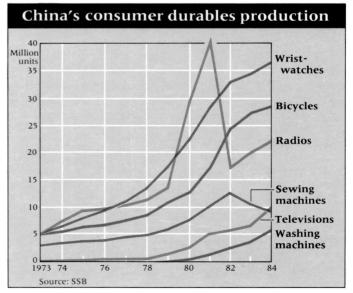

China's consumer durables production

Source: SSB

54

sity. The Dengists, however, expect commodity economy conditions to continue well into the next century, an historical stage that will persist until development of productive forces has eliminated scarcity and so created the preconditions for communism.

The distinction between a capitalist commodity economy and China as a socialist commodity economy, in the Dengist view, is first that land and other important means of production are owned by the whole people, although they are used and operated by collective groups or individuals. Secondly, planning plays a role in the socialist commodity economy, even if only indirectly, through such mechanisms as credit, tax, price, wage and monetary policies, notwithstanding that capitalist societies, forsaking *laissez-faire* doctrines, have innovated and extensively developed these mechanisms.

Some of the questions raised by China's status as a commodity economy are still under debate among the reformists. If labour, for example, can be considered a commodity, then the objections to a labour market vanish. Similar theoretical groundwork is under way to establish the bases for 'socialist' financial markets and 'socialist' stock exchanges.

In a sense, the entire discussion of capitalism in China is more semantic than real, but the reformers' ability to convincingly defend their policies as socialist is in all likelihood essential to the survival of the reforms.

Transportation

Transportation, together with energy, is one of the two critical sectors constraining economic growth. Although China's transport network has been greatly improved in the past 30 years, it has not kept up with expansion of demand. While individual sectors of the transport industry are operated very efficiently, notably the rail service and inland waterway shipping, capacity falls far short of demand and the entire system is burdened by poor short-haul services and inadequate inter-modal connections.

The sheer size of China means that effective inter-regional economic integration requires an extensive long-haul transportation network. This is particularly true with regard to coal, which makes up 38 per cent of railway freight volume. China's most important coal reserves are located in north-western Shanxi Province, while industry and population are mainly concentrated along the coast and eastern river valleys.

Equally serious, however, is the lack of short-haul transport in many rural areas. Human porters, man- and animal-drawn carts, bicycles and poled boats still play a large role in local freight transport in major cities as well as the countryside. In the countryside, reliance on these traditional modes restricts the radius of access to cities and towns, barring over a third of rural communities from markets, while in urban areas they obstruct vehicular traffic.

The limitations of China's internal transport system are complicated by the historical pattern of transportation investment which overly stressed railway development to the neglect of inland waterways and roads, although there have been efforts in the last decade to redress this imbalance.

The problem is not merely the inadequacy of road transport itself, but also its effect on the over-burdened railway system which is called upon to bear high volumes of short- and medium-haul freight and passenger traffic. The railway system contributes to this problem through its tariff structure – artificially low prices for short-run travel and freight have retarded development of short-haul road transport or supplementary local railways.

Poor local road transport also contributes to the inadequacy of inter-modal links, which is further complicated by lack of cooperation between the various bureaucracies governing different modes of transport. Although there has been significant progress in recent years at removing bureaucratic obstacles within the transport system, particularly among regional inland and coastal shipping authorities, routing container or even palletised freight 'door to door' remains extremely problematic even within the most developed regions, and impossible in most of the county.

The Chinese government has devoted considerable resources over the past three decades to the development of railways and roads in the far west. This has been necessary to open the region to economic exploitation, and also for political and military reasons. However, this has been at the expense of needed expansion in the more densely populated east. Long-haul transport links are also weak to the north-east, an important base for heavy industry, petroleum and wheat, and to the heavily-populated Sichuan basin in the interior.

China has fewer than 200 deep-water berths suitable for vessels of over 10,000 dead-weight tonnes (d.w.t.), and all Chinese ports are seriously congested due to this rapid expansion of foreign trade (90 per cent of which is ocean-borne) since the mid-1970s. Apart from oil and bulk items such as grain, most ocean freight is handled in break-bulk form – container facilities are very limited and even where they exist, containers must be stuffed or broken at the dockside due to lack of onward inter-modal container transport by road or rail.

For all these reasons, transport is a high priority for development. State investment in transport, including posts and telecommunications, in 1984 was Rmb10.5 billion, 14.3 per cent of total state capital construction investment, an increase of 34.2 per cent over transport investment in 1983. Preliminary reports suggested for 1985 Rmb13.23 billion, an increase of 26 per cent.

However, the scale of China's transport investment needs far exceeds the financial capabilities of the central government. The construction costs for a single-line railway are currently Rmb2 million per kilometre, and building graded unpaved roads costs an average Rmb300,000 per kilometre. State investment funds are distributed over a wide range of transport projects including railways, waterways, roads, port development, pipelines, posts and telecommunications. Even at the record 1984 level, state investment alone can bring about only modest and gradual expansions in transport capacity, while demand for new facilities is increasing rapidly.

Beyond central state investment, solving China's transport problems will require major efforts by provincial and local authorities to build and improve roads, waterways, bus lines, terminals and intra-urban bus lines and trains. These efforts are now more likely to be successful with recent changes in tariff structures which

make long-term investment in transportation more attractive.

Perhaps the most important policy measure, however, is the liberalisation of controls on ownership of vehicles and boats which is making it possible for individuals and collectives to offer transport services in competition with the state enterprises. In 1983, the number of trucks and buses owned and operated by rural peasants grew from 17,000 to 89,000, reached 130,000 in 1984 and is estimated to top 220,000 by year-end 1985. In addition, peasants now own over two million small tractors which are used for transport as well as field work, and peasants also own and operate 200,000 boats in inland water transport. While still inadequate to meet the need for fast, flexible local transport, these fleets are growing quickly as households using draft animals and other traditional transport means acquire the funds to purchase vehicles.

Railways

The railway system is the most important transportation mode in China, accounting for 50 per cent of total freight volume in 1984. The extent of the rail network has doubled between 1952 and 1983, from 22,900 to 51,600 km.

Rolling stock consists of 11,000 locomotives, of which over 70 per cent are steam driven, approximately 290,000 freight cars and 20,000 passenger coaches. Of this fleet, 652 locomotives, 17,900 freight wagons and 1,180 passenger coaches were newly-built in 1984, and China has purchased an additional 201 diesel locomotives from General Electric Co of the United States for delivery in 1985–86.

Coal movements account for about 35 per cent of rail freight tonnage, followed by cement and other construction materials (15 per cent), ores (11 per cent), iron and steel (6 per cent) and petroleum (5 per cent).

China's railway network is now the fifth largest in the world and one of the most efficient. In 1984, the system carried 724.7 billion tonne-kilometres of freight, 9 per cent more than in 1983, and 204.6 billion passenger/km, an increase of 15.5 per cent, both approximately twice the mid-1970s volume levels. Freight traffic density, an average 13.9 million for tonne-kilometres each kilometre of track, is second only to the Soviet Union and roughly five times higher than on India's 61,230 km rail system, while passenger traffic density is second only to India. This performance is particularly impressive in that there are only 9,000 km of double-tracked lines in the network. Shared use of tracks by passenger and freight trains requires frequent diversion of the slower freight trains to sidings.

However, rail freight service is estimated to meet only 50–70 per cent of demand. Over-loading on passenger trains is severe, and particularly serious on the Beijing-Guangzhou, Beijing-Shanghai, Beijing-Harbin and Beijing-Chongqing truck lines, where even the connecting passages between coaches are often filled with passengers.[41]

China's Ministry of Railways has plans for increasing capacity, building or upgrading 5,000 km of track over the next five years and adding more rolling stock. The most important addition is a 630 km electrified double-tracked railway now under construction between Datong coalfield in Shanxi Province and the port of Quihuang-dao in Hebei Province, designed to carry 100 million tonnes of coal per year.

The ultimate goal is to build four more east-west and two more north-south lines by the year 2000, completing an eight-by-eight grid of truck lines with twice the freight and passenger capacity of the present network, increase network length by 55 per cent to 80,000 km, of which 18,000 km is to be double-tracked (twice the present level) and 20,000 km electrified.

Even this ambitious expansion, however, equivalent to a 4.7 per cent increase in capacity per year, will be insufficient if demand continues to grow at current rates. Demand for passenger services, already far outstripping capacity, is expected to expand by an additional 69 per cent by 1990 and by 165 per cent by the year 2000.[42] The current annual rate of increase for freight services is unlikely to be less than 8.2 per cent which was the average annual rate of freight volume increase between 1976 and 1984.

In addition to expanding capacity, easing the strains on railway capacity will therefore require diversion to other transport modes, e.g. pipelines and water transport for freight movements, roads for short-haul passenger and freight transport, and aviation for long-haul passenger travel. Ten per cent of the 1.12 billion passengers on China's railways in 1984 travelled a distance of 800 km or more, for example, while short-distance travel from city centres to suburbs accounted for 18.1 per cent of all passengers.[43]

China's railways are among the very few profitable rail systems in the world, despite freight tariffs and passenger fares which until recently were far lower than on competing transport modes. Passenger rail fares, for example, averaged only Rmb0.0108 per passenger kilometre, approximately one-sixth the average cost of air-travel. Similarly, bus fares in most areas of China averaged 250 per cent of the corresponding railway hard-seat fares.

Price disincentives to divert short-haul freight to lorries began to be introduced in the mid-1970s and doubled the costs of rail shipments of less than 50 km between 1973 and 1984. New tariff schedules were introduced in May 1985, increasing the charge for passenger tickets on journeys of less than 100 km by 36.8 per cent and adding a special surcharge of Rmb4 per tonne on freight movements of less than 200 km.

Inland waterways and coastal shipping

For centuries, inland waterways were the most important mode of transport in China. All of China's great rivers run from west to east. The 2,500 km long Grand Canal, begun in the fifth century BC and completed in the seventh century AD, provided the crucial north-south communications and transport link integrating the Chang Jiang and its fertile delta with the north.

The Chang Jiang, China's greatest river, is navigable as far as Sichuan using special craft; ocean-going vessels of up to 20,000 d.w.t. can navigate 340 km upstream as far as Nanjing.

The Chang Jiang system includes several tributaries and a dense network of man-made canals (centred on the old Grand Canal) in the eastern provinces of Jiangsu and Zhejiang and the municipality of Shanghai. The

	Double track railways
	Single track railways (+++ under construction)
	Roads
⊕	International airports

system accounts for over 70 per cent of total volume of inland waterway shipping. Portions of the Zhujiang (Pearl River) system in Guangdong and Guangxi Province and the Heilong Jiang (Black Dragon River) system in the north-east are also navigable.

The inland waterway system began to decline in the 19th century with the advent of railways, and further deteriorated during the decades of regional warlords, foreign invasion and civil war. After 1949, inland and coastal shipping were subordinated to railways in terms of investment. Both suffered due to fragmented bureaucratic management and freight tariff structures which made rail shipments 20–30 per cent cheaper, although actual costs of water transport were only 65 per cent of rail costs per tonne/km and energy consumption was 30 per cent less.[44]

Neglect of canals, sluice gates, dredging and facilities reduced the total navigable extent of inland waterways from about 172,000 km in 1961 to only 108,900 km today. Almost a third of the remaining navigable waterways, 34,000 km, consists of the intricate canal systems of Jiangsu and Zhejiang Provinces.

The post-Mao period brought new leaders to transport planning and renewed interest in the advantages of waterborne shipping. From 1976 to 1983, the volume of inland waterways and coastal shipping more than doubled to 181 billion tonne-kilometres, rising from 16.2 per cent to 19.4 per cent of total domestic freight volume. The average increase per year was 11.3 per cent against 8 per cent for railways.

The most important of recent steps to expand inland waterway shipping has been decontrol of the rivers and canals to help collective enterprises and individuals in competing with the state for shipping services and through traffic from local tributaries to major river and coastal ports, particularly since 1983. In early 1985, there were more than 800 different shipping companies, mostly collectives, operating on the Chang Jiang system, as well as 343,000 individuals who owned and operated 173,000 boats totalling 2.06 million d.w.t.

Individuals and collectives now have access to docks operated by state organisations such as the Chang Jiang Shipping Authority, an agency of the Ministry of Communications, or provincial shipping organisations,

whereas previously these docks were only available to state-owned vessels. Privately-owned small boats operating on rivers and canals have played a major role in the expansion of rural industries in the delta regions of Jiangsu and Zhejiang Provinces.

Officials also say that bureaucratic and departmental regulations which previously made it necessary to tranship goods to different vessels when they passed to a part of a system governed by different state or provincial authorities have been eliminated.

Coal is among the most important inland waterways and coastal shipping cargoes — more than half of the coal shipments to Zhejiang Province are moved on the Chang Jiang from Anhui Province, or via coastal steamer from the coal port at Quinhuangdao which is linked to Shanxi coalmines by rail. A joint project is now under way between the Ministry of Railways and the Ministry of Communications to move coal from the north-east inland by rail to the Chang Jiang port of Zhicheng in Hubei Province and then by water to markets in central and eastern China.

Road transport

The weakest link in China's internal transport system is road transport. China's roads total only 930,000 km, about 100 metres per square km of land area, less than one-eighth of the road density in the United States. Rural roads comprise two-thirds of this total. More than 85 per cent of roads are ungraded and unsuitable for heavy trucks or all-weather use, and about 25 per cent are unimproved mud tracks. Such roads also impose high fuel and maintenance costs on vehicles.

Paved or asphalted roads are less than 2 per cent of total road length, and motor vehicles are often obstructed by draft animals, bicycles and handcarts, as well as fairs and use of the road surface for threshing, winnowing and drying grain. As a result, traffic congestion in and around urban areas was already becoming a problem in the late 1970s, before the recent expansion of vehicle fleets, and is now becoming serious.

Except in the western regions, most roads simply feed into urban areas and/or rail nodes and are not designed to function as an inter-urban network parallel to the railway system. Maintenance, however, is well-organised by local political units and is effective, if labour-intensive, although frequently excessive efforts are made to maintain deteriorated surfaces which could more economically be replaced.[45]

In rural areas, access to roads is probably the single most important factor determining prospects for local economic growth. The villages that have prospered as a result of economic reforms since the late 1970s are predominantly those which are located in suburban areas or river deltas with access by road or canal to cities and major marketing towns. 36 per cent of China's rural villages lack suitable roads for motor vehicles, and there is only one truck per 3,375 farmers.

The road construction programme for 1985 includes building 20,000 km of new roads, a third more than in 1984, 72 new road bridges over rivers and widening 30,000 km of narrow roads. Over the longer term, the

---

Workers building a reservoir near Xian are paid by the barrow-loads they move

Ministry of Communications announced plans in March 1985 to complete 96,000 km of new rural roads by 1987, for which the state has allocated Rmb2.8 billion in aid, most of which will consist of subsidies to impoverished areas with annual per capita incomes of less than Rmb120.

Several new expressways or first-class roads, are now under construction or in advanced planning stages:
- Shanghai to a new satellite town in Jiading County, 20 km;
- Shanghai to Hangzhou and the port of Ningbo in Zhejiang Province (planned), 240 km;
- Shanghai to Nanjing in Jiangsu Province (planned), 290 km;
- Guangzhou to the Shenzhen and Zhuhai Special Economic Zones (planned, a joint venture between Guandong Province and Hong Kong's Hopewell Development Company), 240 km;
- Shenyang to Anshan and the port of Dalian in Liaoning Province, 388 km;
- Beijing to Tianjin and the port of Tanggu;
- Jinan in Shangdong Province to the port of Quingdao (planned); and
- Fuzhou in Fujian Province to the Xiamen port and Special Economic Zone.

China's motor vehicle fleet is growing quickly, from 2.05 million at year-end 1983 to 2.4–2.5 million by year-end 1984, of which slightly more than 300,000 are automobiles and the rest trucks, vans, buses and jeeps. The fleet contains very few trucks of more than 8 tonnes capacity, partly reflecting the lack of roads of adequate width and load-bearing construction.

Chinese factories produced 300,000 vehicles in 1984, of which nearly half were medium-sized (2–5 tonnes) trucks and about 15,000 were heavy (8 tonnes) trucks. Automobile production was less than 5,000. Total production was 25 per cent above 1983 levels but met only 60 per cent of the estimated demand. Auto and truck imports exploded in 1985. At least 100,000 and possibly as many as 200,000 vehicles, mostly Japanese automobiles and trucks, were imported in 1984; irregular imports via Hainan Island alone reached 79,000 between early 1984 and March 1985. This contributed to the serious foreign exchange shortages that became apparent in late 1984. New controls on foreign exchange spending are expected to hold vehicle imports to much lower levels in the near future.

China's auto industry has developed joint-venture links with a number of foreign automakers. Joint-venture manufacture and assembly of Volkswagen Santana automobiles is planned to reach 20,000 units per year by 1989 and 100,000 by 1991 (see Chapter 4). A small-scale Peugeot assembly operation is under way in Guangzhou. Fiat has concluded an assembly deal, and Citroen, General Motors, Daihatsu and Nissan are discussing similar arrangements.

Motorcycle production in 1984 was 520,000 units. Demand is estimated at two million, and an expansion of output to 800,000 is planned for 1985. Honda motorcycle technology is used at a motorcycle plant in Chongqing and the company is planning direct production in Shanghai. Licensed production of Suzuki 100 cc motorcycles at three factories in Shenyang, Nanjing and Jinan was scheduled to begin in late 1985.

Ports

Ocean shipping carries over 90 per cent of China's foreign trade goods. Port infrastructure developed during the 1960s and early 1970s, but demand rose rapidly with the expansion of foreign trade in the late 1970s. Despite efforts to expand capacity beginning in 1978, China's ports have been swamped as ship arrivals have mounted to three times the planned handling capacity of the major harbours.

The number of vessels waiting to load or unload reached 540 by July 1985, 164 in Shanghai alone. The situation prompted the government to dispatch military units to the ports of Shanghai, Dalian and Qingdao to assist with cargo handling, and new policies and have been announced to confiscate cargoes left unclaimed in port handling areas for more than three months.

Many ports are located on rivers or estuaries and are relatively shallow. For example, Shanghai, China's most important port, cannot accommodate fully-laden vessels of more than 40,000–50,000 d.w.t. and these only at certain wharves. Large bulk carriers and tankers must unload at an offshore station, a converted bulk carrier, and most container traffic is handled through feeder vessels which meet large container carriers in Hong Kong.

Container capacity is increasing rapidly. It rose from 50–60,000 standard 20-foot units (TEU) in 1980 to 850,000 TEU in 1985, mostly through Shanghai and Tianjin. Planned expansion should bring the total capacity to 1.3 million TEU by 1990. At present, forward multi-modal container movement is limited due to poor roads. Rail container carriers are not used. Modern bulk handling equipment for grain and coal has been installed in Shanghai and other ports.

As of year-end 1984, China's coastal ports had a total of 398 berths, of which only 173 were deep-water berths capable of receiving vessels of 10,000 d.w.t. or more. Total cargo handling at major ports in 1984 was 275.5 million tonnes, up 10.4 per cent over 1983.

Construction of 102 new deep-water berths is under way, and the Ministry of Communications plans for 120 new deep-water berths to be completed by 1990, bringing the total number of berths to 542, of which 319 will be deep-water. 33 new deep-water berths were scheduled for completion in 1985, as well as reconstruction of three crude oil wharves at the ports of Dalian, Qingdao and Nanjing. Investment in port construction in 1984 was reported to exceed Rmb1.13 billion, a quarter more than in 1983.

A total of 99 ports are open to foreign trade, 40 of which were opened between 1979 and 1984. Most of these are small coastal and river harbours with limited shallow-water berthing. The vast majority of China's trade goods pass through one of seven major ports:

Shanghai's river-frontage

60

Shanghai, Dalian, Quinhuangdao, Qingdao, Tianjin, Huangpu and Zhangjiagang.

With 96 berths, of which 45 are deep-water berths, Shanghai overshadows the rest of the China's ports, handling approximately a third of the cargo tonnage in 1984. It is also highly congested – the number of ships waiting to load or unload in Shanghai reached a record 164 in July 1985 – despite rapid recent expansion of handling capacity. The port handled 9.5 million tonnes in January 1985, 23 per cent more than in the first month of 1984.

Shanghai has advanced container handling equipment, although its depth cannot accommodate deep-draft large container carriers. A new 200,000 TEU capacity container wharf was going into partial operation in late 1985.

Dalian is the chief port for the important north-eastern region and the major petroleum export port, linked by pipeline to the Daqing oilfield in Heilongjiang Province. New wharves under construction will expand its crude oil handling capacity from the present 15 million tonnes per year to 20 million tonnes per year, and coal handling capacity to 3 million tonnes per year by 1990, at which time total cargo handling capacity is expected to reach 60 million tonnes, one-third more than at present.

In addition, the State Council has approved plans for a new satellite harbour at Dayao Bay near Dalian. The facility will have 80–100 berths and 50 million tonnes total handling capacity. The first phase of construction, four million tonnes capacity, should be in operation by 1990.

The second phase of construction of the specialised coal port of Qinhuangdao in Hebei Province, developed with Japanese technical assistance and loans, was completed in March 1985, opening two new 50,000 d.w.t. berths with 20 million tonnes capacity. Linked by rail to the Shanxi Province coalfields, the port's total annual coal handling capacity is now 48 million tonnes. The third phase, which will add an additional 30 million tonnes handling capacity, is scheduled for completion in 1988.

The port of Qingdao handles crude oil from the Shengli oilfield in northern Shangdong Province (linked via a 250 km pipeline) and coal from Shanxi which is transhipped to Shanghai. New 50,000 d.w.t. berths, including a timber handling facility and more container handling equipment, were scheduled to go into operation in late 1985. A new satellite port is under construction at Huangdao, 4 kilometres from the present facility, with a planned capacity of 17 million tonnes.

At Huangpu, the main port for Guangzhou 10 new 35,000 d.w.t. berths are to be constructed with World Bank support, five of which are to be completed by 1990 and the rest by 1993. Current throughput at Huangpu, 16.7 million tonnes, is far above its designed capacity of 12 million tonnes.

Zhanjiang port is operating below its capacity of 17 million tonnes, with a throughput of 12 million tonnes in 1984. The petroleum terminal, linked by pipeline to the refinery at Maoming, has four berths for 25,000 and 50,000 tonne tankers and storage tanks for 130,000 cubic metres of oil. Handling capacity is scheduled tor each 20 million tonnes by 1990. Work is under way on a fourth terminal to handle bulk goods, including fertiliser, steel,

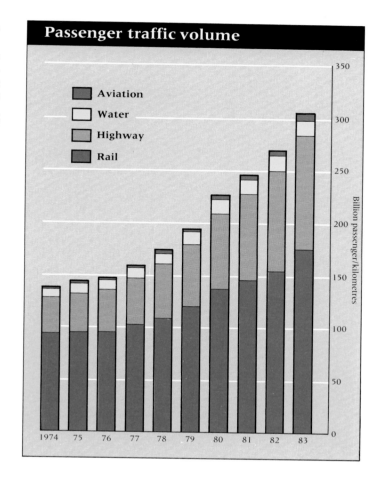

cement, sugar and cereal, and containers with a handling capacity of 2 million tonnes by 1990.

China's biggest deep-water coal wharf at Shijiusuo in Shandong Province, with an annual export capacity of 15 million tonnes, is now in trial operation. Its 2 km long berthing space can accommodate 100,000 d.w.t. bulk carriers and is designed to complete a loading cycle in 18 hours. Official opening was scheduled for late 1985. Development included loans from Japan.

At the Chang Jiang river ports of Nanjing, Zhang-jiagang and Zhenjiang nine new 10,000 d.w.t. berths have been opened with a total handling capacity of 3.1 million tonnes. These ports in the lower reaches of the Chang Jiang, accessible to ocean-going vessels, are being developed to relieve pressure on Shanghai, acting as consolidation and transhipment nodes for shipping to and from the rapidly-growing coastal provinces of Jiang-su and Zhejiang and up-river regions.

Aviation

Civil aviation began its take-off in China in the mid-1970s. Routes were quickly expanded from only 45,000 km in 1974 to 150,000 km in 1978 and 230,000 km by 1983, of which 100,000 km are international services. Passenger volume rose from 1.4 billion in 1974 to 2.8 billion in 1978 and 8.4 billion by 1984. Freight volume, only 40 million tonne-kilometres in 1974 reached 100 million tonne-kilometres in 1978 and 310 million tonne-kilometres in 1984, jumping to 567.7 tonne-kilometres in the first half of 1985 alone.

The quality of service is considered poor, however, and

the Civil Aviation Authority (CAAC) operating all civil air services in China is widely seen as disorganised and inefficient. Guidance equipment at Chinese airports is rudimentary or totally lacking, contributing to CAAC's less than comforting safety record.

Despite the rapid increase in routes and fleet, demand soared in the early 1980s. Over a million customers were turned away from airline booking centres in China in 1984.

A personnel shake-up in early 1985 promoted Hu Yizhou, former deputy director, to head of CAAC, and plans to break up the monolithic carrier into five or six separately-managed regional carriers were announced. The fleet is already being allocated to various regions.[46]

Most striking is the end of CAAC's monopoly with the emergence of independent regional airlines in several provinces. Four independent airlines had been registered by mid-1985 – Xingjian Aerial Transportation, Xiamen Aviation, Ocean Helicopter and Capital Helicopter – but as many as 30 others are being organised or operating with CAAC approval. Xiamen Aviation, operating flights to Shanghai, Guanzhon, Beijing and Fuzhou using leased CAAC aircraft, has agreed to purchase two used Boeing 737s from CAAC.

CAAC made its largest purchases of aircraft in China's history in 1985, starting early in that year with orders for nine Boeing 737-200s, 25 McDonnell Douglas MD-80s, three Airbus A310s and nine Soviet Tupolev TU154s.

Only a few months later, new orders were announced for 10 British Aerospace Bae146s, two more Md-80s and more Boeing jumbos – one 747-200M Combi (passenger/cargo), two 767-200ER (extended range) and five 737-200s, and in July, an additional order for 17 Soviet TU154s was announced.

In addition, two new regional carriers have announced separate purchases. The Xingjiang Autonomous Region announced plans to purchase three 160-passenger Ilyushin 62s in May 1985, and China Southwest Airlines, jointly organised by the provinces of Sichuan and Guizhou and the city of Chongqing, ordered four Boeing 737-300s in July 1986.

Military industries are gearing up to produce small- to medium-sized civil aircraft. Yun 7s (the Chinese version of the Soviet Antonov AN24) is already in service and two other planes, the Yun 8 (the Soviet AN12) and the 17-passenger Y-12 commuter are in flight testing. Licensed production of McDonnell 150-passenger MD-82s is planned to begin in 1987.

Airport improvement schemes are under way at several locations, and sets of ground-based navigation equipment were purchased in 1985 for installation at Dalian, Wuhan, Haikou, Zhanjiang and Beihai. Plans for installing 10 more additional sets will bring the total number of airports equipped for instrument take-off and landing to 25. Imported secondary radar equipment has also been ordered for Xi'an, Wuhan, Chengdu, Kunming, Xiamen and Dalian. Previously, only Beijing, Guanzhou and Shanghai were equipped with secondary radar.

CAAC is also ordering a ticketing and reservation system from the US-based Sperry Corporation in anticipation of passenger loading reaching 13 million by

Beijing's Tiananmen Square at dusk, with the Great Hall of the People in the background

1990. In June 1985, a joint venture between CAAC and West Germany's Lufthansa was organised to provide technology and train managers to upgrade maintenance of Chinese aircraft.

Eight new routes have been added in 1985, including one international route to Singapore, bringing the total to 83 domestic and 24 international routes, and the number of domestic flights increased 38 per cent to 782 per week.[47]

Economic geography

The persistence of an economic dualism between the industrial cities and the rural countryside in China remains evident in the concentration of industry in the coastal areas and the north-east. The coastal provinces and the north-east, comprising 37 per cent of China's population, today account for 57 per cent of total industrial output.

This is a much lower level of concentration than was the case in 1949, due to costly efforts to redistribute industry inland over the past three decades. This policy has established new bases for self-sustaining industrial growth apart from the traditional centres, and thus improved the climate for regionally-balanced economic growth.

The price of those efforts, however, is that cities which had considerable industrial bases and thus were natural centres of industrial development – the coastal cities of Shanghai and Tianjin, as well as riverside cities such as Wuhan and Chongqing – were starved of capital and other resources. As a consequence, their rate of development has fallen behind the national average and far below what would have been expected were China a capitalist economy.

In recent years, and particualrly since 1980, liberalisation of controls on investment has allowed coastal and river cities to take advantage of their natural advantages in transport and human resources.

The east

The lower Chang Jiang delta region, or simply the east, is China's most prosperous region and its most important industrial producer. Comprising the industrial metropolis of Shanghai and the provinces of Jiangsu and Zhejiang, this region has been the economic centre of China for centuries. It accounted for 25 per cent of the country's entire industrial production in 1984, with 10.6 per cent in Shanghai alone and 9.6 per cent in neighbouring Jiangsu.

Jiangsu and Zhejiang have been the fastest growing industrial producers in China in recent years, with average growth rates near 20 per cent in 1983 and 1984, and Jiangsu is likely to overtake Shanghai as the nation's biggest industrial producer in 1985. These two provinces' phenomenal growth rates can be attributed in large part to the explosive growth of rural industry.

Nearly half of Jiangsu's industrial output, 44 per cent, is generated by collective enterprises, primarily commune- and village-run small-scale factories. In Zhejiang, collective enterprises account for nearly half. These enterprises concentrate on light industry, consumer goods and construction materials.[48]

Shanghai is China's largest port and the gateway to the entire Chang Jiang valley region, and it was China's pre-eminent industrial metropolis at the time of the communist takeover in 1949, producing 20 per cent of China's industrial output and probably representing a third of the country's industrial capital and equipment. Shanghai has suffered from the Communists' policy of trying to redistribute industry to inland areas, and their desire to curb the influence of private capitalist firms which retained a dominant role in the city as late as 1953.

Shanghai has been a huge net exporter of capital, technology and trained personnel to the rest of the country. During the critical period of 1953–57, profits and taxes remitted by Shanghai enterprises were equivalent to 64 per cent of all the basic construction investment budgeted for industry for the entire country, while investment in Shanghai was not more than 1–2 per cent of the national total.[49]

The conscious policy of restricting Shanghai's growth in the 1950s, treating the city as a source of funds and human capital, effectively starved the city of needed investment capital for many years. This approach was modified to some degree in the 1960s and 1970s, in part a recognition that any rational national development scheme would have to better utilise Shanghai's unique capabilities and skills.

Like other traditional industrial bases, however, Shanghai's industrial growth continues to lag behind the national average. Net industrial output growth over 1983–84 was 9.7 per cent, against 13.8 per cent nationwide and less than half the phenomenal growth rates of neighbouring Jiangsu and Zhejiang. The state sector in Shanghai generates 85 per cent of all industrial output, and Shanghai's huge state enterprises are much more constricted by ministerial control and bureaucratic red tape than the smaller market-oriented rural industries that have contributed most to rapid growth in Jiangsu and Zhejiang.

The city is also burdened by the failure to upgrade plant equipment and urban infrastructure over the last few decades, in part due to the policies discussed above, although new policies announced in early 1985 should allow Shanghai to retain more of its funds for needed internal investment.

The north-east

The three north-eastern provinces of Liaoning, Jilin and Heilongjiang are a key base area for energy industries and manufacturing. The Daqing oilfield in Heilongjiang accounts for approximately half of China's petroleum production, and proven petroleum deposits in the region, including the Liaohe oilfield in Liaoning, are half of China's total. The north-east has a quarter of China's iron ore deposits and its largest stands of timber.

Total industrial output value in 1984 was Rmb108.1 billion, 15.4 per cent of the national total. Heavy industry is 64 per cent of total industrial output, the highest ratio of any region. In recent years, output growth has been less than the national average – industrial output rose 11.5 per cent in 1984, well below the 15–20 per cent increases recorded in the coastal and central Chang Jiang valley regions.

Development of the north-east began in the 1930s, when the area was a puppet state under Japanese control. The region represented most of China's heavy industrial capacity at the time of the Communist take-over and was a major recipient of Soviet economic assistance in the 1950s. Dalian, in Liaoning Province, is China's second largest port.

The most serious problem in north-eastern industrial development is obsolete equipment. Most industrial plant in the region dates from the 1950s and 1960s, much of Soviet origin. Energy consumption per unit of output is extremely high compared to developed countries. Large state-owned enterprises dominate industrial production, much of which consists of machinery and primary goods, with relatively few consumer goods. The region has become a net importer of coal, and shortages of electricity effectively lay idle an estimated 20 per cent of the region's industrial capacity, a loss of output of Rmb20 billion per year.

Development of small-scale rural collective enterprises in the region has lagged far behind coastal areas which are now showing far higher rates of industrial growth. Relatively under-populated, the north-east is a net grain exporter. Average per capita gross industrial and agricultural output in these three provinces in 1984 was Rmb1,549, over 50 per cent higher than the national average and, together with Jiangsu and Zhejiang, the highest of China's provinces.

The south-east

The high-growth coastal region also includes the provinces of Guangdong and Fujian, with industrial growth of 20 per cent in 1984. China's four Special Economic Zones (SEZs,) are located in these provinces, which have benefited from their proximity and growing trade and investment links with Hong Kong and the overseas Chinese community. Guangzhou, the capital of Guangdong Province, is the centre of the prosperous Pearl River delta area, an important port and the most important industrial centre in the region. Much of China's offshore oil exploration has so far centred on the Pearl River shelf and areas near Hainan Island.

With the autonomous region of Guangxi, the south-eastern region constitutes 12 per cent of China's population and 9 per cent of gross industrial and agricultural output. Much of the terrain is mountainous, which renders transportation links to the rest of China difficult.

North and centre

The vast northern Chinese plain and the inland provinces which flank the Chang Jiang together comprise China's heartland. The wheat-growing northern plain and the rice-bowls of the middle Chang Jiang basin together support nearly half of China's population and generate 40 per cent of all industrial and agricultural output.

Industrial output in the Chang Jiang provinces of Hubei, Hunan, Anhui and Jiangxi grew 15.2 per cent from 1983 to 1984, well above the national average of 13.8 per cent. Gross per capita output of industry and agriculture, however, was only Rmb824, 20 per cent below the national average. The tri-city of Wuhan is the only major industrial centre in the region. Anhui and

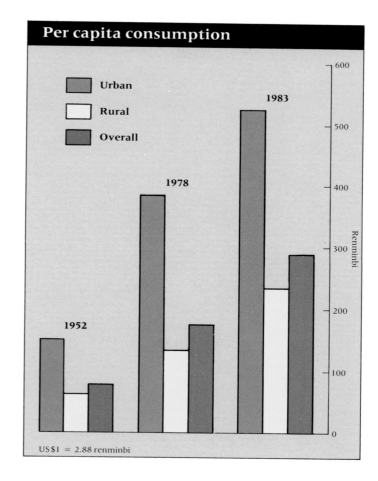

Per capita consumption

Urban
Rural
Overall

1952
1978
1983

US$1 = 2.88 renminbi

Jiangxi are relatively poor, with per capita output levels less than Rmb700, although Anhui is benefiting from rapid growth in neighbouring Jiangsu and Zhejiang.

Beijing, and the port of Tianjin are the biggest industrial centres in the northern plain region. Per capita gross output of industry and agriculture, Rmb 1,055 in 1984, is close to the national average. Industrial growth in 1984 was slightly below the national average.

Shandong Province is the third largest industrial producer and an important energy base with China's second largest oilfield and significant coal production.

The south-west

This region is relatively poor, with the lowest per capita gross output of industry and agriculture of any region – only Rmb612 in 1984, 40 per cent below the national average. The region is dominated by the huge province of Sichuan, a mountain-ringed inland basin the size of France with a population of over 100 million.

Chongqing, the wartime capital of China at the head of the navigable reaches of the Chang Jiang in Sichuan, is a key port, trade and industrial centre in the region, followed by Chengdu, the provincial capital. Sichuan is China's biggest grain producer and the fifth largest industrial producer in the country after Shanghai, Jiangsu, Liaoning and Shandong. Sichuan is China's biggest natural gas producer.

Economic growth in the region has been well above the national average in recent years, with industrial output growth of 15.4 per cent in 1984.

The north-west and far west

The north-western region is relatively undeveloped and poor. Gross output of agriculture and industry in 1984 was Rmb729, 28 per cent below the national average. Total population of the region is 72 million. But the north-west has China's most important coal reserves, in the province of Shanxi and the Inner Mongolian Autonomous Region, and has large mineral deposits.

Mining and related extraction activities are being rapidly expanded in this region. A key problem is the need to develop transport capacity to move coal from this region to the important industrial consumers in the east and north-east.

Qinghai, Xizang (Tibet) and Xinjiang in the far west are vast but extremely poor regions, much of which consists of arid desert or high mountain plateau. Industrially, the far west is insignificant, accounting for only 1 per cent of the nation's total industrial output. The region is heavily subsidised by the central government – government subsidies in Tibet are equivalent to the entire industrial and agricultural output, according to official Chinese sources, although this figure may include some military spending in the region.

Animal husbandry is the most important agricultural occupation in the grassland steppes of the region. The region has considerable mineral resources. Petroleum deposits in Xinjiang are believed to be very large, though they have only been partially explored.

China's international accounts

	US$ million		
	1982	**1983**	**1984**
Current Account			
Trade balance	4,249	1,990	14
Exports	21,125	20,707	23,905
Imports	−16,876	−18,717	−23,891
Services balance	939	1,739	1,574
Credits	3,604	4,028	4,819
Debits	−2,665	−2,289	−3,245
Unrequited transfers	486	511	442
Private	530	436	305
Official	−44	75	137
Current account balance	5,674	4,240	2,030
Capital account			
Long-term account	389	49	−113
Inflows	3,312	2,702	4,128
Outflows	−2,923	−2,653	−4,241
Short-term account	−51	−275	−890
Inflows	244	59	223
Outflows	−295	−334	−1,113
Errors and omissions	279	−336	−932
Change in reserves	−6,291	−3,648	−95
Capital account balance	338	−226	−1,003

Source: Xinhua Newsagency 1 September 1985: People's Bank of China (the first time China has released official international balance of payments information).

Deng Xiaoping, Chairman of the Central Advisory Commission of the Chinese Communist Party

Prime Minister Zhao Ziyang

Bu Ming, Chairman of the Bank of China

Madame Chen Muhua, President of the People's Bank of China, China's central bank

Politics and institutions

Party and government

China, by its constitution, is a socialist state 'of the people's democratic dictatorship led by the working class and based on the alliance of workers and peasants'. Like other states organised on Marxist-Leninist lines, China is governed through a dual bureaucracy – civil state organs and local administrations are penetrated by the Communist party, whose hierarchical embrace reaches from the highest leadership to the individual factory, village and neighbourhood.

The 'leadership role' of the party is not specifically mentioned or sanctioned in the current (1982) state constitution. In theory, that role derives from conception of the party, in the preamble to the party constitution, as the 'vanguard of the Chinese working class,' and 'faithful representative of the interests of the people of all nationalities in China'.

In fact, the civil organ of the state have been all but superfluous at certain times, particularly during periods of intense internal struggle. During the Cultural Revolution in the late 1960s, both party and civil organs were dismantled under assault from the leftists, and the military took on many regional and local governmental functions.

Most, if not all high-ranking government officials are party members, and party members may make up more than half of the personnel in sensitive organisations such as official newspapers.

In theory, the state apparatus is distinct from the party, and the party subordinate to civil law. According to the party constitution, its leadership role 'consists mainly of political, ideological and organisational leadership'. In practice, at the national level the party leadership openly makes all major policy decisions, while the state apparatus is responsible for legislative and executive functions. As Zhao Ziyang, China's Prime Minister, explained in a 1984 interview, 'the party is only concerned with major issues, not concrete issues'.

At the local level, the authority of the party remains paramount, although the operational responsibilities of civil administrations and the authority of the factory director in enterprises have been considerably revived.

There is considerable overlap in the membership of the state and party organs, including the highest levels. Zhao Ziyang, for example, is also a member of the Standing Committee of the Politburo of the party's Central Committee, the top party decision-making organ.

A third organisational structure, known as the Chinese People's Consultative Conference (CPCC), is essentially powerless. The CPCC theoretically represents a 'united front' of the Chinese people including other political parties. The CPCC was founded in 1949 as an interim legislative body to legitimise the establishment of the People's Republic of China.

State organisation

The National People's Congress (NPC) is formally the highest organ of state power. A congress is elected for a term of five years and meets once a year. It is empowered to amend the constitution, to enact and amend laws, to elect the chairman and vice-chairman of the State, the premier (or Prime Minister) and other key state posts. Its powers are vested in a Standing Committee which exercises the functions of the NPC when it is not in session.

The chairman or president of the People's Republic is elected by the NPC and represents the state in its relations with foreign states. This largely ceremonial post is currently held by Li Xiannian.

The highest executive organ is the State Council (SC), which is headed by the premier, and includes various state commissioners and ministers. By law, the SC applies the 'system of decision by the premier'. An unofficial inner cabinet consists of the premier, four deputy premiers and 10 key state councillors.

The SC supervises and coordinates the executive operations of the various ministries and commissions and oversees local state administrations at the level of provinces, autonomous regions and major municipalities. The SC is also responsible for drawing up and implementing State Plans for economic and social development and the state budget, public security operations foreign relations.

The State Council holds regular meetings twice a week, according to Prime Minister Zhao Ziyang, which discusses issues which cannot be resolved within a single ministry or commission. Major issues are proposed to the party secretariat, which may put them forward to the Politburo or its Standing Committee.

China's armed forces, however, are under the control of the (State) Central Military Commission, an organ which is effectively subsumed by its party equivalent, the (Party) Central Military Commission, headed by Deng Xiaoping.

The Chinese Communist Party

The Chinese Communist Party (CCP) was founded in Shanghai in 1921. The party came to power in 1949 with the military defeat of the Kuomintang (National People's Party) led by Jiang Jieshi (Chiang Kai-shek) on the Chinese mainland. The party remains formally committed to the principles of Marxism-Leninism and Mao Zedong thought and, by its constitution, committed to the ultimate goal of creating a communist social system in China. Under the leadership of Deng Xiaoping, however, economic modernisation of Chinese society has become the stated focus of party work, and class struggle is no longer seen as the central contradiction in Chinese society.

The total party membership as of mid-1985 is believed to be 20 million, and includes many who joined the party in the course of the military struggles against Japan and the Kuomintang in the 1930s and 1940s. In recent years, there have been conscious efforts to force superannuated cadres to retire and to recruit more 'intellectuals', defined as anyone with middle-school education or above.

In theory, the highest level of the party is its National Congress, which meets once every five years, and the Central Committee which it elects. The Central Committee, which currently has 210 full members and 133 alternate members, normally meets in plenary (full) session once a year. The most important policy iniatives are normally ratified at a National Congress or Central Committee plenum. The rural reforms, for example, are identified with the third plenum of the 11th National (Party) Congress, held in December 1978.

The National Congress also elects the Central Commission for Discipline Inspection, an internal party organ empowered to investigate and act on breaches of party regulations and discipline, and the Central Advisory Commission, whose membership consists of semi-retired party leaders.

The Central Committee elects its Politburo, the Standing Committee of the Politburo, which exercises the functions and powers of the Central Committee when it is not in session, and a secretariat which handles day-to-day party affairs.

The Politburo Standing Committee is the highest decision-making body in the party. Neither the Politburo nor its Standing Committee hold regular meetings. The Standing Committee has five members following the resignation of Ye Jianying in October 1985: Deng Xiaoping, head of the (Party) Central Military Commission; Hu Yaobang, part secretary-general; Zhao Ziyang, state premier; Li Xiannian, state chairman (head of state); Chen Yun, head of the Party Disciplinary Inspection Commission and an economist.

Zhao Ziyang and Hu Yaobang occupy what is termed the first 'line' or 'echelon', in the sense that they have direct operational responsibilities, Zhao as head of the executive organisations of the state and Hu as the highest-ranking party official and head of the party secretariat.

Deng Xiaoping, Chen Yun and Li Xiannian occupy the second line – a term used to suggest a less direct involvement in the day-to-day operations of the state and party. However, Zhao said, 'as all people know, major issues are determined with the participation of Comrade Deng Xiaoping'.

There is ample to reason to believe, as Bartke and Schier[50] have argued, that Deng and his reformist allies once sought to abolish the Politburo Standing Committee in 1982 and transfer all of its powers and functions to the newly-revived party secretariat. This attempt failed, and the older party leaders Chen Yun and Li Xiannian still represent a powerful conservative element restraining Deng Xiaoping and his younger allies.

The Central Committee also elects the party secretary-general, formally the highest position in the party, and the members of the Party Central Military Commission, which effectively controls China's armed forces. Actual party work in the military is carried out by the General Political Department of the People's Liberation Army under the direction of the Central Military Commission.

The office of the secretariat, revived at the 12th National Congress in 1982, has become increasingly important, taking on some of the policy-shaping functions of the Standing Committee. The secretariat is presided over by the secretary-general.

Decisions on fundamental policy, whether first formulated by the secretariat or the standing committee, must be formally approved at the annual meeting of the Central Committee, or by the National Congress itself, before they become official policy. The only exception to this is that an extraordinary party conference can be called to discuss and decide on major issues that require timely solution. Only two such conferences have been convened at the national level since 1949. The first, in 1955, ratified the purge of the 'anti-party clique' of Politburo member Gao Gang and Rao Shushi, regional leaders with strong ties in the north-east and Shanghai respectively.

The second, in September 1985, approved a large-scale reshuffling of the party leadership – replacing half of the Politburo members and a fifth of the full and alternate members of the Central Committee – and the proposal for a new, reform-oriented seventh Five Year Plan.

Once policy has been decided at the level of the Central Committee (or higher), all party members are bound under the Leninist principle of 'democratic centralism' to support it. In theory at least, open debate on the issue then ceases, although party members may still present dissenting views to higher levels provided they 'resolutely carry out the decision or policy while it is in force'. The practical risks of unsuccessful opposition to current policy can be extreme. Since the internal opposition is effectively limited to passive resistance and indirect criticism unless and until it is ready to present an open challenge, a skilful leader supported at the Central Committee level can bring about dramatic changes in party policy in a relatively short period of time.

That opposition to the current reform policies exists within the party is openly acknowledged in the Chinese press. A popular expression, according to the Beijing *People's Daily*, is 'You (higher central party authorities) may have your policies, but we have our countermeasures'. The Dengists, however, do not wish to adopt the extreme tactics of struggle, purge and imprisonment — tactics used against them by the left during the Cultural Revolution — and so far have relied mainly on persuasion, skilful use of the internal party decision-making structure, self-interest and recruitment.

The party is currently in the course of a rejuvenation campaign designed to recruit younger and better qualified members and retire super-annuated veterans. There is a political component to this campaign, as the Dengists seek to expand the base of support within the party for reformist economic and social policies.

The extraordinary National Party Conference in September 1985 elected 56 new full members and 35 new alternate members to the Central Committee. The average age of the new members is only 50. Ten older Politbureau members were retired at the subsequent Central Committee plenary session, but only six new appointments were made. The new members tend to represent the professional and reformist constituencies of premier Zhao Ziyang and party secretary-general Hu Yaobang. These younger leaders are part of what is sometimes termed the third echelon, a contingent of better educated young and middle-aged party members which Deng Ziaoping and his associates have been grooming for several years. The influence of the military in the new Politburo has apparently been reduced.

New appointments were also made to the party secretariat, Central Advisory Commission and Central Disciplinary Inspection Commission. These changes followed a series of rapid new appointments to provincial posts, a reshuffling of the military command structure and a number of ministerial changes in early 1985.

Nearly 1.5 million new members were recruited in

China's State Council

Premier (Prime Minister)	**Zhao Ziyang**	Minister of Chemical Industry	**Qin Zhongda**
Minister of Foreign Affairs	**Wu Xueqian**	Minister of Textile Industry	**Madame Wu Wenying**
Minister of National Defence	**Zhang Aiping**		
Minister in Charge of the State Planning Commission	**Song Ping**	Minister of Light Industry	**Yang Bo**
		Minister of Railways	**Ding Guangen**
Minister in Charge of the State Economic Commission	**Lu Dong**	Minister of Communications (Transport and Shipping)	**Qian Yongchang**
Minister in Charge of the State Commission for Restructuring the Economic System	**Zhao Ziyang**	Minister of Posts and Telecommunications	**Yang Taifang**
		Minister of Radio and Television	**Ai Zhisheng**
Minister in Charge of the State Educational Commission	**Li Peng**	Minister of Labour and Personnel	**Zhao Dongyuan**
		Minister of Culture	**Zhu Muzhi**
Minister in Charge of the State Science and Technology Commission	**Song Jian**	Director-General of the Xinhua News Agency	**Mu Qing**
Minister of Finance	**Wang Bingqian**	Minister of Public Health	**Cui Yueli**
Minister in Charge of the Commission of Science, Technology and Industry for National Defence	**Ding Henggao**	Minister in Charge of the State Physical Culture and Sports Commission	**Li Menghua**
Minister of Foreign Economic Relations and Trade	**Zheng Tuobin**	Minister in Charge of the State Family Planning Commission	**Wang Wei**
Minister of Commerce	**Liu Yi**	President of the People's Bank of China	**Madame Chen Muhua**
Minister of Water Resources and Electric Power	**Madame Qiang Zhengying**	Minister of Geology and Mineral Resources	**Zhu Xun**
Minister of Metallurgical Industry	**Qi Yuanjing**	Minister of Agriculture, Animal Husbandry and Fishery	**He Kang**
Minister of Machine-Building Industry	**Zhou Jiannan**		
Minister of Nuclear Industry	**Jiang Xinxiong**	Minister of Forestry	**Yang Zhong**
Minister of Aeronautics Industry	**Mo Wenxiang**	Minister in Charge of the State Nationalities Affairs Commission	**Yang Jingren**
Minister of Electronics Industry	**Li Tieying**		
Minister of Ordnance Industry	**Zou Jiahua**	Minister of Public Security	**Ruan Chongwu**
Minister of Astronautics Industry	**Li Xue**	Minister of State Security	**Jia Chunwang**
Minister of Coal Industry	**Yu Hongen**	Minister of Civil Affairs	**Cui Naifu**
Minister of Petroleum Industry	**Wang Tao**	Minister of Justice	**Zou Yu**
		Auditor-General	**Lu Peijian**

1984 of which over 900,000 were said to have middle-school graduate educational level or better. This is a much higher ratio than in the party at large, three-quarters of which were inducted during the late 1960s and early 1970s. There have been one million retirements from the party between 1982 and mid-1985. Family-origin, a euphemism for class background, is no longer to be considered a criterion in evaluating candidates for party membership, according to a decision by the party's organisation department. The new recruitment policy stresses educational and professional attainments.

This reflects in part the fact that the party has lost considerable prestige if none of its power as a result of the tragedy of the Cultural Revolution. In the late 1970s, when Deng Xiaoping was consolidating his influence within the Central Committee, party morale was extremely low. This situation has been complicated by the impact of the economic reforms, which place a higher value on educational and professional skills that many veteran party members lack.

Explaining the Cultural Revolution and the respective roles and responsibilities of the party, and Mao Zedong in particular, has been a serious problem for the party and for Deng's leadership. The official position on this question was hammered out in a 'Resolution on Certain Questions in the History of Our Party since the Founding of the People's Republic of China' adopted at the sixth plenary session of the 11th Central Committee on 27 June 1981.

'Chief responsibilities for the grave "left" error of the Cultural Revolution . . . does indeed lie with Comrade Mao Zedong', the document states, 'but (this) was the error of a great proletarian revolutionary who . . . in his later years . . . imagined that his theory and practice were Marxist and essential for the consolidation of the dictatorship of proletariat. Herein lies his tragedy.' The document also attributes responsibility to the party for 'habitually falling back on the familiar methods and techniques of turbulent mass struggle, and for failing to adequately institutionalise and defend the principles of collective leadership and democratic centralism, thereby facilitating over-concentration of power in individuals'.

The party also suffers from resentment that incomes for cadres remain fixed and very low, while workers' wages have been increased and peasants have doubled and even tripled their incomes as a result of the reforms. 'As cadres, we must let others become well off before ourselves', counselled the influential unnamed 'commentator' of the Beijing *People's Daily* in March 1985. But

some party members have become involved in corruption and illicit business deals.

Regional and local state and party organisations

The dual nature of state and party leadership at the national level is successively replicated at the level of the province or autonomous region, the county, town and village. If anything, the leadership function of the chief party representative is even more explicit at the provincial and local levels.

The top civil official at the provincial and municipal level is the governor (or mayor in the case of an independent municipality), whose party counterpart is the first secretary of the provincial or municipal party committee. Internal party affairs are secret, and understanding of how the formal and informal links between party and government operate in practice remains fragmentary and impressionistic.

It appears that the autonomy of the provincial and municipal civil government is gradually expanding, at least with regard to day-to-day operations within the guidelines of established party policy. But the authority of the party organisation and of the local party secretary probably remains ultimately the more powerful, although the party's role in day-to-day affairs appears increasingly circumscribed.

Key state and party organs are replicated at the provincial and county levels. Each province, autonomous region and independent municipality has its own People's Congress and its standing committee. Economic affairs are administered through Economic Commissions and Planning Commissions which mirror, and are administratively linked to, their national-level counterparts.

Party Congresses also exist at the provincial and county levels, as well as local Commissions for Discipline Inspection. Advisory committees, similar to the national-level party Central Advisory Commission, are also replicated at the provincial, but not the county levels.

Local or primary party organisations extend to individual factories, schools, offices, neighbourhoods, villages and military units – anywhere where there are three or more full party members. It is the responsibility of the primary party organisations to propagate and carry out party policies, to educate and supervise party members and to recruit new members.

Party organisations also exist within important state and other non-party organs, such as commissions, ministries, mass organisations and cultural or educational institutions.

In practice, the party committee and its secretary are frequently the key administrative positions in a factory, office or rural organisation, just as the provincial party committee secretary is ultimately the most important regional official. There has been increasing attention in recent years to the need to separate and distinguish the leadership role of the party from the governmental functions of the state on the one hand, and the administrative and operational leadership of economic enterprises on the other.

Workers following current affairs in Shenyang, Liaoning Province

However, the party openly claims the power of its local congresses and committees to discuss and decide major issues pertaining to that area. In some cases, however, the authority of the party secretary at the factory level has apparently been diminished in favour of the professional factory director.

Party officials clearly remain the important leaders of China's rural townships, the successors to Mao's rural communes, but many of these township leaders appear to have considerable managerial skills, and may identify themselves more closely with the interests of their unit than the often changing policy pronouncements from Beijing. In Sichuan Province, party cadres are now recruited for posts in small towns and rural areas through advertising and are employed on a contract basis. A provincial radio broadcast monitored in August 1985 indicated that over 20,000 party posts had been filled in this manner in the last few years.

Foreign relations

China's foreign relations have gone through four distinct phases since 1949. In the early 1950s, China 'leaned to one side', turning to the Soviet Union for economic and military assistance, a stance reinforced when Chinese and US forces clashed in the Korean War and the United States strengthened its commitment to Taiwan.

However, China's relationship with the Soviet Union began to show strain as early as 1956. Mao and other leaders were wary of excessive dependence on the Soviet Union, and resisted Moscow's claim to supremacy within the socialist bloc. The Soviet Union was nervous about China's programme to acquire nuclear weapons. The split became an open one in 1960 when the Soviet Union terminated all technical and economical assistance to China.

In the second phase, roughly corresponding to the decade of the 1960s, China perceived itself facing both superpowers as 'dual adversaries'. Tensions with the Soviet Union heightened as China criticised Soviet revisionism, denounced the United States-Soviet Union test-ban treaty, and continued its nuclear programme. At the same time, China continued to view the United States as a hostile threat. The United States, while now accepting that the Communists had effectively consolidated their power on the mainland, saw China's support of revolutionary movements elsewhere in Asia and around the world as a dangerous and destabilising force.

China began to assert itself as a leader of the under-developed nations of the Third World. This stance was complicated as China's claims to leadership of the world revolutionary movement against imperialism led to support, both vocal and material, of communist insurgent movements in Asia. The Cultural Revolution reinforced xenophobic tendencies within the party, as well as international perception – including both Soviet and US – of China's leadership as unstable and possibly mad.

The Sino-Soviet confrontation had become a bloody one following a Chinese ambush of a Soviet patrol on a disputed island in the Ussuri River. That incident, probably instigated by Lin Biao in an attempt to counter Zhou Enlai's efforts to cut back the power of the military, was followed by a Soviet counter-attack on the same island and a massive build-up of forces along the border.

The normalisation of China's governmental and economic relations with the rest of the world began in 1970 under the aegis of Mao and premier Zhou Enlai. The critical change was the move toward a rapprochement with the United States. Zhou and Mao apparently felt an understanding with the United States was necessary as a counter-weight to the growing military threat to China posed by Soviet forces. For the United States, opening relations within China similarly presented an opportunity to redefine the balance of world power as the Soviet Union approached parity with the United States in terms of strategic forces, and a means of inducing the Soviet Union to cooperate at the strategic arms limitation talks and in the broader context of East-West detente.

Diplomatic relations were quickly established or restored with other nations of the West, and Beijing assumed representation at the United Nations in 1971. Zhou also agreed to talks with the Soviet Union in late 1969 on the border issue. Those discussions continue today, now taking place at the deputy foreign minister level, and incorporating China's objections to Soviet support of the Vietnamese occupation of Kampuchea and the Soviet invasion of Afghanistan. China cut back its support for Marxist insurgencies, rapidly expanded foreign trade and began to seek foreign investment.

In the 1980s, China has pursued a more equidistant relationship towards the two superpowers. Disavowing support for revolutionary insurrections, China mended its relations with Asian neighbours, expanded the range of countries with which it has diplomatic relations, and presented a new, more responsible profile in international affairs.

China's most dramatic foreign policy achievement has been the signing of the joint Sino-British declaration on the future of Hong Kong on 19 December 1984. Under the agreement, the British colony will revert to China in 1997, the year when the British lease on the New Territories area of Hong Kong will expire. Under the concept of 'one country, two systems', Hong Kong is to retain its capitalist economy and a high degree of autonomy in domestic affairs, including maintenance of the existing legal system, personal freedoms and socio-economic systems.

The cornerstone of China's formal position on international affairs are the Five Principles of Co-existence, first raised by Zhou Enlai in 1953 in the course of Sino-Indian talks. Those principles are: mutual respect for sovereignty and territorial integrity; mutual non-aggression; non-interference in each other's internal affairs; equality and mutual benefit; and peaceful coexistence.

China describes itself as opposed to imperialism, hegemonism, colonialism, and as supporting the oppressed nations and developing countries in their struggle to win and preserve national independence and develop their economies.

There is no need, China's leaders now say, for China to export revolution. 'Because of its own insoluble contradictions, capitalism is bound to be replaced by socialism sooner or later' the Beijing *People's Daily* explained in October 1984. 'Such a process of replacement is not a matter of "exporting revolution" under the "socialist" banner – that kind of "revolution" is actually aggression and enslavement and hegemonism through and through,

The People's Liberation Army has 4 million under arms

and has nothing in common with socialism.'

On this basis, China has cut back if not eliminated, its links and support for insurgent movements in Asia and elsewhere, facilitating a gradual improvement in relations with the Asian nations, with whom China is united in opposition to the Vietnamese occupation of Kampuchea.

Sino-Indian relations have improved dramatically in the 1980s and talks on the long-standing border dispute between the two nations began in 1985. Growing unofficial trade has marked a gradually expanding, though informal, relationship with South Korea.

Current Sino-Soviet relations

The current status of Sino-Soviet relations is subject to widely differing interpretations. Much of the ideological basis of the Sino-Soviet conflict has dissipated, and trade and cultural relations betwen the two countries have improved since 1982 as China seemed to see a position of equidistance, at least rhetorically, between the two super-powers. Leaders of both countries have voiced support for a more substantial normalisation of relations between China and the Soviet Union.

But as yet there has been no real progress on what China terms the 'three major obstacles' to better relations: Soviet troop and missile deployments along the Chinese border, Moscow's support for the Vietnamese occupation of Kampuchea, and the Soviet invasion of Afghanistan.

China's most important objectives in pursuing normalisation is to neutralise or eliminate the Soviet military threat of either a 'pre-emptive' strike against China's strategic forces or a conventional invasion across the Chinese border. China also seeks to maintain its independence of action, avoiding any implication of subservience or dependence on the Soviet Union. While there is scope for considerable expansion of trade, China looks mainly toward the United States, Japan and Western Europe as a source of technology and equipment.

A US$14 billion five-year trade and cooperation agreement between China and the Soviet Union was signed in July 1985. Under the terms of the agreement, two-way trade between the two countries is to reach US$3.5 billion by 1990, about twice the current level. Border trade has reportedly increased sharply in 1985.

The Soviet press has taken a less critical tone of China's economic reforms since Mikhail Gorbachev became head of the Soviet Communist Party.

China has sided with the Soviet position on the US Strategic Defense Initiative, which some have interpreted as evidence of a 'tilt' toward the Soviet Union. However, China has good reasons to be concerned about a race to develop new space-based defensive systems, which would weaken China's less sophisticated strategic forces.

China's Foreign Minister Wu Xueqian met with the

Soviet Foreign Minister Eduard Shevardnadze in New York in September 1985, when the two ministers were attending the General Assembly session of the United Nations.

However, there was no progress reported on the three major obstacles at the conclusion of the seventh round of normalisation talks in October 1985 between Chinese Deputy Foreign Minister Qian Qichen and Soviet Vice-Foreign Minister Leonid Ilyichev. An eighth round is scheduled for April 1986 in Moscow.

According to Den Xiaoping, there are a million Soviet troops on the Chinese border. Western analysts estimate that the total is 600–700,000, in 53 divisions, together with missiles and aircraft. Estimates of Chinese forces deployed along the border are as high as 1.5 million, although Chinese forces are said to have been reduced as part of the military streamlining process. The Soviet forces are believed to have far superior equipment, armour and air support.

China's position on the Soviet Union's growing military presence in the Pacific is somewhat ambiguous. Deng Xiaoping, in a statement in April 1985, apparently conceded any objections to the Soviet use of bases in Vietnam. In early September 1985, the commander of the Chinese naval forces was quoted that 'one superpower focuses its efforts on building up its strategic strike strength and speeding up the modernisation of its navy and air force. At the same time, it takes Cam Ranh Bay and Danang [in Vietnam] as its advance bases so as to extend its combat capacity into the South China Sea and the nearby oceanic areas.'

In an interview with US *Time Magazine* in October 1985, Deng stated that Soviet naval strength in the Pacific is 'the same as their strength in the Atlantic. We realise that removing all [of the three obstacles] at the same time "might be difficult" [so now we say] one at a time. So far we have had no positive response.'

The Kampuchea obstacle is one that China may wish to eliminate quickly. In January 1985, Chinese Foreign Minister Wu Xueqian, on a tour of Southeast Asia, said on more than one occasion that China 'reserved the right' to give Vietnam a second 'lesson' if it continued its provocations along the Chinese-Vietnamese border – an allusion to China's abortive invasion of Vietnam in 1980 after Vietnam occupied Kampuchea. This threat was widely interpreted as a commitment to act if Vietnam intensified its operations against rebel base camps on the Thai border. However, China did not act when Vietnamese forces successfully wiped out the camps a few weeks later.

Current Sino-US relations

The Shanghai Communique signed by President Nixon and Chinese leaders in 1972 essentially deferred resolution of the problems of how diplomatic relations could be restored given the US relationship with Taiwan. In December 1978, the Carter administration announced

Gun powder was invented in China by the seventh century AD. It was not until the 11th century that the Chinese used explosives in warfare

that diplomatic relations would be restored on 1 January 1979, and the United States moved to terminate its diplomatic ties and abrogate its defence treaty with Taiwan. The US Congress, however, enacted the Taiwan Relations Act which obligated the United States to make clear that it 'expected' the future of Taiwan to be determined by peaceful means, and to continue to provide Taiwan with sufficient defensive arms.

On 17 August 1982, the United States and China signed a new joint communique in which the United States stated that its army sales to Taiwan would not exceed either qualitative or quantitatively the level of those supplied during the previous four years, and pledged to gradually reduce those sales over time.

Relations with the United States in the mid-1980s appear to be somewhat cooler than a few years ago. However, it may equally be said that the relationship is now a more realistic one and hence more stable. China will be seen as a 'non-threatening' world power preoccupied with economic modernisation and reform for some time to come, US Ambassador Arthur Hummel explained at the conclusion of his four-year tour of duty in 1985.

This perception undercuts the view that China would be an effective strategic ally against the Soviet Union. Some analysts have questioned how China could have ever been seen seriously in such a role. But China's military weakness and preoccupation do not preclude the strategic dimension of the US-China relationship.

At the most basic level, as Ambassador Hummel explained, the United States no longer need to prepare for the possibility of war in Asia with China. In a broader sense, China and the United States have found and continue to share, a broad range of parallel interests. These include containing the expansion of power and influence by the Soviet Union in the Pacific region and in South and Western Asia; encouragement of a strong Association of Southeast Asian Nations (ASEAN) and curbing the Soviet Union's surrogate, Vietnam, in Indochina; and reducing tensions on the Korean peninsula.

The Taiwan issue, which effectively ceased to be a major obstacle after the United States agreed to gradually reduce arms sales to Taiwan in 1982, continues to be an irritant as the nationalist government in Taiwan resists Chinese overtures. Another irritant was the US cut in aid to a United Nations Fund for Population Activities following charges that China has practised coercive abortion as a means of birth control.

Trade and technology transfer have become the real strength and the most serious source of problems in the US-China relationship. China has become the fourth largest supplier of textiles to the US, and one of the targets of attempts by US industry groups to cut back textile and clothing imports.

The Reagan administration has moved toward direct arms sales to China. To date, China has purchased helicopters and gas turbine engines destined for naval vessels from the US, and discussions on a larger deal, which includes explosives, anti-tank weapons and naval and air defence systems, are said to be close to completion. As of late 1985, however, approval by the US Congress of an agreement to provide China with nuclear materials and equipment remained problematic, following charges that China had contributed to nuclear weapons development in Pakistan and other nations.

Military

General

The People's Liberation Army (PLA) has developed from the peasant-based forces which won China's revolution in the 1940s into the world's second largest standing military force after the Soviet Union. Over a third of its 4 million troops are believed to be deployed along the 8,000 km long border with the Soviet Union and Mongolia, and another 600,000 are based on the southern border with Vietnam.

Backing the PLA is a 10 million-strong civilian militia comprising a core militia of 4.3 million young people who receive regular weapons training, and 6 million ordinary militia (reserves). The military establishment includes an extensive system of factories, railway lines, airports and farms which have developed independently of civilian industry.

China military doctrine since the mid-1960s has combined a modest nuclear deterrent with the strategy of mass-based defence in depth in the event of conventional invasion. The essentially defensive nature of this approach is at least partly dictated by the relatively unsophisticated level of China's conventional forces. The PLA 'lacks facilities and logistical support for protracted large-scale operations at any significant distance outside Chinese borders'.[51] These limitations were underlined by the difficulties Chinese forces encountered in the 1979 war with Vietnam.

Technologically, China's conventional forces have barely advanced since the Korean War of 1950–53, when China received substantial amounts of arms and equipment from the Soviet Union. However, Soviet assistance was halted in 1960. While military spending increased during the 1960s, there were few technical advances.

Military stagnation during this period can largely be attributed to preoccupation with the internal struggles of the Cultural Revolution. As the authority and leadership structure of the party collapsed, the military stepped in to intervene between rival leftist factions and restored local political structures in the form of Revolutionary Committees in the provinces. By 1969, the ninth Central Commitee was dominated by the military with the support of leftist Red Guards.

The post-Mao era has seem the curtailment of the civil role which the military played during the Cultural Revolution. This process began with the death of Defence Minister Lin Biao in 1971, allegedly in the course of an aborted coup attempt. Only 16.4 per cent of the members and alternate members of the current 12th Central Committee (1982) are active military leading cadres.[52]

Military modernisation, however, has been ranked fourth among the 'Four Modernisations', subordinated to overall economic development. This is not to imply that the military's limitations were not recognised – Deng Xiaoping's critique of 'bloating, laxity, conceit, extravagance and inertia' in the military was a central theme of his rise to power in the mid-1970s.[53] 'We must admit that our army is not sufficiently capable of conducting modern warfare', Deng wrote in 1977, 'and that although it is numerically strong, it is of relatively poor quality.'[54]

By 1975, however, Deng had achieved a consensus

among the party leadership that it was impossible to leap-frog military modernisation ahead of scientific and technical advances in a broad-based overall economic modernisation.[55] Nor, apparently, is there any intention of financing wholesale modernisation of China's huge military forces by purchases of arms or technology from abroad.

Military delegations to the West since the late 1970s have expressed considerable interest in sophisticated weapons systems and aircraft such as the British Harrier, but confirmed purchases from Western Europe have so far been limited to small numbers of helicopters, armoured vehicles, communications systems and sidearms. A reported agreement with a British consortium to outfit China's Luda class destroyers with Sea Dart missiles was apparently cancelled in 1983 because of cost.

China has been eligible to purchase certain categories of military equipment from the United States since 1981 and dual-use equipment since 1982, but the only confirmed military sales so far have been for Sikorsky S-70C Black Hawk helicopters for use by the army in 1984 and five General Electric LM-2500 gas turbine engines for naval craft in 1985, although talks are continuing over purchase of US and Italian anti-tank missiles and technology.

Deng Xiaoping replaced Hua Guofeng as chairman of the powerful Party Central Military Commission in 1981. From a high of US$14.6 billion in 1979, the year of the Sino-Vietnamese War, total military spending declined to US$9.5 billion by 1982, dropping from 6.8 per cent to 4.2 per cent of GNP.[56] However, the reformist party leadership's authority over elements in the military who opposed the low priority given to defence spending was limited. Only in 1985, following the consolidation of the economic reform programme in 1984 and significant progress in normalising relations with the Soviet Union, did Deng Xiaoping's 10-year-old master-plan for military reform finally get under way.

Plans for massive military reorganisation including a reduction of the armed forces by 25 per cent – one million men – were announced in June 1985 after an enlarged meeting of the Party Central Military Commission in Beijing. About one half of the personnel to be demobilised will be officers, according to PLA General Chief of Staff Yang Dezhi, of which 100,000 were to be demobilised in 1985. Manning has been cut by 24 per cent in the General Staff headquarters, political department and logistics departments, and by 50 per cent in the remaining regional command headquarters.

Accompanying the reduction of the armed forces was a restructuring of the top military leadership and consolidation of China's regional military commands from 11 into seven. The central Jinan command has been merged with Wuhan, western Lanzhou with Zinjiang, south-western Chengdu with Kunming and eastern Fuzhou with Nanjing, while Beijing, Guangzhou and Shenyang commands remain intact. Guangzhou will take responsibility for Hubei Province, which was previously part of the Wuhan command.

The reduction of the armed forces is unlikely to significantly affect military capabilities as many of the officers and men to be demobilised are believed to be essentially inactive personnel who have remained on the PLA payroll for political or other reasons, while others are staff and workers in military industrial establishments which are being converted into civilian enterprises. (See Defence industries below.)

The reorganisation is expected to result in a more professional and better-educated officer corps, as well as enabling cost savings which can be applied to improving and upgrading weapons systems. A streamlined ordnance industry is expected to concentrate on developing new anti-tank and anti-aircraft weaponry, the new Minister of Ordnance Industry Zou Jiahua announced in June 1985.

China also plans to arm its naval forces, which are currently limited to coastal defence duties, with a new generation of strategic and tactical missiles by 1990, including an anti-ship missile modelled on the French Exocet.

Defence industries

China's military system incorporates an extensive system of factories, railway lines, airports and farms which have developed independent of civilian industry. However, integration and cooperation between military and civilian industry has developed rapidly since 1978, and civilian goods ranging from bicycles and washing machines to radios and foodstuffs now make up 30 per cent of the output of defence industrial establishments.

Defence-related research facilities and factories have long enjoyed priority access to funds, equipment and trained technical personnel, and key installations were relatively insulated from political interference during the Cultural Revolution. The ratio of trained technical staff in defence industries is believed to be two to three times higher than in civilian factories, and many defence-related establishments possess extremely sophisticated tools and equipment.

Military-civilian integration is seen both as a means of using existing industrial capacity more efficiently, and as a form of internal technology transfer to civilian industry supplementing or substituting for technology imported from abroad.[57]

The pace of transfer of military establishments to civilian operation quickened in 1985 with the announcement of large-scale military reorganisation and troop reductions. The military has opened 59 airports, 40 fuel depots and 145 military railway lines to civilian use. Zou Jiahua, appointed Minister of Ordnance Industry in June 1985 when the military reorganisation was announced, called for a speeding up of the switch from military to civilian production, and efforts to develop foreign trade, technology transfer and cooperative ventures with foreign businessmen. China North Industries Corporation the trading arm of the Ministry of Ordnance Industry has been an active exporter of machinery and equipment since the late 1970s and is believed to be a key player in China's growing arms exports.

Notes

1 Alexander Eckstein, *China's Economic Revolution*, London: Cambridge University Press (1977), p.1.
2 Dwight Perkins and Shahid Yusuf, *Rural Development in China*, Baltimore: John Hopkins University Press (1984), p.10.
3 Perkins and Yusuf, *op. cit.*, pp. 10-11.

4 World Bank, *World Development Report 1985*, p. 178.
5 Jürgen Domes, *The Internal Politics of China 1949-72*, London: C. Hurst & Co (1973), p.27.
6 Ralph Thaxton, *China Turned Rightside Up*, New Haven: Yale University Press (1983), pp 39-43.
7 Domes, *op. cit.*, p. 42.
8 Dwight Perkins and Shahid Yusuf, *op. cit.*, pp. 21-24, 34, 69-70.
9 Domes, *op. cit.*, p. 52, and O. Edmund Clubb, *20th Century China* (3rd edn.), New York: Columbia University Press (1978), p. 795.
10 Clubb, *op. cit.*, p. 330.
11 State Statistical Bureau, *Statistical Yearbook of China 1984*, Beijing (1985).
12 Domes, *op. cit.*, p. 43.
13 William A. Joseph, *The Critique of Ultra-Leftism in China, 1958-81*, Stanford, California: Stanford University Press (1984), pp. 62-81.
14 Domes, *op. cit.*, pp. 117-18.
15 David L. Shambaugh, *The Making of a Premier: Zhao Ziyang's Provincial Career*, Boulder, Colorado: Westview Press (1984).
16 Domes, *op. cit.*, p. 125.
17 Domes, *op. cit.*, p. 140.
18 Roderick MacFarquhar, *The Origins of the Cultural Revolution*, volume 2, London: Oxford University Press (1983), pp. 278-83.
19 Domes, *op. cit.*, p. 177-83. See also Jürgen Domes, *China After the Cultural Revolution: Politics between two Party Congresses*, London: C. Hurst & Co (1975).
20 Jürgen Domes, *The Internal Politics of China 1949-72*, London: C. Hurst & Co (1973), pp. 178-99.
21 Based on official Chinese figures. Preliminary results from satellite imaging research indicate that the actual total of cultivated land may exceed official estimates by a considerable amount.
22 World Bank, *World Development Report 1985*, Table 3.
23 Frederic M. Surls and Francis C. Tuan, 'China's agriculture in the eighties' in US Congress Joint Economic Committee, Selected Papers, China Under the Four Modernisations, 13 August 1982.
24 Interview with the author, November 1984.
25 Robert Delfs, 'Back to the market', in *Far Eastern Economic Review*, 30 May 1985.
26 According to a survey of three counties in Hebei Province, published by the Beijing *Gongren Ribao* (Worker's Daily), 8 March 1985, estimating gross costs.
27 Robert Delfs, 'Agricultural yields rise but the boom cannot last,' in *Far Eastern Economic Review*, 13 December 1984.
28 This, and the following comparison figures, are derived from *Selected Indicators of Food and Agriculture Development in the Asia-Pacific Region, 1974-84*, Bangkok: The Food and Agricultural Organisation of the United Nations (1985). FAO production, sown acreage and yield figures differ from official Chinese statistics.
29 World Bank, *World Development Report 1985*.
30 Richard E. Gillespie and Martin Weil, 'China's steel industry' in *China Business Review*, May 1985.
31 Deng Keyun, 'Rural energy development' in *Beijing Review* No. 21, 27 May 1985, pp. 23-25.
32 Martin Weil, 'Coal's promises and problems' in *China Business Review*, March-April 1984.
33 Weil, *op. cit.*
34 Tatsu Kambara, 'Review of China's oil development and export prospects', in *Jetro China Newsletter* No. 51 (Tokyo), August 1984, p. 2.
35 Bernd Knoll, 'China oil: looking downstream' in *China Energy Report 1985*, The American Chamber of Commerce in Hong Kong (1985), pp. 24-25.
36 Knoll, *op. cit.*
37 Martin Weil, 'Hydropower: over budget, over due' in *China Business Review*, July-August 1982, p. 18.
38 Martin Weil, 'Hydropower: project priorities' in *China Business Review*, July-August 1982.
39 Julia Sensenbrenner and Martin Weil, 'Debunking the small hydro myth', in *China Business Review*, July-August 1982, p. 12.
40 Dennis Phillips, 'Peking picks KWU, says Bonn', in *China Trade Report*, July 1985.
41 Li Chunsheng, 'Major strategies for the development of passenger transport by rail', in *Beijing Yanjiu (Peking Studies)*, 20 March 1985, pp. 37-40.
42 Li Chunsheng, *op. cit.*
43 Li Chunsheng, *op. cit.*
44 *China's Socialist Economic Development*, volume II, Annex F, p. 383.
45 *op.cit.*, volume II, Annex F, p. 364.
46 Michael Westlake, 'Change of direction', in *Far Eastern Economic Review*, 13 June 1984, pp. 118-21.
47 Mary Lee, 'Going business class', in *Far Eastern Economic Review*, 18 April 1985, pp. 72-73.
48 Robert Delfs, 'The Delta Factor' in *Far Eastern Economic Review*, 18 July 1985, pp. 93-95.
49 Christopher Howe, 'Industrialisation under conditions of long-run population stability: Shanghai's achievement and prospect' in C. Howe (ed.), *Shanghai: Revolution and Development of an Asian Metropolis*, London: Cambridge University Press (1981), p. 166.
50 Wolfgang Bartke and Peter Schier, *China's New Party Leadership*, London: Macmillan Press (1985).
51 *The Military Balance 1984-85*, London: The International Institute for Strategic Studies (1985).
52 Bartke and Schier, *op. cit.*
53 Deng Xiaoping, 'The Task of Consolidating the Army', speech at enlarged meeting of the Party Central Military Commission on 14 July 1973, in *Selected Works of Deng Xiaoping*, p. 27.
54 Deng Xiaoping, 'The Army Should Attach Stragegic Importance to Education and Training', speech at a forum of the Party Central Military Commission, 23 August 1977, in *Selected Works of Deng Xiaoping*, p. 75.
55 Thomas W. Robinson, 'Chinese Military Modernisation in the 1980s', in JEC Part 1 (1982).
56 *The Military Balance 1984-85*, *op. cit.*
57 Robert Delfs, in *Far Eastern Economic Review*, 25 August 1983, pp. 91-92.

CHAPTER 2

China's changing foreign trade system 1975-85

by Thomas D. Gorman

The period 1975-85 saw dramatic change in every aspect of China's trade and economic relations with the world. During the mid-1970s, China was just emerging from the painful and turbulent decade of the Cultural Revolution, during which foreign commerce was officially viewed as a necessary evil to be conducted principally with friendly socialist states or fellow third-world countries. Sweeping changes were set in motion which introduced pragmatic new management policies into the domestic economy and placed unprecedented priority on expanding the foreign trade sector.

During this period, official policy evolved from a position of endorsing very selective importation of those foreign products and technologies which were essential to China's economic development, to the view that foreign technology, products, management techniques and investment were important catalysts to help China's modernisation efforts. Importantly, the controls on selection of which products and services were to be imported were relaxed, with a significant increase in regional and local-level authority and budgetary discretion. Even more fundamental was the acceptance of foreign investment in China's domestic economy, including the sensitive area of natural resource development, and 100 per cent foreign-owned enterprises.

The new priority assigned to developing the foreign trade sector as rapidly as possible led to changes not only in policies governing foreign trade, but also to structural reforms of the monolithic and monopolistic, highly centralised structure of China's foreign trade apparatus. China's state-owned import and export corporations, created largely on the Soviet model, began to face competition among themselves, and from newly created specialised corporations. Managers with specialised technical skills were recognised and promoted, in some cases at the expense of officials with superior political qualifications. Those experienced old hands within China's foreign trade organisations breathed a sigh of relief as the intense suspicion regarding their loyalties – present by definition because of their constant contact with 'the outside' – was relaxed, and the atmosphere began to favour more efficient and results-orientated performance rather than political purity above all.

The value of China's imports and exports grew from US$10.9 billion in 1973 to US$50 billion in 1984, and planners set their sights on a fourfold increase in foreign trade in the 20 years leading up to the year 2000. Despite the ambitiousness of this goal, exports remain less than 10 per cent of China's GNP, and her abundant supply of manpower, raw materials and energy resources will help the continued rapid growth in trade.

The most significant change in the composition of China's import-export trade has been the decrease in agricultural produce as a component of imports, and their growth as a component of China's exports. Imports are now heavily dominated by machinery, technical products and technology. From being a major market for American farm products, China has become a growing competitor in other export markets. In 1982, China was the largest export market for US cotton, and bought over eight million tons of American wheat and corn; over 50 per cent of US sales to China were in agricultural products. By 1984 that percentage had dropped to 20 per cent and China was exporting both corn and cotton.

Having softened Chairman Mao's extreme position of self-reliance and suspicion of the West, the first historic milestone reached by China's new leadership was the endorsement of foreign investment in China's economy in 1978, followed by the Joint Venture Law in 1979. Given a long history of exploitation by Western powers, including recent memories of domineering behaviour on the part of large foreign corporations, the decision to welcome foreign investment involved considerable political risk for the regime of Deng Xiaoping.

Direct foreign investment grew from zero in 1978 to nearly US$8 billion by mid-1984. This represents Sino-foreign agreements covering some 362 equity joint ventures, 31 offshore oil exploration agreements, 1,372 contractual joint ventures, and several thousand processing arrangements. By the end of 1984 there were also 113 Sino-foreign joint ventures outside China. According to official Chinese sources, China's four Special Economic Zones alone accounted for 4,000 foreign investment projects involving investment worth more than US$4 billion since 1979. Of the US$1.3 billion in direct foreign investment in China in 1984, about one-third went to offshore oil development or related activities. Joint equity ventures between Chinese and foreign firms fall into a broad range of manufacturing, hotel and service industries, including high technology ventures in computer and instrument manufacturing and assembly.

Another milestone which had become clearly identifi-

able by the time the Joint Venture Law was announced in 1979 was the decentralisation of control of both the domestic economy and the foreign trade sector. The intention was to stimulate rapid growth while encouraging controlled competition between regions, bureaucratic divisions, organisations and individuals. Decentralisation of economic management was part and parcel of a much broader policy initiative leading to widespread reform of the central planning system, with the introduction of free market forces and a 'guided' sector of the economy side by side with the main planned sector of the economy. While decentralisation in the foreign trade sector had noticeable effects on foreign companies doing business with China as early as 1979, the combination of decentralisation with the broader package of economic reforms and especially the enterprise management reforms of October 1984 led to excessively rapid growth of imports which made a minor readjustment and reassertion of central control necessary in mid-1985.

The reining in of runaway foreign exchange spending, cutting back on the number of regions with special foreign investment incentives, and the questioning of the Special Economic Zone concept during mid-1985 were typical of the pendulum-like movement which has and will continue to govern central versus local authority in economic and trade matters for many years to come. Debate among Western observers in 1985 centred on whether the economic reforms were destined to fail due to having tried too much too fast, or whether inevitably they would be subject to abrupt and unpredictable start-stop adjustments.

Comparing the minor readjustment of 1985 with the major readjustment of 1980-81, in which dozens of major foreign contracts were cancelled or suspended, it appears that China's leaders are intent on achieving maximum growth while preserving credibility at home as well as abroad. The 1985 readjustment was more timely, although its delayed implementation in some parts of the country was a clear indication of how far the process of decentralisation had been carried. On balance it was far less disruptive to foreign trade, considering that the 1980-81 readjustment damaged international confidence in the China market for three to four years.

The positive results achieved since the late 1970s through decentralised management of the domestic and foreign trade sectors point to a continuation in this direction, allowing for periodic adjustments to cope with runaway growth and dislocations between sectors or regions of the economy. One vexing problem with long historical roots is the disparity in economic resources and living standards between the relatively developed coastal regions of China, with their long trading history and established foreign customer networks, and the relatively underdeveloped provinces in the hinterland, hampered by lack of experience in foreign markets, limited contacts and poor transportation infrastructure.

Another problem associated with decentralisation, but of recent vintage, concerns the apparent disincentive to export for managers of Chinese factories brought about by price reforms, internal exchange rate adjustments and growth in domestic markets. Especially for urban factories, the economic reforms of October 1984 gave the

Mass display of gymnasts at a sports festival

factory managers more autonomy and more impetus to increase profits, but the export market is a complex and possibly more risky prospect than sales at home.

The effects of reforms in the pricing system for all import and export commodities begun early in the 1980s also have a profound impact on the attractiveness of imported products, depending to a large extent on the degree with which domestically produced equivalents are available. The gradual transition from fixed pricing policies for virtually all commodities towards more flexible, market-orientated pricing is a process which bears careful attention by would-be trade partners.

Another effect of decentralisation and rapid reforms has been an explosive growth in the number of organisations involved in trade and investment at the municipal, county, provincial, regional and central government levels. The competition thus created has often been confusing for foreign buyers, sellers and financiers, but it has led to a net growth in the number of potential Chinese buyers as well as suppliers. For foreign investors the growth in the number of potential partners has not necessarily been a positive development, due to confusion over which organisations really have authority, and up to what financial level. This has been especially problematic against the backdrop of very limited legal, tax and regulatory guidelines.

The beneficial effects of decentralisation and economic reform are clearly noticeable in China's import and export trade, with results probably beyond the expectations both of China's leaders and of China's foreign business partners. Few would have expected the speed with which agricultural reforms, aided by several years of good harvests partially due to favourable weather conditions, would have resulted in the decrease in Chinese farm product imports and growth of her exports.

On the foreign investment side, however, both sides underestimated the difficulty and time required to consummate a significant number and range of investment projects, especially those involving international companies as opposed to Hong Kong and Macao compatriots. Also underestimated was the range of complex operational problems a Sino-foreign joint venture has to overcome to function efficiently.

By 1985 Chinese leaders and prospective foreign investors had the benefit of five years' experience, legal, accounting and tax precedents, and a considerably enlarged body of regulations and commercial law to draw upon in forecasting the feasibility of new investment projects, and anticipating their start-up problems. Given relatively slow lateral transmission of information in China, it is still the job of the prospective investor to evaluate carefully the experience of pioneering foreign investors to identify pitfalls and problems in advance. Failure to do so could prove disappointing and costly.

Impact of decentralisation on trade and investment

Decentralisation of authority over the management of foreign trade and investment has had a direct and profound impact on how foreign companies approach the China market, the range of business opportunities open to them and the most effective means of pursuing specific business objectives.

Foreign trade*

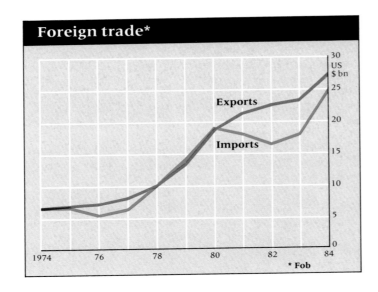

Exports

Imports

1974 76 78 80 82 84

30
US
$ bn
25

20

15

10

5

0

* Fob

Import composition

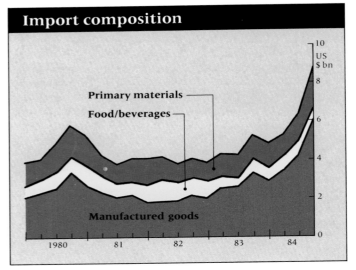

Primary materials
Food/beverages

Manufactured goods

1980 81 82 83 84

10
US
$ bn
8

6

4

2

0

Exports and imports

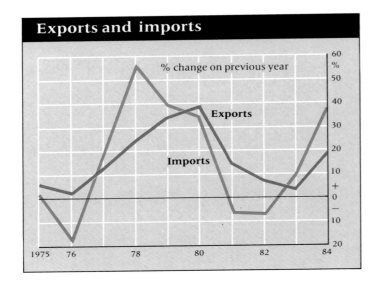

% change on previous year

Exports

Imports

1975 76 78 80 82 84

60
%
50

40

30

20

10

+
0
—

10

20

Export composition

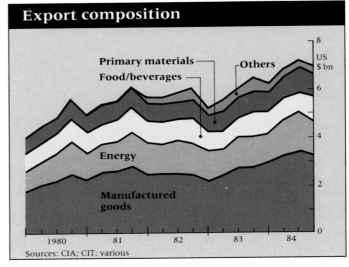

Primary materials
Food/beverages

Others

Energy

Manufactured
goods

1980 81 82 83 84

8
US
$ bn

6

4

2

0

Sources: CIA; CIT; various

Net commodity trade balance

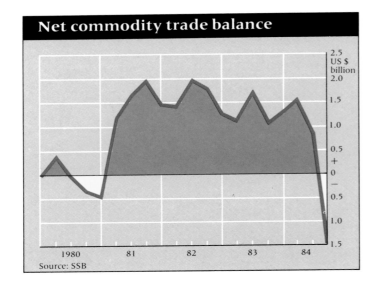

1980 81 82 83 84

2.5
US $
billion
2.0

1.5

1.0

0.5

+
0
—

0.5

1.0

1.5

Source: SSB

Composition of manufactured exports

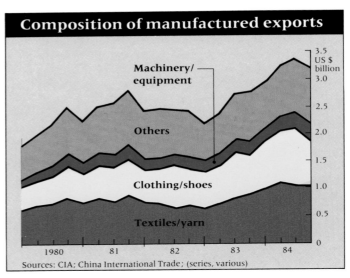

Machinery/
equipment

Others

Clothing/shoes

Textiles/yarn

1980 81 82 83 84

3.5
US $
billion
3.0

2.5

2.0

1.5

1.0

0.5

0

Sources: CIA; China International Trade; (series, various)

84

The traditional, centralised model

Up to 1975, authority governing China's import and export trade was concentrated among a high-level group of bureaucrats in Beijing. There were 12 state-owned import and export corporations, and another seven corporations charged with transportation, insurance and financial aspects of China's foreign trade. These corporations functioned according to plans approved by the State Council and implemented by the Ministry of Foreign Trade. Planning was in strict accordance with foreign policy considerations, reflecting the basic principles of 'equality and mutual benefit'.

A seminar on China's foreign trade and its management, jointly sponsored by the Ministry of Foreign Trade and UNCTAD, was held in China from 16 October to 2 November 1978. In a paper entitled 'Chinese Foreign Trade Policies and Plans', the director of the Foreign Trade Department of the Peking Foreign Trade Institute, Liu Chao-chin, summarised some of the basic principles ruling at the time: 'Equality and mutual benefit and supplying each other's needs are the basic principles of foreign trade of our socialist country. They differ radically from the dumping of goods, monopoly, plunder and expansion that characterises the foreign trade policies of imperialist countries.'

On the subject of planning, Liu outlined the current official view: 'Foreign trade plans include plans for the circulation of commodities, transportation, accounting, foreign exchange, capital construction, labour and wages, etc. The plan for commodity circulation is the centre of all planning in foreign trade.'

Even in 1978, when fundamental policy changes affecting domestic and foreign trade were in their early stages, the rhetoric of past policy was very different from what was to come.

To determine business strategy under these circumstances meant dealing with up to 20 Chinese corporations operating under a unified plan which reflected overall foreign policy and the varying but reasonably consistent priorities contained in the current Five Year Plan and the plan for any given year. There were few surprises. Major decisions were made in Beijing. Most contacts between foreign and Chinese business people were restricted to the twice-yearly Canton Trade Fair, where representatives of the various foreign trade corporations were available for meetings and negotiations. There was no competition between corporations because there was no overlap in product lines. Competition between branches of the same corporation was unimaginable because of unified pricing guidelines and internal restrictions guaranteeing against what was then considered an unhealthy tendency. Between the Spring and the Autumn Canton Fair, foreign trade corporation managers were loath to answer letters or telexes, so the Fair assumed enormous importance. On the opening day crowds of visiting business people from all over the globe gathered at the steps of the trade fair complex, and once the opening ribbon was cut, a frenzied stampede took place.

Political rhetoric dominated the commercial negotiating environment. No Chinese officials or managers carried business cards, and they were generally reluctant to identify themselves except by surname and corporation. This posed major challenges to effective business communications after the meeting, especially in a country of one billion people where there are only about 100 common family names.

Other than the knowledge that everything went according to the plan, the real process of decision-making for import and export business was a mystery to foreign business. Answers to questions such as which departments were involved, what budgeting process was applied, which individuals were key, were not available. Apart from the release of the main details of the prevailing Five Year Plan, no details about annual plans or priorities were released, and few economic or industrial statistics were available. The only market data regularly released was of the sort that claimed large increases in production figures for various commodities without giving base figures.

Prospective buyers and sellers were to be found at the Canton Trade Fair, which drew a truly international attendance. Bankers, lawyers, journalists and government trade promotion officials did not generally attend until the late 1970s. Invitations to the Fair were difficult to obtain and generally were issued in recognition of specific business to be discussed as opposed to a general exploratory visit. Lawyers were considered charlatans under the prevailing xenophobic political ethic, foreign borrowing was out of the question, and journalists and government officials were viewed with the utmost suspicion.

Contracts for buying and selling transactions were signed between the foreign company and the Chinese Foreign Trade Corporation (FTC), following a standard form with few deviations. One notable feature of selling technology or technical products was that the ultimate end-users of the product, whose engineers and technicians would be involved in installation, application, etc., were not only not present for commercial and technical negotiations, but were generally not even identified. This increased the time required to conclude a sale significantly since all important technical questions had to be recorded, translated, relayed to the technical people on the Chinese side, and relayed back again. Apart from the time factor, the potential for misunderstanding was enormous. Many companies who sold technical products during the early or mid-1970s found out, in later years when the atmosphere eased and they were allowed access to their earlier sales' end-users, that huge waste resulted, which sometimes reflected unfairly on their products' reliability and their reputation.

The advent of decentralisation

Decentralised control was a gradual process of reform rather than an overnight directive handing authority to the provinces and municipalities. Its momentum tracked other major changes in policy in the late 1970s, such as the opening to foreign investment and the creation of the Special Economic Zones – part of the broader initiative of Deng Xiaoping's new leadership, aimed at speeding up economic construction, modernising the country and improving the living standard of the Chinese people. Between 1978 and 1983, China's policy for foreign trade and investment was to undergo more dramatic change than in all the years since 1949, so much so that for those used to conducting business with China in the previous era, it now seemed an entirely different market environment offering significantly different types of business opportunities.

The first phase of decentralisation left the 12 state-owned FTCs intact, but gave more authority for import and export decisions to their regional branches, while still maintaining a unified central plan. The Ministry of Foreign Trade remained the predominant central government organisation responsible to the State Council for the planning and implementation of foreign trade, although clear signs emerged by 1978 that units reporting to the various specialised industrial ministries were anxious to handle their own imports, particularly of specialised technical products. In addition to the fact that most of the FTC negotiators had been non-technical people, and negotiated without the benefit of the end-users presence, end-users resented the prices passed on to them by the foreign trade corporation which reflected the old system of fixed pricing for imported commodities. This system was based on a set of prices fixed by ministries as early as the 1950s for certain commodities, which remained largely intact until the late 1970s. For imported goods for which there was no domestic equivalent available, the price paid by the end-user was based on the C&F price plus a fixed percentage (in excess of 100 per cent), plus applicable customs duty and unified commercial tax.

This first phase lasted from 1978 to 1981, and corresponded with major changes in Chinese foreign policy as well as domestic economic policy reforms. Relations with the United States and Western Europe as well as Japan warmed significantly, while relations with the Soviet Union and the Eastern Bloc cooled. The environment for foreign business was relaxed by comparison with the previous 10 years – few if any political comments entered business discussions; Chinese officials readily identified themselves by full name, title and department, and often carried business cards; and invitations and visa procedures became easier. This led to increasing contacts between the Canton Trade Fairs. End-users were brought into negotiations and foreign companies were allowed access to details about planned projects. Advertising was officially accepted as a useful method of business communication and stimulating economic activity. Chinese officials expressed keen interest in learning from Western companies' management techniques. Lawyers were accepted as potentially useful advisors assisting in the negotiation process, and bankers were welcome to discuss extending commercial credits to Chinese enterprises, albeit at extremely thin spreads. Foreign government trade promotion officials were encouraged to spread the word about trade opportunities in China to their constituent business communities. Western business journalists were invited to China and briefed about the mistakes and excesses of the past, attributed initially to the infamous Gang of Four, led by the late Chairman Mao's widow, Jiang Qing.

Although the Canton Trade Fair (formally called the Chinese Export Commodities Fair) is still held twice a year (15 April to 5 May and 15 October to 5 November) and remains an important venue especially for those who buy from China, more and more transactions are made outside the Fair. Many specialised mini-fairs featuring one commodity group or the various commodities available from one province are held throughout the year, not to mention exhibitions of foreign industrial products and equipment on sale to China.

By the early 1980s it was clear that many powerful groups in Chinese industry, the military, as well as some regional and provincial leaders, were not entirely satisfied with the performance of the organisations handling China's foreign trade, and coveted authority to embark in new directions. During this time, the traditional monopolistic structure under the Ministry of Foreign Trade began to be broken down to give new authority to other groups. New specialised or 'end-user' corporations began to appear, usually specialising in the import and export of one commodity or group of commodities. The new corporations were still state-owned, but operated under the aegis of ministries other than the Ministry of Foreign Trade.

Next, cities and provinces with strong roles in import-export trade began to form their own local corporations to handle imports and exports as well as handling foreign trade on behalf of interior provinces. The first were Shanghai, Guangdong, Tianjin and Beijing. This served to exacerbate rivalries between these traditionally dominant trade centres and the provinces in the hinterland who were some of their major suppliers for export markets, but who lacked the authority, experience or contacts to conduct export trade directly. The factor which increased this rivalry more than any other was a series of policy initiatives introduced in the late 1970s which became the driving force behind the rapid growth of Chinese exports; these initiatives allowed local authorities to retain a percentage of the hard currency earned from exports for use in importing needed products, technology and productive capacity. At the same time, other reforms removed obstacles to direct exports by interior provinces outside Ministry of Foreign Trade traditional channels by reducing the number of export commodities under strict licensing and by delegating licensing authority to local-level authorities.

The reforms of import and export pricing in 1980-81 had the effect of greatly increasing the local-level incentive to export more, and thus retain more foreign exchange. Further changes in 1984 opened the door, at least temporarily, to direct imports of consumer goods and components of consumer goods for assembly and re-sale on local markets.

The interior provinces, especially those with strong manufacturing or agricultural export capabilities such as Sichuan and Heilongjiang, thus had a strong incentive to develop direct exports. If they exported as before through their appointed coastal trade centres, their hard currency income would be limited by comparison. Approvals to export were granted to different provinces for various commodity lines at different times in the early 1980s. By April 1985, of 130 commodities under the licensing system, only 15 commodities were subject to sole jurisdiction of the Ministry of Foreign Trade and Economic Relations, 40 were issued by the ministry's special representatives in major ports and 75 were to be examined and approved by local and provincial authorities as designated by the State Council. In cases where a

A colliery in Shanxi Province. China exported 7 million tonnes of coal in 1984

province has near-exclusive control of production of a particular export commodity, full licensing authority may be granted to it. The rise of the Special Economic Zones in Guangdong Province led to complaints by neighbouring provinces at vastly increased volumes of exports of commodities for which licences had not been granted, wreaking havoc on traditional pricing levels and leading to competitive infighting.

For buyers from China the reforms meant an explosive increase in the number of new potential suppliers, depending on the commodity line, and the competition between regions meant potentially attractive pricing. More homework and legwork was required to stay abreast of the market, but the opportunities were significant. The drawback was that suddenly many Chinese enterprises with little or no international trade experience were concluding export contracts. Some needed instruction on rudimentary international trade practices including, for example, letters of credit and insurance.

For sellers to China the reforms had a similar effect: more prospective buyers had hard currency to spend and authority to make purchasing decisions, but a great deal more effort was required to identify and reach this growing range of prospects nationwide. This was a far more preferable state of affairs for marketers, especially given the increasing amount of economic and industrial data made available by the Chinese government enabling at least basic market research, plus the new accessibility of most Chinese organisations to foreign businessmen and wide range of marketing communication options such as advertising, exhibitions and direct mail. A milestone was the first-ever 'Statistical Yearbook of China' published by the State Statistical Bureau in 1982, and updated annually. World Bank studies during the period have also added tremendous depth to available economic data and analysis.

For prospective investors the benefits were less clear-cut. With the exception of natural resource-related projects or others with a clearly defined locality, the new range of organisations with foreign trade authority meant more groups to discuss a project with. Authority levels for approval of joint ventures and other investment projects were not always clear. The real problem was that the speed with which policy changes were made and fine-tuned left local-level officials and managers on the Chinese side confused as to their authority levels at a given time.

For all concerned with China's foreign trade, it is necessary to stay abreast of changing levels of authority governing the spending of hard currency, the allocation of commodities for production of goods for export markets, and the selection of suitable venues for foreign investment and joint-venture projects. All of these functions have varying authority levels which are subject to change from one year to the next; sometimes they inconveniently change during the process of negotiation.

Two conclusions can be drawn. First, the basic trend is clearly towards decision-making authority being handed down to the provincial and major municipal level. But the complexity of this process almost certainly will require cyclical recentralisations depending on economic and political factors. The provinces and municipalities which will obtain the most autonomy and the greatest

amount of local budgetary discretion for imports as well as investment approval will be those with a traditionally strong foreign trade performance: Shanghai, Guangdong, Liaoning, Jiangsu, Tianjin, Beijing and Dalian. In 1984, for example, Shanghai, Tianjin and Guangdong Province had authority to approve investment projects up to US$30 million in value without referring to the central authorities, or sometimes more if no major state energy inputs were involved. Dalian and Shenyang had approval authority in the US$10-15 million range, with lower limits in less developed areas. A parallel situation occurs in Bank of China branches on foreign exchange lending limits for loans to Chinese and foreign-Chinese joint ventures, allowing the local branch in Shanghai or Tianjin to approve loans up to US$10 million, as opposed to lower limits in cities and provinces with less developed foreign trade and investment performance.

Secondly, parallel to decentralisation has been the introduction of a 'guided' as opposed to 'planned' segment of the domestic and foreign trade economy. If a foreign trade or investment transaction is written into the 'plan', it is virtually certain to go through with all the necessary approvals. If the transaction is not written into the plan, but rather approved in the context of the relatively *ad hoc* or 'guided' segment of the economy, its chances of final approval diminish steeply in proportion to the degree its total value exceeds several million US dollars.

Decentralisation increased the complexity of operating in the Chinese market while it exponentially increased the opportunities present. The fact that decentralisation, even subject to periodic adjustments and fine tuning, is likely to be a permanent feature of China's foreign trade and investment picture, vastly increases the number of buying influences and decision-making influences worth the attention of foreign companies, especially those interested in the China market in the long run. The realisation that the picture is subject to constant change argues in favour of investing in expertise located close to or within the China market itself, without which it will be difficult to stay abreast of the adjustments and shifts in where decision-making authority is vested, and what the operative plans are in a given period.

Special Economic Zones (SEZs)

China's open door policy, the brainchild of Deng Xiao-ping, dates from an important policy speech he delivered in December 1978. Little time was wasted in implementing reforms in the domestic as well as the foreign trade sectors, to pursue his stated goal of an open door policy in foreign economic relations while stimulating growth in the Chinese economy overall. In April 1979, Deng spoke of delineating special zones wherein experimental economic management practices would be applied in a controlled manner. The first such zone, then Shenzhen SEZ, was established the same year in the border town of Shenzhen, adjacent to Hong Kong in Guangdong Province. One year later the Zhuhai SEZ was established at the mouth of the Pearl River, adjacent to the Portuguese enclave of Macao. Also in 1980 came the third and fourth SEZ, in Shantou, 180 nautical miles north-east of Hong Kong, and Xiamen (formerly Amoy) on the coast of Fujian Province opposite Taiwan.

Incentives designed to attract outside investment in

the form of joint ventures, compensation trade, processing agreements or counter trade included import tax exemption for supplies, equipment and raw materials, export tax exemption for semi-finished and finished products, free movement of foreign currencies through banks in the zone, 15 per cent corporate profits tax with various tax holiday schemes especially favouring projects with higher capital investment, higher technology and longer capital turnover cycle.

Within five years, the population of Shenzhen had grown from 30,000 to 300,000, and the sleepy agricultural town had been transformed by tall office buildings, hotels, restaurants, department stores, resort facilities and commercial enterprises engaged in a diverse range of activities including raising dairy cattle, food processing and packaging, printing, garment processing and assembly, and assembly of electronics, toys, garments and accessories. Foreign banks were among the first international companies to establish representative offices in Shenzhen, with about a dozen present by 1984. Oil companies were quick to follow with petrol service and supply stations. As a special 'zone within a zone', the Shekou SEZ was established under the jurisdiction of China Merchants Steam Navigation Company (CMSNC) to focus especially on projects connected with maritime and offshore oil support industries.

The apparent success of the Shenzhen experiment led to the two other SEZs being established in Guangdong Province and one in neighbouring Fujian Province. The next major step came following three years of bustling activity in Shenzhen, the largest of the zones, and in the three other zones: Zhuhai, Shantou and Xiamen. After a much-heralded visit of Deng Xiaoping to Shenzhen early in 1984, during which he proclaimed the great success of the SEZ experiment, 14 coastal cities and Hainan Island were opened to foreign investment, allowing them to use many of the same incentives to attract foreign investment as in the SEZs.

Scarcely three months later another 30 cities, 24 of them inland, were designated as open cities with special foreign exchange privileges from the Bank of China to encourage foreign investment. This third phase was clearly a move to satisfy complaints from authorities of inland provinces who felt that the SEZ and coastal cities initiatives did little to benefit them directly, especially in respect to the ability to develop and retain hard currency income.

The Shenzhen SEZ was hailed as a success following Deng's tour of the zone early in 1984. Chinese news media lavished praise on the zone and its managers for achieving rapid growth in economic construction and foreign investment. Deng Xiaoping stated that the zone succeeded in a short time in becoming a window on foreign technology, management techniques, market knowledge and foreign trade policy and practice. In another quote showing the spirit of the day as embodied in the rapid growth of the zone he said 'Time is money. Productivity is life.'

Given the apparent concensus of acceptance of the SEZ concept by early 1984, and bearing in mind the degree of controversy involved in such a radical new experiment, there was widespread speculation about how the lessons learned in these controlled 'laboratories' might be applied elsewhere throughout China.

Shock waves were sent out in late June 1985, when Deng Xiaoping told a visiting foreign leader that Shenzhen was still an experiment, and whether or not it had been a correct one remained to be seen. He described the zone as a product of socialism, and one which he hoped would succeed, but that in the event that it failed, the experience will have been useful in any case.

In the weeks that followed a woeful saga emerged of mismanagement, waste of foreign currency, official abuse of economic authority and violations of Chinese law, involving Shenzhen officials directly and indirectly. At a time when the Chinese economy was overheated, with runaway spending and lending causing erosion of foreign exchange reserves, a spate of economic scandals caused a sudden rethink on Shenzhen. A black cloud hung over what had until recently been a model of success in foreign trade and investment reform, and the conclusion was reached that the experiment had yielded a mixture of failure and success. Some of the negative aspects were embarrassing illustrations of how far out of control the situation had become. The most notable incident was the purchase of US$570 million on Shenzhen's foreign currency black market by senior Communist party officials of Hainan Island. The foreign currency was then used to finance the importation of 89,000 cars for illegal resale at high profits to other parts of China. Other examples included similar schemes whereby precious foreign exchange was wasted on a huge scale to import components for electronic consumer goods and TV sets for assembly in the zone and resale to interior provinces at high prices, a short-lived illegal gambling casino, a thriving and highly visible foreign currency black market, flourishing exports of goods without proper export licences and smuggling of consumer goods. Some analysts estimated that Shenzhen's trade deficit in 1983 reached nearly US$60 million.

Despite a cutback in the number of cities designated as priority locations for new foreign investment from 14 to four, the re-evaluation of the Shenzhen SEZ and related '14 cities' initiative did not produce any dramatic policy shifts either in SEZ policy *per se* or foreign investment in general. Of the original 14 open cities, it was decided that only four – Shanghai, Dalian, Tianjin and Guangzhou – had conditions and infrastructure which were well enough developed to permit significant and immediate new foreign investment. The other cities were relegated to more long-term rather than short-term priority. Even Hainan Island, where the car scandal and other abuses took place, did not lose the special economic privileges which had been granted to it. The Communist party chief on the island was dismissed, however, and two other senior officials were disciplined. Some redefinition of the priorities for types of foreign investment desired took place, and for the first time a list of types of projects which were to be de-emphasised was issued. This underlined the fact that many of the existing projects in Shenzhen did not relate closely enough to the original objective of attracting relatively advanced technology and projects which would generate rather than expend foreign currency. The conclusion seemed to be that the basic direction of the policy was not in error. The open door policy had survived an important crisis.

Among the types of projects specifically discouraged after the Shenzhen scandals were the assembly of TV sets and other electronic consumer goods using imported components, motor vehicle rental and repair, film processing, household appliance repair shops, shopping arcades, beverage and cigarette production – categories in which ventures of a non-essential nature had previously been allowed to proliferate. The list of priority projects placed more emphasis than ever on energy and high-technology ventures.

In a parallel and indirectly related move just prior to the emergence of the Shenzhen scandals, the president of the Bank of China was dismissed and replaced by the former head of the Ministry of Foreign Trade, Madame Chen Muhua. Widely regarded as an exponent of more centralised control of foreign trade, her task was reportedly to bring spending back into control at the local levels, and to implement an improved system of controls nationwide. The first major structural change announced under her direction was in August 1985, when a new decentralised treasury system was set up involving central, provincial and county levels – a move clearly aimed at bringing excessive growth and spending back under control without reversing the direction of decentralised authority.

Ironically, the delayed reaction and reassessment of Shenzhen and the other SEZs may prove of benefit to future foreign investors. The incidents focused the attention of China's top leadership on the experience up to that date of the open door policy in attracting foreign investment, technology, management techniques and market knowledge. Through a careful and timely reappraisal a potential disaster for the open door policy and foreign investment in general may have been averted. More important will be the degree of success achieved in the second half of the 1980s in attracting desired types of foreign investment based on the lessons learned in the first five years.

The common and most important objective of Shenzhen and the other three SEZs – Zhuhai, Xiamen and Shantou – was to attract relatively advanced technology, which would be absorbed, digested and eventually transferred to other parts of the country with less direct access and conditions less suitable to attracting first-generation investment and technology. Their secondary objectives were to generate foreign exchange, and to increase skilled employment; but by most accounts these were to be measured more on a regional than national level, given the relatively small size of the zones. Another goal was to stimulate trade and investment with interior provinces who would open commercial offices in the zones for convenient negotiation with foreign prospective investors and business people. Yet another goal for Shenzhen was the less obvious one of creating an economic buffer zone between the free-wheeling capitalism of Hong Kong and China's Guangdong Province.

Looking back, the projects established in the four SEZs up to 1985 in partnership with Hong Kong and Macao companies, or international companies, did not by and large live up to the objective of acquiring relatively advanced technology. Most were relatively low-technology, land- and labour-intensive projects, or ventures in tourism, local passenger and freight transportation, agriculture, etc. The Hainan car import scandal best illustrates the fact that instead of becoming an earner of foreign exchange, Shenzhen became a thriving outlet for

the import and resale of non-essential consumer goods.

One difference in objectives between the four SEZs and the two groups of so-called open cities – the first group of 14 and the subsequent 30 – was that the emphasis in the open cities was to attract projects which would build upon existing relatively well-developed infrastructure and renovate or modernise existing industrial facilities.

The fact that a large percentage of SEZ projects involved Hong Kong and Macao rather than international companies is not surprising, given that land, labour and other rates were generally competitive with Hong Kong prices, but not necessarily competitive with incentives offered in investment zones elsewhere in Asia or the world. The lack of legal and tax framework also tended to make international companies uncomfortable, in contrast to Hong Kong Chinese business people who had the advantage of ethnic and linguistic ties. This fact tended to spur Hong Kong and other manufacturers forward into Shenzhen in search of lower costs for semi-skilled labour rather than bringing in ventures which would introduce highly technical skills in the workplace.

In introducing outside management techniques, Shenzhen and the other SEZs have been successful in several respects, leading to the development and training of a fairly large semi-skilled labour force in a previously agricultural area, at least in the case of Shenzhen. Part of the philosophy of the SEZ was stated by a Shenzhen official in 1979 who observed that the work force in Hong Kong was ethnic Chinese just like the work force in China, yet the productivity rate in Hong Kong was much higher due to the presence of incentives. Shenzhen became the first place where incentive-based labour management was encouraged, paying workers on the basis of how much they produced, and giving management far more leeway in hiring and firing of staff. The success of this approach in 1979-81 in demonstrating the relative productivity of Shenzhen factories was one factor in the decision to introduce incentives on a widespread basis into Chinese factories in the early to mid-1980s, while attempting to make enterprise management more accountable for profit performance rather than relying on state subsidies perpetuating inefficient operations.

The single most important problem in the first five years of the Shenzhen SEZ was the fact that state expenditure on capital construction, estimated at about Rmb5 billion, far exceeded foreign exchange income through exports or investment, and the trend was widening further as a high percentage of enterprises in the zone were concentrating on imports of consumer electronic components, assembly in the zone, and resale on the domestic market. To curb this trend, authorities tightened lending policies to favour enterprises serving export markets and earning foreign exchange.

The real test for the SEZs will be in the period 1985-90, when they must build upon a reasonably good infrastructure and semi-skilled labour pool, and a fairly comprehensive set of legal, regulatory and tax guidelines, to attract significant foreign investment involving more advanced technology. To do this they will need to compete effectively not only with Hong Kong but with special investment zones and free trade zones around the world, and in particular with their neighbours in Singapore, Taiwan and South Korea who are all anxious to attract the same kind of investment projects.

Shenzhen's position allows ventures to take advantage of Hong Kong's extremely well-developed transportation and communications infrastructure, financial and services sector, international market knowledge and widespread English-language ability. Starting from ventures which utilise Shenzhen's lower manufacturing cost for basic manufacturing processes, with skilled finishing and packaging of products initially done in Hong Kong, it will be possible to expand the range and base of foreign investment in manufacturing while gradually upgrading the level of technology involved. Like a special zone within the Shenzhen economic zone is the Shekou Industrial Zone. Shekou has been the most successful part of Shenzhen in attracting industrial manufacturing projects, and shows continued promise in this direction largely due to the experienced and efficient management of CMSNC.

Zhuhai's fortunes as an SEZ are tied more closely to the search for oil in the South China Sea, but even in the event that no major commercial discoveries are made, Zhuhai is strategically positioned at the mouth of the Pearl River as the gateway to the rich counties of the Pearl River delta, one of China's traditional export processing areas. As Macao reverts to full Chinese administration on more or less a parallel timetable to Hong Kong, Zhuhai will develop in the same symbiotic relation to Macao that Shenzhen will follow in respect to Hong Kong. Competitive in many respects to Hong Kong and Macao respectively, these two SEZs will continue to need the market and management expertise as well as the well-established international business community and trade facilities offered by Hong Kong and Macao.

Xiamen and Shantou SEZs, in Fujian Province and Guangdong Province respectively, share as their common strength close ties with large and prosperous overseas Chinese communities in Southeast Asia and abroad, which have been their principal source of foreign investment during the start-up years. Although this feature is true of all four SEZs, Xiamen and Shantou probably have more native sons in Asia outside Hong Kong – Singapore, Thailand and Malaysia in particular – than the other two. Xiamen is geographically well positioned to develop as an export processing zone for the agricultural and fisheries production of Fujian. Shantou is at the northern reach of the South China Sea oil search and would stand to benefit substantially from a find in that area; road, rail and harbour investments are planned to improve links to the provincial capital of Guangzhou as well as to Hong Kong.

Hainan Island, although not referred to as a Special Economic Zone, has special autonomy in foreign trade and investment. Hainan's strategic position has made it a traditional strong base for the military establishment. It has rich agricultural, fisheries, and mineral resources, and its tourism potential is widely recognised. Its geographical position has given it an important support role in the search for offshore oil in the South China Sea, and foreign oil interests became involved in the search for onshore oil in Hainan in 1985. Despite the scandals involving illegal imports of cars and consumer goods, Hainan looks set to maintain its special status in foreign trade.

Apart from fine-tuning investment incentives, legal, tax and regulatory guidelines, China's planners will need to balance the national objective of attracting higher-technology investment and foreign exchange earnings with the regional, provincial, municipal and SEZ objectives of achieving the same end. The first round of experimentation leading up to 1985 provided useful and fertile experience on which to base the next few years' strategy.

Practical aspects of doing business in China

Planning and positioning

China's size and long-term economic development potential invite exaggerated expectations among businessmen approaching the market. There are companies who have made short-term profits in the China market, especially sellers of specialised industrial products and commodities which are suited to particular Chinese requirements, but these are outnumbered by companies who are still awaiting the return on their investment in market development.

Realistic planning for business development in China should start from the premise that meaningful and profitable business will take many years to develop, but that the failure to begin now will place companies at a great competitive disadvantage. Despite the explosive growth in the number and range of international companies active in China in the late 1970s and early 1980s, the period from 1985 to 1990 will still be a formative stage in the development of China's new foreign trade and investment picture. This creates opportunities to forge and develop new business relationships with the many recently created or recently revamped organisations in charge of importing, exporting, financing, joint-venturing, insuring and transporting China's commerce with world markets.

China is often perceived as a market so complex as to resist most Western efforts to penetrate it. European and American businessmen also tend to perceive Japan's geographical, cultural and linguistic proximity to China as a formidable competitive advantage for a country whose marketing efforts are so phenomenally successful even in remote markets. China will not become overly dependent, however, on any supplier or partner, Japan included, because of the lessons of history. In short, while admittedly a complex market in which returns take time to accomplish, China is approachable for large and small companies, given proper planning and reasonable expectations.

Old China hands generally agree that it is easier to sell to China than to buy from China, obviously depending on the product or commodity line. Buying from China is relatively simple in the case of raw materials or existing products as opposed to new products which are made to the buyer's specifications. In the latter case, a great deal of time is required to obtain satisfactory samples and counter samples and get production to acceptable levels of quality, matched by timely delivery, depending on the degree of experience and efficiency of the particular Chinese producer.

Selling to China will remain more interesting for industrial as opposed to consumer marketers for many years to come because of the scarcity of foreign currency and the higher priority placed on imports of industrial goods to assist in modernisation. China would prefer to develop broader and better manufacturing and distribution capability for consumer goods at home, leading to joint-venture opportunities for foreign companies rather than direct consumer goods marketing.

Most international banks with representative offices in China take a long-term view, given the high costs of operating, and China's limited appetite for commercial borrowing at attractive rates. Leasing business and joint-venture opportunities have offered new business potential for foreign banks operating in China, as have servicing Bank of China's growing foreign currency deposits, and assisting foreign customers and Sino-foreign joint-venture companies with an expanding range of financial service requirements.

International insurance companies were for the most part excluded from the more interesting business opportunities in China, which are dominated by the People's Insurance Company, the state insurer. People's Insurance, employing 30,000 people, wrote business worth US$600 million in 1982 and aims for a gross income of some $2.5 billion by 1990. Foreign insurers cooperate with People's Insurance to indirectly offer many forms of corporate insurance in China, but the promising area of directly insuring foreign investment projects was not available to foreign insurers as of 1985.

Technology licensing opportunities have increased in response to China's new priority of renovating and upgrading existing industrial plants with imported technology and products. Improved relations between China and the United States have led to a far wider range of technology, including defensive military technology, being made available for sale to her. The United States approved US$500 million worth of licences for high-technology product sales to China in 1982, compared with approximately US$1 billion in 1984, and cooperative efforts were under way in 1985 to explore upgrading Chinese air defence, anti-tank and anti-submarine warfare capability.

Sellers of many technical products, such as instruments and meters, have found that to continue selling finished products they must be willing to enter into technology licensing arrangements to manufacture in China for both the domestic and export markets. The degree of production limited to export versus domestic marketing is often a bone of contention and is always subject to negotiation on a case-by-case basis. China's patent law of 1984 was a significant milestone, which helped ease some of the worries about protection of intellectual property rights, but still leaves certain areas of technology in question.

Tourism and hotel business opportunities have also grown as China tapped the enormous foreign exchange earning potential and began admitting more tourist visitors in 1978. The number of tourist visitors to China in 1984 was 11.25 million, compared to 125,000 in 1978; a continuing shortage of hotel rooms is one of the principal constraints to even more rapid growth. By 1985, China Travel Service had an ambitious programme under way for new joint-venture hotels, to expand its growing fleet of taxis and cruise ships, augment its air charter capabilities and expand retail shops catering especially for tourists. Some 100 new hotels are planned for major cities by 1987, including 10 in Shanghai alone.

For business travellers, hotel room shortages are worst in Beijing, where the four existing joint-venture hotels, with a total of about 2,500 rooms in 1985, are the only hotels offering advance reservations through standard travel agency procedures. Accommodation outside these facilities can be obtained through a Chinese host organisation or a representative on the spot. The high priority of expanding tourism resulted in a dramatic increase in the number of cities and provinces open to foreign visitors, and a reduction of the time and red tape involved in obtaining a tourist visa. This is of benefit to business visitors who can now obtain a tourist visa to enter the country on business at major Chinese international airports, or at the China International Travel Service offices in Hong Kong.

Not surprisingly, business opportunities for the short term are often associated with areas, sectors, industries or organisations with export earnings potential. Opportunities further removed from this access to foreign currency tend to be longer-term in nature.

Opportunities for sales in China and joint-venture finance have increased substantially as a result of World Bank, IMF, UNDP and various foreign government low-interest or interest-free development loan programmes in China. In fiscal 1985, for example, the World Bank extended US$1.1 billion in loans to China for projects in education, agriculture, transportation, energy and other sectors of development. Many of these projects create the need for feasibility studies by foreign contractors as well as foreign product and technology imports in areas where foreign exchange would have been lacking without outside financing. Keeping track of World Bank and governmental lending activities and projects in China has become an important task for business planners.

Export of Chinese labour and engineering contracting services has grown steadily since the late 1970s. Once linked only to Chinese foreign aid projects in third-world countries, engineering contracting has been promoted by the China Building and Construction Engineering Corporation more aggressively as a business, leading to a variety of overseas joint ventures. In the first half of 1985, contracts worth US$700 million were signed for overseas projects in this field.

China's goal of the modernisation of science, technology, agriculture and national defence by the year 2000 has created an enormous demand for technical, business, scientific and management information, and for efficient dissemination of this information. Training thus becomes an important component of many companies' business strategies in China. When purchasing technology or technical products, Chinese buyers shop carefully and spend a great deal of effort studying the technical aspects. For sellers, joint-venture partners, technology licensors, financiers and even buyers, willingness to share information, expertise and experience through formal as well as informal training sessions is a means of developing goodwill and cementing relations, and is sometimes an essential aspect of a project's success. Because training can involve significant time and costs, it is also an important item to factor into business plans for budgeting purposes.

Despite the impression that China is industrially 30 or more years behind Europe or the United States, with a low level of technical development, it is a mistake to assume that China is a suitable market only for relatively low-technology, simple products. In many industries and fields of research and development, China has advanced specialists. In some fields, such as nuclear power, rocketry and petroleum, the most advanced research facilities and specialists were largely protected from the ravages of the Cultural Revolution, enabling them to continue while most other research and development workers and facilities were harassed and disrupted. Many American and European companies delivering technical seminar papers have been surprised at questions from Chinese which reflect intimate knowledge of the latest technology in their particular field. The best guideline is to test all assumptions on the level of technology appropriate to a particular business strategy carefully before launching a programme.

Demonstrating commitment to developing a long-term business relationship on a mutually beneficial basis is an important ingredient of success. Chinese officials and trade executives will often stress the fact that China is a developing country with limited resources, and that patience is required to be successful in business there. Although they may sometimes need to be reminded that managers in Western companies need to demonstrate tangible results to maintain the support of their top management for business development efforts in China, they are genuinely appreciative of a long-term outlook and programme which reflect this.

Having invented and developed the concept of a civil service many hundreds of years ago, it comes as no surprise that a country of China's size today boasts the world's largest bureaucracy. Furthermore, the centrally planned structure of the basic foreign trade apparatus favours decision-making by groups as opposed to individuals. As a result business decisions are made relatively slowly. Because of the long hiatus in business relations between China and the West, as well as Japan, companies who are very well known and recognised in their home markets and even international markets may not be known in China; or they may be known only among the older generation, based on their main product of 50 years ago, such as sewing machines or light bulbs. These two factors combined call for good business communications to ensure that targeted groups of Chinese executives involved in decisions relative to a particular project or industry are made aware of the company's history, product range and technical capabilities. Despite the surge in English-language education in recent years, a very limited number of key decision-makers are fluent in spoken or written English; business communications should therefore be translated into Chinese. Mandarin Chinese, known in China as *putonghua* (the common speech), is the national spoken dialect; written Chinese is standard nationwide and has never been subject to the complex differences between the many spoken dialects. Printed materials in Chinese should be prepared in the simplified Chinese script, rather than the older traditional characters still used in Hong Kong and Taiwan.

Sources of market information and assistance

Compared with 1975, access to the China market and availability of information on doing business with China are vastly improved.

The commercial officers attached to Chinese embassies and consulates overseas are a helpful first point of contact, offering advice on some of the Chinese organisations appropriate to a particular product or project interest, as well as advice on how to arrange a visit to China for business purposes.

Many European countries, the United States, Canada and Australia have associations of companies interested in trade with China. These associations are generally supported by membership dues and work closely with their respective government departments of foreign trade to promote exports to China, trade fair pavilions in Chinese industrial exhibitions, business delegations to and from China, etc. These associations (see Appendix) can be extremely helpful sources of more information and contacts.

Many international banks with branches in Hong Kong or representative offices in China offer assistance to their customers in developing trade contacts in China. Some of these banks have well-developed China desks with specialists devoted to the China market, as well as publications on the China market and on doing business with China. A number of international accounting firms and law firms now have offices in Hong Kong and China.

Numerous books and newsletters are produced on the China market and are a useful means of keeping abreast of changes in policy and market trends. Perhaps the best single periodical exclusively devoted to the China market is the *China Business Review*, published bi-monthly by the National Council for US-China Trade in Washington, D.C. Containing analyses of policy trends and reports of US and other company activity in China, it is available to non-members of the Council on a subscription basis. *Sino-British Trade Review*, published monthly in newsletter form by the Sino-British Trade Council in London, is also a good source of market information.

A variety of Chinese and Sino-foreign joint-venture companies have offices and representatives in the United States and Europe, which was not the case until the early 1980s. This makes initiating contacts easier and more convenient, although it does not replace the need to establish some kind of coverage in China itself at least from time to time, and on a regular basis if a major programme is contemplated.

Hong Kong's population of mainland Chinese trade representatives grew a hundredfold between 1979 and 1985, starting from the well-established Hong Kong and Macao agents of the Foreign Trade Corporations in Beijing, such as China Resources Company, Teck Soon Hong, Ng Fung Hong, Nam Kwong in Macao, to include dozens of provincial and municipal representative offices plus a large number of companies with quasi-official or joint investment links to Chinese organisations and officials. In the early 1970s, a small minority of businesses in Hong Kong had active trade links with China. By 1985 most companies in manufacturing, banking, marketing, trading and the service sector had some form of business directly or indirectly related to China. As a result, advice, information and introductions to Chinese trade organisations are plentiful. Many business organisations offer specialised support services for the China market: the China desks of leading banks, and trading agencies, consultants, advertising agencies, translation and printing services and market research organisations. The commercial section of most foreign consulates in Hong Kong has officers who can offer advice and assistance on starting up or expanding business with China. Several chambers of commerce, including the Hong Kong General Chamber and the American Chamber of Commerce, have committees of business people active in trade with China. The number of Chinese business and technical delegations and Chinese product exhibitions visiting Hong Kong has increased dramatically. It is also common for Hong Kong-based China traders to make the convenient day trip to Shenzhen to meet with business associates from interior parts of China who can visit Shenzhen much more easily than Hong Kong. The explosive re-emergence of Hong Kong as a centre for trading with China in the mid-1980s only serves to underline its value as a staging point for international companies who want to do business with China as well as other Asian countries. Many observers concur that Hong Kong's role in this respect will expand even further after 1997, when sovereignty over Hong Kong reverts to China.

Setting up a China office
A challenge in sustaining a business development pro-gramme in China is finding a cost-effective means of maintaining the momentum of initial efforts. Questions which companies typically face are whether or not an office in China is required, and if so what type of executive(s) to staff it with, whether an office in Hong Kong to pursue China and other activities would suffice, where to find an appropriate agent or sales representa-tive and how to obtain expert legal and accounting advice.

Answers to these questions vary according to the industry and type of business objectives. The cost of operating an office in China is comparable to and in most cases probably higher than in Hong Kong. Costs and fees are high by comparison in China for all services required by the international business community, and business offices and accommodations are mainly limited to hotels. In Beijing, for example, approximately 800 foreign companies operated in 1985 in less than 30 different buildings offering rental premises, and these were mostly hotels. Hong Kong is certainly a more popular location among most staff and executives, offers little red tape and maximum operating flexibility in terms of labour, tax, registration, etc., but has the disadvantage of being about three hours' flight from the top decision-makers in Beijing. Counterbalancing this disadvantage is the fact that it is easier to obtain and reconfirm airplane reserva-tions from Hong Kong to any destination in China than from Beijing, due to an awkward system of ticketing and reservations practised by the Civil Aviation Administra-tion of China headquarters office.

Ultimately an office in China is required for companies who are serious about developing business there, and most companies start with an office in Beijing; although the trend towards decentralisation has led some com-panies to open offices in other cities before opening in the capital, to pursue regional marketing and project man-agement goals. Shanghai had 144 registered representa-tive offices of foreign and Hong Kong companies in mid-1985 (of which 76 were from Japan, 20 from the United States and 19 from Hong Kong); Guangzhou also has a thriving representative office community. Many companies take advantage of the mutual strengths and weaknesses of a Hong Kong and a China base to maximise the benefits of both.

The acute shortage of accommodation and suitable office facilities in a range of prices to suit different budgets has been a problem in Beijing and other cities. New construction should help alleviate this situation in Beijing; for example, by 1988 there will be 30,000 hotel rooms in Beijing compared with 16,000 in 1985. In addition, new office and combined office-apartment facilities are opening up, offering a range of non-hotel options. The resident foreign business population in Beijing was estimated in 1985 to be 1,500, out of a total foreign population of about 10,000. As another illustra-tion of how quickly the foreign business presence has grown, 100 companies were registered with the General Administration for Industry and Commerce when foreign businesses were first required to register in 1980. In 1985 this number had swollen to over 600. Author-ities estimate the number will have grown to approx-imately 1,500 by 1990.

Until 1982, all business residents lived in hotels, and in most cases had a hotel room or part of a suite as office. Beginning in 1982, hotel apartments became available which offered more spacious and luxurious accommoda-tion, at prices that would stagger many budget-conscious businessmen. In 1985, the top end of the hotel apartment market featured rental costs in the range of US$75,000 to US$125,000 per year for a three-bedroom suite.

Given the size of China and the decentralised nature of decision-making on many types of business transactions, companies use agents and sales representatives in many cases, even after they have established an office in Hong Kong and in China. For technical product sales it is essential to have sales representatives who are capable of technical sales and some service support. For best results it is advisable to support sales agents with Chinese-language sales promotion materials, advertising, tech-nical seminars and exhibitions.

Good advice from experienced legal counsel can save time and money, and avoid many problems, especially when contemplating a joint venture or licensing arrange-ment. The best counsel will be from legal specialists with experience in the field, either from a Hong Kong or China base. The array of new laws and guidelines continuously issued from various sources in China make it very challenging to keep informed even from Hong Kong.

The same is true of accounting and taxation affecting companies setting up to do business, joint ventures, etc. Several of the leading international accounting firms have active China practices and specialists who concen-trate on Chinese tax and accountancy matters.

The number of Chinese managers who speak English or a European language fluently is very small. One of the benefits of having a fluent speaker of *putonghua* on your company's team is not only to assist with interpreting but to supplement direct interpretation of discussions with the nuance and subtlety so important to understanding the Chinese counterparts' attitudes and reactions. Although *putonghua* is the official spoken language of commerce and government, and is widely spoken among educated people throughout China, knowledge of the regional dialect is still an advantage when doing business in that region, for instance, Cantonese in Guangdong Province and Shanghainese in Shanghai.

Meetings and negotiations

Chinese negotiators are famed for their shrewdness. Their representatives in important commercial negotiations are well trained in the art of positioning, posturing, pricing, psychology and effective use of timing; and they operate from the position of knowing their adversary's strengths and weaknesses well enough to obtain the maximum advantage to their side.

One mistake sometimes made by Western businessmen in negotiations is confusing what they perceive to be Chinese behavioural traits in a general sense – subtlety, indirectness, soft-spokenness, avoidance of conflict – with the behavioural guidelines in force in a negotiating situation. A better approach is to think of entering a negotiation in the same spirit as one would enter a sporting contest which can occassionally be a bit 'rough and tumble'. Both sides are out to win and respect the rules of fair play, but at the end of the day will measure success in the game by who wins or loses the most advantages for their side. Advantages are a kind of point scoring system, so in order to be playing the same game with common currency it is advisable to identify in advance all the advantages desirable to either side in the context of the transaction being discussed. Each time an advantage is traded, the expectation follows that an advantage is owed. A good negotiator keeps careful notes, and may refer months later to an 'advantage owed' that his less vigilant counterpart may long have forgotten.

Business protocol in China is fairly straightforward and in some respects closer to a Western model than Japanese business protocol. The most fundamental rule in meetings and social gatherings is to respect rank, and to match executives of like rank. Because relative rank is not always immediately identifiable from someone's title, it helps to have a trusted advisor on the team, although checking in advance with representatives from the Chinese side is also acceptable.

It is useful to hold top-ranking executives in reserve for important occasions where they may be brought into the business relationship as a sign of its growing importance, to sign a contract, for example, or to officiate at an opening ceremony. Sending the chief executive on the first business mission the company launches into the China market is not harmful *per se*, but it eliminates some valuable options for later roles to be played. It is also likely that despite the chief executive's high rank, a first business visit to China by the company will usually not rate an equally high-ranking welcome from the Chinese side, such a response normally being reserved for 'old friends': companies who are familiar and have established a track record and reputation.

Familiarity and personal contact are very important. Little is achieved in initial meetings other than getting acquainted, but building upon this familiarity becomes easier with each subsequent meeting. This is the cement which holds a business relationship together and enables problems to be solved through frank discussion, which is not possible until a certain degree of familiarity is achieved.

In relationships involving a foreign company and a Chinese organisation, the Chinese side will often delegate a person responsible for liaison and general day-to-day operational matters. Depending on how active the relationship is, it is advisable for the foreign company to nominate a counterpart for liaison. These two then become the focal point not only for operational details, but often for the exchange of views, opinions and topics that more senior executives may find awkward to bring up in face-to-face meetings.

Social gatherings should be informal for the most part. The only strict requirement in a Chinese-style banquet, where the seating is at a round table, is to match the host and the guest of honour. The host, normally seated at the position facing the door, should have the guest of honour seated at his right-hand, and the guest of honour's deputy (if one is present) at his left-hand side. To the right of the guest of honour sits the host's deputy with the next in rank seated to the left of the guest of honour's deputy. The rest of the seating arrangement (normally 12 people per table) is optional. At larger dinners, with more than one table, the formula is followed by the host's number two and three men each acting as a host at another table. Foreign companies entertaining Chinese-style in China should follow this protocol to ensure that everyone feels comfortable. Careful checking in advance is required to make sure that ranks are correctly identified, especially if guests from more than one organisation are invited. At a banquet where the host is Chinese, the host will use serving chopsticks to serve his guest of honour first as each course is served before helping himself; however, Western hosts are usually spared this.

Despite the importance of correct positioning as far as rank is concerned, banquests are usually informal and relaxed once the basic rule has been followed. It is considered poor form for the host to compliment the food and banquet arrangements; instead, if anything, the host speaks somewhat disparagingly of the arrangements made for his guests, apologising mildly for their being insufficient for such honoured guests. As the first course is served, the host will often propose a toast to welcome his guests, after which eating commences. The host may propose toasts before each additional course, and the guest of honour should follow suit by returning a toast or toasts. Moderate drinking is common, and conversation can be lively, but jokes of a political or sexual nature are best avoided.

In planning meetings, one should allow for two to three times longer than would be required if both sides were speaking the same language. Interpretation adds a great deal of time, and even a skilled interpreter familiar with the topic under discussion needs time to explain, since direct translation is not sufficient in many cases. Having a Chinese version of a presentation text can be useful and save time. Ideally, the interpreter should be briefed on the subject matter and any specialised terminology long enough in advance to allow study and familiarisation. Although the Chinese side will usually provide an interpreter for meetings in China and abroad, Western companies should employ their own, especially for negotiations. Because of the importance of the interpreter in conveying and interpreting meaning, it is preferable to have someone with undivided loyalties.

As a general rule of thumb, gifts given in a business context should be practical and related to business as opposed to luxury items. Although business custom has been liberalised tremendously in China during the 1980s, and many cases of extravagant gift-giving and outright bribery can be found, the giving of non-essential presents is officially frowned upon. Short cuts involving under-the-table payments or similar practices are risky exceptions to the rule.

It is common to exchange business cards at the outset of a meeting. Ideally, foreign visitors to China should have a calling card with the Chinese version of their name and company name on the reverse side. This helps the non-English reading Chinese executive and shows special effort and goodwill. As with other printed material, cards should be typeset in simplified Chinese characters, different from the traditional characters used in Hong Kong and Taiwan.

For introductory meetings, a brief company history and description of company size and range of activities is a useful piece of literature to have prepared. In the case of larger companies with multiple divisions or subsidiaries, an organisation chart will assist in identifying where individual executives and product lines fit into the picture.

Colour transparencies and audio-visual materials can be effective in presentations, and can be prepared with Chinese captions or subtitles to speed communications. Video playback units are becoming more common in China, but for special events such as exhibitions it is better to take one's own. The same generally applies to slide projectors and film projection equipment, although 16mm projectors are fairly common. Old China hands often travel with an assortment of electrical plugs and adaptors to cope with the variety of different types of sockets encountered in various parts of China.

Chinese trade and investment organisations

By mid-1985 the number of organisations involved in foreign trade and investment at national, provincial, county and municipal level had grown so quickly that no single Chinese or foreign source could prepare a clear and comprehensive organisation chart or even a complete list of all Chinese corporations engaged in foreign trade. This was in sharp contrast to the situation 10 years earlier when there were only 20 national-level FTCs and their provincial branches, through whom all foreign trade activities were channelled.

Considering the continuing state of flux prevailing in the mid-1980s with regard to organisational structure and authority, the best approach for strategic planners is to begin with a look at the main types of organisations involved on the Chinese side in different types of foreign trade transactions, in order to draw conclusions as to where best to start in cultivating all the necessary business relationships.

Buying and selling

China's traditional import and export corporations numbered about 12 until the late 1970s, when the process of reform and reorganisation began. Each had a monopoly on discussing and contracting imports and exports of a particular commodity line: chemicals; machinery; textiles; technology; native produce and animal by-products; light industrial products; cereals, oils and foodstuffs; publications; metals and minerals; arts and crafts; complete plants; and packaging. All shared the common nomenclature of 'China National . . . Import and Export Corporation', which identified their commodity line. They were variously referred to by foreign businessmen as I/E corporations or FTCs.

Although the range of number of Chinese organisations authorised to conduct import and export transactions has grown explosively since the late 1970s, the new-to-market company is usually better off beginning with the FTCs which offer established infrastructure, experience, knowledge of international trade practice, foreign currency availability for import purchases and better access to supply for export sales. Functioning under the aegis of the Ministry of Foreign Economic Relations and Trade (MOFERT), formerly known as the Ministry of Foreign Trade, each FTC has a head office in Beijing and branch offices nationwide. Although the basic line-up of the FTCs still corresponds to that of the 1970s, experimentation with the division of commodity lines among them, and between them and newer corporations under the aegis of other ministries continues. Since any description of their product line and affiliated or subsidiary corporations is likely to be quickly outdated, the best rule of thumb is to begin with the Beijing head office of the FTC which appears to correspond most closely with a company's product line, and work from there to determine what other alternatives are available.

Despite the confusing range of new entities, the traditional function and role of the China National Textiles Import and Export Corporation, the China National Chemicals Import and Export Corporation, the China National Machinery Import and Export Corporation, and their sister companies headquartered in the Erligou district of Beijing, remains intact.

In almost any buying or selling transaction there will be a variety of prospective Chinese partners. The changing roles and authority levels argue against developing exclusive relationships with any one organisation.

Selling to China requires coverage of more than just the FTC or other intermediary corporation to reach the so-called end-user of the product. The more technical the product, the more consideration sellers should give to locating buyers among some of the newer specialised technical corporations. Examples would be the China National Automotive Corporation, the China National Nonferrous Metals Corporation and the China National Petrochemical Corporation, each of which functions as a kind of super corporation with ministry-level status in areas where previously there had been overlap between two or more different ministries and corporations. Their creation has not eliminated overlap, but reduced it.

Other specialised corporations report to industrial ministries and pursue specialised tasks under ministry guidance. A good example would be the China National Oil and Gas Exploration and Development Corporation under the Ministry of Petroleum Industry. Although most import contracts for petroleum-related products were still signed up to 1985 by the traditional FTCs – China National Machinery Import and Export Corporation in the case of petroleum equipment, China National

Technical Import and Export Corporation in the case of petroleum technology – the growing authority of the specialised corporation in making import decisions underlines the need for sellers to develop good relations among the FTCs as well as the specialised corporations.

A good strategy to follow is to identify the relevant FTC as well as all ministries involved in the import and export of a particular product, and cultivate business relationships with all of them in an even-handed manner. Thorough research is required to determine which industrial ministries are involved in imports and exports of which products because the range usually extends well beyond what would be implied by the ministry name. The Ministry of Railways, for example, has authority and budget to import telecommunication equipment for use in their huge domestic rail network, separate from the overall planning and import authority of the Ministry of Posts and Telecommunications. There are many similar examples.

For buying from China, most important is to determine which organisation is capable of efficiently supplying, on a regular basis, a product which meets the required specifications. Although the established FTCs face a great deal of competition from new specialised and local corporations anxious to develop their own direct export links, many of these groups lack experience and practical market knowledge.

Cities and provinces with significant volumes of foreign trade have established their own local-level import and export corporations, consulting companies and investment companies with varying links to the ministry apparatus in Beijing, and these should be taken into account as a company develops beyond the stage of initial contacts in Beijing. For local-level projects and transactions, this type of organisation, like the Shanghai General Foreign Trade Corporation or the Tianjin General Foreign Trade Corporation, are important and useful contacts. The same applies in the SEZs, where specialised local companies, such as the Zhuhai Special Economic Zone Development Corporation or the Shenzhen Special Economic Zone Development Corporation, are prime contacts for would-be investors.

Investment and finance
Although the Bank of China remains the principal direct counterpart for foreign banks and financial institutions, the rise of China International Trust and Investment Company (CITIC) as well as regional trust and investment companies – GITIC in Guangzhou, TITIC in Tianjin – has opened interesting new possibilities for finance and investment in China.

As in other sectors of the economy, Chinese leaders have taken a series of steps to introduce competition in the finance sector, both domestically and in regard to foreign trade finance. The first step came in 1979 with the formation of CITIC (apparently at the suggestion of Deng Xiaoping) under the direction of former Shanghai industrialist Rong Yiren, one of the pre-1949 capitalists who remained in China when the Communists came to power. CITIC's foundation under the leadership of former capitalists who remained patriotic was seen at the time as a sign that Chinese leaders were impatient with slow growth and a monolithic trade and investment apparatus slow to respond to market opportunities.

CITIC's brief is broad-based: merchant banking, investment matchmaking for foreign companies in China, overseas investment for Chinese companies (especially in the natural resource sector), issuing foreign currency bonds, real estate, leasing, trading and consulting. The company's consulting group evolved into a subsidiary called China International Economic Consultants, which provides market research, and financial, legal and marketing consultation to foreign companies operating in China.

CITIC has been active in the joint-venture field, concluding some 50 joint ventures with foreign companies in coal mining, cement production, elevator manufacturing, food processing and light industrial manufacturing. In about 30 of the ventures the company has taken an equity position in addition to acting as marriage broker. CITIC executives openly speak of the competition they give the Bank of China, and they are proud of their pioneering role in introducing leasing as a means of financing China's equipment and technology acquisition, as well as the publicity made when they launched China's first contemporary bond offering on the international market in January 1982, with a ¥10 billion private issue placed in the Tokyo market.

Similar to the position of the FTCs, the Bank of China faces competition not only from CITIC since the State Council granted it permission to handle foreign currency deposits and other transactions, but also from other sources with increased authority. Having had a virtual monopoly on foreign exchange banking transactions, the Bank of China has to contend with new authority given to the Industrial and Commercial Bank in 1985 to engage in foreign currency transactions in some of its branches. Industrial and Commercial Bank is one of five specialised banks under the People's Bank of China, China's Central Bank; the other four are the Bank of China, the Agricultural Bank, the Construction Bank and the China Investment Bank. All five now compete to some small extent, but the Bank of China, like the FTCs, retains a very well established and dominant position. A tremendous advantage enjoyed by the Bank of China is its growing position in the dynamic Hong Kong market, both directly and indirectly, through its 12 so-called 'sister banks', eight incorporated in China and four incorporated in Hong Kong.

The role of foreign banks in the China market reached a new milestone in mid-1985 when the HongKong Bank (formerly Hong Kong and Shanghai Banking Corporation) became the first foreign bank to open a branch in Shenzhen Special Economic Zone. Foreign banks were permitted to open branches in any of China's SEZs as of April 1984, whereas previous rules had confined their operations to represenative offices unable to engage in banking business *per se*. Several other foreign banks were expected to obtain licences for the Shenzhen SEZ in 1985-86, but high capital requirements (Rmb40 million) and limitations on access to the local market kept many other foreign banks waiting for clarification and additional details on the policy directions governing their operations there. As of late 1984, 63 foreign banks had established representative offices in Beijing.

The first question facing prospective foreign investors is where to start, which Chinese organisation to contact first. The answer depends in part on the type of project.

Depending on the total investment contemplated, local-level authorities may have full decision-making authority. However, the amounts and procedures are subject to adjustment. When projects are referred to the central level for approval, the authority and administrative process is vested in the Foreign Investment Administration of MOFERT under priorities set by the State Planning Commission and the Foreign Investment and Control Commission.

If a planned project appears to be of a size which local authorities have authority to approve and implement, the local-level External Economic Affairs Commission can be approached. It should be emphasised, however, that fast-changing rules and regulations leave significant grey areas, and when in doubt, local authorities are prone to push ahead in discussing a project with a foreign company with an air of authority. Discovering at a later stage that the real authority is higher up can be far costlier for the foreign company than for the local authorities. It pays to do careful homework before entering detailed discussions, and to avoid making or implying commitment to a prospective joint-venture partner until all alternatives have been thoroughly reviewed. Because of the speed with which new rules and regulations are issued, and the experimentation in policy regarding who has authority for what, it is important to obtain advice and guidance from experts close to the market – be they Western bankers, lawyers, accountants, trade commissioners, consultants or others with first-hand experience. It is also important to obtain early advice from sources who do not have a vested interest in promoting one particular organisation or channel of investment.

A checklist of organisations who can be contacted regarding joint ventures, compensation trade, and other forms of foreign investment would include: FTCs and their agents in Hong Kong and Macao; specialised corporations related to industrial or military ministries; CITIC and similar regional organisations like GITIC in Guangzhou and TITIC in Tianjin; Shanghai Industrial Consultants and Shanghai Investment and Trust Corporation; China Merchants Steam Navigation Company for projects in Shenzhen's Shekou special zone; each of the four SEZ Economic Development Corporations; and most provincial or municipal foreign economic and technical exchange commissions. Last but not least, the commercial counsellor at Chinese embassies overseas can be contacted for additional advice.

Service and miscellaneous

The China Council for the Promotion of International Trade (CCPIT), reporting to MOFERT and headquartered in Beijing with branches in the provinces and major cities, is a good starting point for business inquiries which do not immediately fit into obvious categories defined by known FTC or other foreign trade organisation areas of responsibility. In addition to specialised departments handling foreign exhibitions, technical seminars, technical literature and samples, trademarks and patents, CCPIT has traditionally played a liaison role for a wide range of different business lines, helping foreign companies find suitable Chinese counterparts. Unlike many of the newer consulting companies which have been set up in China under various central and local-level

authorities, CCPIT is more service than profit orientated, and is well known and well connected nationwide.

For tourism-related business, the China Travel Service in Beijing is the national-level authority, with branches throughout the country including its affiliate China International Travel Service. For local-level tourism ventures and hotel projects, it is also possible to contact the Foreign Economic Affairs Commission at the local level.

Marketing communications options

China in the mid-1980s offers a wide range of channels through which to communicate company and product information in support of business development strategies.

Advertising

Following a brief period of tolerance in the years after the founding of the People's Republic of China in 1949, advertising was banned for a 20-year period as a capitalist tool. In the late 1970s, the regime of Deng Xiaoping brought advertising back as a controlled means of promoting economic growth. In 1979, China's premier advertising agency, Shanghai Advertising Company, was reopened, and there followed a boom in domestic advertising among Chinese enterprises seeking to sell their wares to each other and to consumers, as well as foreign companies advertising their corporate image and specific products. In a few years, dozens and then hundreds of advertising agencies and specialised contractors sprung up across the country, and several advertising associations were formed.

Advertising in the context of China's foreign trade was approved as a means of stimulating the exchange of product and technical information after years of isolation, not to mention as a means of earning hard currency by allowing foreign companies to advertise in the Chinese media. At the same time, Chinese corporations began to advertise abroad in support of the export promotion drive, and from zero foreign exchange expenditure in 1978, China's FTCs reached an annual hard currency spending level on advertising of some US$20 million by 1984.

An association of state-owned Chinese advertising agencies specialising in foreign advertising in Chinese media as well as Chinese export advertising was set up in 1980. Membership of the China National Foreign Trade Advertising Association, headquartered in Beijing and affiliated with MOFERT, comprises the 27 provincial and major municipal agencies across China. Another group, the China United Advertising Association, is also nationwide, but comprises principally those agencies engaged in domestic advertising. Both groups offer services to foreign advertisers and agencies.

Most foreign advertising in China is corporate or industrial product rather than consumer advertising. Of the estimated US$23 million spent by foreign companies advertising in China in 1983, some 80 per cent was spent by Japanese companies, who unlike their European and American competitors tended to spend on mass media aimed at long-term reinforcement of company and product recognition. Most European and American companies tend to concentrate on trade, technical and business media, where target groups are smaller, costs lower and results theoretically more measurable.

From a mere handful of Chinese media accepting advertising in 1978, the range of printed, electronic, roadside and point of sale advertising options available to foreign companies in China today reaches well into the thousands, ranging from highly specialised technical journals with small circulations to nationwide television with enormous audience reach. In line with decentralisation, most provinces and municipalities offer a variety of local-level advertising media.

One of the advantages to foreign companies of properly planned and executed advertising programmes in China is that response rates tend to be high, especially to colourful and technically informative advertisements offering additional information or literature to respondents. Screening response to eliminate unqualified enquiries poses some challenges, but effective systems have been developed by companies experienced in the market. Advertising can thus become a cost-effective means of building lists of prospects.

Exhibitions and technical seminars

Exhibitions in China were important to companies throughout the 1970s as a means of showing products and technology to prospective Chinese buyers. On average 10 or more national exhibitions were held each year, each showing the wares of all industries from one country, and almost always in Beijing, where the import decisions were made at that time.

Starting late in the 1970s, and increasing at a rapid pace, private sector exhibitions were organised on specific industrial themes, attracting companies from around the world to venues all over China. Suddenly there were more exhibitions scheduled in China than in any mature, well-developed European market; one count in 1985 showed 200 exhibitions on various industrial themes, many organised by Hong Kong trading companies lacking experience in professional trade show management.

The attraction of exhibitions continues to be the opportunity to meet specialised end-users in a particular industry segment and region; but experience has shown that qualified attendance at an exhibition takes effort and investment on the part of the organiser to achieve. Demand for attendance far outpaces demand, with daily visitor numbers exceeding 10,000 attendees in major national shows in Beijing. Some exhibition management companies spend significant amounts of money on nationwide advertising and direct mail to alert as many potential end-users and decision-makers as possible to a coming event, with enough lead time for them to complete the sometimes time-consuming red tape involved in business travel. Others rely on their connections with a particular ministry, to the exclusion of other unrelated ministries or groups who may also be interested in the technology on display.

Participation in exhibitions in China often costs three times as much as in a European or American show, exclusive of travel and freight; the exhibitor should therefore check the track record of the exhibition organiser before committing himself to participate.

Technical seminars were important throughout the 1970s for sellers of technical products and technology, and they are equally important in the 1980s. China rarely makes technical purchases without availing itself of the opportunity to pit its top technical people in a particular field against technical specialists from the vendor organisation. Technical seminars are either single-company events, or are held at exhibitions or symposia.

Direct mail marketing

Direct mail marketing is perhaps the most under-utilised, cost-effective tool for industrial marketers in China. Although premature for marketers of Western consumer goods because of the limited individual purchasing power using foreign currency, it nonetheless enjoys a high degree of impact because of its novelty and the fact that Chinese managers are not bombarded with direct mail offerings. Even so, like advertising, its effectiveness is enhanced in most cases by a straightforward, technical approach rather than an overly slick image appeal without facts and figures to back up performance claims.

List rental sources are most numerous in Hong Kong, where many international companies' China marketing offices maintain their own prospect lists. The more sophisticated rental sources use Chinese computer or word processor equipment to maintain and sort lists. Lists are also available on a rental-only basis from various organisations in Beijing, with fairly limited detail on categories and distribution.

Industrial marketers with an established presence in China use direct mail as a means of circulating Chinese-language newsletters to prospects and customers in China, introducing new products, company activities and company trade events such as exhibitions.

Public relations

If the word 'advertising' conjured up negative connotations in the environment of 1975, 'public relations' was even more tainted. In 1985, the first international public relations consultancy to open an office in Beijing did so in response to increasing needs of major Western client companies, as well as a broad range of new options and opportunities brought about by the relaxed attitudes of the Chinese towards PR and related concepts. Its main rival quickly followed suit by launching a joint venture with an offshoot of the New China News Agency, indicating that public relations may now be a permanent part of the business services available to foreign companies in China.

At the same time as more international print and electronic news media were obtaining accredited status for their journalist representatives in Beijing, Chinese media began to show willingness to receive news releases and product information of a technical nature from foreign companies. Interviews with foreign business representatives and their comments on China's open door economic policy were actively solicited by the Chinese media directly in China, and indirectly through Hong Kong. China's trade and industrial organisations began to show willingness to hold press conferences and appoint press spokesmen as part of an overall process of re-evaluating the role and benefits of press relations and publicity.

Once again Hong Kong had a special role to play as a kind of media test tube through which China followed the reaction of the international business community to new trade and investment policies. Hong Kong's Chinese and foreign press are regularly quoted for limited distribution to senior Chinese officials anxious to obtain a more candid view of how new policies and practices were being accepted.

Public relations has become an accepted part of the marketing communications process through which the interchange of Chinese and foreign economic and business information is promoted.

Market research

Even more than the various forms of market communications, market research has enjoyed a remarkable reappraisal during the 1980s in China. Such apparently mundane subjects as the weather report and the telephone book were classified state secrets until the early 1980s, left over from a time when market research was still viewed as a kind of espionage under the prevailing xenophobic atmosphere. The acceptance of market research as an important tool for Chinese corporations, as well as for foreign companies operating in China, was a major change which improved operating conditions for foreign companies, led to new business opportunities for Chinese and foreign service companies and resulted in a flurry of new Chinese consulting companies being set up

to provide market research and assistance to foreign companies.

Starting in 1981 with the first publication of the 'Statistical Yearbook of China', China has allowed vastly more official economic and industrial data to be publicly revealed than in the previous decades, as well as permitting the World Bank and other international organisations more direct access to statistical data for analysis. The result has been a switch from too little information to a vast sea of information. Market research practioners have been more active in the industrial than the consumer field for obvious reasons, and this is likely to continue to be the case for some time to come.

Although foreign companies cannot expect the kind of research results which they would obtain at home, China does offer a wide range of new research options unimaginable during most of the 1970s. Many local as well as national-level organisations have become involved in consulting work. Some of these groups are capable of taking on research projects on behalf of foreign companies in a specific locale. Fees and methodology are of course subject to discussions on a case-by-case basis. A number of established research companies in Hong Kong have connections with various Chinese organisations who act as local sponsor-partners for specific research projects.

Appendix:
China trade associations

National Council for US-China Trade
1050 17th Street, N.W.
Washington, D.C. 20036
USA

**Australia-China Business
Cooperation Committee**
Industry House
Barton, A.C.T. 2660
Australia

Comité France-Chine
31 Avenue Pierre les De Serbie
75116 Paris, Cedex 16
France

Sino-British Trade Council
5/F Abford House
15 Wilton Road
London SW1V 1LT
England

Canada-China Trade Council
100-199 Bay Street
Toronto
Ontario M5J 1L4
Canada

Netherlands-China Trade Council
Bezuidenhoutsenweg 171
s'Gravenhage
Netherlands

Swedish Trade Council
Styrmansgatan 6
Box 5513, S-114 85 Stockholm
Sweden

Switzerland-China Trade Council
Löwenstrasse 19
8001 Zurich
Switzerland

The Export Council of Norway
Drammensveien 40
N-0255 Oslo 2
Norway

CHAPTER 3

The open door, foreign investment and Chinese law

by Owen D. Nee, Jr

Deng Xiaoping's open door policy has been called the second great revolution of China's Communist Party. This chapter examines from the perspective of a foreign businessman China's remarkable progress in developing an orderly legal system as the foundation for the economic development of the nation.

The published laws of the People's Republic of China now provide an extensive, if not complete, guide to the conduct of business in China by foreign companies and individuals that wish to do business in China. There are laws governing the registration of foreign companies and contractors operating in China, laws related to investment, a contract law governing contracts between Chinese and foreign entities, legislation on taxation and accounting, comprehensive and detailed customs regulations, regulations governing exchange control and banking, and a patent law and a law on trademarks, to mention just a few. Additionally, China has done much to regulate the conduct of its own citizens by published law, rather than Communist Party policy decisions, such as the establishment of a court system by law, the adoption of criminal laws and a law of civil procedure, the resurrection of the legal profession, and the reestablishment of the accountancy profession. Many aspects of the domestic economy are now regulated by law, rather than solely by the state economic planning apparatus. China has a domestic contracts law, regulations on the purchase and sale of industrial products in the domestic economy, price control regulations, regulations governing the registration of domestic commercial enterprises, laws related to environmental protection and an import and export licensing system.

While published Chinese law would only fill a small bookcase, as compared with the rows of volumes in an American or European law library, nevertheless existing Chinese law provides a usable framework for understanding the permitted course of conduct for foreign businesses and Chinese citizens in their day-to-day affairs.

Rather than attempt to describe each of China's laws individually, this chapter examines the broad framework of Chinese law from the viewpoint of a foreign company considering commencing business activity in China. The first question addressed is how a foreign company can register an office in China. The second topic addressed is the forms of investment permitted to foreign concerns

contemplating investing in the China market, and the process whereby such investments are approved. The next part examines China's rules governing foreign exchange control and the lending process, because of the importance of such topics to banks and financial institutions. The fourth section addresses China's laws related to the transfer of technology and the protection of industrial property rights, such as patents and trademarks. After having looked at registering, investing, banking and licensing in China, the chapter describes how Chinese law provides for the taxation of foreign enterprises, and looks at China's Special Economic Zones and coastal cities.

Registration of foreign enterprises

One of the first effects of the open door policy revolution was a flood of foreign businessmen on China's shores scrambling for a foothold in the last major market of the 20th century. In order to sell their wares to China, businessmen during the 1960s and early 1970s were limited to visits to the Canton Trade Fair where Chinese buyers and sellers met with their foreign counterparts twice a year to trade goods. The open door policy increased the opportunities for such business, but businessmen were still required to obtain an invitation from a Chinese enterprise prior to each visit to China. With the increase in the volume of business, it became desirable both from the Chinese perspective and that of the foreign partners to be able to establish permanent offices in China.

This need for permanent representation in China led to some of the first legislation of the open door policy. At the present time, China has laws permitting foreign enterprises to register an office in China to perform representative or liaison activities, or to perform a contract or subcontract in China.

The regulatory framework for representative offices

There are over 930 foreign registered representative offices in China. This is roughly equal to the total number of equity joint ventures. Since such offices handle a large amount of China's foreign trade, they are now an important part of China's foreign trade system. Additionally, since each office must rent office space, hire local employees and provide housing for its expatriates, representative offices provide a substantial amount of foreign exchange to the local economy each year. Over half of such offices are located in Beijing, but there are many in Shanghai, Guangzhou and other cities in China.

With respect to the establishment of such resident representative offices, the applicable legal requirements and procedures are set forth in the Provisional Regulations of the State Council of the People's Republic of China concerning the Control of Resident Representative Offices of Foreign Enterprises (the 'Provisional Regulations'), promulgated by the State Council and put into force on 30 October 1980. After adoption of the Provisional Regulations, experience proved that additional rules were required and additional registration procedures were set out in the Notice of the General Administration for Industry and Commerce of the People's Republic of China concerning Registration Procedures for Resident Representative Offices of Foreign Enterprises (the 'GAIC Notice'), announced on 8 December 1980. Still later, additional measures regarding registration and control of representative offices were pronounced in the Measures of the State Administration for Industry and Commerce of the People's Republic of China concerning the Registration and Control of Resident Representative Offices of Foreign Enterprises (the 'SAIC Measures'), promulgated on 15 March 1983. These regulations as a group govern the registration of representative offices in China with the exception of Guangdong Province, which has adopted its own rules modelled on the national legislation, and the Special Economic Zones, in which there are separate rules for the three Special Economic Zones in Guangdong Province (Shenzhen, Zhuhai and Shantou) and separate rules for the Xiamen zone in Fujian Province.

The registration requirement

Article 2 of the Provisional Regulations provides that foreign companies 'which have a genuine need' for permanent representation in China may apply for registration and, after approval, open a representative office. The same article stipulates that 'a foreign enterprise which has not obtained an approval and registered may not commence the business activities of a resident office'. Article 16 of the SAIC Measures provides for the imposition of a fine of up to Rmb10,000 (US$3,570) on resident representative offices which commence business activities prior to their approval and registration. In fact, in practice it appears that liaison or business activities commenced prior to the obtaining of a registration certificate may be condoned provided that a registration application has been filed and is pending approval.

The Provisional Regulations themselves do not specify when registration is mandatory, optional or unnecessary, and no definitive guidance is given as to when foreign entities must register. In practice, therefore, to date only foreign companies that wish to maintain a long-term presence in China by renting permanent office space, obtaining telex lines, or hiring local office help have generally found it necessary to register, since local Chinese entities in dealing with foreign concerns ask to see the registration certificate before entering into rental or other similar types of contracts.

Registration procedures

The procedures for establishment of a registered representative office in China are set forth in the Provisional Regulations. Basically, three steps are involved in the registration process: (1) application through a host organisation, (2) obtaining approval for registration from the competent authorities in charge, and (3) registration with the local office of the Adminstration of Industry and Commerce (AIC).

Application

Article 2 of the Provisional Regulations provides that before a foreign company is permitted to register a representative office in China it must apply for and obtain an approval for such office. According to article 4(e), 'enterprises shall apply to the relevant commission, ministry or bureau . . . in accordance with the nature of their business'. Most foreign companies must apply to the Ministry of Foreign Economic Relations and Trade (MOFERT), as this ministry is in charge of companies engaged in manufacturing and trading. Financing institutions, however, are under the control of the People's Bank of China, the central bank, and the Bank of China has issued special regulations relating to the registration of representative offices of such financial institutions: Measures of the People's Bank of China concerning the Control of Resident Representative Offices in China of Financial Institutions with Overseas Chinese or Foreign Capital (1 February 1983). Similarly, although there are not any published regulations on the subject, foreign airlines must apply to the Civil Aviation Administration of China and shipping companies to the Ministry of Communications.

Regardless of what the regulations provide, in practice most foreign companies submit their applications through their 'host' organisation, i.e. the Chinese organisation with which they have current business dealings. Therefore, the question of which Chinese 'commision, ministry or bureau' is the 'relevant' one for registration purposes is determined most often by the host organisation, rather than by the foreign enterprise. As the host organisation must write an annual letter to renew a representative's registration and acts as an intermediary with the Chinese governmental structure, the choice of a host organisation that will continue to be friendly in the years to come is of considerable significance to a foreign company planning to open an office in China.

Obtaining approval for registration

Article 3 of the Provisional Regulations sets forth the documents required to be submitted at the time of application for approval to register. Besides the application itself, the foreign enterprise must produce a certificate of good standing from its country or state of incorporation together with its certificate of incorporation, a credit testimonial from a bank with which it has commercial relations, and a statement of the authority of the personnel to be assigned to the resident representative office, along with a brief résumé of each such individual.

Upon approval of the company's application, (MOFERT) or another relevant ministry or bureau will issue a certificate of approval stating the name of the company and the company's representative. Although it is not stated in the Provisional Regulations, the approval document from the ministry is valid for three years and upon the expiration of this period, the foreign enterprise must go through the registration process anew.

According to article 5 of the Provisional Regulations, within 30 days from the date of approval for the establishment of a resident representative office the foreign company must effect the required registration procedures with the local office of AIC. These procedures include the submission of the approval document obtained from the ministry together with a duplicate set of the documents previously submitted through the host organisation to the ministry. There is a national standardised form for registration that must be filled out in triplicate and submitted to the local office of AIC. Presently AIC has authorised its local offices in Beijing, each of the Special Ecomonic Zones and each of the 14 coastal cities to handle the processing of registration documents for foreign resident representative offices. Of course, the company must also pay the registration fee, which is presently Rmb600.

If all these procedures are not completed within 30 days of receipt of the approval, the foreign company's certificate of approval must be returned and, presumably, the applicant would be required to go through the entire procedure once again. However, in practice it appears that AIC authorities will tolerate any reasonable excuse for delayed completion of the formalities.

Registration certificate
In approximately 10 days to two weeks for applications filed in Beijing and several weeks for applications filed in other cities, the local office of AIC will deliver a Registration Certificate of Foreign Enterprises' Permanent Office in China, which is issued by the State Administration of Industry and Commerce and lists the name of the office, address, name of the representative, nationality, the business scope of the enterprise and the period of validity of the certificate. The registration certificate is normally valid for one year. According to article 11 of the SAIC Measures, in order to renew the company's registration certificate, the enterprise must submit an annual report in Chinese on the situation of its business activities in China, as well as a request for extension and surrender the previous year's certificate to the local office of AIC.

Other registration formalities
Immediately after SAIC issues the registration certificate, the designated representative and other foreign personnel are required to comply with several additional formalities.

First, in accordance with article 6 of the Provisional Regulations, all foreign personnel are required to apply for residence permits from the local office of the Public Security Bureau, where the representative registers both his business and residential addresses and is issued an identity card. At the same time, the representative can apply to the Public Security Bureau for a multiple entry visa, which is generally valid up to six months.

Secondly, in accordance with article 9 of the Provisional Regulations, foreign personnel must register for personal income tax purposes and the representative office must be registered for corporate income tax purposes with the Foreign Tax Collection Office of the local Municipal Tax Bureau.

Finally, the representative and other foreign personnel must also register with the local office of the Customs Administration and open a bank account with the local office of the Bank of China or another local bank approved by the State Administration of Exchange Control.

Permissible activities
Article 3 of the SAIC Measures states that 'resident representative offices of foreign enterprises should be representative offices that engage in non-direct business activities', and article 15 provides for penalties including fines of up to Rmb20,000 (US$7,150) and suspension of business activities for representative offices 'directly engaging in business activities'. However, it is not at all clear what is meant by 'directly engaging in business activities'. It would appear that the intention of these regulations is to ensure that foreign representative offices act on behalf of their foreign-based head offices. This is made even less clear by recent tax regulations which impose the Consolidated Industrial and Commercial Tax and income taxes on the business, commission and fee income of such representative offices.

Registering as a contractor or subcontractor
The regulatory framework
The applicable legal requirements and procedures for registration as a contractor or subcontractor in China are set forth in the Notice concerning the Registration of Foreign Companies that come to China to Engage in Cooperative Development and Contract Projects (the 'Registration Notice'), promulgated by the State Administration for Industry and Commerce (SAIC) on 12 March 1983 and put into force on 1 April 1983. After adoption of the measures set forth in the Registration Notice, it was quickly felt that some clarification was required and the Explanations regarding the Notice Concerning the Registration of Foreign Companies that come to China to Engage in Cooperative Development and Contract Projects (the 'Explanations') were promulgated on 4 May 1983. While the Registration Notice and Explanations are generally thought to apply principally to companies engaged in offshore oil exploration, they apply by their terms to any foreign company which has contract work to be performed in China.

Previously, many Chinese enterprises that signed contracts with foreign companies advised those companies that there was no need to comply with the registration procedures set forth in the Notice. Recently this attitude has changed, since the Bank of China now informally applies a rule that all contract payments made by Chinese entities to unregistered foreign companies that are not related to the sale of goods will be treated as payments of passive income subject to China's withholding tax. The foreign contractor must, therefore, either show that it has a registered establishment in China or that the particular payments are either for services performed outside China or not subject to witholding tax for some other reason. This new rule has forced a number of companies with contracts for work in China to comply with the registration rules.

The registration requirement

According to section 2 of the Registration Notice, foreign contractors are supposed to register with AIC by presenting the approval document for their contract issued by the State Council or the department authorised by the State Council, a copy of the signed contract, a certificate of incorporation, an application and a list of the names of foreign subcontractors, subcontract project items and the names of the principal personnel to be resident in China. SAIC upon receipt of these documents issues a Business Licence of the People's Republic of China in the name of the foreign contractor. Registration fees are collected in accordance with the fees charged to equity joint ventures, except in the area of offshore petroleum exploration where there is a reduction during the exploration phase. The business licence, unlike the registration certificate for a representative office, is valid for the period of the underlying contract and therefore may be for many years.

Subcontractors

The registration procedures for subcontractors are very similar. The subcontractor must produce a copy of the subcontract, translated into Chinese, a certifying document issued by an appropriate Chinese enterprise, and an Application Form for Registration of Foreign Enterprises, which is a printed form prepared by AIC. The certifying document required by the Registration Notice serves the purpose of ensuring that the requirements of Chinese law that Chinese enterprises be given preference in the awarding of subcontract work are complied with in full. Subcontractors are issued a Registration Certificate for Foreign Enterprises undertaking Subcontract Projects in China and, as in the case of the contractor, such a certificate is valid for the estimated period necessary to perform the subcontract. Any foreign company intending to perform subcontracting work in China must go through the required registration procedures, regardless of the duration of such company's stay in China. In cases of extremely short subcontracts, the subcontractor may authorise the contractor to perform the registration procedures on its behalf. Each registration is applicable only to the subcontract registered.

Section 3 of the Explanations states that 'in the event that a foreign subcontractor has finished performing one subcontract and signs a new subcontract immediately thereafter, it shall go through the registration procedures again'. However, if a subcontract is extended, such extension may be registered as an amendment to the original registration and the subcontract need not be reregistered.

Contractors and subcontractors are required to register with the tax authorities under the Income Tax Law of the People's Republic of China concerning Foreign Enterprises and must also register with the Customs Administration.

The role of the Chinese host

The attitude of China's bureaucracy in regard to the registration of foreign companies provides an interesting insight into China's open door policy. Chinese companies that are requested to act as 'host' organisations for representative offices only do so reluctantly; it must clearly benefit the host to have permanent representa-tion of the foreign company in China. The reason for the reluctance of Chinese enterprises to serve as hosts arises from the fact that, within the Chinese system, the host carries a continuing responsibility for the actions within China of the guest company. If another Chinese unit or company has a problem with the registered foreign company, they will most frequently contact the host organisation to assist in the resolution of the problem. Contractors and subcontractors are under the same system. Contractors are the responsibility of the Chinese corporation with whom they contract. Subcontractors also have a host, but normally the host is the contractor, and indirectly the Chinese host of the contractor becomes the host for all the contractors' subcontractors. Thus, while the door is open, since over 900 companies have registered representative offices and there are about half that number of registered contractors and subcontractors, each of these foreign companies has a Chinese unit directly or indirectly responsible for its activities in China.

The forms of foreign investment

The possibility that foreign business concerns could participate in China's economic growth through direct and indirect equity investments was first rumoured in the press during 1978. By the end of 1984, just six years later, more than 3,195 Chinese-foreign equity and contractual joint ventures had been approved by the Chinese government. Of this number 931 were equity joint ventures with committed investment totalling US$1.43 billion, 31 were offshore oil exploration, development and exploitation contracts with total committed investment of approximately US$2.42 billion, and 2,213 were contractual joint ventures with a total planned investment of approximately US$4.7 billion. Additionally under the less precise headings of compensation trade and flexible business arrangements, China claimed to have concluded 1,370 compensation trade arrangements valued at US$1.34 billion, 2,412 processing arrangements earning fees of US$129 million and to have authorised 74 wholly-owned foreign enterprises with committed foreign investment of US$740 million to commence production in China. By any standards, such figures represent remarkable success in attracting foreign investment, particularly when one remembers that China had existed in self-reliant isolation for over 30 years and began the process with untrained officials and a legal system inimical to private ownership of the means of production. (See Chart opposite.)

The legal framework

The legal system of the People's Republic of China existing prior to 1979 did not provide any basis for foreign investment in China. The 1978 Constitution described the country as 'a socialist state of the dictatorship of the proletariat' with two kinds of ownership of the means of production: 'socialist ownership by the whole people, and socialist collective ownership by the working people'. Nor did the system of state-owned enterprises, through which China implemented its ownership by the whole people of the means of production, offer a vehicle into which foreign investment could be readily assimilated.

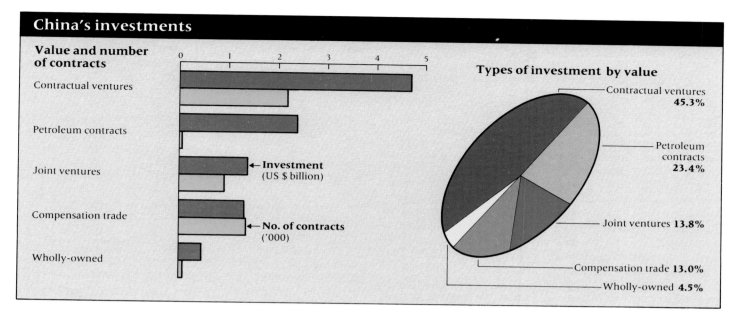

China's investments

Value and number of contracts

Contractual ventures
Petroleum contracts
Joint ventures — Investment (US $ billion)
Compensation trade — No. of contracts ('000)
Wholly-owned

Types of investment by value

Contractual ventures **45.3%**
Petroleum contracts **23.4%**
Joint ventures **13.8%**
Compensation trade **13.0%**
Wholly-owned **4.5%**

Clearly some new category of enterprise had to be created as the legal conduit through which foreign investment could flow. The Law of the People's Republic of China on Joint Ventures using Chinese and Foreign Investment, which was adopted on 1 July 1979, created such an entity called most frequently a 'joint venture', but probably more accurately translated as a 'joint-investment enterprise' – thereby recognising the distinct and separate status of this new form of enterprise from the conventional state-owned enterprise.

The problem was larger than just a new name for a new type of enterprise, however, and quickly the Chinese realised that a host of new laws and regulations would be required in order to properly define the position of this new type of enterprise within the Chinese economic system. Tax laws, accounting rules, foreign exchange regulations, labour regulations and rules on registration would all be necessary. Such a massive legislative programme could only take place gradually, however, if major errors were to be avoided.

In order to make progress with its foreign investment programme and to avoid waiting on the slow process of drafting a complete legislative framework, the Chinese authorities adopted three strategems: (1) adopting new laws and regulations in a piecemeal fashion, correcting prior mistakes as they went along, (2) trying out new proposed laws and regulations through internal guidelines that are made available to Chinese officials responsible for conducting foreign investment negotiations or on occasion adopting such new laws only in Special Economic Zones as an experiment, and (3) adopting model forms or precedents of foreign investment contracts that can be used with minor variations for many different investments. Although only the published laws and regulations are legally binding, the bureaucratic structure of the Chinese government and the foreign investment approval process are such that the unpublished guidelines and model forms are treated by Chinese negotiators with much the same respect as law.

Thus, the practical framework for the regulation of foreign investment in China is much more than just China's published laws and regulations. It also includes future laws that are expected to be published (but appear only as 'internal' guidelines available to Chinese negotiators); it includes legislation from the Special Economic Zones, which is applied by 'analogy'; and it includes model contract forms that have been drafted or approved in prior transactions by the controlling ministry or government agency. A textual analysis of only China's published laws and regulations therefore would lead one to believe that there is both more uncertainty and greater flexibility within the system that in fact exists once one reaches the negotiating table.

Negotiating toward the future

That the legal framework for investing in China is necessarily broader than its published laws and regulations is a product of the developing nature of the legal system itself. Although the 1978 Constitution did not provide for foreign investment with Chinese economic organisations, a number of joint ventures were signed, approved and implemented by the Chinese government under that Constitution. In time, the 1982 Constitution retroactively corrected the earlier deficiency by specifically stating that foreign investment is a permitted economic activity and that the law of the People's Republic of China protects the lawful rights and interests of investors. While Western-trained lawyers frequently queried their Chinese counterparts on the legal basis for foreign investment prior to the 1982 Constitution, the problem seemed of little practical relevance since Chinese negotiators knew that changes in the Constitution, along with a number of new laws covering foreign investment, would be promulgated in due course as part of the evolving open door policy.

Chinese negotiators that apply this broader legal framework in the process of contract negotiation are merely trying to make today's agreement accord with what they feel certain will be tomorrow's law, thereby avoiding future disputes over changed circumstances. The foreign negotiator, however, normally does not have the same insight into future legal developments nor understands why today's transaction should be shaped or inhibited (frequently to the foreign investor's detriment) by some vague, unpublished statement of policy, which may possibly be enacted into law in the future.

The effect of published law on investment

The absence of clearly defined, published laws does inhibit investment in China. Equity joint ventures are a case in point. From 1979 to 1983, China completed less than 200 equity joint-venture contracts. In 1984, foreign and Chinese partners completed 741 equity joint ventures. While other factors also played a role, the promulgation on 20 September 1983 of the Regulations for the Implementation of the Law of the People's Republic of China on Joint Ventures using Chinese and Foreign Investment (the 'JV Implementing Regulations') and the issuance of the Model Contract for Joint Ventures using Chinese and Foreign Investment by the Ministry of Foreign Economic Relations and Trade (the 'Model Contract', see Appendix) in early 1984 were the most significant contributing factors to this enormous expansion in the number of equity joint ventures. With the detailed rules of the JV Implementing Regulations, both the Chinese and foreign negotiator were operating for the first time within the same published guidelines, which each could read and understand. Having a published set of regulations avoided the distrust created by the Chinese negotiator having to repeatedly describe an unwritten Chinese 'policy' as the law, which when announced at the negotiating table was frequently contrary to the interests or desires of the foreign investor. The Model Contract put the JV Implementating Regulations into a usable form; the foreign negotiator knew from the outset what his Chinese counterpart could agree to by way of contract language, so negotiating time was spent on hammering out the additional clauses and articles that the foreign investor wanted or needed to protect his interest, rather than wasting endless amounts of time on the wording of less important provisions.

The other forms of investment in China, with the exception of offshore petroleum investments, do not have the benefit of a developed statutory scheme or model contract like equity joint ventures. The problem remains for such investments that the Chinese negotiator knows the policy as to what is permitted and the foreign negotiator knows what he wants. The two sides must come together at the negotiating table, but it is necessarily a difficult process. It is made even more difficult by the fact that Chinese negotiators are generally unaware of international practice and therefore ask for terms and conditions unheard of in the rest of the world.

China has developed during the past seven years a number of standard forms for business transactions to absorb foreign investment and technical expertise. The following description of these forms differentiates between what is required by the published laws of the People's Republic of China and the broader framework applied by Chinese negotiators in the negotiating process.

Equity joint ventures

The equity joint venture in China has the most complete set of published laws and regulations regarding its creation and operation. The Joint Venture Law of 1 July 1979 sets forth the general principles governing the

establishment and operation of joint-venture enterprises and served as necessary enabling legislation legitimising the numerous joint-venture contract negotiations already in progress at the time of its promulgation. The Joint Venture Law's provisions deal with approval procedures, capital structure, management, profit distributions, labour relations and dispute settlement, among other important issues. The JV Implementing Regulations take the 15 articles of the Joint Venture Law and expand on them in great detail while correcting some errors made in prior legislation.

In attempting to fill in the gaps found in the Joint Venture Law, the Chinese authorities adopted a piecemeal aproach, promulgating a series of more detailed regulations to address specific issues or problem areas. The joint-venture registration regulations (Measures for the Registration of Joint Ventures using Chinese and Foreign Investment), promulgated on 26 July 1980, provide detailed provisions for the registration of joint ventures and the procedures for obtaining a business licence. The joint-venture labour management regulations (Regulations on Labour Management in Joint Ventures using Chinese and Foreign Investment), promulgated on the same date as the registration regulation, provide guidance on issues relating to employment, dismissal and resignation of joint-venture employees, the establishment of labour unions for joint-venture workers, and other related matters. The labour management regulations themselves were found to lack adequate detail, and on 19 January 1984, China adopted more detailed rules in the Provision for the Implementation of the Regulations on Labour Management in Joint Ventures using Chinese and Foreign Investment. There are also separate rules for foreign exchange transactions by joint ventures and their employees, rules for the extension of loans to joint ventures by the Bank of China (Provisional Measures for Providing Loans to Joint Ventures using Chinese and Foreign Investment by the Bank of China), regulations governing the use of land (Provisional Regulations governing the Use of Land for Construction by Joint Ventures using Chinese and Foreign Investment), a special tax law applicable only to joint ventures (The Income Tax Law of the People's Republic of China concerning Joint Ventures using Chinese and Foreign Investment) and special customs rules for joint ventures (Regulations concerning the Supervision and Control, and the Levy and Exemption of Duties on Imported and Exported Goods of Chinese-Foreign Joint Ventures).

In all there are approximately 150 pages of published statute law and regulations relating to equity joint ventures. Scholarly commentators have generally found the published laws and regulations to be unobjectionable and some have gone as far as to publicly applaud the draftsmens' efforts.

Yet no one who has completed an equity joint venture in China would claim that it was an easy process, no matter how much law there is. Examining some of the important issues encountered by investors attempting to complete equity joint ventures in China will make this clear.

Organisation and status

In the establishment of a joint venture in China, one of

the first surprises encountered by the foreign side is the fact the Chinese investor is not legally the government of China. While article 1 of the Joint Venture Law as early as 1979 defined the 'Chinese party' as 'Chinese companies, enterprises or other economic entities', it was generally thought that all Chinese entities were nothing more than instrumentalities of the government and therefore must be backed by and have authority to speak for the government itself. This notion was not so strange, since in fact many Chinese negotiators schooled in the Chinese system before the open door policy thought of themselves as governmental bureaucrats that spoke for and represented the government. It was a shock to both sides to learn that in the area of foreign investment, both the foreign company *and the Chinese company* had limited resources and were unable to speak on behalf of their respective governments in the contract documents.

Joint-venture contracts are signed in the names of Chinese corporations, which may be either national-level corporations reporting to and under the supervision of a central government ministry, or local companies that are under the local provincial or municipal government. Most often such companies have constituent documents constituting their corporate charter allowing them to engage in certain specified types of activities. Moreover, such companies can also have a stated amount of capital, which in some cases is the amount of funds that the state has decided to put at their disposal to back their commercial activities, and in other cases, where the new company is an amalgamation of a number of existing state-owned plants or factories, the original amount of capital construction funds paid out by the state in establishing such plants or factories.

That the Chinese party is not the state itself means many things: first, the contract documents do not bind any administrative portion of the government. Thus, the contract cannot effectively provide for tax or customs relief, since these matters by law are vested in the Ministry of Finance and the Customs Administration. Secondly, the joint venture and both parties to it will be regulated by the governmental bureaucracy in charge of regulating the industry in which the venture does business. While the Chinese party may be well informed about the policy of the relevant ministry to which it reports, it does not control that policy. And if its influence in its own ministry is limited, its influence with other ministries or departments of the government is non-existent.

Therefore, the joint-venture contract creates an entity that must fend for itself within the Chinese governmental structure of approvals and permissions; the Chinese counterpart can assist the joint venture in obtaining necessary approvals, permissions or incentives, but can neither guarantee their availability nor assure the foreign side that the regulatory system will not change.

The Joint Venture Law provides that joint ventures formed pursuant to its provisions should take the form of a limited liability company to exist for a stated duration to be agreed upon in the contract. Joint ventures are created by the parties agreeing upon the text of a joint-venture contract and articles of association, which are submitted to the Ministry of Foreign Economic Relations and Trade (MOFERT) or, within the monetary limits set by the State Council, submitted to the appropriate local government, ministry or bureau for approval. If the contract is approved, MOFERT issues a certificate of approval. Once approved, the joint-venture company must register with the local bureau of AIC in order to receive its business licence. The date of the business licence is the official commencement of the corporate life of the company.

Contract and articles of association
The JV Implementing Regulations specify certain matters which must be covered in the joint-venture contract. In addition to such standard matters as the names of the parties, their addresses, the name of the joint-venture company, and its address, the JV Implementing Regulations require that the contract contain provisions describing the purpose of the venture, its scope and scale of production, the total amount of investment, registered capital, the method of contributing capital, the composition of the Board of Directors, the responsibilities and powers of the management staff, the main production equipment and technology to be utilised by the venture, the means of purchasing raw materials and selling finished products, the ratio of domestic and export sales, principles for finance, accounting and auditing of the venture, matters concerning labour, the duration of the venture and the procedure for its termination and liquidation, liabilities for breach of contract and the method for settling disputes.

Similarly, the JV Implementing Regulations contain a list of matters which must be dealt with in the articles of association. In addition to having to repeat the name, purpose, scope of operation and term of the joint venture, the articles of association must contain detailed provisions relating to the total amount of investment required for the proposed project and the registered capital of the company, and stipulations concerning the assignment of capital and the sharing of risks and profits. The articles of association, as the company's charter, also must contain detailed provisions on the formation and responsibilities of the Board of Directors, the company's management and their removal and replacement. While several of these matters repeat what appears in the joint-venture contract, repetition is required by law.

Fortunately, the task of negotiating a joint-venture contract and articles has been simplified by the issuance of the Model Contract form and Model Articles of Association by the Foreign Investment Bureau under MOFERT. While these forms leave much to be desired, they do establish a framework for the negotiations and address all of the matters which are required by law to be included in the contract and articles.

Agreements and contracts
It is important to note that the principal document which creates a joint venture is the joint-venture contract and not the joint-venture 'agreement'. The JV Implementing Regulations contemplate that the parties may enter into a joint-venture agreement on some of the main principles and provisions of the joint venture before taking the final step of negotiating the definitive joint-venture contract. Only the contract (and not the agreement) can receive a MOFERT approval that permits the registration of a joint venture company. Interestingly, this distinction between

'agreements' and 'contracts' exists in other areas of commercial contracts in China, and a foreign company is always best advised to treat sceptically the binding nature of a document labelled as an agreement.

Limited liability

The entity that is created once the joint-venture contract and articles are negotiated and approved is a limited liability company. Article 4 of the Joint Venture Law and article 19 of the JV Implementing Regulations make clear that the company is to be a limited liability company and the parties are only liable up to the amount of capital for which they subscribe. The straightforwardness of these provisions becomes somewhat blurred at the negotiating table, however. The Chinese side will frequently take the position that if the company needs capital in excess of the amount of registered capital subscribed by the parties, then obviously the joint venture should borrow such amount and the parent companies should either lend or guarantee their respective portions of the loan. This concept of parental responsibility for the welfare of the new child sometimes is the source of humorous exchanges between foreign and Chinese negotiators as to when the joint venture should grow-up and stand alone.

The Bank of China's rules for lending to joint ventures, for example, specifically provide that the joint-venture company must either provide a guarantee from its parent companies or a pledge of collateral security. As China has no mortgage law, except in the Special Economic Zones, or other laws permitting the creation of security interests, the most common solution is for the shareholder to guarantee the venture's loans – although if the investment is one genuinely desired by the Chinese partner to the venture, the Chinese partner on its own can guarantee the loan without recourse to the foreign partner.

Shareholders' role

Another rather unusual fact about Chinese joint ventures is that there is no role for the shareholders in the management of the venture. There are no annual shareholder meetings or any requirement that any matter be referred to the shareholders for decision, other than in the standard arbitration clause where all disputes are to be resolved 'amicably' by the parties. Instead of the shareholders playing a management role, the members of the Board of Directors who are appointed directly by the parties to the venture are supposed to represent both the interests of the company and the interests of the shareholder that appointed them.

Stock certificates

Yet another unusual feature of the entity created by the joint-venture contract and articles of association is that Chinese joint-venture companies cannot issue stock certificates as evidence of the ownership of corporate capital. Instead, a Chinese venture is supposed to issue an 'investment certificate' once the investment provided for in the joint-venture contract has been injected. The investment certificates, which are only issued once a Chinese accountant has issued a report verifying that the contributions have in fact been made, lists the name of the joint venture, the date of establishment of the venture, the names of the partners, the investment contributed and the date of contribution, and the date of issuance of the investment certificate. Although there is no definitive explanation of why investment certificates are used rather than stock, the most likely explanation appears to be that Chinese law does not favour the idea of interests in Chinese joint ventures being negotiable instruments. The JV Implementing Regulations reinforce this view in the provisions which require pre-emptive rights in regard to transfers of investment certificates and require the consent of the other party for any transfer of an interest in the venture.

A solution to the non-transferability of investment certificates has been to put the certificates into and make the investment through a single-purpose foreign holding company, the shares of which could be transferred freely without encountering the pre-emptive rights problem. Recently, however, both MOFERT and Chinese negotiators at the lower levels have been insisting that the ownership of such holding companies be disclosed and that transfers of the shares of the holding company be approved by the Chinese party to the venture and MOFERT.

However, recently Chinese negotiators have been talking about selling stock in their own enterprises, and in Shanghai a few such corporate securities have been issued. If the issuance of stock becomes more commonplace in China, the restrictions on the transferability of joint-venture investment certificates will probably disappear.

Corporate scope

The scope of a joint-venture company is also much narrower than the modern notion of a Western corporation, which by its constituent documents is most often formed for any lawful business purpose. A joint-venture enterprise in China is formed for a single specific purpose, such as constructing and operating a hotel on a specific site, or operating a specific service enterprise or factory. Moreover, a general purpose such as cooperation in a particular industry has not been acceptable on the grounds that the approving authorities were unable to determine the feasibility of the venture, unless a specific project was proposed and evaluated. In the initial ventures approved under the Joint Venture Law the Chinese negotiators were even reluctant to include incidental powers related to the performance of the stated primary objective, such as the power to sue and be sued, open bank accounts, make contracts, etc., but this reluctance has been overcome in more recent years. Any amendment or expansion of the venture's original purpose has to be approved by the same formalities as the original joint-venture documentation.

Capital contributions

The Joint Venture Law specifically allows the contribution of capital either in cash or in kind. In kind capital contributions may include industrial property rights and know-how, land usage rights, buildings, plant, equipment and trademarks. Capital contributions in kind (other than the site) are to be appraised, and agreed upon values specified in the joint-venture contract and articles of association. In accordance with the ratio of the mutually agreed contribution values, the parties are to share in the venture's profits, risks and losses.

Appraisal of in kind contributions

Appraising capital contributions has proved quite difficult, partially due to inherent problems of the Chinese economic system and partly due to internal guidelines applied by the Chinese to the process. If the Chinese contribution consists of existing plant and equipment, the carried cost for such property in the state-owned enterprise method of accounting is seemingly difficult to compute, either due to an absence of accurate records or a reluctance to produce those records for foreign inspection. Moreover, since the assets of state-owned enterprises are owned by the government, there is no free market mechanism for their transfer, and market values cannot therefore be determined.

The Chinese side in a negotiation would always prefer to value its plant and equipment at original capital cost less depreciation funds held by the Chinese unit, since this is (or should be) the amount shown on the Chinese enterprise's books. Such an appraisal method does not, however, take into account the actual state of the plant and equipment or its value to the proposed new venture.

Pursuant to the JV Implementing Regulations it is now possible to appoint a third party agreed upon by the joint-venture parties to evaluate the respective worth of each party's contribution. While this method of appraisal has only been used on a few occasions to date, with the increasing sophistication of Chinese accountants and their willingness to work with foreign accountants and appraisers it should become more common in the future.

The most common procedure to date for determining equity shares has been to proceed exactly in the reverse of the method contemplated by the Joint Venture Law and JV Implementing Regulations. Rather than appraising assets to be contributed and setting the investment ratio based on a comparison of values, the first letter of intent or memorandum of agreement states what the investment ratio should be and the types of assets the parties will contribute. For example, the memorandum of agreement may call for a 50/50 joint venture with the foreign side contributing all necessary foreign equipment, technology and raw materials, and with the Chinese side contributing a building and an initial inventory of locally available raw materials. After exhaustive negotiations to determine the true market value of the foreign capital items, during which the Chinese act more as buyers than joint investors, the Chinese contribution is then mutually assumed to be of an equal value in order to maintain the 50/50 investment ratio. Occasionally this method leads to out-of-date plant and equipment in China being appraised at values higher than new plant and equipment in the investor's own country. In this case, the negotiations can occasionally shift capital items from the foreign side to the Chinese side, if the Chinese party has the necessary foreign exchange; but still the touchstone of the appraisal is the market value of the foreign items provided, and not the true value in China of Chinese supplied items. The JV Implementing Regulations provide, for example, that in kind equipment contributions by the foreign side 'shall not be higher than the current international market price for similar equipment . . . ', which is fair, but there is no similar restriction on the value of in kind contributions of equipment from China.

The problem of evaluating the true value of Chinese contributions can be partially remedied by providing for cash capital contributions, with which the new company buys the necessary machinery and equipment. This solution does not help much in the case of buildings, since there is not a free market in real estate, nor does it help when the Chinese side wants to sell an existing factory to the new joint venture.

Although the negotiation of capital contribution values is frequently the subject of acrimonious debate, it seems the only alternative until some rational and uniform method of appraising Chinese plant and equipment is developed by the Chinese for their own enterprises. As Chinese state-owned enterprises are converted to the profit system, some progress should be made in this field. Recently MOFERT has indicated that buildings and capital goods of an existing state-owned enterprise that has been run at a profit should be appraised based on the value to be realised by the venture from the use of such productive assets. Specifically, the average profit of the state-owned enterprise over the three previous years of operation should be taken into account when appraising the value of the plant and equipment to be contributed.

Another valuable step in resolving this problem is that several Chinese consulting companies are now preparing their own preliminary feasibility studies before approaching foreign investors. Such Chinese preliminary feasibility studies are required by the JV Implementing Regulations as a precondition to project negotiations and will help to ascribe a value to both parties' respective contributions, thereby providing a starting point for the negotiations.

Value of land

The valuation of land usage rights has also proven to be a difficult problem in the past. For political reasons, ventures cannot own land, but may be granted either the right to use the land by the local government or pay rent to the local government for its use. The Joint Venture Law indicates that the value of contributed land is to be determined unilaterally by the Chinese side. At the time of the Joint Venture Law's promulgation, it was stated that the Chinese government would soon publish additional regulations defining the value of various types of land. In fact, such regulations were adopted as internal guidelines in 1980 and various investors were told that the land usage rates stipulated by the government had to be followed. The Provisional Regulations concerning the use of Land for Construction by Joint Ventures using Chinese and Foreign Investment have now become available, although by the Regulations' own provisions it is an internal document not to be shown to foreigners. These regulations provide that the annual land use fee shall not be less than Rmb5 nor more than Rmb300 per square metre per year. The actual amount is negotiable. Starting first in the Special Economic Zones, there has been a trend over the past several years for local governments to adopt and sometimes publish standard land rates. The rates vary throughout the country and vary within each locality based upon the purpose for which the land is to be used, but fortunately the trend across the country has been for land use rates to come down in price rather than escalate. Many local areas are now publishing their standard land use fees in promotional brochures and the Shekou Industrial Zone near Hong Kong has published its rates as a law.

The capital value of the contribution of land usage rights is to be determined by multiplying the area of the site times the length of the joint venture. When the venture exceeds 15 years, it has been possible to limit the valuation of the capital contribution of land to the annual standard land use rate times 15 years. In this calculation, no discount for present value is given.

The justification for what is frequently considered the high value placed on the land is that the local government has to spend considerable sums on new infrastructure to support the venture and is therefore entitled to be compensated for the infrastructure costs. It is interesting to note that if the Chinese side contributes the land, what happens in effect is that the Chinese side pays the land use fee out of its share of the profits.

The Provisional Regulations, although still a starting position, are no longer mandatory and recent experience indicates that the subject is negotiable, depending upon the local government's support for the proposed venture.

The JV Implementing Regulations have done much to formalise prior practice in regard to land use. Specifically, local governments are now required to adopt standard land use fees and file them with MOFERT for the record. Once agreed upon by contract, land use fees are not supposed to be adjusted for five years, and thereafter only adjusted every three years based upon the development of the local economy and current supply and demand.

Technology contributions

The contribution of technology from the foreign investor's perspective remains attractive and is sometimes used to balance high land values. Regulations on technology in the Shenzhen Economic Zone near Hong Kong specify that the amount of the foreign side's capital contribution attributed to technology cannot exceed 20 per cent of the total foreign contribution. Although a similar provision does not appear in the national regulations on technology, the Shenzhen rule appears to be applied by analogy in other parts of China. Thus the instances in which the foreign side's contribution to capital is solely technology are very limited.

The Chinese concern that the technology be truly advanced is reflected in the Joint Venture Law and JV Implementing Regulations. The Draconian nature of the penalty involved, if the technology is not up to world standard, has discouraged some investors from contributing technology as capital; such investors have opted to enter into licence agreements under which the venture pays for the technology, and the agreement specifies the extent of the licensor's liability.

The JV Implementing Regulations provide that any technology contributed must either be capable of producing new, urgently needed products in China or products for export, or improve productivity, or be capable of saving raw materials, fuel or power. Moreover, the foreign investor contributing technology has to provide copies of the relevant patents and trademark certificates, as well as documentation supporting the mutually agreed upon evaluation. MOFERT or the lower-level approving authority must specifically review and approve such in kind contributions.

Registered capital and total investment

The JV Implementing Regulations distinguish between registered capital and total investment. The registered capital of a joint venture is the total of the capital contributions to be made by the parties, either in cash or in kind, and is verified by a Chinese accountant who issues a verification report that provides the basis for the company's issuance of its investment certificates. Total investment, on the other hand, is the total amount of investment including loans required to be invested to achieve the stated scale of production specified in the joint-venture contract.

The preferred position of many Chinese negotiators is to have registered capital and total investment equal to each other, since in this case the two investors provide all the funds needed to develop the project. Such contribution eliminates the need for bank financing during the capital construction period and may entirely eliminate the requirement for any debt during the term of the venture.

Capitalists, who are more used to leverage and the benefits of debt finance, generally prefer to limit registered capital and wish to borrow whatever excess funds are required. In industrial joint ventures, the most common debt to equity ratios are initially 60/40 to 70/30. Because of the absence of mortgage or collateral security laws in most of China, other than in the Special Economic Zones, such debt requires a guaranty or guaranties from the sponsors of the project. While it is still the position of most Chinese corporations that debt like other risks in the venture should be shared by the parties in accordance with the capital contribution ratio, in several recent cases the Chinese side has agreed to arrange on its own the necessary guaranties to finance the difference between total investment and registered capital. Previously a number of hotel deals were done on 100 per cent debt financing, but this is now becoming increasingly rare since the Bank of China expects that the hotel projects which require the bank's support should have at least 30 per cent equity. Interestingly, the Bank frequently refuses to include the value of contributed land as part of the equity when calculating the amount of debt the project can support.

Management and control

The Joint Venture Law and JV Implementing Regulations provide that the venture is to be managed by a Board of Directors, which is to be the 'highest authority' of the venture, the composition of which is to be specified in the joint-venture contract and articles of association. The chairman must be Chinese, and the vice-chairman a foreign-appointed director. The Board of Directors is empowered, according to the Joint Venture Law, to discuss and determine all important issues concerning the joint venture. While the amendment of the articles of association, decisions on termination of the venture, approvals for the increase or assignment of registered capital and the merger of the joint venture must be approved by the Board unanimously, the articles of association may state the required number of votes necessary to approve any other matter.

The Board of Directors must consist of at least three directors, although normally the number is larger, and the distribution of directors among the parties is to be based upon the parties' respective capital contributions. A director's term of office is for four years, but a director may be reappointed by the party that originally appointed him. The Board is required to meet at least once a year, although more frequent meetings, particularly during the construction and start-up phases, are common. The chairman of the Board calls all meetings of the Board, although the JV Implementing Regulations provide that he 'may' convene an interim meeting at the request of one-third of the directors; most commonly the articles make the calling of such a meeting mandatory. Unless increased by the articles of association, the quorum for a Board meeting is two-thirds of all directors, who must be present in person or by proxy.

The chairman of the Board is by law the legal representative of the joint venture. What in fact this means, no one is sure, including the Chinese draftsmen who have attempted to explain the meaning. Most frequently this position is said to be necessary in order to give the chairman the status to deal with the various departments of the Chinese government on behalf of the venture.

Management

Below the Board of Directors, offices for a general manager, deputy general manager, chief engineer, chief accountant and auditor are referred to in the Joint Venture Law, together with the stipulation that the positions of the general manager and deputy general manager shall be assumed by the separate parties to the venture, just as each party appoints its own designated number of directors. Article 39 of the JV Implementing Regulations confers considerable power on the general manager:

'The general manager shall implement the various resolutions adopted at the Board meetings and shall organise and conduct the day-to-day operation and management of the joint venture. The general manager shall, within the limits of authority vested in him by the Board, represent the joint venture in external affairs, appoint and dismiss his subordinates within the joint venture, and exercise other responsibilities and rights as authorised by the Board.'

Board members may also serve as managers or deputy managers of the venture, but any such appointment must be approved by the Board of Directors as a whole. The manager and deputy manager may not participate by law in commercial competition with the joint venture itself.

What is not apparent in the Joint Venture Law or JV Implementing Regulations is the system of managers and deputy managers that appears in most joint-venture contracts. The management staff is effectively doubled by the Chinese requirement that each foreign-appointed manager have a Chinese deputy to act as his counterpart. Since the vast majority of the labour force will be Chinese, the system of deputies makes some sense in order to ensure that the foreign manager's instructions are carried out by the workforce. The deputy system, however, has two faults: first, the Chinese negotiators would prefer to have each manager's decision arrived at jointly by the manager and his deputy; second, the deputy system undermines the authority of the appointed managers, since the workforce naturally tends to follow the instructions of the Chinese deputy who will remain in China long after the expatriate advisor has returned home.

The deputy system is symptomatic of another problem experienced in operating joint ventures. Too many decisions are made by committees, where equal numbers of foreign investor appointees and Chinese appointees are supposed to negotiate and decide all issues. While such a management principle corresponds to the much valued Chinese maxim of equality in all things, it is a difficult and time-consuming way to run a business. This is particularly true since Chinese members of lower-level committees do not wish to make decisions unless they have instructions from their own higher-level authorities, which in turn means many decisions of a routine nature are referred to the Board of Directors.

The Board of Directors is not the easiest place to make management decisions either. First, the Board is supposed to act for the benefit of the investing parties when handling any important matter, rather than deciding issues in the interest of the venture itself. Secondly, on the Chinese side there is always a great reluctance to go further than or act on any matter outside the basic premises of the joint-venture contract, since Chinese bureaucrats know that under their system such actions should first be approved in writing by higher authorities. Thirdly, decisions on important matters are supposed to be unanimous. Board meetings can last several days, even when the parties thought the agenda and issues were settled before the meeting. Issues that are not decided are held over until the next meeting, and those that are decided are minuted in the vaguest of language in order to avoid problems with higher authorities that monitor the venture's progress.

Recent experience indicates that where the venture has been thoroughly and professionally negotiated prior to signing the contractual documents, management and control of the venture is far less acrimonious. Moreover, with greater experience in the operation of joint ventures, Chinese Board members and managers at the day-to-day operations level are beginning to exhibit true professionalism.

Operational matters

The Joint Venture Law contains only a few scant provisions relating to operational matters. The venture's production and operation plans are to be filed with the authorities concerned and implemented through economic contracts. The venture is supposed to give priority to the sourcing of its raw materials and supplies in China, although it may also purchase such items from abroad if it has the foreign exchange to do so. The venture is supposed to export its products, but may also distribute them on the local market.

One of the reasons why there were few joint ventures before 1984 was that the Joint Venture Law's provisions on how the venture would operate within the Chinese domestic economic system were too vague to provide any definite answers. Attempts to write detailed provisions into the contract failed because the Chinese negotiators were afraid to commit in the contract to a system that was not authorised by either law or policy guidelines.

The paucity of direction provided by the Joint Venture Law in regard to the planning for construction, purchasing of local raw materials and the sale of finished products has to a large extent been remedied by the JV Implementing Regulations. These regulations solve the interesting problem of how a profit-motivated company, the joint venture, fits into a state-planned economy like China's. The system used is that for state planning purposes: the joint venture becomes a unit of the 'department in charge', which is the parent organisation of the Chinese partner. For example, pursuant to article 54 of the JV Implementing Regulations, the joint venture must develop a capital construction plan in accordance with the plans contained in the feasibility study. This plan, once developed, becomes part of the department in charge's capital construction plan. The significance of this provision is that in China construction materials are allocated in accordance with the state plan. By including the joint venture's construction plan within that of the Chinese parent unit, the joint venture's needs for construction materials becomes a small part of the overall national planning process.

Similarly, the joint venture must work out annual production and operating plans. After being approved by the joint venture's Board of Directors, this plan is incorporated in the annual plan of the department in charge and in turn becomes part of the overall national planning process. Materials which are under planned distribution in China are allocated to the joint venture through the incorporation of its annual production plan into that of the department in charge. Other necessary materials that are not under the national distribution plan can be purchased at state enterprise prices from the commercial departments, local markets or, if necessary, imported.

Once finished products are produced, the joint venture sells its products in much the same way. If the product is one that is under planned distribution in China, the output is incorporated in the annual plan of the department in charge and the national economic planning mechanism handles its distribution by allocating the output to specified end-users. If the product is one that is handled exclusively by the commercial departments in China, the commercial department will enter into annual purchase contracts with the joint venture to purchase its output. Output that is either not under planned distribution or handled by the commercial department, or output in excess of the planned amounts, can be sold by the joint venture itself through its own sales efforts.

In purchasing goods of Chinese origin, the joint venture is under constraints. Gold, silver, platinum, petroleum, coal and timber used by the venture in the production of export products are priced at international market levels (rather than the lower Chinese prices) and paid for in foreign currency or renminbi. More troublesome is that when the joint venture needs materials which China presently exports, it must negotiate a price based on the international market price and pay foreign currency for the purchase. Because balancing the foreign exchange account is frequently difficult, the added burden of paying for such commodities in foreign exchange frequently is a hardship to the foreign investor. The Chinese authorities justify this by pointing out that if the joint venture had not purchased the product, it

would have been exported anyway so it is only fair that the price be paid in foreign exchange. Other than the above, joint ventures in general pay the same prices for their raw materials as state-owned enterprises.

Treating the joint venture as a subsidiary organisation of the department in charge has both advantages and disadvantages to the joint venture. The most obvious advantage is necessity: without such a system, the joint venture would have no place in China's state-planned economy. The joint venture could not compete successfully with Chinese enterprises for raw materials in short supply, such as steel or cement, and would therefore have to import all of its supplies. The most obvious disadvantage is that the performance of the joint venture can be no better than the surrounding state-planning apparatus that must provide the raw materials for its production and take the products produced for the domestic economy.

Import and export licences are another example of the impact of the state-planning process on joint ventures. China has both an import licensing and export licensing system, under which the central government controls all imports into and exports from the country. Equipment imported as part of the foreign investor's capital contribution may be imported without an import licence, based solely on the MOFERT approval of the contract. In regard to imports necessary for the venture's annual production, an annual plan for imports is to be prepared each year, and six-month import licences are to be requested. While considerable flexibility is shown to joint ventures in allowing them to import whatever is needed, since the venture must spend its own foreign exchange, the issuance of the six-month import licences is not automatic, and the requested list may be amended or reduced. Should the venture require to import items outside its contractually stipulated scope of production, it must apply for a special import licence, the granting of which is purely discretionary.

Similarly in the case of exports, joint ventures are encouraged to export their products, but must apply for export licences in case the particular products require an export licence under state guidelines. In the textile field or other areas where China participates in a voluntary restraint programme, it cannot be assumed that the joint venture will receive all of the quota required to manufacture at its full scale of production, since the venture must compete with domestic enterprises for quota allocations.

Labour

The Joint Venture Law states that the employment and dismissal of workers should be provided for in the joint-venture contract in accordance with law. Regulations on labour management, however, extensively amplify and correct the Joint Venture Law by mandating the use of a labour contract and the formation of a joint-venture trade union, stipulating minimum wages to be paid and procedures for hiring and firing workers. The first of these regulations was adopted in 1980: Regulations on Labour Management in Joint Ventures using Chinese and Foreign Investment. Subsequently, additional rules were found to be necessary, and in January 1984, China issued the Provisions for the Implementation of the Regulations on Labour Management in Joint Ventures using Chinese and Foreign Investment.

The joint-venture contract itself normally does not contain much detail about the employment of workers or their management. Most frequently the contract contains brief provisions to the effect that labour matters will be handled in accordance with the regulations referred to above, that the workers will form a trade union, and the joint venture will enter into a labour contract with the union and pay the union 2 per cent of the venture's total wage costs to fund the union's activities. Occasionally, there is a reference to the average, overall wage to be paid by the venture for each member of the workforce.

Wages and wage payments in a joint venture are not simple matters, however, and the situation differs throughout the country as to the labour system for joint ventures. In essence, the labour regulations provide that joint ventures should pay to their workers 125 per cent of the basic wage that such workers would earn in local state-owned enterprises. Such basic wages vary throughout the country, based upon the assumed cost of living in the area and the particular skill levels of the workers involved. Fortunately, as most Chinese joint-venture partners are engaged in the same line of business as the potential joint venture, and will in the first instance probably be providing workers to the venture, Chinese negotiators are fully familiar with local labour costs. Such costs can change, however, as recently occurred when the central government decided to cut the subsidies for the agricultural markets in the central cities and therefore had to give across-the-board wage increases to city dwellers.

In addition to the basic wages paid to the workers as take-home pay, the joint venture must make an additional subsidy payment to the labour department or the unit from which the workers come in order to cover state subsidies for housing, medical care, education and retirement that are built into the state-owned enterprise system. This additional payment can be as much as 100 per cent of the basic wages.

Certain cities such as Shanghai have adopted their own labour regulations that generally conform to the national system, but add some new requirements. For example, joint ventures must participate in a state insurance fund by buying insurance for their workers, and must also contribute to a state-run pension plan. Such costs should logically reduce the amount of the payment of the subsidy to the labour department, but do not always do so.

The labour contract between the joint venture and the trade union is sometimes negotiated as part of the joint-venture documentation, but is more often negotiated after the venture is established. The negotiations, which are supposed to be between the new venture and the trade union, are almost always between the foreign and Chinese parties. While the regulations indicate that the labour contract should cover the important matters of hiring and firing workers, the number of days of holiday and general conditions of employment, the form of contract most frequently offered by the Chinese side is a document codifying existing practices in state-owned enterprises regarding labour. Some of the more unusual clauses include the right of a retiring worker to nominate a member of his family to take his place, the fact that the venture should care for the worker and handle his medical bills during his lifetime, and a system of three warnings before dismissing any worker. Fortunately, such contracts are not mandatory and the provisions of the labour regulations are more accommodating to a Western system of labour management, so that most joint ventures with detailed labour contracts have a document that clearly establishes management's ability to manage the venture, including labour matters, without undue interference either from the union or governmental authorities in charge of labour matters.

Equal pay for equal work

Although there are certainly problems with the labour regulations and labour contracts, the most constant source of frustration related to labour matters is the internal guideline to the effect that Chinese counterparts or deputy managers must receive the same basic pay as expatriate staff on the basis of equality. While article 94 of the JV Implementing Regulations handles the issue gingerly by saying that the Board of Directors will determine the salary and benefits of high-ranking management personnel, the policy guideline is firm on equal pay for equal work. No rational means for avoiding this requirement has been discovered so far, other than hard bargaining at the negotiating table. In several recent joint ventures, the Chinese side has agreed to use Hong Kong wages as a reference point for managers appointed by the Chinese side or a reduced percentage of the expatriate managers's base wage level.

Workers' bonus and welfare fund

Joint ventures are also supposed to maintain a bonus and welfare fund for workers and staff members out of the after-tax profits and before distributing net profits to the investing partners. This fund, together with the Chinese negotiating preference that bonus payments should be based on the profitability of the enterprise and be shared equally among the workers, cause consternation to investors interested in taking home their profits and promoting worker productivity. Such a system does avoid the problem of worker envy of higher-paid fellow workers, which seems the justification for the equal bonus system.

While labour problems, such as strikes and work-to-rule, do not appear to be a problem in China so far, motivating the workforce to achieve Western productivity rates is. The time-clock so far exists in only one joint venture, but a number of managers of other ventures have commented how useful such a clock would be in combating the 'iron rice bowl' philosophy of the average worker.

Foreign exchange control and banking

China's foreign exchange regulations contain specific provisions relating to joint ventures. All receipts of a joint venture in foreign currencies must be deposited with the Bank of China (or other banks approved by the State Administration of Exchange Control). Payments of foreign currencies are to be made out of the foreign exchange account, but payments to local entities should be made from the venture's renminbi account. Both the repatriation of operating profits after tax and payments upon termination of the venture should also be made from the foreign exchange account.

The new implementing rules for the foreign exchange

regulations offer one very important benefit to joint ventures. Earnings in foreign currency for exported products may now be converted to renminbi at the prevailing internal rate of exchange, rather than the standard tourist rate. At the moment, the internal rate of exchange varies throughout China, but in some cases (particularly the interior, as compared with the coastal cities) it can be significantly higher than the official rate.

Balancing the foreign exchange account

Both the JV Implementing Regulations and the foreign exchange control regulations require that the proceeds of the venture's domestic sales be deposited in the venture's renminbi account and the proceeds arising from export sales must be deposited in the venture's foreign exchange account. Funds standing in the foreign exchange account can, in practice, be freely used to pay any foreign exchange liability, such as the costs of importing production materials, paying foreign currency loans or royalty payments on licence agreements, and declaring dividends to the foreign investor in hard currencies. The problem arises with the use of the funds in the renminbi account for the same purposes. The renminbi is not a convertible currency, and only on special approval will the State Administration of Exchange Control authorise the conversion of funds in the renminbi account to hard currencies.

This problem is particularly vexing in manufacturing joint ventures where the purpose of the joint venture is to sell on the domestic Chinese market, an objective which is much desired by most foreign manufacturers of industrial and consumer goods. The Joint Venture Law and the JV Implementing Regulations both emphasise the fact that 'the Chinese government encourages joint ventures to sell their products on the international market . . .', but also state that sales on the domestic market will be permitted. The factor that restrains the development of ventures solely for the purpose of exploiting the local market is the policy of MOFERT to approve only joint ventures which show a likelihood of balancing their foreign exchange earnings and expenditures.

In this regard, article 75 of the JV Implementing Regulations apparently opened a new door to foreign businesses that sought to participate in the domestic Chinese market through joint ventures:

'The foreign exchange receipts and expenditure of a joint venture shall in general be kept balanced. When a joint venture whose products are mainly sold on the domestic market, based on the approved feasibility study report and contract, has an imbalance of foreign exchange, the people's government of the relevant province, autonomous region, or municipality directly under the central government or the department in charge in the State Council shall regulate and solve such imbalance from its retained foreign exchange; if the imbalance cannot be solved, it shall be solved through inclusion in the plan after the examination and approval by MOFERT together with the State Planning Commission of the People's Republic of China.

The wording of article 75 apparently puts the burden on the local government or department in charge of the venture to balance the venture's foreign exchange account, if the venture and its feasibility study had been approved by MOFERT. Unfortunately, to date only a very few joint ventures have been able to take advantage of this article, since feasibility studies that showed a foreign exchange deficit have routinely been disapproved. In two instances such ventures were approved, but in each case the venture showed a positive foreign exchange balance after a few years of operation and, in regard to the early years of deficit, the Ministry of Finance in Beijing had to give an undertaking to the local government that the ministry (and not the local government) would be responsible for the deficits.

One obvious problem with article 75 is that in most instances it is the local government that shoulders the burden of making up any foreign exchange deficits, unless the venture is proposed and supported by a national ministry. In such cases, the question always arises as to why a particular locality should spend its own foreign exchange to support a venture that will benefit the nation as a whole. This apparently is the reason that, in the few instances where the benefits of article 75 have been obtained, the Ministry of Finance in Beijing was asked to underwrite the local government's obligations in regard to foreign exchange deficits in the early years.

Although imaginative foreign companies have struggled with ways of solving the foreign exchange problem, no one has yet developed a satisfactory solution. Attempts to make joint ventures go into side-line trading activities, thereby using their renminbi to buy local products for export, and proposals to sell renminbi to foreign companies that needed local currency for other projects, have been blocked either by policy decisions of MOFERT or foreign exchange control regulations.

Loans to joint venture

Although the Joint Venture Law and JV Implementing Regulations indicate that joint ventures can deal with foreign banks directly to obtain financing, the Chinese partner has in most cases raised numerous obstacles. First, since the finance is coming from abroad, the Chinese partner frequently says that the foreign investor should provide the loan itself, as the Chinese partner does not wish to deal with banks it does not know. Secondly, no financial security devices exist in China (outside the Special Economic Zones) such as mortgages, pledge of shares, or assignment of receivables, and no joint venture has so far been able to secure its borrowings. Thirdly, if all else fails the Bank of China can lend the money for projects of national importance, but the Bank of China under its own lending regulations must take security, which normally works out to be a parent company guarantee, thereby supporting the Chinese view that the venture really is not a separate and distinct independent company after all, but instead the child of two parents who must support it. Again, the Chinese appear to be making progress in this area, since secured mortgages of a contractual nature can be obtained and the Special Economic Zones are experimenting with security devices like mortgages over real property and chattel mortgages over movable assets.

Joint-venture accounting

The JV Implementing Regulations provide that joint

ventures must prepare their accounts in accordance with relevant Chinese law, which in the case of joint ventures is the Accounting Regulations of the People's Republic of China for Joint Ventures using Chinese and Foreign Investment, promulgated on 4 March 1985 (the 'Accounting Regulations'). The Accounting Regulations contain detailed provisions relating to the joint venture's accounting office and staff, general accounting principles, accounting for capital contributions in cash and in kind, accounting for cash and current accounts, inventories and long-term investments and liabilities, accounting for fixed assets and intangible assets, and accounting for sales and profits and for costs and expenses. Although the Accounting Regulations are too recent to have received much critical comment from Western accountants, the principles expressed in the regulations have been seen as conforming to generally recognised international accounting principles.

The purpose of the Accounting Regulations is to provide a detailed framework for accounting in joint ventures, rather than to address every possible situation. Article 4 of the regulations permits joint ventures to work out their own 'accounting system in accordance with these regulations . . .' and to file the accounts with the local public finance department and tax authority for the record. The Accounting Regulations took effect on 1 July 1985, but since then one hotel joint venture has received permission to use the Uniform System of Accounts for Hotels, which contains certain provisions that are different from the requirements of the Accounting Regulations.

The Accounting Regulations confirm many aspects of joint-venture accounting that were formerly practised, but not covered by law, and in other cases answer questions that were outstanding and unresolved under prior practice.

The fiscal year for joint ventures is the calendar year under the Accounting Regulations, but the tax law permits the tax authorities to approve a different fiscal year in cases of need. All joint ventures must practise the double entry method of bookkeeping and the accrual system of accounting. Accounting records must be kept in Chinese, but it is also permissible to keep such records concurrently in a mutually agreed foreign language.

The Accounting Regulations, just like the JV Implementing Regulations, indicate that in general, joint ventures should use the renminbi as the unit for accounting, but if the joint venture parties agree, a foreign currency can be used. Assets of a joint venture are to be stated in the accounting records at their original cost and asset revaluations are in general not permitted, although the language of the regulations would indicate that with special permission such a revaluation might be allowed.

The Accounting Regulations confirm prior practice that the value of in kind contributions to capital will be the value stipulated in the joint-venture contract and that the registered accountant, who by law must certify such contributions before the issuance of investment certificates, will not attempt to second-guess or revalue the amounts contractually agreed upon by the parties to the venture contract.

A joint venture is permitted to use first-in-first-out (FIFO), shifting or weighted average methods in valuing its inventory, but the last-in-first-out (LIFO) method would presumably require special approval of the local public finance authorities.

The Accounting Regulations finally put to rest one issue that had proved troublesome ever since the promulgation of the joint-venture tax law. The tax law provided that 'interest on capital' was a non-deductible expense of a joint venture. While at first it was thought that this provision simply meant that capital stock in the nature of preferred shares would not have deductible dividends, the tax authorities subsequently said that interest on any loans taken by joint ventures for the purchase of equipment during the capital construction phase would not be deductible. Article 36 of the Accounting Regulations now clarifies that interest on such loans should be capitalised as part of the construction cost of the fixed assets and, after transfer of the assets to operations, such interest is deductible as a current expense. The capitalisation portion of such interest not related to fixed assets may be amortised as a pre-operational expense over five years.

Depreciation in joint ventures is supposed to be done using the straight-line method, but if the joint venture can justify its case, it may apply to the tax authorities for the right to use the accelerated method. The specific useful lives of joint-venture assets are to be determined by the joint venture in accordance with the depreciation periods set forth in the joint-venture tax law, which stipulates 20 years for buildings, 10 for machinery and equipment, and five for electronic equipment and transport vehicles, but again in special cases the tax authorities can be requested to approve a different schedule. All items subject to depreciation should assume a residual value of 10 per cent before calculating depreciation.

Intangible assets such as proprietary technology, patents, trademarks, copyrights, land use rights and other franchise or organisational expenses that are contributed to the joint venture should be amortised over their useful life as stipulated in the joint-venture contract, but such period cannot exceed the term of the joint venture, and in the absence of a stated period of use should be amortised over 10 years.

The Accounting Regulations specifically provide that the additional payments made by joint ventures in order to cover labour insurance, health and welfare benefits and government subsidies for Chinese staff, as well as any direct bonus or incentive payments to workers, are charged as wages and salaries.

The Accounting Regulations confirm prior practice in regard to the use of the three funds established out of after-tax profits: the reserve fund is to be used as a financial cushion to protect against possible future losses by the venture; the staff and workers' bonus and welfare fund is restricted to payment of bonuses and collective welfare for the staff and workers; and the enterprise expansion fund may be used to acquire fixed assets or increase working capital in order to expand production of the venture.

Joint ventures are required to retain the services of a certified public accountant registered with the Chinese government to conduct an annual audit of the venture's books of account and issue an auditor's report. Each participant in the joint venture may independently audit the books and records of the venture, but the cost of any such additional audit must be paid by the participant requesting the audit. Since only Chinese accountants are registered by the government to carry out such work, foreign joint-venture partners must pay for their foreign auditors if they want a separate audit performed. Most Chinese accounting firms, however, will cooperate in such audits by performing them jointly with a foreign accounting firm.

To date, very few joint ventures have experienced any serious problems in their accounting work, other than a severe shortage of qualified Chinese accountants. Audits of the first-year accounts have proved to be a problem in a few joint ventures but this was most often the result of the failure by the venture to keep accurate books and records during the initial start-up period. Because of a shortage of computer-trained Chinese accountants, joint ventures using computerised accounting systems have found it advisable to train both the venture's staff, the local tax authorities and their Chinese accountants in the use of the system at the same time. There is, however, no resistance to computerised accounting systems.

Duration, termination and liquidation

The term of the joint venture must be stipulated in the joint-venture contract after negotiation between the parties. The JV Implementing Regulations suggest that the normal term for a joint venture is between 10 and 30 years, but also recognises that in special situations it may be necessary to have an even longer term. The JV Implementing Regulations also recognise that the parties may wish to extend the term of the venture, but to do so an application must be filed with the original approving authority at least six months before the scheduled termination date for the venture.

Reasons for early termination of a joint venture

The JV Implementing Regulation recognise a number of specific circumstances under which a joint venture can be brought to an early termination:
– inability to continue operations due to heavy losses;
– inability to continue operations due to force majeure;
– inability to achieve the desired objectives for which the joint venture was formed and no reasonable prospects for development; or
– breach of the contract by one of the parties causing the joint venture to be unable to continue operations.
Additionally the regulations permit the parties to stipulate in the contract other grounds for termination.

In such cases the Board of Directors may decide to terminate the venture. If one of the parties has caused the termination by defaulting on its contractual obligations, that party is liable for the losses so caused. Although the JV Implementing Regulations do not provide any standard for the measurement of damages, the Law of the People's Republic of China on Economic Contracts involving Foreign Parties (21 March 1985), which applies to joint-venture contracts, limits such damages to foreseeable losses at the time the contract was signed and requires that the non-defaulting party seek to mitigate any possible damages. Liquidated damages clauses are also permitted, but by Chinese law, the party affected may request the arbitration tribunal or a court to raise or lower the amount of damages, if excessively greater or less than actual damages.

In case of a decision by the Board of Directors to terminate the venture early or upon the scheduled termination date, the Board of Directors is required by the JV Implementing Regulations to appoint a liquidation committee. Although the JV Implementing Regulations were not entirely clear on the subject, the Accounting Regulations have now confirmed that the liquidation committee acts as its name implies: that is, assets are sold to satisfy the outstanding debts and liabilities of the venture and the remaining property is distributed in kind to the investors in accordance with the capital contribution ratio.

Some foreign investors would prefer to see the venture sold to the Chinese side for some stipulated price that took into account the future profits of the venture appraised as a going concern. While the regulations do not approach the subject in this way, recent joint ventures have in fact been documented so as to give the Chinese side a right of first refusal to buy the venture as a going concern. If the Chinese side elects not to purchase, then the venture is liquidated, the assets distributed and the business ends in the manner contemplated by the JV Implementing Regulations.

Governing law and dispute settlement

All Chinese joint ventures are governed by Chinese law; the JV Implementing Regulations do not permit any other alternative.

Disputes, however, may be settled by third-country arbitration, even though the JV Implementing Regulations reflect a bias toward Chinese arbitration. The most frequently selected country is Sweden, since the Chinese prefer it, but other places that have been chosen are Switzerland, the United Kingdom or Hong Kong, and in some cases, Beijing under arbitration conducted in accordance with the UNCITRAL arbitration rules.

A typical arbitration clause in a Chinese joint-venture contract normally permits the parties at the time the dispute arises to settle the dispute through consultation or mediation by a third party. In the event that consultation or mediation fail to resolve the parties differences, if both sides agree, then arbitration may be held in China by the arbitration commission under the China Council for the Promotion of International Trade. If the parties do not so agree in writing within 60 days, then the dispute must go to arbitration in Stockholm.

While foreign investors have shown a reluctance to commit themselves to Chinese arbitration, there are some advantages to arbitration in China. First, under the civil procedure law, the award of a Chinese arbitration tribunal may be enforced as a matter of right by Chinese courts. Secondly, there is an eagerness among Chinese arbitrators to show that Chinese arbitration is both fair and prompt. The disadvantage of Chinese arbitration is that it is conducted in the Chinese language and there are a limited number of qualified arbitrators that the parties may appoint. Foreign arbitral awards have been honoured by Chinese parties in the past, and Chinese lawyers have issued legal opinions to the effect that such awards would be recognised in China.

Contractual joint ventures

Whereas by Chinese standards there is a mass of

regulations governing the equity joint venture, there is little published legislation specifically governing contractual joint ventures. There is not even a law which states how a contractual joint venture is to be approved by the Chinese government.

The Chinese legal framework, however, is once again much broader than the published laws and regulations. A draft of a Cooperative Enterprise Law has been circulating among Chinese officialdom for over two years, but it has still not been promulgated. Promulgated or not, provisions of the draft law are used as guidelines by Chinese negotiators in hammering out the terms of important contractual joint ventures at the negotiating table.

One authoritative publication issued by the Chinese government simply states (without referring to any statutory authority) that in contractual joint ventures

. . . the liabilities, rights and obligations of both parties are stipulated in the agreements and contracts signed by them. Contracts should be authorised by the Chinese government and the ventures are subject to protection and jurisdiction of Chinese laws.'

Unfortunately too many Western businessmen believe that this means one can negotiate anything into the contract. Instead, it really means the Chinese side can only agree to what it knows to be Chinese policy in regard to contractual joint ventures as spelled out in the draft law and additional guidelines from MOFERT. In addition, the rules and regulations applicable to equity joint ventures are applied by analogy to contractual ventures. Quite frequently projects that start out as equity joint ventures at the letter of intent stage may be converted to contractual ventures if the parties run into conflict with some provisions of the JV Implementing Regulations or other laws applicable to joint ventures. In such a case, the contractual venture complies with all aspects of the Joint Venture Law, except for the specific provisions where the parties mutually desire to achieve a different result.

Even without a clear legal framework, there were 2,213 contractual joint ventures by the end of 1984 in China with more than US$4.7 billion pledged as investment from foreign investors. The number of contracts is more than twice the number of equity joint ventures and the amount of committed investment is more than three times as much as for equity ventures. Also the average value of each contractual joint venture is greater than that for equity ventures.

While these figures would indicate that the contractual joint venture was a more popular investment vehicle than the equity joint venture, the trend may be changing. Prior to 1984, contractual joint ventures outnumbered equity ventures almost 10 to one, but during 1984 the number of equity joint ventures completed roughly equalled the number of contractual ventures.

Organisation and status

There are two distinct forms of contractual joint ventures: in the first an entity with the status of a legal person is created, while in the second no legal entity is created and the business relationship takes the form prescribed by the venture contract.

The first form of contractual joint venture is most often referred to as a cooperative venture and is very much like the equity joint-venture company created under the Joint Venture Law. The parties may in fact limit their liability to the amount of their capital contribution. Three elements are different in a cooperative company, as compared with an equity joint-venture company: (1) labour services are a permitted capital contribution, (2) the capital contribution ratio and the sharing ratio for profits and losses can be different, and (3) capital can be returned to the parties during the term of the venture, but capital so returned is always subject to recall in case the venture suffers losses.

The documentation required to establish a cooperative joint venture is substantially similar in practice to that required for an equity joint venture: there must be a cooperative or venture contract and the cooperative company is supposed to have articles of association. The form of such documentation is often substantially similar to the MOFERT Model Contract for equity joint ventures, except for those specific sections that must be changed to account for the company's status as a cooperative.

In practice, MOFERT has authority to approve and disapprove cooperative contracts and the related articles of association. Although no law specifically confers this power upon MOFERT, the general acceptance by Chinese lawyers that MOFERT has such powers has made foreign negotiators concede the point.

Although there are no provisions in Chinese law for partnerships, the second form of contractual joint venture has many of the attributes of a partnership. Such contractual joint ventures do not have articles of association generally, and the contract is the only constituent document establishing the relationship. Such ventures are hereinafter referred to as 'contractual ventures'.

Under true contractual ventures, the foreign contracting party must register itself in China. Foreign investors in either an equity joint venture or a cooperative need not register an establishment in China, since the new legal entity formed by their joint investment is registered. But a contractual venture creates corresponding rights and obligations directly between the contracting parties and it is therefore necessary for the foreign company contracting for the contractual joint venture to register. In practice the contractual joint venture, although not a legal person, must also register with AIC since it will be conducting a business within Chinese territory.

Capital contributions

Capital contributions are treated in both forms of contractual joint ventures much the same as in equity joint ventures, since there seems to be a general trend to apply the provisions of the Joint Venture Law and related regulations to contractual joint ventures, unless there is an internal guideline in the draft law indicating a contrary rule.

There are, however, some notable differences. In both forms of contractual joint ventures, the Chinese contribution may include natural resource rights, labour and utilities, which under the equity joint venture regulations may not be counted as capital contributions. While natural resources belong to the state on behalf of the whole people and title cannot therefore be contributed to the venture or severally to the parties, the permission to exploit China's natural resources directly affects the sharing ratio, although technically the permission is not treated as a capital contribution. The Chinese appear to be somewhat touchy, however, if the foreign side proposes the mortgaging of such rights to its banks. It is also interesting to note that when labour is contributed to the venture by the Chinese, the labour regulations applicable in equity joint ventures do not necessarily apply, and the parties are free to negotiate some other basis (normally higher) for valuing the contribution of labour.

In the true contractual venture, since there is no legal entity formed, capital contributions are most often contributions in kind rather than in cash. Moreover, the venture itself does not have equity or registered capital.

Profits arising in a cooperative joint venture, where a legal entity is formed, are to be distributed in the same manner specified by the Joint Venture Law; that is, after payment of taxes, deductions for the venture's reserve fund, the workers' bonus and welfare fund and the venture expansion fund should be made before distributing net income. All distribution of foreign exchange dividends are subject to the foreign exchange regulations.

Non-entity contractual joint ventures have more flexibility. According to the foreign exchange regulations, they may distribute net profits, gross revenues, or products manufactured or produced, so long as a reasonable method for assuring the payment of taxes and operational expenses has been found.

Management and control
Cooperatives tend to have a Board of Directors and a separate management office with at least a general manager and one or two deputies. The provisions for Board of Directors' meetings and the powers and responsibilities of the general manager closely follow the similar provisions for equity joint ventures.

In true contractual joint ventures, the management structure is more flexible, although some form of joint committee is necessary in order to maintain liaison between the parties and control their respective efforts in accomplishing the project goals. Because of the absence of a legal entity in a true contractual joint venture, many matters that normally are decided by the Board of Directors in an equity joint venture must be approved by the parties, either through regularly convened meetings of representatives or a committee structure. Most frequently this committee structure is merely set forth in the contractual joint-venture contract, but in one instance the power and duties of the committee members had to be confirmed by a power of attorney published in China. Necessarily this structure requires that somewhat greater authority be given to the day-to-day management personnel in order to avoid all decisions being referred back to the parties or their committee representatives.

Operational matters
In the cooperative format, a contractual joint venture follows closely the rules regarding management found in the JV Implementing Regulations. In true contractual joint ventures, it is necessary to pay close attention to the provisions in the contract regulating day-to-day operational management, since there is no statutory framework to rely upon.

Just as in the case of the equity joint venture, both cooperatives and contractual joint ventures are increasingly relying on management contracts for the purpose of conferring management duties on a nominated, independent third party. Equity joint ventures and cooperatives have adopted the management contract device because of the great number of hotel ventures done in this way. In the case of contractual joint ventures, management contracts are less frequent, but probably of equal use, since day-to-day management of contractual joint ventures is a difficult problem to solve in the contract itself.

Taxation
Cooperative joint ventures may be taxed by analogy under the Joint Venture Income Tax Law, so the effective rate of taxation is 33 per cent, with a further 10 per cent repatriation tax applied to distributions sent abroad. At the moment, in order to qualify for such treatment, the articles of association must specifically state that the cooperative is a Chinese legal person. The foreign party to a true contractual joint venture, however, is taxed under the Foreign Enterprise Income Tax Law, which provides for progressive taxation rates from 30 to 50 per cent (with no repatriation tax applied to remitted earnings), but the venture itself is not taxed on profits. The taxation of cooperatives and contractual joint ventures is described below in the section on taxation.

Foreign exchange control
Cooperative joint ventures and contractual joint ventures are subject to the general foreign exchange rules of China. In true contractual joint ventures involved in coal, petroleum or other natural resources, where the method of profit-sharing is through the distribution of output, special rules apply permitting the free export of the foreign partner's portion of the output. Moreover, the implementing rules for foreign exchange control appear to allow the foreign participant to keep foreign exchange earnings in foreign bank accounts, so long as a reasonable method of assuring the payment of venture operating costs is allowed for in the contract.

Joint development

Joint development is similar to the true contractual joint venture and to date has been used solely for the granting of cooperative offshore oil exploration, development and exploitation contracts. Thirty-one such contracts have been signed so far and the amount of investment pledged by the foreign oil companies is over US$2.4 billion.

Unlike the true contractual joint venture, where it is common for both sides to contribute capital during the investment phase of the contract, in projects for joint development, the exploration stage is funded at the sole risk of the foreign investor. If oil is found in sufficient quantities for commercial development, both the Chinese side and the foreign oil company invest in the joint development of the resources. Once production has begun, the recovered oil is divided between the parties as stipulated in the joint-development contract.

The Model Contract proposed by the China National Offshore Oil Corporation (CNOOC) for its dealings with foreign oil companies in the cooperative development of China's oil resources is the best example to date of how a 'model' contract can take on certain attributes of a law. Negotiators which have successfully concluded oil contracts with CNOOC acknowledge the reasonableness of China's desire for uniformity with all oil companies, and have (after lengthy negotiations) grown to appreciate the benefits of CNOOC's treatment of the draft as a law unto itself. To the extent that the contract has the effect of a law, the parties' rights and obligations are fixed permanently.

The Model Petroleum Contract divides the foreign contractor's operations into three separate phases: exploration, development and production. As part of the bidding programme, foreign oil companies were asked to bid on blocks within certain areas designated by the Ministry of Petroleum Industry (MOPI). The form of the bidding is a commitment by the oil company to complete a minimum exploration work programme, including a specified amount of seismic work and a number of wildcat wells, together with a minimum exploration expenditure obligation denominated in US dollars. Exploration costs required for the exploration operations are to be provided solely by and at the risk of the foreign oil company, and exploration costs required for the fulfilment of the mutually agreed minimum exploration obligation must be either equity capital or non-interest-bearing loans. Exploration costs accumulated during the exploration period will, it is hoped, be recovered after commercial production.

In the event that the foreign oil company discovers oil and agrees with CNOOC upon an overall development programme, which must be approved by MOPI, the costs required for the development will be shared by CNOOC and the foreign contractor in proportion to their respective participating interests, which unless otherwise agreed are 51 per cent for CNOOC and 49 per cent for the foreign contractor. Such shared development costs are accumulated by the respective partners, together with deemed interest at the rate of 9 per cent on expended funds, to be recovered out of crude oil allocations after the date of commencement of commercial production.

Similarly, during the production phase, operating costs are shared in accordance with the partners' participation interests and recovered in kind by the parties out of crude oil produced from the oilfield during the calendar year in which they are incurred.

Starting with the date of commencement of commercial production, crude oil produced from the field is allocated in the following manner, according to the Model Petroleum Contract:
(a) 17.5 per cent to payment of the Consolidated Industrial and Commercial Tax and royalty;
(b) 50 per cent to operating cost recovery oil, which is used to pay in kind first actual operating costs incurred in all producing oilfields, with the remainder of such 50 per cent in any year being treated as investment recovery oil;
(c) investment recovery oil is then used to pay in kind exploration costs incurred by the contractor and thereafter to recover development costs, together with deemed interest on development costs;
(d) the remaining oil, including the remainder of any operating cost recovery oil, is then treated as profit

oil, which is divided between share oil of the Chinese side and allocable profit oil;
(e) bidders for contracts were then asked to bid competitively on an 'x' factor, which divides share oil of the Chinese side from allocable profit oil through a series of production tiers for each producing oilfield;
(f) once determined, the allocable profit oil is divided between CNOOC and the contractor in proportion to their participating interests in the development costs.
Therefore, the foreign oil company is to receive its portion of operating cost recovery oil, investment recovery oil (including exploration costs and development costs with deemed interest), and allocable profit oil; the Chinese Government or CNOOC is to either receive or recover in kind the Consolidated Tax, the royalty, operating costs, development costs and deemed interest, Chinese share oil and CNOOC's portion of allocable profit oil.

In order to convert quantities of crude oil into values for the purpose of payments in kind to recover costs and investments, the Model Petroleum Contract adopts the standard of 'the prevailing price in arm's-length transactions of the long-term contract sales of similar quality crude oil on the main world markets' with adjustments for quality, terms of delivery, transportation, payment and other items. The standard is implemented practically by the contractor proposing a price quarterly to CNOOC, which may either approve or further negotiate such price, and in the event no price is agreed by the end of a calendar quarter, the crude oil is valued based upon the weighted average net realised f.o.b. price of sales of offshore China crude oil to third parties during the quarter.

Although joint development probably affords the greatest flexibility of any of the presently available forms of investment, its usefulness has so far been limited to the offshore oil area. Moreover, it is not at all certain that joint-developments contracts will not be regulated in the future by new laws applicable to enterprises operating in China. Because MOPI developed the joint-development form of model contract, it is likely that this form will be used for the development of onshore oil- and gasfields, where China is presently seeking foreign investment. The joint-development model therefore will be of continuing importance, although probably only to foreign companies involved in the oil and gas business.

Compensation trade

When China's open door policy was first announced, by far the most popular form of foreign investment was compensation trade. In all, 1,370 compensation trade contracts were signed by the end of 1984 and each was valued at approximately US$1 million of foreign investment. Compensation trade was particularly popular with Hong Kong textile manufacturers who wanted to move a portion of their production to China. Compensation trade dropped off dramatically in 1984, however, in part due to the increasing severity with which the United States applied its country of origin rules to textile products: the rules prohibited Hong Kong manufacturers from using Hong Kong's quota allocation when too much of the value of the garment was produced in China.

Compensation trade is basically a loan transaction

where both the initial advance and subsequent loan repayments are made in kind. The foreign compensation trade partner either sells the Chinese party new equipment or technology on credit or lends the equipment and technology to the Chinese enterprise. The purchase price, the value of which is mutually agreed upon in the compensation trade contract, is repaid in instalments of products, either produced by the equipment or technology or less frequently by the provision of other goods manufactured by the Chinese partner. Compensation trade contracts also stipulate an interest rate, which is added to the installment repayments and is also paid in kind.

Compensation trade arrangements are normally for short periods of time and seldom exceed five years, although one notable US project has operated in Beijing for almost 12 years.

There is no formal joint-management structure in compensation trade transactions. The inability to participate in management of the Chinese enterprise at first led to many problems in receiving the compensation goods on time and of the right quality. Many of these problems were resolved, however, when the foreign investor, either through formal or informal agreements, was permitted under the compensation trade framework to render technical and management assistance to the Chinese enterprise involved.

Probably the most attractive aspect of compensation trade is that to date such arrangements have not been subjected to tax either under the Joint Venture Income Tax Law or the Foreign Enterprise Income Tax Law. The Chinese party earns its profit by taking over ownership of the new plant and equipment at the end of the compensation period. The foreign side technically does not receive profits at all, but instead goods in kind in payment of the debt.

The most difficult contractual aspect of a compensation trade project is always the formula for pricing the compensation products returned to the foreign investor. Although recent contracts have incorporated formulae for the pricing of such products, in early contracts the most the Chinese would agree to was that the contract could stipulate the first year's price, but thereafter the price was a subject for annual 'friendly negotiations'. For this reason, very few American or European companies did compensation trade contracts and only the Hong Kong entrepreneurs seemed able to make the system work well.

Compensation trade has proved particularly attractive in southern China where Hong Kong industrialists have found the method of investment to be a generally cheap and efficient means to obtain simple subcontract work for production of textiles, component materials and parts.

Foreign investment approval process

The approval process for foreign investment proposals is as important as the published laws and regulations governing such investments, since the approval process determines how the investment project will be integrated within the Chinese economic system.

State planning of the national economy is required by the Chinese constitution. The State Council is responsible for ensuring the proportionate and coordinated develop-ment of the national economy as a whole through the national economic planning mechanism, supplemented by market regulation in limited areas. The compilation of the annual and five-year State Plans is a process of adjusting and consolidating at the national level the economic plans of the ministries, provinces, municipalities directly under the control of the State Council and autonomous regions. The seventh Five Year Plan (1986-90) was presented to the National People's Congress in 1984, where it was adopted along with long-range economic planning goals that extend into the 21st century.

Once approved, a foreign investment project becomes part of the State Plan with both its planned production and necessary inputs of raw materials and utilities accounted for within the plan. Since the state planning process predicts future economic needs and goals, and since at any particular point the Chinese authorities are operating with an existing State Plan, a major foreign investment project that is not contemplated in the existing plan will be subject to lengthy delays before it can be implemented. Any major foreign investment project that will require the utilisation of substantial power, utilities, transportation or raw material supplies should therefore be part of the existing State Plan before a foreign investor spends time and money pursuing the project.

Letters of intent

The approval process for foreign investment projects is meant to ensure that the requirements for overall national economic planning are met before the investment programme is implemented. What is normally thought of by the foreign investor as a non-binding letter of intent is, in fact, the initial stage of the foreign investment approval process.

Under the Chinese system, the Chinese party is supposed to submit a written proposal together with a preliminary feasibility study on the project to the appropriate authorities at the provincial, independent municipality, autonomous region or State Council level, depending on the size and type of project. The proposal should include information on the object of the proposed investment, sphere of operation, scale of production, total amount of investment, technology to be employed, sources of raw materials, fuel, power and equipment, market studies, economic effects and basic terms of the venture. If the preliminary feasibility study and proposal are approved, the Chinese party is authorised to begin serious negotiations on the joint venture and is authorised to conduct a joint feasibility study with the selected foreign partner.

Most letters of intent touch on many, if not all of these subjects. In some cases, the letter of intent is required to be submitted at the same time the proposal is sent in for approval in order to evidence the fact that the project is worth being considered as a foreign investment project.

The foreign investor may consider that all subjects in the letter of intent are left open for further study, refinement and possible amendment, but since the relevant higher authorities act on the written approval and authorise negotiations based on the signed proposal, it becomes very difficult to change the terms stated in the initial letter of intent, even though such terms are not legally binding. In particular, items that could not be included in the letter of intent because the Chinese side said their inclusion would not be approved by the higher authorities are virtually impossible to negotiate back into later agreements and contracts.

The level to which the initial written proposal must go for final approval is still subject to confusing interpretations. As a general rule, it has been stated that the Provinces of Guangdong and Fujian may approve investments up to any level without higher approval, that independent municipalities directly under the State Council such as Beijing and Tianjin may approve investments up to US$10 million without higher approval and Shanghai may approve investments up to US$30 million, and ministries and certain coastal provinces have authority to approve investments between US$3 and 5 million without higher approval; all other investments must go to MOFERT for prior approval. Even in the areas where the lower-level economic authorities have apparent approval power, they must report to the higher-level organisation for the record (and the higher-level authority can intervene with an objection, if it chooses) and, in cases where the national economic system is to be called upon to support the venture through the supply of raw materials or utilities, or where a national-level organisation is necessarily involved (such as the CNOOC in offshore oil matters), the lower-level economic authority must receive the central government's approval.

Feasibility studies
Once the initial approval is received, the Chinese party and the foreign investor are supposed to jointly conduct an economic feasibility study. This study should include all technical aspects of the project and predict future income and expenses. Again this feasibility study is supposed to be submitted for approval through the relevant chain of command.

It is this stage of the negotiation process that frequently creates the greatest difficulties. The foreign investor will by now have studied Chinese laws and regulations governing foreign investment and trade and learned something of the likely operating expenses to be incurred in China. In order to achieve an acceptable return on investment, the foreign investor will want to write into the feasibility study tax concessions or holidays, reduced customs duties on imports, favoured treatment as to the pricing of Chinese-supplied raw materials or utilities, lower land use costs or reduced local or consolidated taxes. But since the original letter of intent said nothing about such concessions, the Chinese side will be very reluctant to go beyond the initial mandate granted by the higher-level economic regulators.

The Chinese side has certain additional responsibilities in the second stage of the approval process beyond preparing the 'joint' feasibility report. The Chinese party sponsoring the investment must separately report on the concrete arrangements that it has made for performing its portion of the proposed investment. Under current practice this may include such matters as initial commitments from Chinese financial institutions like the Bank of China or the Industrial and Commercial Bank to lend the Chinese party its portion of the equity investment, proof that the required raw materials and utilities necessary for the venture are available in the locality and

that the sources of supply have been confirmed, and that the percentage of the production to be sold locally can be distributed efficiently and absorbed by the local market. Normally this secondary report prepared by the Chinese side is not shown to the foreign investor.

It is also at the feasibility report stage that the Chinese and foreign negotiators must address the difficult question of how to balance the foreign exchange account of the venture. The data accumulated for the cashflow projections necessarily must show how much income is in renminbi and how much in foreign currency; similarly, operating costs must be shown in the relevant currency of their payment. The feasibility study cashflows, therefore, clearly demonstrate whether the joint venture will have to rely on the local government or department in charge to balance the foreign exchange under article 75 of the JV Implementing Regulations.

Negotiating and approving the contract
Once the 'joint' feasibility report and secondary report are approved by the higher-level economic regulators, the Chinese side is authorised to finalise the investment contract and related legal documents. The documents have probably been under negotiation for some time, as the Chinese side likes to begin the contract process shortly after the original approval for the letter of intent is received. The Joint Venture Law indicates that once negotiated and signed, such documents are submitted to MOFERT for approval within three months. While this was the system in China in 1979, the early experience led to a modification of the system since the foreign investment control authorities found that they must either renegotiate the contracts causing delays longer than three months or approve contracts that did not fully conform to China's internal guidelines. Therefore, now before any contract which constitutes a final and binding legal document for a major project can be signed, it must be submitted to and approved by MOFERT or its lower-level equivalent organisation as a matter of policy. The Chinese side submits the contract itself before signing and MOFERT may comment. This preliminary approval by MOFERT or its lower-level equivalent organisation is non-binding and, even with this system, there have been embarrassing incidents where the signed final contract was not approved when formally submitted under the law's formal requirements.

The general experience with MOFERT review is that the mutually agreed contract draft will normally require some amendments before MOFERT authorises signature. Common areas where this occurs include matters relating to the balancing of the foreign exchange account and the terms of technology licence agreements.

Formal approval
Once MOFERT or the relevant lower-level authority has approved execution of the contract, it is signed but then must be formally resubmitted in technical compliance with article 3 of the Joint Venture Law. The formal submission in the case of an equity joint venture is supposed to include:
1 an application for the establishment of the joint venture;
2 copies of the contract and articles of association;
3 the feasibility report;

4 a name list for the joint venture's chairman, vice-chairman and other members of the Board of Directors; and
5 comments on the joint venture from the province, municipality, autonomous region or ministry proposing the venture.

A formal approval certificate is supposed to be issued by MOFERT within three months of formal submission, but recently (because the ventures are subject to approval prior to signing) this procedure has been shortened. After the formal approval is granted, the joint venture is required to register with the national office of AIC or its agency in the locality where the joint venture is situated, according to the special provisions on registration applicable to equity joint ventures.

Although in certain circumstances ministries, provinces and municipalities acting through their own lower-level economic control organisation have the power to approve joint ventures, AIC will only register the enterprise and issue the business licence against a MOFERT-granted approval, since the registration regulations require presentation of the approval document of the Foreign Investment Bureau of MOFERT. MOFERT, not having had to approve the contract prior to signing, can insist on some amendments before issuing the approval required by AIC. In such a case, either the relevant ministry must use its powers of persuasion with MOFERT or, more likely, the parties will have to amend the contract to satisfy MOFERT's requirements.

The effect of foreign investment on China

The forms for investment in China and the regulations governing such investment have been clarified during the first six years of the open door policy. Whether foreign investment capital will play a meaningful role in China's economic development is still unclear: the total of all committed foreign investment to China from 1979 to 1984 was less that 6 per cent of China's investment in fixed assets and, during that period, the actual amount of committed investment paid into China was only slightly more than 2 per cent of China's own investment in fixed assets. Yet the final result of its foreign investment programme may not be the amount of capital received, but instead the effect of learning how Western joint ventures are managed, how their products are produced and how, once produced, they are sold.

The allure of China as a country in which to invest is still not substantiated by the facts; few joint ventures other than hotels have shown respectable profits and many industrial ventures are suffering start-up problems. But the China market remains to be tapped and, if anything is clear, investment conditions have improved over time rather than worsened, so it is likely that foreign companies will continue to seek investment opportunities in China.

Foreign exchange and loan transactions

As a state-planned economy, China practises strict control of its foreign exchange transactions. The principal piece of legislation in this area is the Provisional Regulations of the People's Republic of China governing Foreign Exchange Control (the 'exchange control regulations') promulgated by the State Council in December 1980. The exchange control regulations contain chapters regulating exchange transactions of domestic Chinese organisations, individuals, joint and cooperative ventures, as well as containing provisions in regard to the carrying in and out of China of foreign exchange, precious metals and foreign exchange instruments.

Domestic organisations

The stated policy of the exchange control regulations is to implement 'centralised control and unified management of foreign exchange by the state'. This policy is most rigorously enforced against domestic Chinese organisations, which by the terms of the regulations includes all local organisations and stated-owned enterprises in China. Unless approved by the State Administration of Exchange Control (SAEC), a domestic organisation cannot privately possess foreign exchange, deposit foreign exchange abroad, offset foreign exchange receipts against foreign exchange expenditures or borrow or transfer the foreign exchange belonging to Chinese organisations outside of China. Without the approval of SAEC, domestic organisations are not supposed to issue negotiable securities with a foreign exchange value and, except for that specifically approved portion, must sell all of their foreign exchange earned to the Bank of China for non-convertible renminbi.

The exchange control regulations state that the measures for examining and approving loans shall be stipulated separately. What is know about the process for approving foreign loans makes it clear that the procedures are not simple and that control is tight.

The planning process for foreign loans and credits is one small part (though a complicated one) of the overall national economic planning process. Ministries, provinces, autonomous regions, municipalities and enterprises which contribute to the general budget of the national plan by submitting proposed budgets must estimate anticipated foreign exchange income and expenditures. Similarly, they must also generally request allocations from the central planning authorities permitting them to expend foreign exchange or to borrow from abroad. Certain provinces, municipalities and enterprises that have earned foreign exchange previously through exports are allowed to retain a portion of such foreign exchange for discretionary expenditure and, as part of the central planning process, these units are only required to notify the central authorities of planned expenditures. At the end of the planning process, the State Council decides on the overall permitted level of foreign exchange expenditure and allocates such expenditures between the subordinate units that contribute to the planning process.

Two separate administrative departments play an important role in the administration of foreign loans. The Bureau of Foreign Investment Control under MOFERT, in addition to approving foreign investment projects, also manages in cooperation with the Ministry of Finance the utilisation of credits from foreign governments and international financial organisations, such as US Exim-bank loans or World Bank loans.

The second administrative body that plays an important role in the administration of foreign loans is the People's Bank of China (PBOC), which serves as the central bank. PBOC has as its subordinate agency the State Administration of Exchange Control (SAEC), which is formally vested with the power to control and administer all aspects of the country's foreign exchange control programme. PBOC has set up an authoritive council to act as its policy-making organisation for loans. The council consists of the president of PBOC, its vice-presidents, several advisors and specialists, a vice-minister of Ministry of Finance, vice-ministers of the State Planning Commission and the State Economic Commission, the presidents of each of the specialised banks, and the general manager of the People's Insurance Company. The council submits on behalf of PBOC the recommended allocations for foreign loan authorisations requested by Chinese enterprises to the State Council for approval. Once the State Council approves the allocations, the formal allocations are issued by SAEC to the borrowing units.

These planned loan allocations make it imperative for a foreign bank when doing business with a state enterprise to determine that such enterprise has received authorisation from the appropriate authorities governing all foreign exchange aspects of the proposed transaction. By virtue of article 7(1) of the Economic Contracts Laws of the People's Republic of China (1981) and the specialised regulations governing loans issued in 1985, a loan agreement providing for a loan outside the approval of the State Council plan would not be legally binding. While the annual credit plan will not be provided to a foreign bank, the Bank of China will, upon request, provide a letter of confirmation of foreign exchange quota allocation.

Generally speaking, prior to beginning detailed negotiations with a foreign bank, the state enterprise will have submitted a general proposal outlining the contemplated transaction to the appropriate authorities for their approval. A foreign bank should as a routine matter request the state enterprise to inform it as soon as the necessary approval has been given. Under present practice, a copy of the actual approval by SAEC is not given to a foreign bank, since the approval document is considered an internal Chinese government document. Instead, the practice has been for the Bank of China or another independent organisation (such as a Chinese law firm) to issue a letter confirming that the state enterprise has complied with China's foreign exchange control regulations and that all necessary foreign exchange approvals have been obtained.

Individuals

Individuals, except for foreigners residing in China on behalf of a foreign enterprise, are also subject to very strict foreign exchange control regulations. In general, they must sell their foreign exchange holdings to the Bank of China, except for that portion which they are allowed to keep under unpublished regulations. At the moment, it is understood that this amount is normally 10 to 30 per cent of their foreign exchange receipts, and even this foreign exchange must be deposited with the Bank of China in special foreign exchange accounts.

Joint and cooperative ventures and foreign enterprises

The exchange control regulations are more liberal in their treatment of joint ventures and cooperatives. Joint ventures must deposit all of their foreign exchange receipts with the Bank of China and all of their foreign exchange expenditures must be paid out of their foreign exchange account with the Bank of China. Indirectly this provision confirms that renminbi earnings of a joint venture cannot be converted into foreign exchange.

The actual procedure for the transfer of profits out of China is to request the Bank of China for permission to debit the venture's foreign exchange deposit account for the transfer. In practice the procedure is so simple that most joint ventures are unaware that they have made the application, but the fact remains that any such outward remittance may only be made from the venture's foreign exchange account. In order to remit capital, which only occurs in equity joint ventures upon termination of the venture, the venture must apply to SAEC for permission and again, the amount can only be paid from the venture's foreign exchange deposit account. It is for this reason that many joint-venture partners seek in the joint-venture contract a commitment from the Chinese side to purchase their interest in the joint venture for foreign exchange upon the termination of the venture.

The expatriate workers in a joint venture or cooperative are also subject to one unreasonable restriction. Their wages must in general be paid into a bank account in China and they may only remit out of China 50 per cent of their 'net wages and legitimate earnings'.

The difficulties caused by the exchange control regulations in handling the standard payment problems encountered by joint ventures was the source of a considerable number of complaints from foreign investors. The situation has been partially remedied by the Detailed Rules and Regulations for the Implementation of Foreign Exchange Control governing Enterprises with Overseas Chinese Capital, Enterprises with Foreign Capital and Joint Ventures using Chinese and Foreign Investment adopted on 19 July 1983. In particular, the implementing regulations announce a procedure under which the foreign worker can apply to SAEC for permission to repatriate more than 50 per cent of his wages. According to officials of SAEC and general practice, such permissions are routinely granted.

Foreign exchange instruments and precious metals

Chinese law is also strict on the exportation of foreign exchange instruments and precious metals. In general, the export of such items, whether made by domestic enterprises or foreign enterprises, may only take place after an application has been filed with and approved by SAEC.

Special regulations govern the handling of gold and silver. In general, the regulations provide that gold and silver may only be transported out of China pursuant to special requests made to PBOC. Gold and silver needed for industrial purposes or for the making of jewellry must be purchased from PBOC, but such approval will only be granted for a legitimate business purpose.

Currency and foreign exchange control

In 1980 the Bank of China issued special regulations relating to a new currency called the foreign exchange certificate (FEC). An FEC is only created by the inward importation of foreign exchange, most frequently by tourists. Such certificates are denominated in renminbi, but actually have a higher value than the non-convertible renminbi since they may be used by local Chinese to buy foreign goods at the various Friendship Stores or other outlets for foreign goods.

The Bank of China has also issued special regulations relating to accounts denominated in foreign exchange rather than in renminbi. These accounts, called Category A Accounts, can be denominated in US dollars, pounds sterling, Hong Kong dollars, Deutschemarks and Japanese yen. Amounts standing to the credit of any such account may be freely remitted outwards upon the instruction of an authorised signatory. There is a second similar set of rules for individuals (Category B Accounts).

Under the Regulations of the Bank of China for Special Renminbi Deposits, it is also possible for a foreign company desiring to do so, to convert its foreign exchange income into renminbi and hold it in a special renminbi deposit account. The advantage of such a system is that special renminbi can be automatically converted into foreign exchange if needed to pay any foreign exchange costs of the venture.

Article 10 of the implementing regulations contain one very interesting provision in regard to such accounts and the conversion of foreign exchange into renminbi:

'. . . [foreign ventures] dealing in exchange between renminbi and foreign currencies must make the currency conversion according to the official rates of exchange published by SAEC; their foreign exchange receipts from exports may be converted into renminbi in conformity with Chinese government regulations governing foreign trade exchange conversion.'

At first, this simple clause would seem innocuous enough not to warrant attention. But the foreign trade exchange conversion system is a method pursuant to which the Chinese government encourages exports by granting a higher exchange rate for foreign currency generated by foreign industrial sales as opposed to tourist revenues. Affording the same treatment to joint ventures which export a portion of their production effectively means that, for export products, China is willing to reduce the cost of sales by granting a higher value to the foreign currency income received by the venture but expended to meet local operating costs. Although the difference between the tourist rate and the internal rate has narrowed substantially (and in most of the coastal provinces does not exist at all), still this concession can be quite valuable to ventures located in remote areas.

Trademarks and patents

The importation of advanced technology has long been viewed in China as the means to modernise the country's economy, but the absence of industrial property laws made potential suppliers of technology reluctant to deal with Chinese enterprises. Much has been done to alleviate these fears. First, in 1982 China modernised its Trademarks Law, and in the following year issued new detailed regulations implementing the new law. In March 1984, China adopted a patent law, and on 14 November 1984, the Standing Committee of the National People's Congress decided that China should join the Paris Convention for the Protection of Industrial Property. From 19 March 1985, China has been bound by the Paris Convention.

Trademarks

Article 1 of the Trademark Law is quite interesting and shows the fundamental distinction between China's Trademark Law and the trademark laws of many other countries:

'This law is enacted for the purposes of improving the administration of trademarks, of protecting the exclusive right to use a trademark, and of encouraging producers to guarantee the quality of their goods and maintain the reputation of their trademarks, with a view to protecting consumer interests and to promoting the development of socialist commodity economy.'

The law, therefore, aside from providing traditional trademark protections, is intended to be used in a novel manner as a mechanism for quality control and consumer protection. Under article 31 of the Trademark Law, the Trademark Office is authorised to impose sanctions, including the revocation of a registered trademark, if a registered trademark is used in respect to goods which have been roughly or poorly manufactured, or whose superior quality has been replaced by inferior quality so that consumers are deceived. Other sanctions, which may be imposed by the local bureau of AIC, include, for a minor offence, criticism or education or an administrative order to remedy the situation within a specified period of time and, for a major offence, 'order the making of self-criticism, circulate a notice of criticism or impose a fine not exceeding Rmb2,000'.

The Trademark Law also grants to the trademark registrant protection for its exclusive ownership of the trademark. Article 39 of the law allows the trademark holder in the case of an unauthorised use of the registered mark to protest to the local bureau of AIC, and the bureau has the administrative power to issue an order stopping the unauthorised use and awarding compensation to the trademark owner equal to 'the profit which the infringer has earned through the infringement during the period of the infringement or the damages that the party whose right was infringed has suffered through the infringement'. In addition to the administrative remedy, which is available through the local bureau of AIC, the trademark holder can proceed directly in the People's Courts.

Registration of trademarks

The Trademark Law permits the registration of trademarks used in connection with goods manufactured, produced, processed or marketed in China. Service marks cannot be registered in China, although some enterprising foreign companies have registered their service marks as marks used in connection with stationery and paper products.

The process of registering trademarks of a foreign

company in China is relatively simple and straightforward. First, the foreign company must file an application with the Trademark Registration Agency of the China Council for the Promotion of International Trade (CCPIT Trademark Registration Agency), which acts as the agent for the foreign applicant; in Hong Kong this agency work may be handled through CCPIT Trademark Registration Agency's sister company, China Patent Agent (HK) Ltd (CPA-HK). After preliminarily examining the application CCPIT Trademark Registration Agency will submit the application on behalf of the foreign applicant for approval of the Trademark Office of AIC under the State Council (the 'Trademark Office'). The Trademark Law provides for a two-step approval procedure. If the trademark for which registration is applied for is in conformity with the Trademark Law's provisions and is not identical with or similar to another trademark that has already been preliminarily approved, then the Trademark Office will preliminarily approve the trademark and publish it. During the three-month period following its publication, any person may file an opposition against the trademark with the Trademark Review and Adjudication Board. If no opposition is filed, or if it is decided that the opposition is not justified, registration shall be approved and a trademark registration certificate will be issued and publication of the approved trademark made.

Once a trademark is finally approved, it is still possible for a person who wishes to dispute the validity of the trademark to do so within one year of the date of approval by filing an application with the Trademark Review and Adjudication Board. If the trademark was subject to an opposition during the preliminarily approval period based on the same facts and circumstances, no such application can be made.

By joining the Paris Convention. China was required to grant the priority required by the Convention to trademark applicants from signatory countries. On 15 March 1985, the State Council approved provisional regulations permitting applicants from signatory countries to claim priority of filing within six months from the date of first filing in another Paris Convention signatory country.

Renewal, assignment and licensing
Registration of a trademark is effective for 10 years and may be renewed for additional 10-year periods. There is no limit on the number of renewals that may be requested. An application for renewal should be filed with the Trademark Office during the six months prior to the expiration of the trademark period, although the Trademark Office will accept applications for renewal during the six-month period following the expiration of the prior term.

When a trademark is to be assigned, both the assignee and the assignor must jointly file an application with the Trademark Office. It is worth noting that the assignee is obligated to guarantee the quality of the goods produced under the trademark.

Article 26 of the Trademark Law permits the licensing of a registered trademark. While no approval is required for such licensing, copies of the licence contract must be submitted to the Trademark Office for the file. In addition, it should be noted that under the Trademark Law, a licensor is required to supervise the quality of the goods in respect of which the registered trademark is used. Such supervision can include seeking administrative assistance from the local bureau of AIC to require one's licensee to comply with the product quality control conditions imposed by the trademark licence.

Patents

The Patent Law of the People's Republic of China was adopted by the fourth session of the Standing Committee of the National People's Congress on 12 March 1984, and came into effect on 1 April 1985. The Standing Committee also decided on 14 November 1984 to join the Paris Convention and since 19 March 1985, China has been bound by the provisions of that convention. The Patent Law and China's ratification of the Paris Convention will, it is hoped, increase China's ability to attract advanced technology for the modernisation of its industrial enterprises.

Prior to the Patent Law's coming into effect, foreign licensors of technology had to rely upon the confidentiality provisions written into their licence contracts with Chinese licensees. Although the general experience with such clauses was favourable, most foreign licensors of technology, particularly where patents were involved, were reluctant to rely solely upon the provisions of the contract to protect their technology. Besides the inherent difficulty of negotiating meaningful restrictions in such licence agreements, foreign licensors were never sure that a breach of one or more of its terms, such as a failure to provide technical documents on time or to provide the required amount of training, would somehow constitute an excuse for the Chinese side to avoid the restrictions on the transfer of the technology that was subject to the licence's restrictive terms.

This concern has largely been alleviated by the Patent Law in regard to technical transfers involving patents. Although the new law only relates to new inventions after the date of its effectiveness (so that existing technology protected by patents in other countries as of 1 April 1985 may not in general be patented in China), still the broad protections of the Patent Law indicate that it is China's legislative policy to protect all imported technology in a meaningful manner.

Conditions for the grant of patent rights
The law provides for the protection of three types of patents: inventions, utility models and designs. Inventions are protected by the law for a period of 15 years and utility models and designs are protected for a period of five years, but the patent holder may request a further extension for an additional period of three years.

Article 22 of the law requires that inventions and utility models must possess 'novelty, creativity and utility'. 'Novelty' is defined by the law to mean that the invention or utility model has not been previously published or publicly used prior to the date of application. 'Creativity' is defined by the law to require that the invention possess outstanding substantial characteristics and is a marked progress over technology that existed prior to the date of application. The law defines the requirement of 'utility' to mean that the invention or utility model can be manufactured or used and can produce positive results.

The Implementing Regulations of the Patent Law, which were promulgated by the Patent Bureau on 19 January 1985, further define the meaning of inventions, utility models and designs. According to rule 2 of the Implementing Regulations, an 'invention' means any new technical solution relating to a product, a process or improvement thereof; a 'utility model' is any new technical solution relating to the shape, the structure, or their combination, of a product, which is fit for practical use; and a 'design' means any new design of the shape, pattern, colour, or their combination of a product, which creates an aesthetic feeling and is fit for industrial application.

The law prohibits the grant of patent rights to a number of items, such as:

– scientific discoveries;
– rules and methods of intellectual activities;
– methods of diagnosis and cure of diseases;
– food, beverages and seasonings;
– pharmaceuticals;
– animal and plant varieties;
– substances derived from nuclear variations.

The most controversial exclusion from patent protection relates to the non-patentability of pharmaceuticals, which a number of foreign companies have complained about, but China's policy on the subject, which is made clear in the law, is that, for the present anyway, pharmaceuticals cannot be protected by patent rights.

Application process

The State Patent Bureau (or Patent Office) is charged by the law with the responsibility for handling the examination of all patent applications and is empowered to grant patents to inventions and creations that conform to the stipulations of the law.

One of the more interesting provisions of the law is article 6, which provides that inventions and creations made by an individual as part of his employment either by a state enterprise, a foreign-Chinese joint venture or other foreign enterprise belong to the enterprise and not to the individual. In the event that an individual makes an invention or creation while employed by his employer and that invention or creation is commercially practised, the individual is supposed to be rewarded under the terms of the law. According to the Implementing Regulations, the inventor should be given a monetary reward of Rmb200 when the patent is granted for an invention and, if the invention is commercially exploited, the inventor should be paid between 0.5 and 2 per cent of any increase in profits after taxation arising from the exploitation of the invention or, if the patent holder licenses others to exploit the patent, then the inventor should be paid 5 to 10 per cent of the licence fees received by the enterprise holding the patent.

The Patent Law employs the system of deferred examination of patent applications to determine their substance. Except in cases where the Paris Convention applies or there is a bilateral agreement between China and a foreign country, the date of application for a patent is taken to be the date of receipt of the application by the State Patent Bureau. Upon receipt of the patent application, the Patent Office will conduct a preliminary examination to determine whether the application conforms to the law. According to the law and the Implementation Regulations, the preliminary examination is primarily to determine whether the requested patent 'violates the laws of the state or social morality or jeopardises the public interest' or that the invention or creation for which the patent is requested is not of one of the types for which a patent can be granted. Normally the Patent Office will publish the patent application for comment within 18 months of its receipt. After the publication of the patent application, any person desiring to do so may file an opposition with the Patent Office within three months of the publication of the application. According to article 35 of the law, the State Patent Bureau may, on the basis of a request made at any time by the applicant, conduct an examination of substance. If the applicant fails to request an examination as to substance within three years from the date of filing, the application will be regarded as having been withdrawn.

In the event of an opposition being filed within the three-month period, the State Patent Bureau will examine the opposition and notify both parties of its findings. Either the applicant or the party in opposition may take the decision of the Patent Office to the State Patent Re-examination Commission for a rehearing and, if such party is still not satisfied, may refer the matter to the People's Courts.

Once the patent is granted, any third party that has not made an opposition after the publication of the initial application can request the Patent Re-examination Commission to conduct an examination for a request of nullity of a patent. Again, if either party is dissatisfied with the decision of the Commission, that party may take the case to the People's Courts.

Compulsory licensing

Article 51 of the Patent Law creates in the patent holder an obligation to work the patent in China. A patent may be worked in China by the patent holder's setting up an enterprise in China to manufacture the product, entering into a joint venture in China to produce the product, or licensing a Chinese enterprise, joint venture or other enterprise in China to manufacture the product. In the event that an invention or utility model patent holder fails without proper reason to perform the obligation to work the patent in China for a period of three full years from the date the patent is granted, the State Patent Bureau may, on the basis of an application by any unit that possesses the conditions for working of the patent, grant a compulsory licence. The patent holder is still entitled to a royalty for the use of the patent and the law provides that after the grant of the compulsory licence, if the licensor and licensee cannot agree upon a royalty rate, then such rate will be determined by the State Patent Bureau. Pursuant to article 53 of the law, the State Patent Bureau also has the right to grant compulsory licences to a subsequent patent holder whose new patent relies upon or must necessarily use the invention or utility model of a prior patent holder. In such case, the State Patent Bureau has the power to grant a reciprocal licence to the prior patent holder to use the new invention for which his prior technology is to be licensed.

Infringement actions

The Patent Law strictly protects the exclusive right of a patent holder to determine the use of his invention, utility model or design. In this regard, China has an additional administrative remedy to the normal ones found in the West. A patent holder who has knowledge of an infringement of his patent rights may request the patent administration organisation in the local area of the infringing party to take administrative action. Such action includes the power to order the stopping of the infringement and to require the payment of money damages to the patent holder to compensate him for loss. A patent holder may also choose to go directly to the People's Courts for the enforcement of his patent rights.

There is a two-year statute of limitations on the commencement of patent infringement actions. The statue of limitations runs from the date on which the patent holder knew or should have known of the infringement.

Licensing

In addition to the Patent Law, one other piece of legislation plays an important role in the transfer of technology to China. The Regulations of the People's Republic of China governing Contracts for the Importation of Technology (24 May 1985) codify much of China's recent practice in regard to licensing of technology to Chinese enterprises. Technology agreements are also under the approval authority of MOFERT, so that central government discipline can be imposed on all commercial units around the country in order to maintain low royalty rates and preserve certain important contract clauses in all licence contracts. The most objectionable part of the new regulations is that the licensor of technology is required to guarantee that the 'technology as provided will be . . . capable of achieving the targets stipulated in the contract' (article 6). Article 9 of the Regulations also prohibits the licence agreement from containing clauses to the effect that the licensee (a) must buy raw materials, spare parts or equipment from the licensor, (b) must not export the products or (c) stop using the technology at the end of the licensed period.

The new technology regulations are already beginning to influence the willingness of foreign owners of technology to licence into China. It is particularly unfortunate that, given the degree of precision and fairness in the Patent Law, the technology regulations should now be discouraging the importation of technology. Fortunately, MOFERT has stated that if a technology agreement contains provisions contrary to the technology regulations, the Chinese licensee may apply to MOFERT for a waiver of the particular requirement. While this administrative procedure does provide an escape clause to the more burdensome provisions of the regulations, Chinese negotiators are very reluctant to make the special applications required.

The Chinese tax system relating to foreign business activities and individuals

Since 1980, China has adopted several pieces of tax legislation affecting foreign business activities. These include the Individual Income Tax Law, the Joint Venture Income Tax Law and the Foreign Enterprise Income Tax Law. This section discusses the Chinese tax system as it relates to the more common forms of business activities in China, such as equity joint ventures, contractual or cooperative ventures, technology transfer agreements, compensation trade arrangements and representative offices, so that the reader will be aware of the principal tax laws affecting such transactions. The Individual Income Tax, as it relates to foreign individuals in China, is also briefly discussed at the end of this section.

Equity joint ventures

Equity joint ventures with Chinese and foreign investment are required by Chinese law to be organised as limited liability companies. In general, these joint-venture companies are taxed on their net income under the Income Tax Law of the People's Republic of China concerning Joint Ventures using Chinese and Foreign Investment (10 September 1980), on their sales and imports under the Consolidated Industrial and Commercial Tax Regulations (13 September 1958) and on their land and buildings by the Provisional Regulations governing Urban Building and Land Taxes (8 August 1951).

Taxable income

Taxable income for a joint venture is defined as 'net income' after deduction of costs, expenses and losses, and includes income derived from production, business and other sources. Income from other sources includes dividends, bonuses, interest, royalties, rental and other income.

Neither the joint venture tax law nor the regulations specify what may be included as deductible costs, expenses or losses, but the recently announced Accounting Regulations discussed above do clarify the Chinese view of 'net income'. The Detailed Rules and Regulations for the Income Tax Law concerning Joint Ventures using Chinese and Foreign Investment (10 December 1980) issued under the Joint Venture Income Tax Law list certain items that are disallowed as deductions in calculating taxable income. These include national and local income tax, surtax, fines and penalties, expenditures that must be capitalised, and interest on capital. Business-related entertainment expenses are limited to 0.3 per cent of total sales income or 1 per cent of total operational income.

The Joint Venture Income Tax Law provides that the net profit of a joint venture can be distributed after the joint venture income tax is paid and after payments are made into the venture's reserve fund, bonus and welfare fund, and expansion fund; the payments made into these funds are not deductible as they are after-tax items.

The Joint Venture Income Tax Law also provides for the depreciation of fixed assets and for the amortisation of intangible assets according to general schedules included in the regulations. Generally, such depreciation periods cannot be accelerated, except in cases where either the term of the joint venture is shorter that the useful life of the items to be depreciated, or such items can be shown to have a shorter useful life because of corrosion, vibration, high utilisation period or other destructive causes. Losses may be carried forward for five years.

Income taxes paid abroad by the joint venture on

income earned outside China may be credited against taxes to be paid in China. The credit cannot exceed the Chinese tax payable on the income earned abroad.

Tax rates for joint ventures

The Joint Venture Income Tax Law provides for a basic 30 per cent tax rate. In addition, a local surtax of 10 per cent of the tax paid is levied by the local governments, bringing the total basic tax rate to 33 per cent.

A further tax of 10 per cent is levied on a foreign participant of a joint venture that remits its share of profits out of China. Accordingly, a dividend that is reinvested within China without first being remitted outside China will be free of this 10 per cent tax.

A newly-established joint venture that is scheduled to operate for a period of 10 years or more may apply for a full exemption from tax in its first two profit-making years and a 50 per cent reduction from tax in the following three years. The first profit-making year is defined as the year in which a joint venture begins to make a profit after taking into account any loss carry-overs.

Tax incentives

Under the Joint Venture Income Tax Law, a participant in a joint venture that reinvests in China a portion of its share of profits from the joint venture for at least five consecutive years may obtain a refund of 40 per cent of the national income tax paid on the reinvested funds (although this is not available for the local income tax paid). The refund is granted upon the taxpayer's application to the relevant authorities that it intends to reinvest for the five-year period. The amount refunded is not subject to the 10 per cent tax on the remittance of profit abroad. If the funds are withdrawn before the end of the five-year period, the taxpayer must pay back the refunded tax.

The Consolidated Industrial and Commercial Tax

Certain activities of equity joint ventures are subject to the Consolidated Industrial and Commercial Tax. These activities include the production of industrial products, the importation of foreign goods, commercial retailing, communications, transportation, and the rendering of services. Tax is imposed on the gross amount of proceeds received from the sale of goods and services. Under a new Chinese policy, equity joint ventures may pay tax according to the lower rates of the 1972 Industrial and Commercial Tax Act, which ordinarily only applies to Chinese domestic enterprises.

Taxable items and rates

The tax schedules of the Consolidated Industrial and Commercial Tax Regulations list over 100 categories of taxable industrial and argicultural products. Rates range from 1.5 per cent for cotton greige cloth to 69 per cent for grade A cigarettes. A 5 per cent rate applies to any industrial product that is not listed specifically in one of the categories. Raw or semi-finished materials are subject to the lowest rates of tax and industrial goods are generally taxed at lower rates than are consumer goods.

Taxable items under the categories of services and commercial retailing are subject to tax rates ranging from 3 to 7 per cent.

Exemptions

Machinery, equipment, parts and other materials imported under a joint-venture contract as part of the foreign party's capital contribution to the venture are exempt from the Consolidated Industrial and Commercial Tax, as well as from customs duties. Raw materials, auxiliary materials, components, parts and packaging materials are also exempt from the consolidated tax and duties when imported by a joint venture for the production of export products. If a joint venture sells in China any items imported tax free, or incorporates these items into products for sale in China, it must make up the appropriate tax payments.

With the approval of the Ministry of Finance, joint ventures may be exempted from the Consolidated Industrial and Commercial Tax as applied to exports, except in the case of export items which are restricted by the state.

Provisional urban real estate tax

Equity joint ventures may also be subjected to the Provisional Regulations governing Urban Real Estate Tax levied on buildings that the Chinese party contributes as part of its equity in the venture. The annual tax rate for buildings is 1.2 per cent based on an assigned standard value. Exemptions from this tax are routinely requested by and granted to joint ventures.

Contractual joint ventures

In contractual joint ventures, where the documents establish a legal person in China as the cooperative company, the company may apply to the tax authorities to be taxed in the same manner as an equity joint venture. To date, few such applications have been granted, since the documentation establishing the cooperative was generally found to be unclear as to the nature of the entity as a separate and distinct legal person.

In true contractual joint ventures, the Chinese and foreign parties contribute resources or technology and share profits according to contractual terms. Typically, the Chinese and foreign parties calculate and pay their own taxes – the Chinese under relevant domestic tax legislation and the foreign party under the Income Tax Law of the People's Republic of China concerning Foreign Enterprises.

The Foreign Enterprise Income Tax Taxpayers

The Income Tax Law of the People's Republic of China concerning Foreign Enterprises (the 'Foreign Enterprise Income Tax Law') divides taxpayers into two categories: foreign companies, enterprises and other economic organisations having 'establishments' in China, and those which do not. Foreign partners in contractual joint ventures which are considered to have establishments in China are taxed at progressive rates on their income from production, business and other sources. 'Establishments' are defined as organisations, sites, or business agents engaged in production or business operation either independently or in cooperative production or joint business operations with Chinese enterprises. Sites include factories, sites where natural resources are being exploited and sites where construction, installation and other projects take place.

Taxable income and rates

The definition and calculation of taxable income under the Foreign Enterprise Income Tax Law are generally the same as those in the Joint Venture Income Tax Law.

The tax rates for foreign companies with establishments in China range from 20 per cent on the portion of annual net taxable income up to Rmb250,000 to 40 per cent on net income over Rmb1 million. In addition, the localities levy a tax of 10 per cent on the amount of taxable income; therefore, the total tax rates range from 30 to 50 per cent.

The Consolidated Industrial and Commercial Tax

As with equity joint ventures, the foreign participants in a contractual venture, or the cooperative itself in the case of a cooperative venture, are also subject to the Consolidated Industrial and Commercial Tax and customs duties on goods imported for the venture unless there is a special exemption, and on business or service income earned by the venture. Such taxes may be paid either by the venture or the parties directly depending upon the provisions of the contract. Many of the tax exemptions and reductions available to equity joint ventures can be obtained by contractual or cooperative ventures upon application.

The taxation of transfer of technology

China signed over 1,600 contracts during 1984 which included provisions for the importation of advanced technology, valued by the Chinese authorities at MOFERT at over US$1.56 billion.

Taxpayers without establishments in China are taxed on certain categories of China-sourced income at a flat rate of 20 per cent which is levied on the gross amount of the income. The 20 per cent tax is withheld at source. China-sourced income includes dividends, interest, rentals, and fees for the use of proprietary rights in China and other income as determined by the Ministry of Finance. The use of proprietary rights includes royalties, licence fees for patented or other proprietary technology, trademarks and copyrights. In addition, fees for technical training, technical services and technical documentation provided by a foreign company to an entity in China would fall within this category of income.

As discussed above, the Foreign Enterprise Income Tax Law includes as taxable income licensing fees, royalties, technical training fees and fees for the use of other proprietary information. The 20 per cent withholding tax on such income may be reduced to 10 per cent on the transfer of nuclear technology, certain types of computer technology, agricultural technology and energy exploration and conservation technology, among other things. A licensor of technology may even be exempted from tax if the technology transferred is 'advanced' and offered at 'preferential' terms. However, to qualify for the reduction or exemption, the foreign companies have to apply for approvals from the local authorities and the Ministry of Finance respectively. Companies from countries that grant a tax credit for such withholding taxes are seldom able to receive a total exemption, since the withholding tax can be credited against their home country tax liability. Unfortunately, Chinese tax authorities will only give a definitive tax ruling after a particular contract is signed, except in regard to the most important contracts. This means that before a contract is signed, a company could not effectively determine whether it would be subject to a 20 or 10 per cent withholding tax or totally exempt from withholding for the transfer of technology under the contract.

China has signed tax treaties with the United States, Japan, France and Germany, and other tax treaties are under negotiation. The United States treaty has not yet been ratified. Each of the tax treaties automatically reduces the withholding tax or royalties, as well as other passive income, to 10 per cent. The existing national legislation permitting the reduction of withholding taxes to 10 per cent or total exemption could be eliminated at any time, in which case the withholding tax could be 20 per cent except for countries with tax treaties.

Compensation trade

Compensation trade as described above refers to the type of project where a foreign company provides machinery, equipment or technology to a Chinese party and receives payment in kind. The in kind payment usually consists of goods produced from the foreign company's equipment and technology. These goods are almost always resold by the foreign company outside China.

There are two ways in which a compensation trade project can be set up. It can be set up as a loan of equipment with repayment in kind for both principal and interest. It can also be set up as an instalment sale of equipment, with each in kind payment as an instalment payment of the purchase price of the equipment. If technology or services are provided by the foreign company, a portion of the in kind payment may be designated as fees for 'the use of proprietary rights'.

Chinese tax officials have stated that although a compensation trade project usually involves a 'site' in China, the project is not viewed as an 'establishment' in China. Therefore, when the Foreign Enterprise Income Tax Law was first announced, the in kind payments representing interest and service fees to the foreign company were taxed under the 20 per cent 'non-establishment' tax under the Foreign Enterprise Income Tax. The amount of this tax was withheld in kind.

In 1983, the Ministry of Finance exempted from the Foreign Enterprise Income Tax those interest and leasing fees paid in kind. However, exemption was not given to technology service fees paid in kind. Again, the local tax authorities have to approve the exemption for a particular contract. Therefore, for the moment, most foreign companies engaging in compensation trade projects are exempt from Chinese tax.

Taxation of representative offices

Under the Foreign Enterprise Income Tax Law, a representative office of a foreign company can be an 'establishment' for tax purpose only if it engages in 'production or business operations'. Most of the foreign companies' representative offices are viewed by the Chinese as liaison offices engaged in the development of business and negotiation of contracts in China on behalf of their home offices. However, some representative offices do in fact engage in true business operations (which may be contrary to the regulations permitting their registration) and must now pay taxes according to the Foreign Enterprise Income Tax Law. Moreover, representative offices of professional service or trading companies are viewed as 'establishments' in China because they generate fees for professional services performed by the representative offices and such offices also must pay tax.

That resident representative offices were subject to the Foreign Enterprise Income Tax Law and the Consolidated Industrial and Commercial Tax on their China-sourced income was made clear in the recent Provisional Regulations of the Ministry of Finance of the People's Republic of China on the Levy of Consolidated Industrial and Commercial Tax and the Enterprise Income Tax on Resident Representative Offices of Foreign Enterprise (14 May 1985). These regulations define the types of income on which representative offices must pay the enterprise income tax and the consolidated tax. Primarily the type of income subject to the regulations is fee income generated by the performance of services for third parties in China. Whether or not a representative office is treated as an establishment for purposes of the Foreign Enterprise Income Tax, it has to pay Consolidated Industrial and Commercial Tax and duties on office equipment imported into China.

Representative offices of foreign banks are generally not viewed as 'establishments' for purposes of the Foreign Enterprise Income Tax Law, since the regulations permitting their establishment and by agreement with PBOC, the central bank, such offices are not to engage in the business of banking. It is interesting to note that certain tax regulations of the Ministry of Finance encourage lending through such representative offices, but so far no bank has had the nerve to run contrary to the restrictions imposed by PBOC prohibiting lending through representative offices. Since some banks do provide advisory services to their clients for fee income, they are now required to pay tax on such income pursuant to the May 1985 regulations. Therefore, in general, interest on China loans earned by banks is subject to the withholding tax under Foreign Enterprise Income Tax Law and their service income is subject to both the income tax and the consolidated tax. Banks lending to the Bank of China and other state banks at 'preferential' rates are exempt from the withholding tax on their interest income.

The Individual Income Tax Law

Taxpayers
The Individual Income Tax Law provides that individuals who reside in China for 90 consecutive days or less are exempt from individual income tax on compensation paid by an employer outside China. Individuals who reside in China more than 90 days are subject to taxation in China on all income gained within China.

'Residency' is interpreted as the right to remain in China, as evidenced by a taxpayer's visa. Consequently, holders of visas valid for more than 90 days are treated as residents of more than 90 days and are subject to taxation on all their wages and salaries for the entire period of the visa, even if they should temporarily leave China and return during the period of the visa. There-

fore, a foreigner with a six-month multiple-entry visa who only spends four of the six months in China is considered a resident for six months and is taxable on six months' wages and salaries. At the same time, foreigners who enter China on short-term visas (30-60 days' duration) would be subject to taxation on all their wages and salaries from their initial date of entry if they accumulate a total of 91 days in China with no absence of more than 30 days between visas.

Source rules
Under the regulations, income gained in China includes compensation for services performed in China, dividends and bonuses gained in China, fees for use of proprietary rights rent from the leasing of property in China and interest earned in China. Included in China, in an individual's wages and salary are per diem or other subsidies on personal expenses paid by the individual's employer. Therefore, payment of an employee's Chinese tax by the employer should result in taxable income to the employee, but frequently does not due to the tax collection apparatus. Payments by the employer of housing, transportation and business expenses from general funds of the company are not included in salary income subject to tax.

Tax Rates
A standard allowance of Rmb800 per month is exempted from an individual's taxable income. Wages and salaries are taxed at the following rates:

Monthly income in Rmb	Tax rate (%)
0 — 800	
801 — 1,500	5
1,501 — 3,000	10
3,001 — 6,000	20
6,001 — 9,000	30
9,001 — 12,000	40
More than 12,001	45

Income other than wages and salaries are taxed at a flat rate of 20 per cent with the first 20 per cent of each such payment being exempted.

China's Special Economic Zones and 14 coastal cities

On 26 January 1984, while on a visit to the Shenzhen Special Economic Zone (SEZ), China's leading comrade, Deng Xiaoping, took brush in hand and in his best calligraphy wrote out these words of encouragement complimenting the local authorities on the successful implementation of China's open door policy:

'Shenzhen's development and experience prove that our policy for setting up Special Economic Zones is correct.
Build the Special Economic Zone still faster and better.'

But less than a year later, Comrade Deng had something else to say about the Shenzhen SEZ:

'We have yet to see whether this course is right or not

... We hope it will succeed, but if it fails then we can draw experience from it.'

There is no question that Deng's earlier congratulatory statement on the development of the Shenzhen SEZ was fully warranted by the facts. Shenzhen, which became an SEZ in 1980, has been transformed in less than five years from a sleepy, coastal fishing village to a city of 330,000 people with a bustling trade and vigorous industrial base. Between January 1980 and June 1984, the Shenzhen SEZ signed 3,018 contracts with foreign firms representing a total investment of US$2.05 billion, of which over US$450 million has already been invested in the 327 square kilometre enclave.

If one compares the national figures for foreign investment with those of Shenzhen, the dominant position of Shenzhen in leading China's open door policy toward foreign investment is clear:

Total national to 31 December 1984

	Number	Investment (US$m)
Joint ventures	931	1,430.00
Cooperatives	2,213	4,700.00
Petroleum	31	2,420.00
Processing	n.a.	n.a.
Compensation trade	1,370	1,340.00
Wholly-owned	74	470.00

Shenzhen to June 1984

	Number	Investment (US$m)	Shenzhen percentage of national
Joint venture	213	307.77	21.5
Cooperatives	340	1,269.23	27.0
Petroleum	0	0	0
Processing	2,412	129.50	
Compensation trade	7	6.02	0.4
Wholly-owned	46	339.74	72.2

The Shenzhen Special Economic Zone, which borders Hong Kong, is only one of four zones established by enabling legislation of the National People's Congress in 1980. The other three zones are Zhuhai, next to Macao, Shantou, on the coast of Guangdong Province well to the east of Hong Kong, and Xiamen in Fujian Province across the Taiwan straits from the Republic of China.

While the economic growth of these other three SEZs has not been as rapid as that of Shenzhen, they are beginning to catch up and can boast some impressive statistics. Zhuhai has signed more than 65 contracts with foreign investors and the total pledged investment exceeds US$1.3 billion. Xiamen has signed 67 contracts with foreign firms, which have committed over US$300 million of investment to the zone. Shantou has signed 24 such agreements, but the value of such investments is not available.

Yet Deng Xiaoping's statement of July 1985 is also correct – the SEZ experiment might fail. While the economic achievements are genuine, socialist discipline has paid a heavy price. There is a rampant black market in Shenzhen and most of its investment has been in real estate projects, rather than high-technology industrial ventures. It is logical therefore that the leadership might question whether the economic progress justified the inroads of capitalism.

Role of the SEZs in China's modernisation

As reflected by the remarks of Deng Xiaoping, it has never been clear what China's precise goals for the SEZs were, nor the role that the SEZs are supposed to play in China's overall modernisation plan. The concept of forming special zones was first raised in China in 1978 at the very beginning of the country's modernisation drive, and during 1979, even while the zones were beginning to operate, the Academy of Social Sciences did research on established export processing zones and free-trade zones in other countries. While such studies have led to a substantial amount of legislation to establish the SEZs and regulate the business affairs of foreign and Chinese enterprises within the zones, there has never been a definitive policy statement by the Chinese government as to the particular purpose the zones are to serve.

Foreign commentators have speculated on the purpose of the SEZs and come up with possible rationale such as increasing employment, earning foreign exchange, and importing Western technology. The problem with each of these objectives is that they are just as true for other places in China that are seeking foreign investment as they are for the SEZs. A more political analysis has suggested that the zones are to serve as half-way houses for the economic reintegration of Hong Kong, Macao and Taiwan into the mainland's economy. By providing a suitable environment for capitalists in the special zones, China would prove that its announced policy of 'one country, two systems' was workable. Such a rationale for the SEZs, however, necessarily means that they will always be kept quite separate and distinct from the mainland of China and not play an important or integral role in China's modernisation programme.

At the same time Chairman Deng was penning his words of encouragement to the economic leadership of Shenzhen, one of China's leading economists, Xu Dixin, was trying to rationalise some of the peculiarly unsocialistic features of the SEZs in an essay in *Beijing Review*.

After pointing out that the role of SEZs in capitalist countries poses no inherent contradiction since their purpose is to develop capitalism, Xu stated that in a socialist country like China, SEZs, in nature and in function, do pose contradictions with the unified policies of state socialism. In particular, Xu pointed to the fact that in the SEZs, the law of value is the driving economic regulator, rather than state planning. Moreover, while under socialism goods are to be priced based upon the value expended in their production (no profits), goods in the SEZs are priced at values set by the market, which may greatly exceed the cost of production.

'In the Special Economic Zones, it is not only the law of value but also the law of surplus value [meaning prices greater than the costs of production] that is operating. There is exploitation of surplus value in the form of profits earned by guest investors, whether joint ventures or foreign-owned enterprises. The exploitation of surplus value exists objectively in China's Special Economic Zones, which is in contradiction with China's socialist system. However, in the long term, the exploitation of surplus values in the special zones is a 'buying-out' policy. During the early post-liberation years, China adopted a policy of redemption to get the cooperation of the national bourgeoisie. Under today's buying-out policy, China is cooperating with foreign and overseas Chinese investors – using their funds, importing advanced technology, learning their managerial skills and more – so as to develop the special zones and increase the country's earnings in foreign exchange. All this will benefit China's modernisation drive. That is what we mean by 'unified' relationship . . . The buying-out policy serves as the theoretical basis for China's protection of guest investments.'

While the 'buying-out' rationale for the SEZs may not be appealing to potential investors, it probably does correctly express the views of many of China's leaders. The freedom of development given to foreign investors in the zones will benefit China at almost no cost and the lessons learned will be used to modernise the truly socialist portions of the country, so that they can in time compete in the capitalist free markets.

Liang Xiang, the former mayor of Shenzhen and a Vice-Governor of Guangdong Province, has summarised the advantages of the SEZs in a slightly different way. The advantages of establishing the zones are:

1   Through preferential policies these zones can use large amounts of foreign investment in a better way, import advanced technology, and acquire scientific techniques and management skills – all of which will enable the country as a whole to develop economically at a quicker pace.
2   By dealing regularly with foreign capital, we can further observe and understand the development of and changes in the modern capitalist world, and keep abreast of the changes on the international markets and in science and technology.
3   Through cooperation, we can learn modern urban construction and management methods, and train professionals.

The purpose of the SEZs therefore appears to be to serve as a university for the training of Chinese officials, who will learn Western technology and management methods that will in time be used to modernise all of China. Rather than being unique, isolated enclaves cut off from the rest of China that were formed to prove that a 'one country, two systems' policy is workable, the SEZs are instead the places to which all of China can look to see the road to modernisation. But the road to modernisation presently displays for all to see an enormous black market in goods and currency. If the experiment fails due to excesses and poor planning, the modernisation programme itself must also be in trouble.

Role of the 14 coastal cities

During Comrade Deng's historic visit to the four SEZs in January 1984, he also proposed to extend the flexible business procedures and preferences found in the SEZs to a number of additional cities along China's coast. The decision to open the 14 coastal cities was taken in April 1984 by the State Council, and an investment seminar was held in Hong Kong to promote each of the new open cities in November 1984.

The coastal cities are to adopt many of the same laws and preferences that already exist in the SEZs. There is one striking difference, however, between the coastal cities and the SEZs: whereas the SEZs were each established in relatively underdeveloped areas, the coastal cities are already established manufacturing and commercial centres in their own right. The total cargo-handling capacity for the coastal cities presently accounts for 97 per cent of all of China's capacity and their industrial production presently accounts for 23 per cent of all of China's industrial production. Thus the new coastal cities add a substantial new dimension to the philosophy which was first experimented with in the SEZs: now China will try in a unified way to match the flexible business attitudes and preferential treatment that have encouraged the economic development of the SEZs with the established industrial base of its major trading cities along the coast.

SEZs and open cities

It is the contention of the author that the role of the SEZs in China's overall modernisation plans has been changed, partly by the further opening of the 14 coastal cities and partly by the increased awareness at the national level of the SEZ experiment. The role of the 14 coastal cities will be to adopt the economic policies that have been proven to be successful in the SEZs and hopefully improve on the development pace of the SEZs by blending together flexible policies with an established manufacturing and trading base. The role of the SEZs, on the other hand, will be enhanced even further to include acting as a controlled environment for legislative experiments regarding potential measures that may, if proven successful in the SEZs, be applied nationwide in China. Thus, the SEZs will become the experimental ground for new economic legislation so that policies can be tested first on a small scale before being applied to the 14 coastal cities and elsewhere in China.

Regulatory and legal framework of the SEZs

On 26 August 1980, the 15th session of the Standing Committee of the National People's Congress adopted Regulations on Special Economic Zones in Guangdong Province (the '1980 Regulations'). These regulations stated the objective of the Guangdong SEZs to be 'to develop external economic cooperation and technical exchanges' so as to promote 'socialist modernisation construction'. The 1980 Regulations set the framework for the SEZ concept by establishing the principle that the zones were to provide a favourable environment for foreign investment by making the local government responsible for the necessary infrastructure in exchange for providing that all business activities within the zones were to be subjected to the laws and decrees of the People's Republic of China.

The 1980 Regulations contained a number of surprises that made the SEZs unique within China. First, foreign companies were allowed to establish their own wholly-owned enterprises in the zones by applying to the Administrative Committee for the SEZs of Guangdong Province (the 'Committee'), as well as being able to enter into joint ventures with Chinese enterprises which was already permitted in other parts of China. Secondly, while the goal of the zones was clearly export oriented and the products produced there were to be sold on the international markets, still upon application to and the approval by the Committee, an SEZ joint venture or wholly-owned enterprise could sell a portion of its products on the domestic Chinese market. Thirdly, all 'necessary machinery, equipment, spare parts, fittings, raw and other materials, transport vehicles and other materials required for production' were exempted from import duties, as compared to the rather cumbersome and laborious internal rules for obtaining custom duties and other tax exemptions in the rest of China for foreign investment projects. Fourthly, and most surprising of all at the time, was the clear promise in the legislation that 'staff members and workers employed by enterprises in the special zones shall be managed by the enterprises in accordance with their operational requirements and, if necessary, may be dismissed'. When compared with the labour management regulations for joint ventures in the rest of China that had just been issued the previous month, which provided for dismissal of workers only if it could be shown that they had become redundant due to technical transformations or that they were incapable of learning the necessary skills, the bold and very unsocialist provisions regarding the dismissal of workers in the 1980 Regulations were seen by foreign investors as one of the principal attractions of the Guangdong SEZs.

The 1980 Regulations also established an administrative framework for the Guangdong SEZs. Rather than administering the foreign investment programme at the national level, the Guangdong Committee was given the power to:
- draw up development plans for the SEZs and organise their implementation;
- examine and approve investment projects in the zones;
- process registration papers for foreign enterprises that wished to establish wholly-owned operations in the zones;
- coordinate the work of banking, insurance, tax, customs, border inspection and other national regulatory agencies in the zones;
- take responsibility for providing the necessary qualified workforce within the zones to meet the needs of foreign investors; and
- supervise health, education, and cultural affairs in the zones and take responsibility for public security.

By entrusting the overall supervision of the zones' investment programme to the Committee formed at the provincial level, the National People's Congress did much to overcome the delays inherent in other parts of China where each of the various arms of the governmental administrative structure had to report to its own head office in Beijing for resolution of new questions, rather than solving problems or misunderstandings regarding investments at the local level.

The 1980 Regulations also conferred a number of investment incentives on foreign companies that chose the Special Economic Zones as the place to do business in China. The tax rate on profits was in general lowered to 15 per cent, land use fees or rental rates were also to be lower than in other parts of China, and the entrance and exit formalities for businessmen were to be simplified.

While the 1980 Regulations set the guiding principles for the SEZs – that is, favourable tax rates, low land use fees, the right to hire and fire, wholly-owned foreign factories and most importantly local administration of all aspects of the business bureaucracy – nevertheless, the regulations themselves were no more than guidelines and many early investors found the going rough. Several early investors suffered from a continuance of the previous mental attitudes of Chinese bureaucrats. Harpers International, a Hong Kong subsidiary of the Sime Darby Group that planned to invest in a bus and truck production factory, found the labour force supplied, rather than being competent to carry out the work, were in fact local farmers from the nearby communes who had no industrial experience whatever. But more troublesome still was that the guidelines of the 1980 Regulations required more detailed legislation to implement their provisions and there was uncertainty as to which legislative body in China was responsible for formulating and adopting such implementing legislation. The Guangdong Committee for the SEZs clearly had administrative authority, but did it also have legislative authority?

Slightly more than one year after the 1980 Regulations, the National People's Congress took a bold move to solve the problem of legislative authority. On 26 November 1981, the NPC adopted a resolution authorising the People's Congresses and their Standing Committees in Guangdong Province and Fujian Province to formulate various specific economic regulations for the Special Economic Zones in their respective provinces. Besides resolving the question of legislative authority for the SEZs, this resolution had another profound effect: it gave to the local authorities in the SEZs who administered the day-to-day activities of investors the power to propose to their local provincial congresses draft legislation to regulate the activities of their investors. Rather than drafting new laws in committees of academics and leading cadre in Beijing, economic legislation would be proposed and drafted by the cadre that were dealing with foreign businessmen on a day-to-day basis. Following this authorisation, a whole host of legislation began rolling off the presses in Guangdong Province.

Regulations regarding eased entry and exit formalities, the procedures for registering business enterprises, the determination of labour rates and procedures for hiring and firing workers, and land use or rental rates and the system for contracting for land, were all issued under the authority of the Guangdong People's Congress after being proposed by the economic planners of the zones.

With the November 1981 resolution in place and the new detailed regulations issued shortly, the Shenzhen SEZ began its rapid expansion. While it would be an overstatement to say that the clarification of the legal system in Shenzhen was the sole cause of its growth, clearly the existence of a reasonably detailed set of rules for the establishment of enterprises, the hiring and firing of workers, the rental of land and the tax and other preferences available assisted substantially in the attraction of foreign capital. Such rules were particularly welcome by Hong Kong Chinese investors, who were able businessmen but accustomed to operating in the Hong Kong environment of clear rules of the game. While the whole of China was only able to attract 190 joint-venture projects during the period 1979-83, the Shenzhen SEZ on its own attracted over 89 joint ventures and Xiamen in Fujian Province a further 10. By the end of 1983, US$786,045,000 had been pledged in joint ventures in all of China, and of this amount US$151,499,700 or 19 per cent was invested in the Shenzhen SEZ alone. With the publication of the JV Implementing Regulations in September 1983, the rest of China had a legal framework that to a large extent matched the specificity and certainty found in Shenzhen and the other SEZs. A similar phenomenon took place in China itself after the introduction of this higher level of legal precision: over twice as many joint ventures were negotiated, signed and approved in 1984 in China as compared with all previous years taken together.

SEZs as experimental laboratories for new legislation

The fact that the Shenzhen zone had an established track record also permitted the normally cautious Beijing authorities to adopt two more important measures. First, the legislation that had been prepared and implemented in Shenzhen as a limited experiment was extended uniformly to the other three zones, while permitting the local authorities in those zones to adopt measures and amendments that they felt necessary for their own zones.

Secondly, and more radical still, the November 1981 resolution authorising the Provincial People's Congresses to adopt economic measures for their zones, which had proved so successful in 1982 and 1983, was extended in spirit (if not by law) to permit the zones to experiment with truly radical legislation modelled on business practices in the West. The zones – rather than being 'special' areas cut off from the rest of China – are to become the experimental laboratory for legislation that could eventually become national in scope.

Technology rules

Probably the best example of the new legislative role of the SEZs are the Shenzhen Technology Regulations adopted in early 1984 (the 'Technology Regulations'). Formulated in accordance with the 'relevant laws and regulations of the People's Republic of China' and the 1980 Regulations, the Technology Regulations were in fact a first for China. The regulations lay down some basic requirements, such as that all technology transfer contracts must be in writing, for technology transfers made for consideration to enterprises within the special zones.

In general, the Technology Regulations' requirements are quite stringent:

1 patented technology must be supported by issued patents or, in the case of pending patents, by the patent applications;

2 there is a very detailed list of documents, data and equipment that must be provided when transfering technical know-how;

3 if the technology has been licensed before, the licensor must produce copies of other licence agreements;

4 the licensor must guarantee the legal validity of the imported technology and that the desired technical results will be obtained;

5 the technology must be capable of producing products saleable on the international markets and in the event of any losses caused by the failure to meet such a requirement, the licensor is responsible; and

6 the licensor shall compensate the licensee for damages in the event that the licensed technology does not meet the requirements stipulated in the contract 'due to factors caused by' the licensor.

The Technology Regulations are not all unfavourable, however; they contain a specific requirement that the licensee maintain the confidentiality of the licensed technology as specified in the contract and that such restrictions not only apply to the licensee but also to all staff members that are exposed to the confidential information. Also, in cases where the technology is of an 'advanced world standard' according to the Scientific and Technological Development Centre of Shenzhen and the relevant state scientific research departments, the local tax authorities can confer special tax treatment and the land department can grant preferential treatment in regard to land use fees.

The Technology Regulations also set forth the procedures to be followed by the licensee in seeking approval to import technology: first, a feasibility study is required; secondly, an application for the import of technology; thirdly, the execution of a contract; and fourthly, the submission of the contract in triplicate to the Shenzhen municipal government along with the proof of authority of the licensor and the licensee and the approved application. According to the regulations, the Shenzhen municipal government is the approving authority for all technology imports, and only after issuance of its approval can the contract come into force.

It is interesting to note that the Technology Regulations when they first appeared had a scope much wider than just Shenzhen; they were being used extensively by analogy by other units in mainland China when negotiating technology transfer agreements. Although at first it would seem strange that such regulations, which by their terms only apply in the 327 square kilometre zone of Shenzhen, should be applied by analogy elsewhere in China, it was in fact such 'application by analogy' that was the main purpose of the legislation. Although Shenzhen was supposed to be a centre for the importation of advanced Western technology, the zone has not in fact attracted much high-tech investment. While several recent joint ventures with US and Japanese investors do have a documented technology content, Shenzhen's showcase projects are not of an 'advanced world standard', investors seldom contribute patents or know-how as part of their capital contribution, and few joint ventures have licence agreements from or pay royalties to foreign investors.

If the purpose was to promote the importation of high technology into Shenzhen, the Technology Regulations would have only authorised the Shenzhen municipal government to grant tax and land use preferences and guaranteed the protection of industrial property rights, while leaving the rest of terms of transfer to be worked out by the licensor and licensee in contract negotiations. Instead, the purpose of the Technology Regulations was to serve as an experimental model for China as a whole. By publishing the regulations in written form, China prompted constructive criticism from foreign legal commentators as to the merits of the legislation. More importantly, Chinese enterprises negotiating technology transfer contracts in other parts of China could refer to the regulations as 'the law', but if the licensor was intractable, still have the flexibility to make concessions since 'the law' only applied to Shenzhen. In this way, Chinese units gained first-hand experience in negotiations as to where the Technology Regulations were acceptable and where they should be amended before being formalised as national legislation.

Much of the experience learned from the Shenzhen experiment is reflected in the Regulations governing Contracts for the Importation of Technology issued by the national government on 24 May 1985. While many of the objectionable provisions of the Shenzhen Technology Regulations were removed in the national legislation, some critics feel that the Chinese should have studied the Shenzhen experiment more closely. Nevertheless, whether used effectively or not, it is clear that in the case of technology, Shenzhen was used by the national government as an experimental proving ground.

It is also of interest to note that apparently the Technology Regulations are not mandatory even in Shenzhen itself. A recent licence agreement concluded between an investor and its Shenzhen joint venture required prior approval from MOFERT in Beijing for certain provisions of the agreement, including the governing law, terms and damages clauses, which did not correspond with the Technology Regulations. If a foreign licensor of technology cannot live with one of the regulations' provisions, it is always possible to request that the Technology Regulations not be followed in full and, if the local authorities in collaboration with the national Foreign Investment Bureau of MOFERT agree, such provision can be ignored in the final contract. It appears that this practical attitude experienced in dealing with the Shenzhen Technology Regulations is to be copied at the national level.

Other experimental legislation
Shenzhen has and is experimenting with legislation in a number of other fields that either has been or may in the future be incorporated into national legislation.

Foreign economic contracts
On 7 February 1984 the Guangdong provincial authorities promulgated regulations governing foreign economic contracts (the 'Contract Regulations'). Unlike the national Economic Contracts Law, which is of national application, but only applies to contracts between Chinese legal persons, the Shenzhen regulations apply to all agreements between Chinese enterprises or other economic organisations in the SEZ and foreign enterprises and also apply to agreements between wholly-owned or joint-venture enterprises in the SEZ and Chinese enterprises. The Contract Regulations are not a contract law in the Western sense, but instead a series of specific provisions dealing with such issues as contract formalities, the contents of certain specified types of contracts, and penalties to be imposed in case of a breach of contract.

The Contract Regulations are unlikely to promote the economic growth and development of the zone. Provi-

sions that are particularly burdensome include (1) the requirement that both parties of the contract must deliver a guaranty, (2) that if one of the contract parties fails to deliver goods or pay money when due a penalty of 0.1 per cent of the total value in arrears is levied per day (a per annum interest rate of 36.5 per cent which is high when one considers the standard rate of interest for renminbi loans is only 7 per cent), and (3) a provision that if the contract is in two languages, then the Chinese language version governs.

The Shenzhen experiment with the Contract Regulations proved valuable to China when the national Law on Economic Contracts involving Foreign Parties (21 March 1985) was drafted. Each of the objectionable provisions mentioned in the preceding paragraph was eliminated in the national law on foreign economic contracts. While beneficial to the rest of China, one must ask where this leaves the experimental Special Economic Zone, since it now has a contracts law less favourable than the rest of China.

Fortunately, the Shenzhen Contract Regulations are more often ignored than enforced, and so far have not appeared to be a barrier to the negotiations of more sensible contracts. It is hoped that this flexibility in application will continue to be the case, but the Draconian nature of the regulations is now a major incentive for foreign companies to insist upon a foreign governing law clause. It is also interesting to note that since the adoption of the Contract Regulations, Shenzhen Chinese enterprises have been more willing to accept a foreign governing law and to sign contracts only in English.

Property management
The Rules of the Shenzhen SEZ on Property Management promulgated by the Guangdong provincial government on 23 January 1984 have a sounder basis in commercial practice and should help to develop the zone. The Property Management Rules attempt to organise the ownership, sale, mortgage, lease and registration of residential, commercial and industrial property of foreigners and SEZ joint and cooperative ventures. Moreover, the rules reduce the likelihood of a reoccurrence of some of the abuses that took place in the first Shenzhen apartment development schemes, since purchase money funds prior to completion must be placed on deposit with a bank in China.

Mortgages
The Provisional Procedures for Bank Mortgage Loans promulgated on 5 December 1984 reintroduces to China the capitalist tool of mortgage lending. Banks may now lend against not only real estate, as contemplated by the Property Management Rules, but also commodities and negotiable securities.

Non-bank financial institutions
The Provisional Procedures of the Shenzhen SEZ for non-banking state-owned Financial Institutions, which were drafted by the Bank of China and also promulgated on 5 December 1984, encourage China's national and provincial trust and investment companies, leasing concerns, insurance enterprises and, most surprisingly, 'stock exchanges' to set up in Shenzhen. Apparently the purpose of these procedures is to encourage the inland

areas of China to attract investment for their local areas through use of Shenzhen's close geographic connection with Hong Kong's international financial market. The procedures set capital requirements for the local offices, another experimental first for China.

Foreign branch banking

On 2 April 1985, the State Council issued new legislation governing foreign banks and Chinese-foreign joint-venture banks that wish to engage in banking in the Special Economic Zones. Although the impact of the legislation is not known, it is anticipated that a number of foreign banks will open branches in Shenzhen or go into joint ventures with Chinese banks in Shenzhen in order to capitalise on Shenzhen's close geographic ties with the Hong Kong financial market.

Reduced land use fees

The Measures of the Shenzhen Special Economic Zone for the Adjustment and Preferential Reduction and Exemption of Land Use Fees promulgated by the Shenzhen municipal government on 25 December 1985 carry forward a more traditional facet of the SEZs — low land rentals — but also add seven additional specific categories for even further reduction of the new low rates.

There is therefore a great deal of experimental legislation in Shenzhen on new ways to liberalise and modernise China's economic system. Although businessmen and investors in other parts of China may be annoyed by the tendency of Chinese negotiators to apply these experiments 'by analogy' to projects outside Shenzhen, this can also be a two-way street. The preferences and privileges announced for application in the SEZs can be requested for other projects in China 'by analogy'. Such requests are particularly likely to be granted in the 14 coastal cities, but have also been granted in cities such as Beijing and Xian which are not newly opened cities.

The 14 open coastal cities

The State Council decision of 6 April 1984 to open 14 coastal cities to foreign investment represents a strong endorsement by the central authorities of the Special Economic Zone concept. The newly opened cities — Dalian, Qinhuangdao, Tianjin, Yantai, Qingdao, Lianyungang, Nantong, Shanghai, Ningbo, Wenzhou, Fuzhou, Guangzhou, Zhanjiang and Beihai — will couple the preference system developed for the SEZs with economically developed areas that possess reasonably good industrial, scientific, technological and managerial infrastructure.

Certain of the cities are more developed than others; the gross industrial output of Shanghai and Tianjin was Rmb67 billion (US$33.5 billion) and Rmb23 billion (US$11.5 billion) respectively in 1983, while the industrial output of Wenzhou and Beihai for the same year was only Rmb1.8 billion (US$900 million) and Rmb0.14 billion (US$70 million). The same is true for their experience in handling foreign investment: Shanghai completed 237 foreign investment contracts in 1984 with US$6,355.3 million of committed foreign investment, and Tianjin 167 investment contracts with US$255.3 million of investment from abroad; Qinhuangdao completed only two foreign investment projects for

US$40,000 of foreign investment. Some of the coastal cities are better in getting foreign investment than in producing export products. Guangzhou received commitments for US$816.9 million of investment in 1984, but only did US$354 million worth of foreign trade.

Because of the disparity in the development of the coastal cities, Beijing decided in May 1985 to limit the 14 coastal cities to four for the time being: Shanghai, Dalian, Tianjin and Guangzhou. While the other 10 coastal cities may continue offering preferential terms to foreign investors, their development is supposed to be delayed for several years while their infrastructure is developed and their foreign trade experts trained. (See Chart.)

Preferential investment terms

While the investment record of the 14 coastal cities prior to their 'opening' in 1984 does not compare favourably with the success of the SEZs, there is tremendous interest from abroad. In November 1984, the Bank of China and several other Chinese enterprises in Hong Kong hosted an Open Cities Investment Symposium in Hong Kong. The symposium was attended by more than 1,174 foreign delegates from 22 countries and a combined total of 441 letters of intent and preliminary agreements were signed, pledging investments of more than US$4.95 billion.

Although specific legislation is not yet in place for each of the coastal cities, the symposium promoters promised that a number of investment preferences will be available in each of the coastal cities. Business preferences promised to investors include such SEZ preferences as allowing a degree of access to the Chinese domestic market for each contract negotiated, the ability for joint ventures to adopt their own system of financial management and accounting, the right to hire and fire workers, and easier entry and exit formalities.

The pattern found in the SEZs of delegating investment approval authority to lower levels has also apparently been adopted for the new coastal cities. According to Wei Yuming, Vice-Minister of MOFERT, Shanghai and Tianjin have authority to approve projects of up to US$30 million in total investment, Guangzhou and Dalian can approve projects up to US$10 million in total investment, and the other coastal cities may approve projects of US$5 million.

The most important preference relates to tax and customs treatment. The State Council in mid-November 1984 adopted Provisional Regulations of the People's Republic of China concerning the Reduction and Exemption of Enterprise Income Tax and Consolidated Industrial and Commercial Tax for the Special Economic Zones and 14 Coastal Port Cities (the '1984 Tax Regulations'), thereby taking the opportunity of clarifying the 1980 Regulations for the SEZs as well as establishing the tax preference system for the coastal cities. The portion of the 1984 Tax Regulations relating to the SEZs confirms a number of practices that were already being followed in Shenzhen, including the grant of a two-year tax exemption followed by a three-year tax reduction of 50 per cent for most special zone enterprises which plan to operate over 10 years, and a shorter period of preference for foreign investors in the service trades, an exemption from the dividend withholding or remittance tax, a reduction to 10 per cent of the withholding tax on other passive income, and substantial reductions in the Consolidated Industrial and Commercial Tax.

Economic development zones and old urban areas

The 1984 Tax Regulations make a distinction between the Economic and Technology Development Zones (ETDZs) to be established in the 14 coastal cities and the older urban areas of those cities. Investors in the ETDZs receive the most preferential treatment. The stated purpose for the distinction is that the higher capital costs involved in building new factories in the ETDZs, as compared with the renovation of factories in the old urban areas, justifies more preferential treatment for investors in the ETDZs.

Each of the 14 cities has or is in the process of designating an ETDZ area, which is typically only a few square kilometres of good industrial and commercial land on the outskirts of the older urban area. Once the open city selects its ETDZ, the location of the site must be submitted to the State Council Office for the Special Economic Zones for approval, since this office has been given the responsibility for coordinating national policy in regard to the 14 coastal cities. Shanghai, Dalian, and some others have already designated their respective ETDZ areas, while the other coastal cities are still formulating their development plans.

ETDZ enterprises will enjoy the 15 per cent tax rate applicable to the SEZs and also receive most of the same tax and customs breaks. The old urban areas may also receive the advantages of a 15 per cent tax rate, if the amount of foreign investment exceeds US$30 million, the investment recovery period is long, the project is technology-intensive, and the Ministry of Finance in Beijing approves the concession. Investment in the old urban areas that do not qualify for the 15 per cent tax rate can qualify for a tax rate of between 24 and 26.4 per cent if they are engaged in certain types of business and the Ministry of Finance and the local development authorities approve the application.

The 1984 Tax Regulations provide an overall framework for all SEZs, ETDZs and old urban areas. The local authorities have the power to supplement the 1984 Tax Regulations' concessions, however, by providing additional incentives, if the proposed incentives are approved by the State Council's Office for the SEZs. The Dalian ETDZ was the first coastal city to release its lists of preferences, which include such concessions as (1) a possible extension of the tax holiday period specified in the 1984 Tax Regulations for a further one to two years if the investment exceeds US$45 million, (2) farming and forestry ventures may receive a 15 to 30 per cent reduction in enterprise tax for up to 10 years, and (3) an exemption for the first three years and a 50 per cent reduction in the following five years from the local enterprise tax for all productive enterprises established in the eight-year period commencing 15 October 1984. It can be expected that each of the other ETDZs will over time issue regulations of the same type as Dalian's, thereby creating a very complicated patchwork quilt of tax rates, exemptions, reductions, preferences and concessions in the SEZs, coastal cities and the rest of China.

Future developments

It is interesting to speculate on the future of the SEZs and coastal cities.

SEZs

The SEZs will continue to be used as an experimental laboratory for new economic legislation and policies. The most likely next step will be a severe crackdown on the black market and other illegal practices, followed by an increased liberalisation permitting the adoption of more Hong Kong business practices.

The types of future legislation most likely to be issued

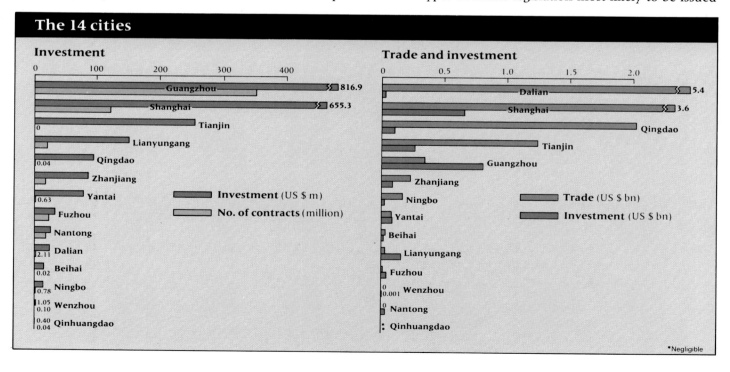

The 14 cities

137

are rules and procedures for an arbitration body to be located in the SEZs to handle cases between foreign and local litigants, and laws relating to companies, accounting procedures and trade unions.

Coastal cities

During 1985 the four principal coastal cities will issue their own legislation on special preferences and publicise their approved development plans. Guangzhou and Dalian have already done so, and the rules for Shanghai and Tianjin have been prepared. It is also likely that the coastal cities will increasingly apply new Shenzhen and SEZ legislation to their own areas by reference, so that the differences between the SEZs and coastal cities will lessen over time.

Probably of greater significance to foreign businessmen is that during 1985, the SEZs and EDTZs will begin to compete for the foreign investor's capital. Competition between willing host cities, more than legislated preferences, will encourage foreign investors to come to China. In the competition between the coastal cities and the SEZs, the coastal cities have the advantage of an existing industrial base. The SEZs, on the other hand, have the advantage of having trained professionals. China Merchants Steam Navigation, for example, which is in charge of the Shekou Industrial Zone in the Shenzhen SEZ has done more equity joint ventures than any other commercial entity in China. Such experience is a very important positive factor in the competition for new investment.

Appendix

Model contract for joint ventures using Chinese and foreign investment

CHAPTER I

General provisions

In accordance with the 'Law of the People's Republic of China on Joint Ventures using Chinese and Foreign Investment' and other relevant Chinese laws and regulations, _____ Company of China and _____ Company of [Country], adhering to the principle of equality and mutual benefit and through friendly consultations, agree to jointly invest to set up a joint venture in _____, _____ Province of the People's Republic of China and enter into the contract hereunder.

CHAPTER II

Parties to the joint venture

ARTICLE 1
The Parties to this contract are:

_____ Company of China (hereinafter referred to as 'Party A'), registered in China, with its legal address at [No.], [Street], [District], [City], China.
Legal representative: Name:
    Position:
    Nationality:

_____ Company of [Country], (hereinafter referred to as 'Party B'), registered in _____, with its legal address at _____.
Legal representative: Name:
    Position:
    Nationality:
[Note: In case there are more than two parties to the joint venture, they will be referred to as Party C, D... in proper order.]

CHAPTER III

Establishment of the joint venture company

ARTICLE 2
In accordance with the 'Law of the People's Republic of China on Joint Ventures using Chinese and Foreign Investment' and other relevant Chinese laws and regulations, Parties A and B agree to set up _____ joint venture limited liability company (hereinafter referred to as the 'Joint Venture Company').

ARTICLE 3
The name of the Joint Venture Company shall be _____ Limited Liability Company in Chinese, and _____ in foreign language.
The legal address of the Joint Venture Company is: [No], [Street], [City], [Province].

ARTICLE 4
All activities of the Joint Venture Company must be in compliance with the laws, decrees and pertinent rules and regulations of the People's Republic of China.

ARTICLE 5
The form of organisation of the Joint Venture Company shall be a limited liability company. Party A and Party B shall be liable to the debts of the Joint Venture Company within the limit of the capital contribution subscribed by each respectively. The profits, risks and losses shall be shared by the Parties in proportion to their respective amount of contribution to the registered capital.

CHAPTER IV

Purpose, scope and scale of production and operations

ARTICLE 6
The purpose of the joint venture between Parties A and B is: in conformity with the desire to strengthen economic cooperation and technological exchange, to adopt advanced and appropriate technology and scientific methods of operation and management to raise product quality, develop new products and be competitive in the international market both in quality and in price so as to raise beneficial economic results to enable the investing parties to obtain satisfactory economic benefits.
[Note: This article shall be written in accordance with specific conditions in a specific contract.]

ARTICLE 7
The scope of production and operation of the Joint Venture Company shall be:

to produce _____ products; to carry out maintenance services for products after sales; to research and develop new products.
[Note: This article shall be written in accordance with specific conditions.]

ARTICLE 8
The production scale of the Joint Venture Company shall be as follows:

1 The production capacity after the Joint Venture Company is put into operation shall be _____.

2 The production scale may be increased up to an annual output of _____ with the development of the production and operation. The product varieties will be developed into _____.
[Note: It shall be written in accordance with specific conditions.]

CHAPTER V

Total amount of investment and the registered capital

ARTICLE 9
The total amount of investment of the Joint Venture Company shall be Rmb _____ (or a foreign currency agreed upon by both parties).

ARTICLE 10
The capital contribution to be made by Parties A and B shall be Rmb _____ in total which will be the registered capital of the Joint Venture Company.
Of which: Party A shall contribute _____ yuan, accounting for _____ per cent; Party B shall contribute _____ yuan, accounting for _____ per cent.

ARTICLE 11
Party A and Party B will contribute the following as their investment:

Party A: cash _____ yuan
machinery and equipment _____ yuan
factory premises _____ yuan
the right to the use of the land _____ yuan
industrial property _____ yuan
others _____ yuan, _____ yuan
in total.

Party B: cash _____ yuan
machinery and equipment _____ yuan
industrial property _____ yuan
others _____ yuan, _____ yuan
in total.
[Note: In the event of contribution in kind or in industrial property, Party A and Party B shall conclude a separate contract which shall be an integral part of this Contract.]

ARTICLE 12
The registered capital of the Joint Venture Company shall be paid in _____ instalments by Party A and Party B in accordance with their respective proportion of contribution.
The amount payable in each instalment shall be as follows:
[Note: It shall be written in accordance with specific conditions.]

ARTICLE 13
In the event that either Party A or Party B intends to assign all or part of his capital contribution to a third party, consent must be obtained from the other party to the joint venture, and approval from the examination and approval authority is required.
When one party to the joint venture assigns all or part of its capital contribution, the other party shall have the right of preemption.

CHAPTER VI

Responsibilities of each party to the joint venture

ARTICLE 14
Party A and Party B shall be respectively responsible for completing the following matters:

Responsibilities of Party A:

— to handle applications for approval, registration, business licence and other matters concerning the establishment of the Joint Venture Company from relevant Chinese departments in charge;
— to go through application procedures at the department in charge of land to obtain the right to the use of land;
— to organise the design and construction of the factory premises and other engineering facilities of the Joint Venture Company;
— to provide cash, machinery and equipment and factory premises ..... in accordance with the stipulations in article 11;
— to assist in going through import customs declaration procedures for the machinery and equipment contributed by Party B as investment and arrange for transportation within the Chinese territory;
— to assist the Joint Venture Company in purchasing or leasing equipment, materials, raw materials, office appliances, means of transportation and communication facilities, etc.;
— to assist the Joint Venture Company in coordinating and ascertaining the infrastructural facilities such as water, electricity, transportation, etc.;

- to assist the Joint Venture Company in recruiting local Chinese operation and management personnel, technical personnel, workers and other personnel required;
- to assist foreign workers and staff in going through necessary procedures for obtaining entry visas, work permits and making travel arrangements;
- to be responsible for handling other matters entrusted by the Joint Venture Company.

Responsibilities of Party B:

- to provide cash, machinery and equipment, industrial property ..... in accordance with the stipulations in article 11, and be responsible for shipping capital contribution in kind such as machinery and equipment, etc. to a Chinese port;
- to handle matters entrusted by the Joint Venture Company relating to the selection and purchase of machinery and equipment, materials, etc. outside China;
- to provide necessary technical personnel for installing, testing and trial production of the equipment, as well as the technical personnel for production and inspection;
- to train the technical personnel and workers of the Joint Venture Company;
- in the event that Party B is also the technology licensor, he shall be responsible for the stable production of qualified products at the design capacity by the Joint Venture Company within the prescribed period;
- to be responsible for other matters entrusted by the Joint Venture Company.
[Note: It shall be written in accordance with specific situation.]

CHAPTER VII

Transfer of technology

ARTICLE 15
Both Party A and Party B agree that a technology transfer agreement shall be entered into by and between the Joint Venture Company and Party __ or a third party so as to obtain advanced production technology, including product design, process, method of testing, materials prescription, standard of quality and the training of personnel, etc. required for accomplishing the production and operation purpose and the scale stipulated in chapter IV in this Contract.
[Note: To be specified in the contract.]

ARTICLE 16
Party B shall provide the following guarantees on the transfer of technology: [Note: This article shall be contained in the joint venture contract only when Party B is responsible for transferring technology to the Joint Venture Company.]

1 Party B shall guarantee that all technology such as the design of _____ [Note: Specify product name], manufacturing technology, technological process, testing and inspection, etc. provided to the Joint Venture Company shall be complete, accurate, reliable and in conformity with the requirements of the operational purpose of the Joint Venture Company, and shall guarantee that the product quality and production capacity required by this Contract shall be attained.
2 Party B shall guarantee that the technology specified in this Contract and the Technology Transfer Agreement shall be fully transferred to the Joint Venture Company, and that the technology to be provided shall be the most advanced technology among similar technology of Party B, that the models and performance quality of the equipment shall be excellent and that they meet the requirements of technical

operations and practical usage.
3 Party B shall prepare detailed lists with regard to the technology and technical services to be provided at various stages under the Technology Transfer Agreement, which shall be attached to such agreement as an annex and Party B shall guarantee the implementation of the same.
4 Drawings, technological conditions and other detailed information shall be an integral part of the technology to be transferred, and timely delivery shall be guaranteed.
5 During the effective term of the Technology Transfer Agreement, Party B shall promptly deliver to the Joint Venture Company, without extra charge, any improvement to such technology as well as the information and technical data of such improvement.
6 Party B shall guarantee that the technical personnel and workers of the Joint Venture Company shall be able to master the technology so transferred within the period prescribed in the Technology Transfer Agreement.

ARTICLE 17
In the event that Party B fails to provide equipment and technology in accordance with the stipulations of this Contract and the Technology Transfer Agreement or in case any deceiving or concealing act are found, Party B shall be responsible for compensating for the direct losses of the Joint Venture Company.

ARTICLE 18
The technology transfer fee shall be paid in the form of royalties. The royalty rate shall be _____ per cent of the ex-factory net sales value of the products.
The term for royalty payment shall coincide with the term of the Technology Transfer Agreement as stipulated in article 19 of this Contract.

ARTICLE 19
The term of the Technology Transfer Agreement to be entered into by and between the Joint Venture Company and Party B shall be _____ years. After the expiration of the Technology Transfer Agreement, the Joint Venture Company shall have the right to use, research and develop such imported technology continuously. [Note: The term of a technology transfer agreement is generally not longer than 10 years, and the agreement must be approved by the Ministry of Foreign Economic Relations and Trade or other examination and approval authorities entrusted by the Ministry of Foreign Economic Relations and Trade.]

CHAPTER VIII

Sales of products

ARTICLE 20
The products of the Joint Venture Company will be sold both on Chinese domestic markets and on overseas markets; the export portion shall account for _____ per cent and the domestic sales portion shall account for _____ per cent.
[Note: An annual percentage and amount for domestic and export sales may be specified based on practical situation. Under normal circumstances, the amount of export sales should at least meet the requirements of foreign exchange expenditure of the Joint Venture Company.]

ARTICLE 21
Products may be sold on overseas markets through the following channels:

_____ per cent to be sold directly by the Joint Venture Company outside China.

The Joint Venture Company shall enter into a sales contract with a Chinese foreign trade company, entrusting it to be the agent for sales on commission basis or the Chinese foreign trade company shall act as sole agent, which accounts for _____ per cent.

_____ per cent to be entrusted by the Joint Venture Company to Party B for sales.

ARTICLE 22

Products of the Joint Venture Company for domestic sales may be sold on a sole agency or commission basis by Chinese departments for supplies or commercial departments, or may be sold by the Joint Venture Company directly.

ARTICLE 23

In order to sell products and to carry out maintenance and repair services for products after sales both in China and abroad, subject to the approval of the relevant Chinese department, the Joint Venture Company may set up branch organisations for sales, maintenance and repair service in China and abroad.

ARTICLE 24

Products of the Joint Venture Company shall use _____ as the trademark.

CHAPTER IX

The Board of Directors

ARTICLE 25

The date of registration of the Joint Venture Company shall be the date of the establishment of the Board of Directors of the Joint Venture Company.

ARTICLE 26

The Board of Directors shall consist of _____ directors, of which _____ shall be appointed by Party A, _____ by Party B. The Chairman of the Board shall be appointed by Party A, and its Vice-Chairman by Party B. The Directors, Chairman and Vice-Chairman shall have a term of office of four years, and their term of office may be renewed if they are reappointed by the relevant party.

ARTICLE 27

The Board of Directors shall be the highest authority of the Joint Venture Company. It shall decide all major issues concerning the Joint Venture Company. Major issues [Note: The main contents shall be listed in accordance with article 36 of the Regulations for the Implementation of the Law on Joint Ventures using Chinese and Foreign Investment] shall require unanimous approval before any decisions may be made. With respect to other matters, resolutions may be made upon an affirmative vote by majority or simple majority. [Note: It shall be explicitly stipulated in the specific contract.]

ARTICLE 28

The Chairman of the Board of Directors shall be the legal representative of the Joint Venture Company. In the event that the Chairman of the Board of Directors cannot perform his duties for any reason, he may temporarily authorise the Vice-Chairman or any other Director to act as his representative.

ARTICLE 29

The Board of Directors shall convene at least one meeting every year. Such meetings shall be called and presided over by the Chairman of the Board. The Chairman may convene an interim meeting of the Board of Directors based on a proposal made by more than one-third of the Directors. Minutes of the meetings shall be kept on file.

CHAPTER X

Operation and management organisation

ARTICLE 30

The Joint Venture Company shall establish an operation and management organisation which shall be responsible for its daily operation and management. The operation and management organisation shall have one General Manager, who shall be nominated by Party _____; _____ Deputy General Manager(s), of which _____ shall be nominated by Party A and _____ by party B. The General Manager and Deputy General Manager(s) shall be appointed by the Board of Directors for a term of _____ years.

ARTICLE 31

The responsibility of the General Manager is to carry out the various resolutions of the meetings of the Board of Directors, and organise and direct the daily operation and management work of the Joint Venture Company. The Deputy General Manager(s) shall assist the General Manager in his work.

The operation and management organisation may have several department managers who shall be respectively responsible for the work of the various departments of the enterprise, handle matters delegated to them by the General Manager and the Deputy General Manager(s) and be responsible to the General Manager and the Deputy General Manager(s).

ARTICLE 32

In the event of graft or serious dereliction of duty on the part of the General Manager and the Deputy General Manager(s), they may be removed and replaced at any time upon a resolution passed at a meeting of the Board of Directors.

CHAPTER XI

Purchase of equipment

ARTICLE 33

In its purchase of required raw materials, fuel, parts, means of transportation and office supplies, etc., the Joint Venture Company shall give first priority to purchase in China where conditions are the same.

ARTICLE 34

In the event that the Joint Venture Company entrusts Party B with the selection and purchase of equipment from overseas markets, Party A shall be invited to send personnel to participate.

CHAPTER XII

Preparation and construction

ARTICLE 35

During the period of preparation and construction, the Joint Venture Company shall set up a preparation and construction office under the Board of Directors. The preparation and construction office shall consist of _____ persons, among which _____ persons will be from Party A, _____ persons from Party B. The preparation and construction office shall have one manager who shall be recommended by Party _____, and one deputy manager who shall be recommended by Party _____. The manager and deputy manager of the preparation and construction office shall be appointed by the Board of Directors.

ARTICLE 36
The preparation and construction office shall be specifically responsible for examining the designs of the project, signing project construction contracts, organising the procurement, inspection and acceptance of relevant equipment, materials and other supplies, working out the general schedule of project construction, preparing plans for the application of funds, controlling project financial payments and final accounts of the project, drawing up relevant management measures and carrying out work for safekeeping and collating documents, drawings, files and material, etc. during the course of construction of the project.

ARTICLE 37
A technical group comprised of several technical personnel appointed by Party A and Party B shall be organised. The group, under the leadership of the preparation and construction office, will be in charge of the examination, supervision, inspection, acceptance and performance assessment of the design, the quality of the project, the equipment and materials and the imported technology.

ARTICLE 38
After approval by Parties A and B, the organisation, remuneration and the expenses of the staff of the preparation and construction office shall be covered in the project budget.

ARTICLE 39
After the construction of the factory as well as the turning over procedures have been completed, the preparation and construction office shall be dissolved upon the approval of the Board of Directors.

CHAPTER XIII

Labour management

ARTICLE 40
After the Board of Directors has studied and formulated plans with regard to matters concerning the employment, resignation and dismissal, wages, labour insurance, welfare, rewards and punishments, etc. of the staff and workers of the Joint Venture Company in accordance with the Regulations of the People's Republic of China on Labour Management in Joint Ventures using Chinese and Foreign Investment and its implementation measures, the Joint Venture Company and the trade union organisation of the Joint Venture Company shall collectively or individually enter into labour contracts covering such matters.

After the labour contracts have been executed, they should be filed with the local labour management department for the record.

ARTICLE 41
The appointment of senior management personnel recommended by Parties A and B as well as the standard of their wages and remuneration, social insurance, welfare and travel expenses, etc. shall be discussed and determined in a meeting of the Board of Directors.

CHAPTER XIV

Taxes, finance and auditing

ARTICLE 42
The Joint Venture Company shall pay taxes in accordance with the stipulations of relevant Chinese laws and regulations.

ARTICLE 43
Staff members and workers of the Joint Venture Company shall pay individual income tax in accordance with the Individual Income Tax Law of the People's Republic of China.

ARTICLE 44
The Joint Venture Company shall set aside the reserve funds, the development funds of the venture and the bonus and welfare funds for staff and workers in accordance with the stipulations in the Law of the People's Republic of China on Joint Ventures using Chinese and Foreign Investment. The proportion to be set aside annually shall be discussed and decided by the Board of Directors according to the business situations of the company.

ARTICLE 45
The fiscal year of the Joint Venture Company shall be from 1 January to 31 December. All accounting vouchers, bills, statements and reports, and books of accounts shall be written in Chinese. [Note: May also be written in a foreign language agreed upon by both Party A and Party B.]

ARTICLE 46
An accountant registered in China shall be engaged to examine and verify the financial and auditing matters of the Joint Venture and the results thereof shall be reported to the Board of Directors and the General Manager.
If Party B deems it necessary to engage an auditor from another country to examine the annual financial matters, Party A shall give its consent. All expenses required shall be borne by Party B.

ARTICLE 47
During the first three months of each business year, the General Manager shall organise and prepare the balance sheet, profit and loss statement and profit distribution plan for the preceding year and submit the same for examination and approval at the meeting of the Board of Directors.

CHAPTER XV

Term of the joint venture

ARTICLE 48
The term of the Joint Venture Company shall be _____ years. The date of establishment of the Joint Venture Company shall be the date on which the business licence of the Joint Venture Company is issued.
At the proposal of one party and upon unanimous approval in a meeting of the Board of Directors, an application may be filed with the Ministry of Foreign Economic Relations and Trade (or its delegated examination and approval authority) six months prior to the expiration of the joint venture term for an extension of the joint venture term.

CHAPTER XVI

The disposal of properties upon the expiration of the joint venture term

ARTICLE 49

Upon the expiration of the joint venture term or early termination of the joint venture, the Joint Venture Company shall carry out liquidation in accordance with law. The properties after liquidation shall be distributed in proportion to the respective investment of Party A and Party B.

CHAPTER XVII

Insurance

ARTICLE 50

Insurance policies of the Joint Venture Company on various kinds of risks shall be purchased from the People's Insurance Company of China. The types, the value and the term of insurance shall be discussed and decided at a meeting of the Board of Directors of the Joint Venture Company in accordance with the stipulations of the People's Insurance Company of China.

CHAPTER XVIII

The amendment, alteration and discharge of the contract

ARTICLE 51

Any amendment to this Contract and the annexes hereof may enter into effect only after a written agreement is signed by both Party A and Party B and approved by the original examination and approval authority.

ARTICLE 52

In the event that the Contract cannot be performed due to force majeure or that the Joint Venture Company is unable to continue operations due to successive years of losses, the term of the joint venture may be brought to an early termination and the Contract discharged upon the unanimous adoption of such a resolution by the Board of Directors and approval by the original examination and approval authority.

ARTICLE 53

Should the Joint Venture Company be unable to continue its operations or achieve the business purpose stipulated in the Contract due to the fact that one of the contracting parties fails to fulfil the obligations prescribed under the Contract or the Articles of Association, or seriously violates the stipulations of the Contract or the Articles of Association, such defaulting party shall be deemed to be unilaterally terminating the Contract. The other party, in addition to having the right to claim compensation from the defaulting party, shall also have the right to terminate the Contract upon approval by the original examination and approval authority in accordance with the provisions of the Contract. In the event that Party A and Party B agree to continue the operation, the defaulting party shall be liable to compensate the Joint Venture Company for its economic losses.

CHAPTER XIX

Liabilities for breach of contract

ARTICLE 54

Should either Party A or Party B fail to make the capital contribution on schedule and in the amount as stipulated in chapter V of this Contract, the defaulting party shall pay an overdue fine to the other party, for every month in arrears, at _____ per cent of the amount of contribution due starting from the first month payment is overdue. Should the defaulting party fail to pay after three months, in addition to payment by the defaulting party of the accumulated overdue fine at _____ per cent of the amount of contribution due, the other party shall also have the right to terminate the Contract and to claim damages from the defaulting party in accordance with article 53 of this Contract.

ARTICLE 55

In the event that this Contract and its annexes cannot be performed or fully performed due to the fault of one party, the party at fault shall bear the responsibility for default. Should it be the fault of both parties, the parties shall bear their respective responsibilities for default based on the actual situation.

ARTICLE 56

In order to guarantee the performance of this Contract and its annexes, both Party A and Party B shall each provide the other with a bank's letter of guaranty for performance.

CHAPTER XX

Force majeure

ARTICLE 57

In the event that the performance of the Contract is directly affected or that the Contract cannot be performed in accordance with the terms and conditions agreed upon as a result of earthquake, typhoon, flood, fire, war or any other event of force majeure that is unforeseeable and the occurrence and consequence of which is unpreventable or unavoidable, the party that encounters the abovesaid event of force majeure shall immediately notify the other party of the conditions of the event by cable and shall, within 15 days, provide details of the event and valid certifying documents evidencing the reasons as to why the Contract cannot be performed in full or in part or the performance of which needs to be postponed. Such certifying documents should be issued by a notary organisation in the place where the event occurred. Based on the extent of the effect such event has on the performance of the Contract, the parties shall consult and decide whether or not the Contract should be discharged, or part of the responsibilities for the performance of the Contract should be relieved, or the performance of the Contract should be postponed.

CHAPTER XXI

Applicable law

ARTICLE 58

The execution, validity, interpretation, performance and settlement of disputes of this Contract shall be governed by the laws of the People's Republic of China.

CHAPTER XXII

Settlement of disputes

ARTICLE 59

Any disputes arising from the performance of, or in connection with this Contract shall be settled through friendly consultations between both parties. In case no settlement can be reached through consultation, the disputes shall be submitted to the Foreign Economic and Trade Arbitration Commission of the China Council for the Promotion of International Trade for arbitration in accordance with its provisional rules of arbitration procedures. The award of such arbitration shall be final and binding upon both parties.

Or

Any disputes arising from the performance of, or in connection with this Contract shall be settled through friendly consultations between both parties. In case no settlement can be reached through consultations, the disputes shall be submitted to _____ Arbitration Organisation in [Place], [Country] for arbitration in accordance with its rules of arbitration procedures. The award of such arbitration shall be final and binding upon both parties.

Or

Any disputes arising from the performance of, or in connection with this Contract shall be settled through friendly consultations between both parties. In case no settlement can be reached through consultations, the disputes shall be submitted for arbitration.

Arbitration shall take place in the defendant's country.

If in China, arbitration shall be conducted by the Foreign Economic and Trade Arbitration Commission of the China Council for the Promotion of International Trade in accordance with its provisional rules of arbitration procedures.
If in [Name of defendant's country], arbitration shall be conducted by [Name of arbitration organisation of defendant's country] in accordance with its rules of arbitration procedures. The award of such arbitration shall be final and binding on both parties.
[Note: When formulating contracts, only one of the abovementioned three ways can be used.]

ARTICLE 60

During the course of arbitration, this Contract shall continue to be performed except for the part which the Parties are disputing and which is undergoing arbitration.

CHAPTER XXIII

Language

ARTICLE 61

This Contract has been written in Chinese and in _____. Both languages are equally authentic. In the event of any discrepancy between the two aforementioned texts, the Chinese text shall prevail.

CHAPTER XXIV

Effectiveness of the contract and miscellaneous

ARTICLE 62

The following ancillary agreements and documents concluded in accordance with the principles stipulated under this Contract including: the Articles of Association of the Joint Venture Company, project agreement, the technology transfer agreement, the sales agreement ....., shall all be an integral part of this Contract.

ARTICLE 63

This Contract and its annexes shall be subject to the approval of the Ministry of Foreign Economic Relations and Trade of the People's Republic of China (or its entrusted examination and approval authority) and shall become effective as of the date of approval.

ARTICLE 64

With respect to the methods by which Parties A and B send notices, all notices given by cable or telex should be followed by a notice in the form of a written letter if the contents of such notices involve the rights and obligations of the Parties. The legal addresses of Parties A and B set forth in this Contract shall be the posting addresses of Parties A and B.

ARTICLE 65

This Contract has been executed by the authorised representatives of Party A and Party B in _____, China on this _____, 198___.

For_____
Company of China
(Signature)

For_____
Company of [Country]
(Signature)

CHAPTER 4

China International Non-Ferrous Metals Leasing Company Inc

by First Interstate Bank Ltd

On 7 December 1984, a joint-venture agreement signed in Beijing made American banking history. With the agreement to form China International Non-Ferrous Metals Leasing Company with five joint partners, Los Angeles-based First Interstate Bank of California became the first US bank to form a joint venture based in China.

Harold J. Meyerman, First Interstate's Executive Vice President and International Division Manager, and Antonio E. Marti, Senior Vice President and Asia-Pacific Area Manager, signed the agreement to import capital equipment from the United States and other countries and, in turn, lease the equipment to joint ventures and Chinese enterprises involved in the non-ferrous metals industry in China. The deal was timely, as projections from the goverment's official state plan call for the doubling of China's non-ferrous metals production capacity by 1990.

The partners

In addition to First Interstate Bank, which holds a 20 per cent share, the partners and their holdings are: China National Non-Ferrous Metals Industry Corporation (30 per cent), Bank of China Trust and Consultancy Company (20 per cent), Industrial and Commercial Bank of China (10 per cent), and Banque Nationale de Paris (20 per cent). Initial capitalisation in the new venture was US$3 million.

First Interstate Bank was invited to the project following the signing of a business cooperation agreement between the Bank of China Trust and Consultancy Company and the First Interstate Trading Company.

The success of the new leasing company will depend heavily on the expertise of the five partners. The First Interstate Trading Company will work with the large network of First Interstate's 22 affiliate banks and 35 franchised banks to develop contracts with US and overseas equipment manufacturers needed in the non-ferrous metals industry.

The China Non-Ferrous Metals Industry Corporation (CNNC) is responsible for the development of the industry throughout China. Lessees are primarily the 819 enterprises formed under the corporation.

The Bank of China Trust and Consultancy Company, a wholly-owned subsidiary of the Bank of China, is responsible for attracting foreign investment and making its own investment in high-priority Chinese enterprises. The Industrial and Commercial Bank of China was spun off from the People's Bank of China on 1 January 1984. With assets at year-end 1984 of approximately US$100 billion, it is a state institution specialising in industrial and commercial banking. Together with the Bank of China and CNNC, the Industrial and Commercial Bank of China will be instrumental for the quality of the assets and liabilities of the balance sheet.

Banque Nationale de Paris, along with First Interstate, will bring international financing, management and leasing expertise to the venture.

A tombstone announcing the formation of the China International Non-Ferrous Metals Leasing Company

announces the formation of

China International Non-Ferrous Metals Leasing Co., Ltd.

A joint venture leasing company based in Beijing to import capital equipment

for the

Non-Ferrous Metal Industry

from the United States, France, Japan and other countries

to China

In Association with

*China National Non-Ferrous Metals Industry Corporation
Bank of China Trust and Consultancy Company
Banque Nationale de Paris
Industrial and Commercial Bank of China*

Leasing in China

In China, leasing is becoming a very attractive method of financing the import of equipment needed for the modernisation and technological advance of local enterprises. Cash flow of the lessees is not tied up in large capital outlay, as in the case of outright purchase of the equipment. The approval level is also less cumbersome as many entities at provincial level have the authority to approve lease transactions, which require a small down-payment.

First Interstate believes that by specialising in one industry, it will focus its leasing expertise in China and increase the profit and success potential of the venture. Through the leasing company, First Interstate believes it will enhance its relationship with its customers, specifically equipment manufacturers.

The negotiations

The negotiations in the venture began to take form in late 1984. The discussions began in Paris, and were continued in Los Angeles, where drafts of the joint-venture contracts and articles of association were initiated. Some of the key issues of negotiations centred on the control of the Board of Directors, the minority partners having equal representation and veto power on key issues, and on the accounting practices, the availability of hard currency and the convertibility of renminbi, and the targeted return on equity and dividend remittance.

First Interstate appointed J. K. Barrington to be a director and Vice Chairman resident in Beijing, because of his familiarity with Chinese and American business practices. Previously he was Senior Vice President of First Interstate Bank of Washington's International Division.

Oil exploration in China

by Cluff Oil plc

Cluff Oil plc (Cluff) is one of the British oil exploration companies formed during the last 20 years as North Sea oil and gas operations were opened up. Many US companies, large and small, were attracted by the opportunities offered by the North Sea, and J. G. (Algy) Cluff, the eponymous Chief Executive of the company, decided that North Sea oil was too important to the British economy to be left to large companies and foreigners. Cluff Oil was formed in 1973 and acquired an interest in a third-round block in the North Sea, where the Buchan Field was discovered.

Cluff began to search for opportunities elsewhere and when the Chinese economy was opened up, was attracted by the oil prospects offshore China. First contacts were made in 1973 with the Embassy of the People's Republic of China in London, and these were regularly pursued. In the early 1980s, seismic surveys were carried out offshore China, and the companies which participated became qualified to apply for offshore acreage when bids were invited by the Chinese government in 1983. Cluff participated in three of these surveys, and so qualified to apply. In the meantime, Cluff formed a Hong Kong company, in which it held 20 per cent of the equity; the balance was held by six major Hong Kong financial and industrial enterprises.

Exploration and production rights

In 1983, the Chinese government invited companies to bid for acreage on offer in the three areas covered by the seismic surveys – the Gulf of Beibu, the Pearl River delta basin (off Guangzhou) and the South Yellow Sea (off Shanghai). Bids were to be made on the basis of a draft agreement covering the grant of exploration and production rights. Qualified companies were free to form bidding groups among themselves if they wished. Each group or company then offered, in respect of the blocks it sought, a work commitment – in terms of seismic surveys and wells to be drilled – which it would carry out during the exploration period, and the split between the China National Offshore Oil Corporation (CNOOC) and itself of oil produced after commercial discovery.

The general scheme of the oil agreements concluded with CNOOC under these first-round awards was as follows:

(a) Initially, the contract is for an exploration period of five or seven years, depending on the size of the area, with work and expenditure obligations specified for each phase of the period. The foreign company (the 'contractor') has the right, at the end of each phase (two or three years), to terminate the agreement provided that the work obligations have been completed. All work during the exploration period is for the sole account of the contractor.

(b) If a commercial discovery is made:
(i) CNOOC has the right to take up a working interest in the venture not exceeding 51 per cent and, at any time thereafter, to assume operatorship;
(ii) the development period will start, during which, at the joint expense of the parties, the necessary facilities to produce and export oil/gas will be installed.

(c) On completion of the development period, the production period will commence and continue for 15 years.

(d) Once production has started, the oil produced each year will be allocated to the parties in the following proportions:

17½ per cent in kind to the government (via CNOOC) by way of royalty;

up to 50 per cent as payment of past and current costs, allocated initially against current operating costs and then against the operator's exploration costs and the parties' investment in development of facilities;

the balance ('remainder oil') is divided between CNOOC and the contractor in accordance with a formula set out in the agreement, the terms of which are confidential to the parties and critical to the Chinese side in deciding to whom to award any particular area. The contractor's share of remainder oil represents his profit and is taxable.

While the expenditure burden during the exploration period is borne only by the contractor, the project is treated from the start as a joint venture between CNOOC and the contractor. Ultimate control is vested in a Joint Management Committee (JMC) which meets quarterly to approve work programmes and budgets and to decide on all other matters of principle concerning the operations. The JMC is chaired by the senior representative of the Chinese side, who is usually a senior management member of the subsidiary of CNOOC in whose area the contract area is situated. The JMC does not reach decisions by voting; it is required to seek by a process of conciliation a unanimously acceptable solution to any problem. Where unanimity cannot be achieved, it is laid down that, in the last resort, the decision shall be made by the operator. In Cluff's case, in the South Yellow Sea (contract area 10/36), the chairman is Wu Yao-Wen, Deputy General Manager of the South Huanghai Oil Corporation (SHHOC). SHHOC is based in Shanghai and is responsible for all operations in the South Yellow Sea. In the case of contract area 22/22 in the Gulf of Beibu, the chairman is Xu Yao Qan of the Nanhai West Oil Corporation. In all JMCs, the Chinese side has the majority of members, but where the contractor consists of a number of companies (as in the Idemitsu-managed consortium in area 22/22), each company has a representative on the JMC.

Cluff's bid for exploration rights

Of the areas on offer, the most highly regarded were the Gulf of Beibu (because of its closeness to recent offshore oil discoveries) and the Pearl River delta basin. Cluff, however, was attracted by the South Yellow Sea where the larger blocks on offer contained indications of sizeable structures. Cluff, therefore, submitted a bid to operate one of the South Yellow Sea blocks, conditional on its being granted a minority interest in a block in the Gulf of Beibu. The first reaction to its bid (and Cluff suspects it was not unique in this regard) was that the split of oil production proposed was not sufficiently favourable to CNOOC — but no indication was given of what would be considered a satisfactory level.

After a preliminary discussion with CNOOC of its offer in Beijing in April 1983, Cluff undertook to submit a final offer very shortly. This revised offer was sent to Beijing at the end of April; tension mounted as other companies were seen visiting China but no call came for Cluff. Finally (on 26 August) Cluff was invited for further discussions, and a speedy conclusion was then reached.

First, in the Gulf of Beibu Cluff was invited to join a consortium consisting of Idemitsu (of Japan) as operator, and Natomas, a US corporation. Cluff's interest in this venture was 5 per cent and the area involved was contract area 22/22 in the Gulf of Beibu, adjoining the block in which Total, the French major oil company, had already made a discovery (the Weizhou field). Secondly, Cluff was offered 100 per cent of a block (contract area 10/36) in the South Yellow Sea covering some 4,450 square kilometres, in less than 50 metres of water; the nearest port of any size on the mainland was Qingdao, some 150 kilometres from the contract area.

Transfer of technology

The main objective of the Chinese side in seeking the assistance of foreign companies in the search for offshore oil was to profit from the expertise and experience gained elsewhere. This transfer of technology figures largely in the contract and in the manner in which the operation is organised. Subject to the directives of the JMC, the responsibility for the conduct of operations is entrusted to the operator, who is free to provide his own staff. The Chinese company, however, has the right to appoint 'professional representatives' who, at the operator's expense, work in the operator's office to monitor the progress of operations. In addition, the contractor is required to spend a sizeable sum each year to provide an agreed training programme for employees of the Chinese company.

In Cluff's case, it was recognised that Chinese employees had to be able to speak English if they were to assimilate training in the international oil business quickly. The first major step in the training programme was to arrange English courses at different levels for employees. Modern language teaching aids were brought in, and the classes were organised and taught originally by the manager's wife and later, following a change of manager, by a teacher of English as a foreign language.

The importance of the transfer of technology was also shown by the requirement that the contractor should, entirely at his own expense, make a contribution to China. In most cases, this has provided for the overseas training of students nominated by CNOOC or the provision of some facility within China for further training of Chinese graduates. Cluff undertook, in its contract for area 10/36, to pay each year for postgraduate courses at British universities for two Chinese graduates in disciplines relevant to a career in the oil industry. The Idemitsu group in area 22/22 undertook to spend an annual sum on providing a computer system for CNOOC. Once again, particularly in the case of the area 10/36 contribution, the need for ability to speak and understand English was apparent. In its first year, Cluff sent one student on a law course at Dundee university, and CNOOC are discussing with the Shanghai office of Cluff possible students for future years.

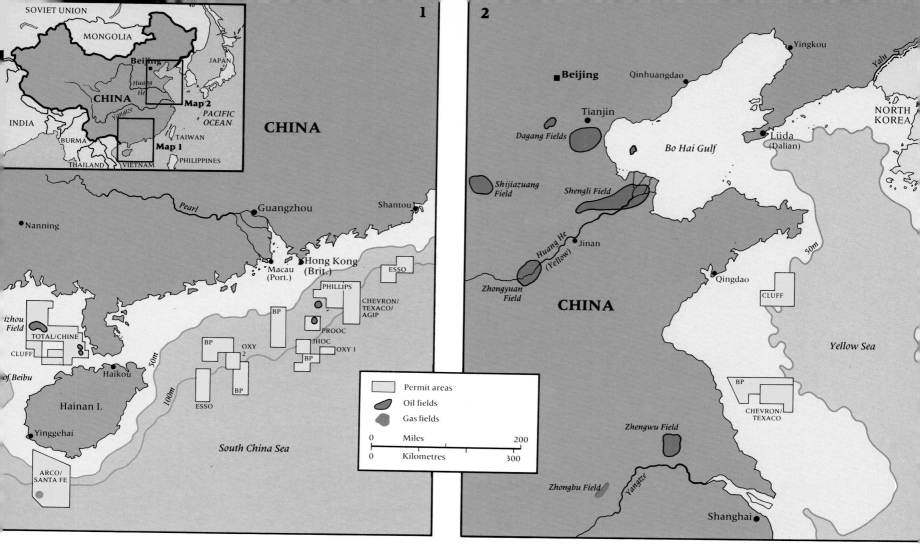

Role of Cluff Oil in China

Cluff's part in the development of contract area 22/22 has necessarily been limited. Cluff has, of course, been informed as fully as all the other interest holders, and has been able to take part in discussions at meetings of the JMC and also at meetings of the industry contractor. On the other hand, with an interest as small as 5 per cent, it has only been able to speak with a small voice.

However, Cluff's role in area 10/36 is considerably greater. Although most of the technical operations have been, and will be, contracted out to specialist geophysical, drilling and other companies, Cluff is responsible for inviting tenders at each stage of the operations, for deciding in conjunction with SHHOC which tenders shall be accepted, for concluding the resultant contracts and for supervision of the performance of the contract. Many contracting firms now available in China are joint ventures formed by Chinese state-owned companies and foreign companies. For example, the geophysical contractor employed in the seismic survey of area 10/36 is a joint venture between CNOOC and Geco, a Norwegian company, while the positioning equipment and service for the survey was provided by a joint venture between Bohai Oil Corporation and Racal. All substantial contracts have to be put out to tender, and it is understood that, other things being equal, preference will be given to Chinese companies or joint ventures. These joint ventures represent a further example of the importance China attaches to the transfer of technology.

By mid-1985, Cluff had shot a seismic survey of some 1,350 line kilometres in area 10/36, which greatly increased its knowledge of the area and confirmed its attractiveness for an oil company. While the final proof will depend on the results of drilling, nothing so far discovered about the area has discouraged Cluff. In area 22/22, following a seismic survey over some 1,500 line kilometres, three wells have been drilled on separate structures, but unfortunately, despite the presence of oil shows, no oil discovery resulted.

Looking at the China offshore areas as a whole, while some 20 wells have been drilled, there have so far been only one substantial gas discovery off Hainan Island in the south, three oil discoveries in the Pearl River delta basin and the Weizhou discovery in the Gulf of Beibu. While these results may seem disappointing both to the Chinese and the foreign companies involved, the results bear comparison with the results of oil exploration in the North Sea in its early stages.

Cluff Investment and Trading Ltd

One side benefit of exploring for oil in China has been the opportunity for many oilmen to visit China and to develop relationships with the Chinese authorities. Equally, JMC meetings held outside China have given companies the chance to show Chinese colleagues developments in the oil industry in Europe, the United States, Canada and elsewhere. Furthermore, as more Chinese official visitors visit Europe, interesting developments can arise.

149

In the autumn of 1984, Xu Guang-Lei, Deputy Chairman of the State Administration of Industry and Commerce, visited London. Over lunch Xu suggested that Cluff should broaden its connection with China by adding trading activities to its oil activities. The possibility seemed interesting, but a little remote; nevertheless, Cluff enquired later whether the suggestion could be taken as a serious indication of interest. This was confirmed, but it was suggested that major cities such as Beijing, Guangzhou and Shanghai probably had all the trading links with the outside that they needed. There were, however, 14 coastal cities which were granted a degree of economic autonomy by the government, and it was suggested that Cluff might be interested in trading in one or two of these.

Rather diffidently, Cluff approached the municipal authorities of two cities, Ningbo and Wenzhou. These were chosen because their recent inclusion among the open port cities meant that established China traders were not yet present, and their proximity to Shanghai meant that the Cluff office opened there in connection with oil operations would be able to give a degree of support to the trading activities. Both cities welcomed the approach and, after a short negotiation, contracts were signed between each of them and a newly formed Cluff subsidiary, Cluff Investments and Trading Limited (CIT). These contracts gave to Cluff, for a period, exclusive rights to introduce British (and in one case, Scandinavian and Swiss) suppliers and contractors to meet the requirements of the two cities. The response in the United Kingdom to the announcement of these contacts was immediate and encouraging; a number of concerns who recognised in China a potentially valuable market suddenly saw in CIT a road into that market. An office has been opened by CIT in Hong Kong, and visits to both Ningbo and Wenzhou have taken place to see what the 'shopping list' is likely to contain. Further visits have been made in which representatives of CIT were accompanied by representatives of interested suppliers. While it is early days yet, it is, for a small company, a challenge and an exciting prospect.

Conclusion

To anyone who watched the changes in the Middle East which followed the explosive growth of the oil industry, China presents a challenge at once similar and totally dissimilar. There is in China, as there was in the Middle East, a determination to master technically the business of the oil industry so that techniques learned from outside can be developed internally. At the same time, in China one sees an ancient civilisation and a vast population adjusting to the same stimuli as were felt in the Middle East, by a small, nomadic population, yet a population with in many cases an almost equally old civilisation. It is both a privilege and a pleasure to visit China, to enjoy the warm friendliness and courtesy of its people and the beauty of its countryside and its culture. It would be rewarding to think that the oil industry could help the government of China achieve its goal — the modernisation of China — as it has been able to do elsewhere.

China's countertrade

by Robert Henriques Girling

To some observers the People's Republic of China is one of the most promising markets for countertrade. Since 1978 Chinese organisations have entered into countertrade agreements worth well over US$20 billion and possibly as high as US$60 billion, and the trend is toward an increasing use of countertrade vehicles to finance the country's modernisation campaign.

Others are far more sceptical of the countertrade potential, focusing instead on the myriad pitfalls which await the unsuspecting foreign company. Countertrade specialists decry the lack of a central infrastructure and note that traditional countertrade is infrequent and often poorly understood by the Chinese traders.

Some have found it surprising that China is at all interested in countertrade in view of its extensive gold and foreign exchange reserves (estimated at US$14.4 billion in mid-1985).

Susan Welker provided valuable research assistance for this article.

Chinese motivations

Western companies report that the Chinese view countertrade as a sort of moral obligation of Western businesses. 'If you sell us something you should buy something as well.' It is a sign of friendly intent. In addition, China uses countertrade as an alternative source of capital and raw materials. There are several motives. The first is to interlink Chinese and Western businesses in order to acquire access to Western technology. China's ambitious modernisation goals will require large-scale transfers of modern technology and management skills. Countertrade agreements tie the Western partner in to the success of these ventures in a manner which is more thorough than straight arms-length trade. Secondly, countertrade provides access to worldwide marketing and distribution channels for China's exports, gaining exposure in important markets. Thirdly, countertrade is particularly compatible with China's planned economy. Self-liquidating ventures are preferable and easier to justify to government planners who must allocate slim resources. Moreover, it provides an important avenue for utilising China's new joint-venture law and the Special Economic Zones. Finally, countertrade is in some instances a valuable tool of international politics, such as when China swapped rice for Pakistani jute to promote foreign goodwill.

The biggest countertrade deal to date is a 13-year Sino-Japanese agreement (US$20–40 billion) which involves the supply of whole smelters, electronic plants, fishing equipment and other machinery in exchange for the outputs of the new Chinese factories and Chinese crude oil and coal. In addition, US firms have traded power systems for electronic goods, a container plant for marine containers, and textile machines for blouses and shirts. General Motors took a quantity of tourist trips in exchange for truck engines, using the trips as a dealer sales incentive. And one novel British deal provided geo-thermal equipment and technical advice in exchange for electricity transmitted to Hong Kong.

For Western businesses countertrade can provide a competitive advantage. An executive of a major chemical exporter stated 'We have participated in countertrade and financing and are finding that this is not just a theoretical avenue of trade but a realistic way of approaching the Chinese.' Knowledgeable Western businessmen report that they 'buy in support of their sales'. The advantage of countertrade according to official Chinese internal guidelines is that an enterprise which accepts a countertrade contract may find it easier to obtain approval to pay higher wages and thus employ better workers.

Forms of countertrade

The Chinese definition of countertrade covers a wide variety of arrangements from barter to cooperative joint ventures. However, the major vehicles for Western countertrade have been processing and assembly agreements in contrast with the more familiar counterpurchase. The most common forms include compensation, export processing, counterpurchase and cooperative joint ventures.

Compensation

Compensation transactions involve payment for the original purchase, say textile machinery, with resultant products. In a typical compensation (also called buyback) agreement one party imports machinery or a complete factory from a second party. The supplier then agrees to buy back some fraction of the output produced by the equipment and this repurchase finances the original sale. It is not uncommon for three to five years to elapse before the purchases by the supplier begin.

From the Chinese viewpoint this is one of the most desirable types of countertrade. The terms of compensation agreements usually stretch over a long period of time, say 10 to 20 years, during which the Western party purchases the products. Currently the Chinese are seeking compensation agreements primarily to upgrade some obsolete plants; there is a moratorium on turn-key factories. One example of a successful compensation accord is the operations of Samash and Sons.

Steps in setting up a compensation agreement

1	The Western firm contracts for sale of plant and equipment with the Chinese Foreign Trade Corporation (FTC)
2	The FTC contracts to sell goods to the Western firm, generally under a separate contract from the original Western export contact.
3	The Western bank extends credit to the Western firm for the hard currency against a promissory note from the FTC with guarantees from the Bank of China.
4	The Western firm provides the FTC with the plant and equipment required.
5	The Western firm receives the goods specified in the contract.
6	The FTC remits payment of the outstanding credit to the Bank of China which repays the Western bank.

In 1983 Samash and Sons agreed to enter an equal joint venture with China's premier silk manufacturer to dye and finish silk. Samash invested US$1.5 million for purchase of new machinery, Cortaulds will provide manufacturing and technical know-how and the China Silk Corporation will build a new plant and provide land and workers. According to Samash, most of the equipment used in the Chinese silk industry is very much out of date. China, supplier of almost half the world's silk, is anxious to acquire modern equipment and technology, and to gain information about Western tastes and needs to strengthen its international marketing. For Samash the venture offers an opportunity to sell within China where it sees a large growth potential.

Negotiations took two years. According to *Business China*, 'The three big negotiating issues were: how to value the land and buildings (they will be leased on to the joint venture), what kind of equipment would go into the factory (a mix of Chinese-made and imported) and compensation for the workforce.' Countertrade enters the picture since the foreign exchange credits generated by silk sales will repay Samash's initial investment. Additionally, these earnings may be used to support equipment for other ventures. Chinese entities wishing to import equipment may purchase silk in China for renminbi, sell the silk to Samash and use the foreign exchange credits to import equipment.

Export processing

Export processing involves the import of materials or samples from abroad for manufacture in China. The Chinese distinguish between two types of processing contracts: *lailiaojiagong* and *laiyangjiagong*. The former refers to the import of raw materials and packaging for Chinese processing, while the latter involves the import of samples from abroad for production in the Chinese factory. In the case of *laiyangjiagong* the Chinese supply the raw materials and build to foreign specifications.

Many of the export processing transactions are small, usually less than US$50,000. This is because the majority of the deals are carried out by Hong Kong and Macao firms doing business with friends and relatives living in the Special Economic Zones. Most of the arrangements involve textiles and clothing since China's technological base and thus quality standards are highest in this economic sector.

Counterpurchase

Counterpurchase transactions are often referred to as triangle trade and involve exchange of goods which are not the result of export of technology. Usually two separate but linked contracts are negotiated, with the Western exporter receiving payment in cash and manufactured goods, raw materials, and machinery from the importer.

Counterpurchase agreements are generally discouraged by the Chinese government as they often require cumbersome negotiations with separate and sometimes competing agencies. However, recent changes in joint-venture legislation, which have eased restrictions on the repatriation of foreign exchange earnings and the distribution of profits, have given a boost to this type of arrangement. In the past all production had to be exported, but some recent contracts have involved compromises in which one-third of the output was sold locally, one-third exported and one-third sold in tourist centres in China for hard currency. This latter arrangement allows both partners to develop new markets for their products.

A deal which is being negotiated between 3M and China involves 3M's construction of a wholly-owned subsidiary to produce telecommunications and electric power distribution equipment, as well as electrical machinery. 3M will lease a newly constructed facility in Shanghai and employ about 30 workers. It is the first wholly-owned foreign venture in China.

The agreement calls for the state-owned Shanghai Electrical Machinery Corporation to recruit the initial production work force for 3M. In return, 3M will send employees to China to train managers and oversee initial operations.

John Marshall, director of China affairs for 3M, visited the Chinese company nearly 50 times in setting up the deal. Chinese officials warmed to the deal after visiting other foreign subsidiaries of 3M. In payment for its investment 3M will receive a number of products from China including Chinese silk; these will be distributed through the company's US countertrade units.

Ron Hafter, President of the Venerable Seal Co (VSC), a California-based import-export company, reported problems he experienced in attempting to put together a deal with China. VSC tried to exchange electrical hand tools for Chinese seals (hand carved figurines) with four different Chinese companies, but was unable to interest any of the firms. Even though electric hand tools were in short supply and a high priority for the Chinese government's national development programme, the firms preferred to obtain unencumbered foreign exchange for their exports.

Cooperative joint ventures

In cooperative joint ventures both the Chinese and the Western company agree to supply a portion of the components to be assembled, the technology and the equipment. The Chinese may supply land and a factory shell. The proceeds from the production are then distributed according to contractual arrangements. This is distinct from compensation, where a specific sum is paid.

One of the more successful countertrade agreements was a cooperative joint venture between Schindler Holding AG of Switzerland, Jardine Shipping of Hong Kong and the government of China's Beijing and Shanghai elevator plants.

Since its establishment in 1980, China-Schindler Elevator Co Ltd has exported over 400 elevators. Schindler-Jardine invested US$4 million for upgrading the technology of the obsolete plants, while the Chinese invested the equivalent of US$12 million. China's elevator industry is 30 years out of date, and the Chinese motivation was to acquire access to Schindler's advanced technology in design, manufacturing, installation, marketing and post-sale service. The goal was to mass produce and sell a competitive product.

An important feature of this countertrade agreement included exchange of Schindler's technology and technical training to be paid out of the proceeds of the export sales. The inclusion of technical assistance and training was essential to concluding the agreement. In the first year of the venture, the Chinese sent a number of engineers to Switzerland for training, while the Swiss sent technical personnel to China to offer on-site instruction. This exchange of personnel was crucial to designing and rebuilding workshops, and developing technology and equipment.

Schindler-Jardine recovered its investment within four years. Schindler's share of the profits over the 10-year life of the joint venture is projected at four times its initial investment. China-Schindler elevators are sold to Hong Kong, in Southeast Asia and the Middle East. They have also gained a dominant position in the Chinese market.

When deals go awry

In the early 1970s Shell International attempted to put together deals which got entangled in the maze of Chinese bureaucracy and ultimately failed to materialise. On outward appearance these were model transactions. The proposals involved exchange of a range of petroleum products, including marine oils and lubricants, aviation fuels, industrial chemicals, plastics, agricultural chemicals as well as the necessary process licences and expertise. These products were to be offered for bentonite, furfural and other products required at various points in the vertically integrated oil company's production, refining and manufacturing operations. It was also hoped that the buying power of Shell's affiliate, Billiton, could be incorporated in the form of purchases of metals.

Proposals were put to several Chinese Foreign Trading Corporations (FTCs), the China Ocean Shipping Authority, the Civil Aviation Administration of China and other official bodies for many months. The clear advantage of such deals would have been the netting out of payments between the multinational oil company and China. However, the compartmentalisation of government agencies at that time proved insurmountable. (Subsequent efforts have apparently been more successful and Shell-China Ltd is now established in Beijing.)

All trade within the People's Republic of China is

conducted through FTCs which act as agents to coordinate trade between China and foreign governments, companies and agents. Working for the producers in China, they help locate and connect distributors and companies outside China who want to use their products. They may also operate as end users of imported products and technology. Each corporation specialises in one type of commodity, and most have branches in those regions most involved in the production or use of that product.

While each FTC which dealt with Shell was able to see the benefits for itself, lateral communication with other agencies were non-existent. The Maritime Shipping Agency was more than ready to cut its hard currency costs through compensation, but other government agencies were unwilling to give up their claim on the right to export mineral products and the resulting foreign currency earnings. As a result the deal came to nothing.

The problem is that while the Chinese have established a range of corportions to deal with foreign trade, no single organisation handles countertrade arrangements. It is possible, however, that in the near future the newly created Export Import Commission may coordinate countertrade arrangements.

Negotiating countertrade in China

Negotiations are normally conducted in Beijing during normal business hours. Western negotiators have found Chinese counterparts to be straightforward, thorough on details, and above all, excellent hosts. The Chinese negotiating team will expect the Western exporter to have detailed information on the potential product. It is important to note that once a firm has been invited to China, the odds are that a sale can be made, provided flexibility is shown by the Western company in accommodating Chinese contractual clauses. Chinese negotiators usually insist on concluding all contract points while Western representatives are in China.

The Chinese prefer to keep the countertrade transactions simple and, as Shell discovered, almost never involve linkage of goods outside the negotiating parties' jurisdiction. Contrary to many Eastern European negotiators, the Chinese will indicate at an early stage of negotiation whether countertrade is necessary.

The Chinese regard the Western company's technical competence to train factory personnel and upgrade the quality of China's exports as primary negotiating strengths. In addition they are anxious for their products to gain entry to new markets. They will refuse to grant exclusive marketing rights to a Western firm unless the level of the investment or the projected volume of exports are judged to be substantial.

In carrying out negotiations it may be important to make several visits to China. The Chinese believe in long-term relationships, and they have special regard for 'old friends'. The development of an atmosphere of trust is crucial.

The countertrade contract

As a result of the Chinese attitude of regarding business acquaintances as old friends, the contract is a technicality. The minimal regard for contracts stems from the low regard the Chinese have for the legal profession. As a Chinese proverb says, 'It is better to enter a tiger's den than a court of law'. Consequently, the preferred mechanism for solving disputes is through friendly negotiation, and only as a last resort through arbitration. A typical contract may be unlikely to include any arbitration provisions. The Chinese countertrade export contract is apt to be simple and brief. The Chinese contract will insist on detailed description of the Western party's contractual obligation regarding equipment, technology and services to be provided. Any penalty provisions, if these do appear, are vague.

Secrecy agreements will be resisted by the Chinese negotiators, but they will agree to protect technologies. Nevertheless, enforcing infringement of patents may be difficult since until 1985 the Chinese had no patent law. Trademarks may be registered by companies whose home countries have a bilateral trademark agreement with China. The new patent law will provide no help to existing products but may help with new products developed in the future.

Quality and quality control

A major problem in countertrade deals often arises with respect to the quality of products offered in exchange. The Chinese have a central agency for inspecting the quality of both imports and exports, the China Commodities Inspection Bureau, which is generally noted for its thoroughness. Any requests for quality control inspections in countertrade or joint ventures should be handled diplomatically. It is best to couch these in the form of an offer to provide technical assistance and training.

Financing

The financing of countertrade activities may take several forms:

- Supplier credits granted by Western banks have been used by some firms to finance exports paid for in Chinese counterdeliveries.
- Since 1979 the Bank of China was granted authority to guarantee foreign investment in China involving compensation agreements.
- Bank to bank credits are supporting a US$20 billion US-Chinese trade agreement.
- Export-import financing is available to firms from the US Exim Bank.

Exports requiring countertrade

While countertrade is seen as important to China's modernisation, the guidelines for implementing it are still being developed. The general emphasis is on industrial production capacity primarily where volume, variety and sophistication of Chinese production is restricted. In exchange, the Chinese will offer light manufactures and foodstuffs. Counterdeliveries from expanded production lines are the fastest-growing form of countertrade in China. The Chinese are concerned about the potential disruptive effects in their export markets which might be caused by Western dumping of goods obtained under counterpurchases agreements.

Guidelines for successful countertrade

Patience is the most important single ingredient for negotiating with China. The Chinese are superb negotiators and it takes patience to become an old friend. Occidental Petroleum Corporation's negotiations for a coal operation took two-and-a-half years. This can be costly: one expert who expected to spend two weeks in China initiating a turn-key plant spent two months.

Secondly, companies dealing in China should always go prepared to expect countertrade demands even if no previous mention of it has been made. In addition, the Chinese prefer that the Western counterpart take along one staff member with expertise in countertrade and Chinese culture, ideally a Chinese speaker.

Thirdly, the best time to make countertrade deals in China is late in the year, when high-quality goods which have been reserved for hard currency exports but remain unsold become available.

Fourth, the Chinese select products carefully and will purchase only those which are urgently needed for their economy. They expect to be given detailed information on the potential import item and will conduct an intensive investigation of it beforehand. It is essential to be prepared to adapt the product and plans to the Chinese requirements.

Finally, it is important to know the types of products that would be acceptable in exchange. It is also important to be aware that familiarity with the import-export business is necessary.

AMF's compensation trade deals

by Leo G. B. Welt

AMF Inc, the sports and industrial equipment manufacturer, decided in the early 1970s to take up China's potential for economic growth, in spite of the dislocations of the Chinese political and economic system. This decision was taken despite the failure of several large development projects with foreign firms, deliberate decisions on the part of the Chinese to slow down economic development, and Chinese reluctance to borrow on the capital markets. These factors had lead to the disenchantment of US investors with business in China.

Ignoring popular projections that the Chinese economy would stagnate, AMF expanded into the Chinese market by adopting the practice of countertrade. While smaller countertrade deals had been concluded with China by the French before the 1970 debt crisis, AMF's proposal was a pioneering effort for such a large US multinational.

The most common form of compensation trade is 'direct compensation', whereby foreign firms modernise existing plants by providing capital equipment, technology and know-how, and are compensated with the output of these refurbished plants. The foreign partner is responsible for marketing the finished product outside China. The Chinese view this operation as foreign investment which enables them to modernise obsolete industries without an outlay of foreign exchange. Normally, compensation trade calls for two separate agreements linked by a protocol: one contract governs the sale of machinery, the other covers the purpose of the resulting product.

The first compensation agreement

In 1980, AMF entered into a cooperative production arrangement with the city of Shanghai to produce at least US$50 million worth of AMF Volt basketballs, footballs and volleyballs. AMF would provide compensation for the economic advantages of low labour costs by sharing technology, improving Chinese managerial skills and modernising the Chinese production facilities.

Internal compensation agreements had been common practice in China for a long time. They allowed interior provinces to trade their agricultural output and raw materials for manufactured goods from the industrialised coastal areas. AMF and Shanghai officials hoped that their agreement would provide opportunities for international trade without the need for hard currency reserves.

The 1980 AMF compensation agreement to produce sports balls included a partial buy-back commitment, with the finished product expected to be imported into the United States and other overseas markets. AMF was already a large importer of sports balls from other Asian countries; the contract with the Chinese allowed AMF more control over the quality of the merchandise it purchased, and the opportunity to introduce new products.

AMF used countertrade to enter the Chinese market before any of its competitors, because it regarded the operation as a starting point for future expansion and diversification in China. China viewed the deal primarily as a source of foreign exchange through overseas sales.

For both partners it was an historic opportunity to benefit. AMF hoped to market better-quality Chinese-made goods, and to make closer contact with Chinese economic leaders. China could again enter the world market, despite the handicap of limited foreign exchange. Although there was little real evidence that the deal would guarantee the success hoped for, AMF took the risk.

Operations in China have so far been smooth for AMF, but pitfalls remain. The rigid, and often uncoordinated, political bureaucracy is a particular problem. Although the central government in recent years has given more autonomy to provincial authorities, vertically integrated national import-export corporations continue to wield strong influence in all areas of Chinese trade and investment. Trading under one corporation's jurisdiction in exchange for goods under the jurisdiction of another is nearly impossible.

Legal aspects of ownership raise further problems for firms, as the Chinese, who view compensation trade as essentially a foreign investment, expect the foreign supplier to cover financing during the period between installation of the equipment and compensation in output.

The second agreement

However, AMF has found that overcoming the barriers to investment in China and the bureaucratic hurdles can lead to success. In 1982, two years after signing the sports contract, AMF's Porter and Brumfield relay-producing division announced a compensation agreement to supply modern machinery and technical expertise to improve the production facilities of the Electronics Component Industry Corporation's ageing factory in Shanghai.

Under the second agreement, the Chinese are sole producers of an electrical relay with a wide range of industrial application. Factory output is expected to be millions of units, aimed at penetrating a large part of the market both inside and outside China. AMF will supply quality control and testing equipment, in addition to retooling standard machinery which is already in place. AMF has accepted responsibility for training the work-force and Chinese managers in the use and maintenance of the equipment, including training in AMF factories in the United States, and will provide its own engineers to oversee the technical aspects of production upgrading. However, AMF personnel will not be allowed to stay permanently in China. AMF will buy back the product under an agreed pricing formula for marketing outside China. In return, the Chinese will provide the production facility, basic equipment and most of the raw materials.

This agreement provided AMF with a new product, an additional supply of low-wage labour to aid the firm's international competitiveness, and an important expansion into the Chinese internal market.

The negotiations on the second compensation project in China benefited little from the experience gathered on the first, as an entirely separate import-export corporation was involved. However, the Chinese commitment shown in the sports deal encouraged AMF throughout the lengthy, often frustrating negotiations.

AMF is now preparing a third compensation agreement with China. This involves the production of geo-phone equipment, a seismic device used in oil exploration, to be distributed both within and outside China.

Negotiations

Negotiations with the Chinese are time-consuming, but once completed, long-lasting relations are established. This spurred AMF into considering further investments. Now, on the eve of the third compensation announcement, the company remains 'comfortable' with the Chinese way of doing business. AMF's usual battery of lawyers at the negotiations were met by Chinese trade and industrial experts, and AMF has found that tight contracts are written which protect Chinese interests. The Chinese are assured that their factories retain their benefits, while AMF is guaranteed the economic returns it expects. The dual contract processes resulted in clear and precise documents, and the Chinese have not yet changed substantially any aspects of the agreements.

China is, however, still uncomfortable with the all-important arbitration clauses in countertrade contracts. These clauses were rarely included before 1980, but since then arbitration has been negotiated, either in the country of the defaulting party, or in a third, neutral country.

In the export clause of a countertrade agreement, the Chinese insist on a description of the partner's contractual obligations relating to the equipment, technology and service to be provided. By contrast, the Western import contract is kept brief, and is usually phrased so as to be of little use in arbitration.

The Chinese want up-to-date technology, and their technicians, usually strongly involved in the purchasing process, are likely to be extremely well versed in all relevant technological details. Western negotiators are expected to be equally conversant with technology. This also reduces the need to make changes in technical details toward the end of negotiations. Negotiations with the Chinese have convinced AMF of the importance of having competent and experienced technical personnel involved from the start.

Previous negotiations have also shown the importance of entering into negotiations with a realistic draft contract. AMF found it advantageous to present at the outset a draft more favourable to the Chinese than would usually have been thought prudent. This reduced the time spent in negotiating, and allowed a quicker start of the project.

Nevertheless, AMF encountered problems despite careful planning and negotiating. Among these were a lack of urgency among the Chinese managers towards missed production goals, and frequent shortages of raw materials. AMF has also had to stress the importance of product quality and appearance, and the necessity of keeping tight delivery schedules.

Quality control

The Chinese usually refuse to grant exclusive marketing rights to Western firms, but are eager to have their products marketed abroad. Therefore, the Chinese will usually allow foreign firms to take an active role in quality control. However, quality control is still a problem in China. Compliance with standards is specially important where production is beyond the technical capabilities of the Chinese partners, and should be an integral aspect of the dual contract.

AMF has spent much time and money on training Chinese managers and installing the most up-to-date quality control equipment in all three operations. The contracts allow for an AMF representative to inspect the standard of the finished product, and employees of the company at many levels offer feedback from the market-place to the Chinese.

Conclusion

Countertrade still comprises a small portion of China's trade, but it will continue under present policies. China's Compensation Trade Bureau of the State Import and Export Commission (SIEC) has stated that counter-trade is 'indispensable' to China as a tool of economic planning. This position has been echoed in recent public pronouncements by the most important political leaders. Priority areas for countertrade deals are:
– energy projects;
– textiles and light industry;
– food;
– the electronics industry;
– building materials;
– the machine tool industry;
– iron and steel;
– the chemical industries; and
– agriculture.
Unforeseen offshoots can evolve from successful countertrade relations: for example, the recent opening of Beijing's first bowling lanes in the famous Lido Hotel. The new venture is initially aimed at tourists, but its sponsors, Chinese and Singapore interests and AMF, are hopeful that the sport will become popular among the urban Chinese.

R. J. Reynolds' tobacco venture

by Ronald J. Field

In the spring of 1979, Lester W. Pullen, then Chief Executive Officer of R. J. Reynolds Tobacco International's Asia-Pacific operations in Hong Kong, learned of the existence of a cigarette factory in a south-eastern province of the People's Republic of China. He was determined to visit the factory and to explore areas of common interest between his company and the operation in China.

Pullen first secured an invitation to visit the factory in the port city of Xiamen in Fujian Province. He met with the management team of the Xiamen Cigarette Factory led by its manager Madame Liu Weican and saw the equipment and facilities for the first time. From the beginning, he was impressed by the friendship, enthusiasm and confidence of the people of Xiamen, a city that is one of China's four Special Economic Zones.

Despite a variety of cultural and social differences, Pullen soon learned that the Chinese were very interested in developing a business relationship with R. J. Reynolds.

The two cigarette ventures

The relationship established in 1979 eventually led to two major projects between the Xiamen Cigarette Factory and the Winston-Salem based international tobacco company. The agreements establish RJR Tobacco International as a participant in China's future economic growth, giving RJR a strong position among international tobacco companies in a market where more than one trillion cigarettes are sold each year.

The first tobacco agreement led to the contract manufacture of the company's Camel Filter brand in the existing factory in Xiamen. In 1981, Camel Filters became the first American cigarette produced in China under the new open door policy, primarily for sale to tourists in foreign currency outlets.

The second agreement was announced in May 1984, when RJR Tobacco International became the first foreign company invited to participate in the cigarette market in the People's Republic of China through a joint venture.

Under the second agreement, RJR Tobacco International and its Chinese partners will construct a new factory in Xiamen producing R. J. Reynolds brands and new jointly-owned brands. As part of the agreement, the new factory will use equipment and manufacturing technology supplied by R. J. Reynolds.

Both agreements were developed with mutual trust, cooperation and the firm commitment of RJR Tobacco International and its parent company. They required constant teamwork and cooperation between negotiators in Winston-Salem, Xiamen and Hong Kong.

Negotiations and agreements

Soon after the initial relationship was established in 1979, meetings were held in Xiamen and at RJR world headquarters in Winston-Salem. In 1980, a Chinese delegation led by representatives of the Xiamen Cigarette Factory and the Tobacco Division of the Light Industry Ministry (now China National Tobacco Corporation (CNTC), the government body that regulates the tobacco industry in China) visited Winston-Salem.

The Chinese delegation met with RJR Tobacco International's senior management and with the highest levels of Reynolds' corporate management. These meetings and those that followed established RJR's corporate commitment to a long-range, multi-faceted relationship that was instrumental in achieving the tobacco agreements.

As part of the first agreement, RJR Tobacco International provided equipment to the factory in Xiamen to produce Camel Filters. The company also sent a team of technicians to Xiamen to provide training and technical assistance. Although none had ever been to China and communications were mostly through interpreters, the RJR technicians built strong personal and professional relationships with their Chinese colleagues as they worked together at the factory in Xiamen.

In combination, corporate commitment at the highest level and the relationships developed by RJR negotiators and technicians created a strong bond between the US company and its Chinese partners.

That bond led to negotiations for the second and more ambitious joint venture. Its development required patience and understanding to help the parties negotiate a successful agreement, then guide the joint venture through China's complex governmental approval process which included the following bodies: authorities of the Xiamen Special Economic Zone; the local CNTC representative in Xiamen; authorities of Fujian Province, including the Fujian Office of the Ministry of Foreign Economic Relations and Trade (MOFERT); national officials of CNTC and MOFERT; the Ministry of Finance; the Bank of China; and the Chinese customs authorities.

While the process has been complex and time-consuming, the Chinese are making substantial progress in streamlining approvals for foreign joint-venture agreements.

To expedite RJR's agreement, drafts were sent to CNTC and MOFERT officials during various stages of the negotiations. As a result, government authorities were familiar with components of the proposal before they began reviewing the completed version.

The agreement represents an equity investment of US$20 million shared equally by both parties. Most of the RJR Tobacco International investment is in US dollars and is earmarked for machinery, equipment, engineering design and project management. Most of the Chinese investment is in renminbi targeted for construction of the new factory and locally available machinery, equipment and support facilities. Land for the new factory is being leased from the Xiamen Special Economic Zone.

A long-range commitment

Throughout the process, the key to RJR's success has been the strong bond between the company and its Xiamen partners, a bond that has been strengthened by corporate support to a long-range commitment.

For example, the company co-sponsored a China tour by the Washington Ballet to encourage greater understanding between China and the United States through cultural exchange. A special benefit performance was held at the Kennedy Center in Washington two months before the tour. It was attended by Vice-President George Bush, Chinese Ambassador Zhang Wenjin, RJR executives and a number of US and Chinese dignitaries. Later, the tour received rave reviews in China.

RJR Tobacco International is also creating an educational exchange programme by establishing scholarships for qualified Xiamen students to study at Wake Forest University in Winston-Salem. The programme enables two Chinese students to study business administration at the university for two years; they then will return to Xiamen to put their business training to practical use.

Such cultural and educational exchange programmes help emphasise the company's total commitment to a long-term relationship with its Chinese partners.

Other opportunities

That relationship has helped create opportunities for other units of R. J. Reynolds Industries Inc, a diversified, international corporation with major interests in a wide range of consumer products and annual sales of over US$19 billion.

During the early stages of negotiations between RJR Tobacco International and the Xiamen Cigarette Factory, Chinese officials learned of RJR's diverse interests in consumer products.

Subsequently, Chinese officials visited the headquarters of Del Monte Corporation, a subsidiary of RJR, in San Francisco. Those meetings led to the establishment of an agricultural research programme in Shanghai where fruit and vegetables are being produced in a joint project. Opportunities exist for additional projects in which Del Monte can provide the technology and expertise to help China achieve new agricultural and economic goals.

As a beginning, Del Monte will build a US$1 million food processing plant in the Shanghai economy zone scheduled to begin operating in the summer of 1986.

Another RJR subsidiary, Kentucky Fried Chicken Corporation, is considering a joint venture in China where chicken is a favourite dish and quick-service restaurants are in high demand.

Conclusion

RJR is in a strong position to participate in the future economic development of the People's Republic of China, due in part to the relationship that was established in Xiamen in 1979 based on mutual trust and cooperation.

When the RJR Tobacco International joint-venture agreement was announced in Beijing in May 1984, Lester Pullen, who is now President and Chief Executive Officer of RJR Tobacco International, put the relationship into perspective. 'This is a project for the long term', Pullen said. 'We and our Chinese partners are committed to substantial growth over the longer term. We are especially pleased that our joint venture will help in the development of the Xiamen Special Economic Zone where the relationship with our Chinese partners began in the spring of 1979'.

The Great Wall Sheraton Hotel

by The Sheraton Corporation

The signing on 18 March 1985 of an agreement to manage the Great Wall Hotel in Beijing was the culmination of nearly 10 years of Sheraton's efforts to develop hotels in China.

The Chinese government is concerned about the inadequate facilities for tourism – infrastructure, transportation and accommodation – and encourages development of hotels, mostly through the use of joint ventures. The first example, the Jianguo Hotel in Beijing, was a joint venture of China International Travel Service (CITS) and expatriate Chinese in San Fransisco. The hotel has been very successful, recouping the investment in three years, and is seen as an example of the type of hotel China needs: one meeting the expectations of foreign travellers, and generating healthy financial returns for its owners.

Sheraton's performance since assuming the management of the Great Wall Sheraton Hotel will be another example of the realisation of China's needs in the development and promotion of tourism and business alike.

The negotiations

The Great Wall Hotel was already open when the owners, a Sino-US joint venture, invited a number of hotel management companies to submit their proposals. Sheraton received the invitation late September 1984, and a team of executives travelled to Beijing early October to introduce the company, its facilities, services and systems, and to make an initial proposal for business conditions.

The owners of the hotel established criteria for judging the five short-listed hotel management companies. The criteria included the terms of business, training and development of staff, image, food and beverage, services, quality, sales and marketing activities and reservation capabilities. Sheraton and the other short-listed companies were invited to negotiate further the contract conditions for operating the hotel. Sheraton executives again travelled to Beijing to negotiate in detail the terms of business, and at the conclusion of these meetings Sheraton was invited to submit a draft management agreement for contract negotiations.

In most points the proposals of the five short-listed companies were fairly close, although Sheraton was probably more aggressive in its terms of business. However, the key points in Sheraton's favour were its extensive sales and marketing network and its worldwide central reservation system. The owners recognised the need to have an international office and the ability for customers to make reservations directly with the hotel, rather than through intermediaries or through CITS and its inefficient reservation system.

Sheraton won the contract, and assumed the management of the Great Wall Sheraton Hotel on 18 March 1985. This modern hotel with its up-to-date facilities has all the necessary attributes to make it the leading hotel in China. Since starting the management of the hotel, Sheraton has increased occupancy to approximately 95 per cent, and improved the average room rate by about US$20.

Outline of the agreement

Under the agreement Sheraton manages the hotel as the agent of the owners. The agreement is for 10 years, with options for renewal. Under the terms of business Sheraton receives a basic management fee, calculated as a percentage of turnover. In addition, there is an incentive management fee, calculated as a percentage of gross profits, as negotiated, taking into consideration the owners' financial obligations.

Sheraton appoints the personnel for the five key management positions. The General Manager of the hotel nominates the expatriate heads of departments and sub-departments, and the Chinese personnel who will be trained for these positions. All appointments and nominations are confirmed by the owners' Board of Management. Sheraton is fully committed to train and develop the Chinese staff in order to reduce the number of expatriate employees as soon as possible.

Some key observations

Interpreters
Probably the most important asset for successful negotiations in China is a good interpreter, who should be fluent in Mandarin or the local dialect, and should preferably have a good Western education and familiarity with the Western negotiator's type of enterprise.

The Chinese always retain their own interpreters, who in most cases are fluent in 'textbook' English. However, they are often limited to translating literally, and consequently may miss more subtle concepts or principles. The presence of an interpreter acting for the Western negotiator is therefore essential to communicate a proper joint understanding of positions and requirements.

Chinese negotiators
The Chinese are generally very astute negotiators with a keen sense of business, but it must be remembered that the fundamental principles and ethics of Western business – profit making, employee rewards, promotion for good performance, etc. – are new concepts in present-day China. However, the Chinese are adapting quickly, and are attempting to make the necessary adjustments in their attitude.

At the same time, the Chinese negotiators must deal internally with a well-defined hierarchy and a committee-orientated organisation composed of superiors and associates who must be convinced that what is proposed is the best means to achieve the desired results.

As a result of this complex internal review system one may encounter reversals of position or even attempts at renegotiation of points which were believed to have been agreed upon only the previous day. Another approach often used by Chinese negotiators is to introduce one or more new members to their team, possibly each day. This in effect re-opens the negotiations as each new member needs to review, question and agree on the points which had been agreed previously.

Very few of the Chinese negotiators and business managers Sheraton has dealt with wish to be innovators. The task of obtaining internal approval is much easier for a Chinese negotiator if the terms of the deal being negotiated have a precedent. This also means that one must be very careful in assessing the merits or value of any deal, since the provisions of all future transactions will be structured similarly, or even reduced.

In its negotiations with the Chinese, Sheraton has found both the younger and the older generation equally keen and astute, but for different reasons. Negotiators from the older generation have survived the turbulent years since 1949 by not taking risks, and they will insist on staying within parameters approved in previous deals. The younger generation will negotiate very hard in order to establish a reputation for themselves by appearing not to make too many concessions.

Expatriate Chinese partners
Sheraton receives on average one communication each day regarding a hotel project in China. In many of these cases an expatriate Chinese person or business entity is involved in the project. This can be very advantageous when the expatriate Chinese is fluent in Mandarin and comes from a family which still has strong ties with China. In addition, the expatriate Chinese partner's association with the project may facilitate the negotiation of favourable tax treatment, or an improvement in the terms of business, or help bring about an improved guarantee of loans by the Bank of China.

It is important to determine at the start the influence of an expatriate Chinese partner, and also the role he intends to play, in order to fully recognise all possible exposures as well as the potential benefits of such an association.

Letters of intent
This term is used widely throughout China but is often misunderstood. Some Chinese believe that Westerners want a letter of intent so that they can justify their trip to China with this 'trophy'.

To the Chinese, a letter of intent is simply an expression of interest or a non-exclusive memorandum of understanding. In several cases Sheraton discovered that the same Chinese agency had signed at least five letters of intent with different developers for one hotel site. The intention of the Chinese was to compare all the letters of intent, and then to select the developer with the model most advantageous to their agency.

As a result Sheraton has not recognised these letters as representing any formal commitment, and consequently has never made an announcement of a pending project based solely on a letter of intent. Such a premature announcement could cause a negative reaction from the Chinese, as was demonstrated in the case of one of Sheraton's competitors some years ago: this company has not signed a management contract with the Chinese to this day.

Documentation
Sheraton's negotiations were prolonged, and at times tedious, because it insisted on having a management agreement which essentially conforms to those signed for other Sheraton hotels around the world.

The Chinese prefer to write a fairly simple document, covering only the basic principles that have been negotiated and upon which there is agreement. If all issues are not formulated precisely, the inherent danger is that each new event could give rise to negotiation or renegotiation. Sheraton's approach is more demanding and time-consuming initially, but it avoids potential problems for those members of staff who must enforce or operate under the agreement.

Legal aspects
Chinese laws for commercial activities are being revised and rewritten. Many types of ventures and business activities currently under negotiations are not yet covered by laws. Chinese negotiators may try to persuade Westerners to accept existing laws as binding for a venture under discussion. This should be resisted: if new laws are passed after a deal has been signed, it may well be possible to use the deal as a precedent in future negotiations.

It is very important to use capable local legal counsel, who will monitor changes in the law, and who are familiar with the day-to-day processes of doing business in China.

Taxation and accounting
Local counsel is also needed for taxation aspects. Special considerations have been and are continuing to be negotiated. It is essential to explain to the Chinese tax authorities in detail the nature and conditions of the agreement before it is finalised. If the tax position is unsatisfactory, one can either attempt to renegotiate or abandon the deal before being locked into an unfavourable agreement.

It may take some time to review the acceptability of maintaining separate accounting for bookkeeping, i.e. in accordance with Hotel Industry Uniform System of Accounts, and for tax purposes. The latter aspect requires the involvement of a Chinese accounting firm, since only they are allowed to confirm records for tax filing purposes.

Repatriation of earnings
Before the final agreement is signed, every effort must be made to ensure that earnings can be repatriated. However, the Bank of China is reluctant to provide any such assurances in writing. Sheraton met with the appropriate Chinese authorities, during the later stages of the negotiations, to discuss the remittance of funds outside China. Sheraton accepted the authorities' advice, and

made the necessary adjustments to ensure smooth transfers of funds.

Sheraton is in the advantageous position of being able to generate earnings in foreign currency. Because of the nature of its business, Sheraton needs to maintain foreign currency bank accounts in order to pay foreign expenses and fees. Foreign currency deposits are not placed in the local currency bank accounts, since reconversion to foreign currency is impossible.

Having a foreign currency bank account does not, however, eliminate the need to obtain prior approval by the Chinese authorities for each transfer of foreign currency out of China.

Conclusion

Sheraton has been active in a number of negotiations involving both wholly-owned Chinese projects and joint-venture projects in which foreign investors are partners. The tone and strategy of these negotiations did not differ substantially except that, in the latter cases, the foreign investor often proved helpful in convincing his Chinese partners that Sheraton's conditions were acceptable Western business conditions and were not unfair to the owners of the project.

Some of the previous Chinese conditions, e.g. length of agreement not to exceed seven years, inability to use the Sheraton name on hotels, and obligation to promote Chinese personnel to management position after three years whether ready for promotion or not, are now regarded as negotiable.

An invitation to the Chinese to visit the Western negotiator's facilities outside China can serve to demonstrate sincerity. It will also provide an excellent opportunity to acquaint the Chinese with one's methods of doing business.

Sheraton's negotiations in China, which have involved several projects and many discussions with a variety of authorities and interest groups, have been very rewarding, even when a deal could not be concluded. Sheraton believes that, once an agreement is signed, trust grows rapidly as Sheraton is now able to demonstrate its commitment to its responsibilities under the agreement, rather than merely 'selling its point'.

Shanghai Volkswagen Automotive Company Ltd: a German-Chinese joint venture

by Volkswagenwerk AG

The first automobile joint venture in China is now under way in Shanghai and will involve the annual production of up to 30,000 Volkswagen motor cars in the Chinese plant from 1987. The agreement between the German company and the Chinese involves the transfer of technological and industrial expertise, and the opening up of a potentially huge market both within China and throughout Southeast Asia. The success of the partnership has been fuelled by the realisation on all sides of the immediate as well as long-term benefits that the manufacturing partnership could bring.

The following press release, issued on 10 October 1984 at a press conference held by Volkswagenwerk AG in Beijing, gave the details:

'Volkswagenwerk AG, Wolfsburg, and the Chinese partners Shanghai Tractor and Automobile Corporation (STAC), Bank of China Trust and Consultancy Company, a subsidiary of the Bank of China (BOC), and the China National Automotive Industry Association (CNAIC), signed a contract on 10 October 1984 to establish a German-Chinese joint venture. The company's name is to be Shanghai Volkswagen Automotive Company Limited (SVAC). The length of the contract is initially set at 25 years.

Each partner's share in the joint venture is as follows: Volkswagenwerk AG 50 per cent, the Chinese motor manufacturer STAC 25 per cent, the BOC subsidiary 15 per cent, and the association of Chinese motor manufacturers CNAIC 10 per cent. The company's starting capital is 160 million renminbi, about DM200 million.

Volkswagenwerk AG, BOC and CNAIC are contributing their share of the venture in the form of investments. STAC's share is mostly in the form of material investments, mainly two factories near Shanghai and the manpower to install the necessary machinery and capital equipment.

The first stage in the joint-venture agreement is the construction of a vehicle factory with an annual capacity of 20,000 Santana models by 1989, and an engine factory with an annual capacity of 100,000 engines by 1990. By this time the planned investment programme of 500 million renminbi should have been carried through. Further stages of the joint venture will be discussed by the partners at the appropriate times. . . .

The highest executive body in the joint venture will be a board of 10 directors, with equal representation. Because of domestic regulations, the chairman has to be a representative of the Chinese partners. The day-to-day running of the company is to be entrusted to an Executive Committee of Management, consisting of four directors. The Chinese partners will appoint the managing director and the head of personnel, while Volkswagenwerk AG will nominate the finance, purchasing and technical directors.'

The negotiations over this joint-venture contract took more than five years. The first initiative for the automobile project was taken in 1978, when the Chinese Minister for Machinery Manufacturing visited Wolfsburg. The negotiations and definitions of the project were made against the background of the readjustments in Chinese economic policies, and with regard to the financing and foreign currency demands necessary for the project.

The first step

After the responsible government departments in Beijing and Shanghai gave their approval for the automobile project at the end of 1981, an 'agreement on trial manufacturing' was signed by STAC and Volkswagen in mid-1982. This cooperation agreement saw the assembly of the Santana model in a STAC factory as the first step towards working together in a joint venture. The trial

manufacturing agreement allowed Volkswagen to gain experience, particularly of working with the other partner, without incurring great financial risk. Specifically, Volkswagen could gather first-hand experience of the Chinese partner's organisation, the Chinese components industry, the Chinese customer service industry, and living and working conditions in China. At the same time the first steps could be taken to modernise STAC's factory in Shanghai.

Under the terms of the trial manufacturing agreement STAC has assembled over 2,000 Santana in Shanghai. These vehicles are exclusively for the Chinese market; buyers are mostly civil servants and taxi companies.

Realisation of the project

Immediately after signing the trial manufacturing agreement, the technical and economic viability of the automobile project was jointly examined. A feasibility study was made and the contract – consisting of a joint-venture contract, a technology transfer agreement and articles of association – was negotiated. The contract, which has over 500 pages, was signed in October 1984, and was approved by the Chinese Ministry of Foreign Economic Relations and Trade at the end of 1984.

In mid-1985, the Shanghai Volkswagen Automotive Company (SVAC) was established. Its first objective was to initiate the realisation of the investment programme.

Enthusiastic workers in the Anting factory near Shanghai

Two Chinese workers proudly displaying the label that identifies them as VW inspectors

Production of the Santana is being transferred to SVAC.

Engine production is to begin in 1989, and full annual capacity of 100,000 units should be reached by the end of 1990. Production of four-cylinder petrol and diesel engines common to the VW and Audi range is planned. Engines not required for Chinese car production will be exported to Volkswagen in Germany, thus integrating the joint venture into the worldwide manufacturing network of the company.

Once the vehicle and engine plants have achieved full production, SVAC will employ a labour force of about 2,500. The local content level in the manufacturing process is already 30 per cent, and will be increased to between 80 and 90 per cent by 1991. A precondition for this is the development of an adequate components industry. Components initially supplied by the Chinese are tyres, radios, rubber components and seats.

Conclusion

The joint-venture automobile project underlines the commitment of the Chinese government to industrial modernisation and liberalisation.

Some of the reasons why Volkswagen was chosen as partner for this joint venture were:
– the fundamental aim of the Chinese in modernising their industry is to achieve export potential, and non-Japanese motor manufacturers with small market shares in Asia therefore enjoy an advantage;
– Volkswagen was attractive to the Chinese partners because of its experience in building up national automobile industries, e.g. in Brazil and Mexico;
– Volkswagen from the beginning suggested a joint venture for the project, thereby indicating its readiness to make a considerable financial contribution and to take the responsibility for realising the project;
– production of engines in China and their export to Germany, thus locking the joint venture into Volkswagen's worldwide manufacturing network, is a guarantee for the Chinese that the company will continue to transfer technology to the joint venture.

For Volkswagen the joint venture represents the first step into a market with enormous future potential, as well as the development of a bridgehead to Southeast Asia. The fact that it was decided at the first board meeting of SVAC to produce 30,000 Santana annually from 1987, and to include the Audi 100 in the product range, clearly shows the future prospects of this German-Chinese joint venture.

One of the statues flanking the avenue leading to the Ming tombs

東亞銀行
THE BANK OF EAST ASIA

Bank of East Asia: leading contender in the China market

For more than 66 years the Bank of East Asia has enjoyed a close relationship with China. Since its founding in 1918, the bank has proved an unqualified success in fulfilling its original objective: to serve the international financial needs of Chinese communities in Hong Kong and Southeast Asia. In so doing it has captured a major share of Hong Kong deposits, and now has 49 local branches. In addition, it has built an expanding network of international branches and a series of correspondent banking relationships throughout the world, and through joint-venture agreements offers representation in other financial services fields.

The bank's association with China dates primarily from its establishment of a Shanghai branch in 1920. Since then the branch has provided full banking services in Shanghai without interruption, and today is the only overseas Chinese or foreign bank in China that owns — and operates from — its own premises.

In addition to the usual banking services, the Shanghai branch maintains a correspondent relationship with more than 160 banks throughout Canada, the United States, Europe, Australia and Asia. Because of its special status in China, the Shanghai branch is able to efficiently process documentary credits for correspondent banks in all parts of China. The Shanghai branch is thus well placed to assist foreign businessmen in locating and exploiting investment opportunities in China.

Recent expansion

The bank's China-related activities have expanded significantly in recent years, stimulated initially by China's adoption of the open-door policy in 1978. Since then the bank has participated in several loan syndications for projects in China, such as the construction of the first phase of the China Nanhai Oil Centre in Guangzhou (formerly Canton), the Lido Hotel complex in Beijing and the Shenzhen New Overseas Chinese Hotel in the Shenzhen Special Economic Zone.

In 1979 the bank entered the first of a number of joint ventures giving it direct business links with China. The bank took an 18 per cent stake in China Air Catering Limited (CACL), a company established in Hong Kong to participate jointly with the Civil Aviation Administration of China (CAAC) in setting up aircraft catering facilities at Beijing's International Airport and in providing in-flight kitchen service to all CAAC-operated airlines as well all foreign airlines with access to this airport. The

The Bank of East Asia's head office in Hong Kong

joint-venture company, Beijing Aircraft Catering (Joint Venture) Ltd, was in fact the first joint venture between China and a foreign participant.

The bank also reached an agreement with the Bank of China in 1979 to honour the East Asia Bank Americard/VISA in Guangzhou and Shanghai. The card, originally launched by the Bank of East Asia and the Bank of America in Hong Kong, was the first to be allowed into China, and is now accepted in about 47 Chinese cities.

In 1982, the Bank of East Asia, in conjunction with the Bank of China group and several other Hong Kong banks, formed the Joint Electronic Teller Service Limited (JETCO) to share over 300 automatic teller terminals. JETCO will install ATMs in the Special Economic Zones of Shenzhen and Zuhai in the near future, creating the first shared ATM network that geographically covers China, Hong Kong and Macao.

In 1984 the bank, in a joint venture with the Bank of China and Société Générale, formed Trilease International Limited with the aim of promoting plant and equipment leasing as a modern financial tool in China. As foreign exchange is scarce for many Chinese enterprises, leasing is considered an effective way to import the Western technology and equipment urgently needed for modernisation of China's industries. Trilease has already won numerous leasing contracts in China.

The bank's China programme took a major step forward in 1984 with the establishment of the China Division under the International Department. The China Division, in addition to coordinating all China-related activities within the bank, administers the Shanghai branch and the Shenzhen representative office, identifies financing opportunities in China, assists clients in barter trade and various business dealings with Chinese enterprises and provides other counselling and information services. The division is being expanded to keep pace with an ever-increasing volume of business.

A colourful past

When the Bank of East Asia was formed in 1918, the idea of a Chinese bank operating with Chinese capital on an international scale was unprecedented. The Revolution of 1911 had forged a new economic structure in China, and, as trade and industry developed, the former 'Imperial Mints' were converted into municipal, provincial and national banks. In Shanghai, commercial banks appeared and rapidly assumed importance in the conduct of business affairs, a trend soon repeated in other leading Chinese cities.

While Hong Kong banking was ruled by British and foreign banks, the need for banking services specifically tailored to local and overseas Chinese business interests was recognised by a group of prominent Chinese businessmen. This group founded the Bank of East Asia on 14 November 1918, and two months later the bank commenced business at a Hong Kong Central District site with an authorised capital of HK$2 million.

The response of Chinese business interests was immediate and widespread, rapidly leading to a network of international services with agencies in various parts of the world. During the first year, deposits rose to HK$4 million and net profit to HK$370,268. In its first decade the bank increased its staff from 20 to more than 200. By the mid-1920s branches had been established in Kowloon, Canton (Guangzhou), Shanghai and Saigon. Growth continued despite periodic economic problems in mainland China and throughout the world.

In 1935 the bank completed a new 10-storey building in Central Hong Kong. Business increased with the outbreak of the Sino-Japanese war in 1937, the cause of extensive industrial movement from Shanghai and other Chinese cities into Hong Kong. The Canton branch was forced to close in 1938 with the Japanese occupation of the city, but the bank continued to prosper. In November 1938, its 20th anniversary, deposits had exceeded HK$25.5 million and profits had reached HK$2.6 million.

The bank was able to continue operations during the World War II occupation of Hong Kong, from December 1941 to August 1945, although trade and banking activities were severely restricted.

Growth resumed in post-war years, generated primarily by Hong Kong's evolution from a trading port largely dependent on business with the mainland to a major financial and industrial centre.

Sound policies through the years helped guide the bank through various crises, including a bank run in 1965 which threatened Hong Kong's economic stability. The bank's position actually strengthened during this period. Expansion continued through a stock market boom and collapse in 1973 and the global economic uncertainties of the late 1970s and early 1980s.

In September 1983 the bank completed redevelopment of its headquarters in Hong Kong's Central District. The bank now occupies 10 floors of the 24-storey building.

By 1985 the bank's staff had grown to more than 1,630, and the number of Hong Kong branches had increased to 49. Issued capital totalled HK$214,599,000. Published reserves totalled HK$616,245,000 and total assets exceeded HK$12 billion.

Looking ahead

Increasing trade and economic ties between China and Hong Kong, especially after the signing of the Sino-British agreement in 1984, have enabled Hong Kong banks to play a greater role in China's modernisation drive. As China seeks to quadruple its total industrial and agricultural output by the end of this century, a large amount of funding will be required to import the machinery and equipment the country needs to establish

The Shanghai branch of the Bank of East Asia

advanced-technology industries, renovate old enterprises and upgrade infrastructure. Moreover, as China becomes more familiar with Western economic and financial systems, modern financial tools such as leasing and the issuing of bonds and shares as methods of raising capital can be expected to find wider acceptance in China.

In recognition of these developments, the Bank of East Asia is preparing a substantial expansion programme in China. It is planning a branch in the Shenzhen Special Economic Zone, immediately north of Hong Kong, and will reopen its branch in nearby Guangzhou. Also under consideration are branches in the 14 open coastal cities of China.

Additional joint ventures with various foreign and Chinese financial institutions are being evaluated in an effort to provide China with a broader spectrum of modern financial services. Further development of existing joint ventures is also planned. For example, Beijing Aircraft Catering Ltd is exploring opportunities for expanding its business in Shanghai, Guangzhou, Xiamen and other areas.

The Bank of East Asia's Shanghai branch, a pillar of the Bank's China activity for more than six decades, anticipates new growth with China's recent decision to relax controls on the scope of business conducted by the four overseas Chinese and foreign banks (including the Bank of East Asia) in Shanghai.

Beginning 1 December 1984, these banks have been permitted to offer the following services:
- launching foreign exchange deposit accounts for three types of capital enterprises (i.e. foreign capital enterprises, overseas Chinese capital enterprises and Chinese-foreign joint-venture capital enterprises) in China, as well as enterprises, organisations and individuals outside China;
- providing foreign exchange loans to both state-owned enterprises and institutions and the above-mentioned three capital enterprises in China;
- handling inward and outward remittance for both Chinese and foreign enterprises, organisations and individuals;
- settling accounts and trade bills for exports and imports (including letters of credit) for Chinese state-owned export and import corporations and the three capital enterprises mentioned above;
- attracting foreign exchange trust deposit accounts from abroad and trust investments;
- providing letters of guarantee for the establishment of loans;
- consultancy;
- safe-deposit boxes.

The bank is planning to introduce all of these services at its Shanghai branch in the near future. Initially, it will offer outward remittance, foreign currency deposits of five major currencies (US dollar, Hong Kong dollar, Japanese yen, pound sterling and Deutschemark) and safe-deposit boxes.

In addition, the Shanghai branch will continue its established business lines, including export bill negotiation and collection, inward remittance, consultancy and credit information. Also, as an agent of the China Industrial and Commercial Bank, the Shanghai branch has for many years been accepting deposits in renminbi (yuan) currency.

David K. P. Li, Director and Chief Manager

In January 1985 the Shanghai branch was one of the 23 financial institutions in China officially approved to provide foreign exchange guarantee services. According to China's regulations on foreign exchange control, only those banks or financial institutions which have been set up in China subject to approval by the People's Bank of China and have obtained the 'Business Licence on Foreign Exchange' issued by the State General Administration of Exchange Control can provide foreign exchange guarantee services.

The satisfactory and amicable resolution of the question of Hong Kong's future in September 1984 set the scene for the Bank of East Asia to operate and grow in a stable business environment until the year 2047. It also convinced many foreign companies that their efforts to gain access to lucrative Chinese markets would be best served through a Hong Kong bank.

With its long history of sucessful operations on the Chinese mainland, its thoroughly tested role as a leading bank is the strategic Hong Kong market, and its widely acknowledged position in international banking, the Bank of East Asia is well equipped to offer what may be the world's most comprehensive range of China-related services.

CORNELIUS
BERENBERG
1634–1711

Berenberg Bank:
a German merchant bank's history
and its links with China

The Berenberg family emigrated from Antwerp to Hamburg during the Spanish-Dutch war of independence. The records of the City of Hamburg show that Hans and Paul Berenberg founded the firm in 1590, when they established themselves as cloth merchants in the city. Later entries in the records indicate that the Berenberg brothers were successful merchants.

In the 17th century, the third Berenberg generation added general importing and exporting to the family's trade. After the 30 Years' War, Cornelius Berenberg – a grandson of Hans – expanded the business throughout Europe. Family relations of the Berenbergs were instrumental to this development, especially in Lisbon, a centre for trade with the colonies, and in Livorno, whose merchants traded with the Orient.

The Portuguese had been the first Europeans to reach the Chinese coast by sea in 1513. In the 1550s they were allowed to settle in Macao which thus became the first place where maritime trade between China and the West developed. About 1600 the Spanish and Dutch arrived at the south China coast, and in 1635 the British followed. Guangzhou (Canton) soon became the major port where European merchants could be active. Towards the end of the Ming Dynasty (1368-1644) trading contacts between Europe and China had been well established, although on a limited scale. These contacts, however, were reduced during the early Qing (Manchu) Dynasty (1644-1911) when China, on the whole, was not interested in overseas trade. In the late 17th century Sino-European trade was resumed in specially designated ports such as Guangzhou, Xiamen (Amoy), Fuzhou and Ningbo, only to be confined to Guangzhou in the period from 1760 to 1842.

Merchants financed their own trading activities: they gave credit to their customers, and advanced money to their suppliers. There was a considerable trade in the many different currencies, which produced additional profits for merchants, and gradually merchant houses became semi-bankers. Cornelius Berenberg realised that the family fortune made in trade could be increased by banking business, and he developed the financial activities within his operation.

In the 18th century, major parts of the firm's activities were investment business and acceptance credits, as well as discounting of bills and mortgage financing. When Paul Berenberg died in 1768, five generations of Berenbergs had given their name to the firm over 175 years.

**A contemporary portrait of Cornelius Berenberg
(1634-1711)**

Joh. Berenberg, Gossler & Co

To ensure the continuity of the firm, Johann Berenberg took Johann Hinrich Gossler – a descendant of a family which had settled in Hamburg in the 14th century – into the firm when he married Johann Berenberg's daughter Elisabeth, and became a partner in 1769.

In 1791 the firm's name was changed to – and has been since – Joh. Berenberg, Gossler & Co. Cornelius Berenberg's business philosophy continued under Johann Hinrich Gossler: while fostering the trading activities of the firm, he further developed its financial operations. The firm's reputation as a discount and acceptance house was established far beyond Hamburg, while shipping and insurance were added to the existing trade business.

The business relations between China and Joh. Berenberg, Gossler & Co go back to the 18th century, when ships carrying Chinese goods docked regularly in Hamburg, and Joh. Berenberg, Gossler & Co participated in financing these shipments and trading in the goods. Members of the family maintained close connections with their Chinese trading partners through visits to China.

After the occupation by the French revolutionary armies, Amsterdam ceased to be an important trade centre, and Hamburg took its place. During the French Revolution, England subsidised Russia and Austria in their war against France, and part of the transfer of funds was handled by Joh. Berenberg, Gossler & Co. The Continental blockade by the French severely affected the economy of Hamburg. However, after the end of the Napoleonic wars, trade and business recovered remarkably quickly. Hamburg retained its strong links with England, but business with other European countries diminished. Instead, business was focused on the new states in South America, on North America and on East Asia. Hamburg regained its role as an economic and financial centre.

A substantial change in Sino-Western trade was brought about by the Opium War (1839-40) and the ensuing Anglo-Chinese treaty of Nanking (1842), which initiated the process of opening relations between China and the West. Further treaties followed in which China step by step accepted the Western demands for increased trade relations. From the mid-19th century onward, the Western nations competed in securing their share of the China trade. Trading houses and shipping lines, banks and industrial enterprises were founded in the Chinese treaty ports which became more and more integrated into the international commercial system.

In the mid-19th century Joh. Berenberg, Gossler & Co was among the founders of two major shipping lines – Hamburg-America Line (HAPAG) and Norddeutscher Lloyd – and participated in forming financial institutions and insurance companies. The Norddeutscher Lloyd in 1885/86 became Germany's official shipping line between Bremerhaven and Shanghai.

When the German Empire was founded in 1870, there was considerable reservation in the Hanseatic Cities of Hamburg and Bremen about the economic and political consequences. Hamburg did not join the Customs Union of the German Empire until 1880. John Berenberg-Gossler had supported Hamburg's entry into the Customs Union, partly because of its important relations towards international trade, and in recognition of his services he was made a member of the Prussian nobility in 1889, and was created Baron in 1910.

Two World Wars

John v. Berenberg-Gossler's son Cornelius, who inherited the title and the firm on his father's death in 1913, had the difficult task of leading the firm through World War I, and of overseeing its reconstruction after the war. The German economy was rebuilt but inflation, which reached its peak in 1923, and the subsequent reflation resulted in the economic crisis of 1931. In 1935 Cornelius' son Heinrich became a partner in the firm.

A meeting of officers of the International Banking Division: (left to right) Michael Schröder-Castendyck, Joachim H. Wetzel (Managing Partner), Carsten Sönnichsen, Claus-G. Budelmann (Executive Manager), Rüdiger K. Schultz, Dieter Rusch

Germany's disclaimer of all her former privileges in China after World War I created favourable conditions for Sino-German relations, because Germany was among the first foreign nations to cooperate with China as a true partner. Despite China's internal struggle for national unity and Germany's economic difficulties in coping with the provisions of the Versailles Peace Treaty, trade relations between Germany and China developed to a considerable extent.

After World War II the firm, by then 350 years old, resumed active banking business, and the bank developed a wide range of activities. Industrial reconstruction and the gradual rebuilding of foreign trade brought back a large number of old clients. The foreign connections of former years were revived, and the firm was again active in German and international business.

After the death of Cornelius v. Berenberg-Gossler in 1953, the bank was lead by his son Heinrich. With the increasing activities and rising business volume Heinz A. Lessing and Joachim H. Wetzel joined the bank as personally liable partners in 1961 and 1967 respectively. In 1967 The Philadelphia National Bank, and in 1974 Norddeutsche Landesbank-Girozentrale, as successor to the former partner Norddeutsche Kreditanstalt AG, joined the bank as limited partners.

Berenberg Bank

Since recommencing its banking business after World War II, Joh. Berenberg, Gossler & Co, now also known as Berenberg Bank, has increased its scope and volume of business. In the first balance sheet after the German currency reform in 1948, the bank's capital was shown as DM500,000 and its business volume was about DM2

million. In 1984, the capital of the bank had reached DM80 million and the business volume DM2.1 billion. Berenberg Bank plays an important role as private bankers in German and international banking, and its partners are committed to maintain its character as a private bank.

The bank is now led by Joachim H. Wetzel, partner since 1967, Baron Peter v. Kap-herr, partner since 1976 and Hans-Joachim v. Berenberg-Consbruch, partner since 1978 – and representing the 12th generation of the Berenberg-Gossler family.

In its fourth century, and bound by the tradition of a Hanseatic family enterprise, Berenberg Bank is a modern, dynamic private bank which owes its position to the commitment of its partners and staff, and to the large number of domestic and international loyal clients.

The bank's services

The main activities of the bank are financial and credit services for commercial and industrial companies, portfolio management for institutional and private investors and advising on merger and acquisition opportunities. The handling and financing of international trade transactions has traditionally been one of the bank's primary activities. The major services provided in this area include:
– import and export financing;
– documentary business;
– foreign exchange advisory services and dealing;
– international money market business and cash management services;
– information about foreign markets;
– credit inquiry service and introductions to potential business partners.

An experienced team with regional responsibilities and close contacts with foreign correspondent banks is available to advise both German and foreign-based clients on financing, risk evaluation and operational matters. The close personal contact maintained by the account officers, and their knowledge of the client's business and the foreign trading partner's country, enable the bank to advise clients promptly and accurately on the structuring of transactions, individual financing requirements, and the covering of foreign exchange risks. Although foreign lending is mainly orientated toward short-term financing and processing of cross-border trade in commodity goods, Berenberg Bank offers some specialised financing schemes for medium-term transactions. The bank is also active in arranging cover for foreign risks to promote German exports.

Based on economic and political factors, Berenberg Bank has focused its business activities on selected geographic regions in order to concentrate the bank's expertise; and since the client deals directly with an account manager who is familiar with the foreign country, thorough and expert counselling is ensured.

Smooth and efficient execution of business transactions is guaranteed by an electronic data processing system, and by utilising SWIFT, of which Berenberg Bank is one of the founder members. With the most up-to-date equipment in technology and telecommunications, Berenberg Bank is able to offer clients specialised services in monitoring and processing their

Berenberg Bank's modern office building in Hamburg

payments traffic, providing high-yield instruments for investing short- and medium-term excess liquidity, and extending special conditions for operating the account itself, in order to optimise the client's cash management. For some specific functions Berenberg has developed programmes to match given requirements.

Hamburg and China

The City of Hamburg maintains traditionally close links with China. As one of the major European ports, Hamburg has developed into one of the centres for China trade with Europe. As early as 1845 a regular shipping service from Hamburg to China was established. Moreover, Hamburg ships were active in the China coastal traffic. In the past as well as in the present the major part of Sino-German trade has been handled by the port of Hamburg. In 1984 about 80 per cent of Germany's exports to China and 75 per cent of its imports from China – about 1.4 million tonnes – were shipped through the port of Hamburg. In 1985 the German trade volume with China will be about DM6.2 billion.

As a reflection of the significance of Hamburg the first General Consulate of the People's Republic of China in Germany was opened in Hamburg early in 1984. A year later the Chinese European Trade Centre was established in Hamburg. Meanwhile Hamburg has signed a partnership agreement with Shanghai.

Shortly after the foundation of the People's Republic of China in 1949, Berenberg Bank became one of the first correspondent banks of the Bank of China in Germany. Following the introduction of new economic policies at the end of the 1970s, the first loan raised by the Bank of China in Germany was arranged through Berenberg Bank in Hamburg.

Conclusion

One of the main goals of Berenberg Bank is to build on the strength of its internationally experienced team to design customised financing schemes, and to offer efficient processing of China trade and other international transactions. Berenberg Bank will constantly strive to improve on the high-quality services it renders in this traditionally important area, particularly with its orientation to the Sino-German trade in mind.

Coudert Brothers' experience in China

A century after the establishment of Coudert Frères as the first American law firm in Europe in 1879, Coudert opened its office in the People's Republic of China. Coudert Brothers' experience in China owes much to its history and heritage as a firm. The original Coudert Brothers were the sons of Charles Coudert who was born in Bordeaux, France, in 1795 and joined Napoleon's army at the age of 15. He rose to become a cavalry lieutenant in the Imperial Guard of Honour, and in 1820, still faithful to Napoleon's cause, was sentenced to death for his involvement in a conspiracy against Louis XVIII. After a dramatic escape from prison, he fled to New York in 1824.

Charles Coudert continued to be an ardent Bonapartist: he frequently entertained Louis Napoleon and Joseph Bonaparte during their visits to the United States and visited them himself in France. It was only natural, therefore, that when Frédéric Coudert, his son, took up the practice of law in 1853, after graduating from Columbia College at the head of his class, his clients were predominantly French, Spanish and other European investors in America. The volume of European business grew quickly after the Civil War, and by 1879 it was both desirable and necessary to establish the Paris office of the firm to assist in these internationally oriented European investments. Today the firm's 270 lawyers are still primarily engaged in the practice of international law through its 15 offices on five continents.

While the early pioneers of the China practice did not come to China under 'sentence of death', it was probably as brazen to believe that there was a role for the international practice of law in Beijing in 1979 as it was for three French brothers to believe that they could successfully practice law in New York of the pre-Civil War period. Yet the history of the firm had shown that to properly advise foreign clients on doing business in a foreign country one must be there and both know and be a part of the local environment.

The involvement in China

From its office in Hong Kong, which was established in the early 1970s, Coudert Brothers was involved in a number of trade-related transactions with China, when Hong Kong was the only open vantage point for China and the rest of the world to engage in normal commercial relations. The firm was first invited to the Canton Trade Fair in 1974, when American companies began to attend

(Above) The Occidental delegation
(Below) The signing ceremony after the successful completion of the deal

the bi-annual event on a regular basis. It was not until 1978, however, that the United States and China established formal diplomatic relations, and it became possible for US and foreign companies to freely trade with and invest in China following Deng Xiaoping's open door policy. This change in the business environment of China and its relations with the United States encouraged the firm to explore the possibility of establishing a permanent presence in Beijing.

Coudert Brothers organised a seminar with the China Council for the Promotion of International Trade, China's leading organisation for contacts with the West, in February 1979. Led by Charles Torem, the head of the firm's Paris office, Coudert's team lecturing on joint ventures and foreign investments included the head of the firm's Japan practice, Charles R. Stevens, and Owen D. Nee and W. Gage McAfee of the Hong Kong office. The materials for the course were widely distributed in China. One month later the firm established its first contact with the Ministry of Finance, which led to a two-month seminar on US and international tax law problems, held in Dalian during the summer. Professors from Columbia, Harvard, New York University and Connecticut taught portions of the course, which was attended by Ministry of Finance officials from all over China.

In the autumn of 1979 the firm began teaching a small class of students organised under the supervision of the municipality of Beijing about international trade and investment law problems. Students in the course came from a number of ministries, such as the Ministry of Justice, Ministry of Petroleum and Ministry of Coal, as well as from the trading departments of many of the import and export corporations of Beijing municipality. This course lasted for two years and ended in 1981 with more than 65 students having attended.

Setting precedents

Fortunately, the firm's experience in China was not solely academic. The firm did the pioneer legal work for the Great Wall Hotel joint venture, which was the first hotel venture in China. The hotel now stands as the most impressive example of a completed, operating joint venture in China's capital city. The firm also assisted the Atlantic Richfield Company (ARCO) in concluding the first exploration agreement between a US oil company and the China National Offshore Oil Corporation. Coudert also did the first joint-venture contract in the offshore oil service area just two weeks later.

The most difficult transaction of all, and in many ways the most interesting, was Occidental Petroleum Corporation's US$650 million coal mine in Shanxi Province with the China National Coal Development Corporation. This

Owen D. Nee, Jr, partner in Coudert Brothers, Hong Kong

project, which is the largest contractual joint venture, the largest US investment and the largest amount of direct foreign capital investment in China, took over three and a half years to conclude. The perseverance of Dr Armand Hammer in seeing the transaction to its conclusion and the skill of the Occidental negotiating team saved this surface mine from many a deep pit. The form of the venture, the coal sales contracts and the financing arrangements for the project all were firsts in documentation of Chinese investment projects.

The recent PPG Industries (Pittsburgh Plate Glass) float glass joint venture in the Shekou Industrial Zone was another precedent-setting transaction for Chinese equity joint ventures, since the transaction involved both the transfer of complicated, high technology and difficult questions regarding domestic and export sales of the venture's products. China Merchants, the Chinese partner in the venture, proved willing to adopt advanced, Western management methods for the joint venture.

Coudert Brothers has been involved in many other equity joint ventures in China, including investments in hotels, textiles, food and beverage, toys, pharmaceuticals, computers, radios and offshore oil services. The firm has also prepared and negotiated technology transfer agree-

ments relating to paint, air-conditioning, medicines, foundries, boilers, and other technologies. In the financial area, the firm has assisted many banks with representative offices in obtaining their licences, and documented the first syndicated loan to the Bank of China, the first syndicated note purchase agreement for a Chinese issuer and the first foreign bank loan to a Chinese joint venture. In addition to working with ARCO on their petroleum contract, the firm has helped Exxon Corporation, Occidental, Phillips Petroleum and Pennzoil on various aspects of their offshore oil drilling programmes in China. The total value of China investments projects that the firm is currently working on exceeds US$2 billion and, during 1985, the firm's China Group should complete contracts for approximately half of this amount.

The China practice

The firm's China practice is headed by Owen D. Nee, Jr, who has been visiting China since 1974. He is the editor of a looseleaf service on China's business and commercial laws and has written part of this work on China's laws related to foreign investment. The China team at Coudert

174

includes six full-time lawyers and five translators. Lucille Barale is the firm's resident in Beijing, and Norman Givant is in charge of the firm's presence in Shanghai. In Hong Kong, W. Gage McAfee, Thomas E. Jones, Laura Cha and Florence Li work with Owen Nee on China matters. Altogether the firm has 13 lawyers who speak Chinese in its New York, San Francisco, Singapore, Hong Kong and China offices. The translation department is an integral part of the China team, since all investment contracts in China must be in both English and Chinese.

The work performed by the lawyers of Coudert's China Group is varied and interesting. Principally the firm assists clients by advising on the structure of transactions, drafting investment and licensing contracts, preparing Chinese-language translations of the documents and assisting in the negotiation of the final contracts. The majority of this work is done in Hong Kong, because of the availability of English- and Chinese-language word processing and typists. Usually Chinese contracts are negotiated either in Beijing or in one of China's other major commercial cities, although recently Chinese negotiators, recognising the difficulty of producing documentation in China, have shown a willingness to travel to Hong Kong to negotiate the final agreements. When the negotiations are held in Beijing, Coudert Brothers can revise the documentation at its office there, which has proved invaluable in many transactions with central government-level corporations.

The firm also maintains an extensive library of practical business information related to China. Based on its previous experience in other transactions and statistics available from Chinese government sources, the firm can provide such basic information as land use rates, utility costs, trade volumes and levels of investment for the major cities of China.

Probably the most important aspect of the firm's work of general significance is the ongoing commitment of the firm to translate important Chinese legislation into English for use by its clients. Much of this material is published in a looseleaf service edited by Owen Nee, but other regulations of limited applicability are only provided to clients interested in the particular legislation.

The firm has prepared a series of model contracts for use in joint ventures, cooperatives, compensation trade and licensing transactions, which are based on the preferred Chinese forms, but seek to answer common, recurring problems. These model forms smooth the negotiation process by adopting much of the language of the Chinese model form contracts and only include additional provisions that have previously been approved by the Ministry of Foreign Economic Relations and Trade.

Coudert Brothers cooperates closely with the major law firms of China, such as the China Global Law Office and the China Legal Consultancy Centre and many of the local law firms in Shanghai, Dalian, Shenzhen and Guangzhou. The firm also works with important Chinese consultancy companies such as China Consultants of Accounting and Financial Management and the China International Economic Consultants.

Predicting the future in China is always difficult, except that the open door policy will be around for a long time to come. Since the open door policy is what makes it possible for foreign companies to participate in the re-emergence of China as a commercial power, it is likely that someone will have to be in China to document the transactions. Coudert hopes to be there about as long as the sons of a French emigré have managed to survive in the hospitable legal circles of New York, which should give it at least another 125 years.

Dr Hammer and Deng Xiaoping

First Interstate Bank's presence in China

First Interstate Bank, Ltd, part of First Interstate Bancorp, is a major financial organisation with a substantial branch and corporate financial network worldwide. First Interstate Bank, Ltd, formerly the World Banking Group of First Interstate Bank of California, has had significant business interest in China for several years.

In 1979, First Interstate Bank of California (then called United California Bank) was among the first group of US banks to establish a correspondent relationship with the Bank of China. Soon after, in early 1980, a delegation from the Bank of China were the guests of First Interstate Bank in both its Los Angeles and San Francisco International Division offices, acquainting the visitors with on-site operations in both Southern and Northern California as well as introducing the systemwide network of banks located throughout the United States. Subsequently, relations between the two organisations grew, with First Interstate's involvement in servicing trade-related transactions expanding steadily and substantially.

Opening of the Beijing office

In late 1981, the bank first inquired about establishing an office in China. After selecting a location for its first banking office in the People's Republic of China, First Interstate Bank of California formally opened a representative office in Beijing in October 1983. At that time, First Interstate became one of only seven US banks with an office in Beijing, and one of only two US banks west of the Mississippi River with a Beijing office.

The initiation of involvement by bank holding company subsidiaries in export trading activities marked an additional avenue for First Interstate to expand its China-related activities. In 1983, First Interstate Trading Company initiated business cooperation agreements for referral of trading opportunities with both Bank of China Trust and Consultancy Company in Beijing and with the Shanghai Foreign Trade Consulting Corporation.

First Interstate's business activities with China are not restricted to its California operations. Business activities extend throughout its North American-based international offices. This multi-state, multi-provincial network gives First Interstate a unique ability to cover a wide variety of business in China, from correspondent banking with the Beijing and New York offices of the Bank of China to working with US and Chinese timber exporters through First Interstate's Seattle and Portland offices.

In addition to direct business activities, First Interstate executives have served on the boards of the Los

---

First Interstate Bank's head office at 707 Wilshire Boulevard, Los Angeles, California

Angeles-Guangzhou and San Francisco-Shanghai sister city committees as well as chairing the Washington State China Trade Council which promotes trade between the western United States and China.

Further significant Chinese business is transacted through First Interstate's global network including its Edge Act offices in the United States and its branches in Hong Kong, Tokyo, Singapore and London as well as the representative office in Frankfurt.

The Chinese have a new sign for expertise.

第一聯美銀行

(First Interstate Bank.)

On September 26, First Interstate Bank opened a new office in Beijing. Now, as one of the few American banks based in the People's Republic of China, we can help you expand your trade with that vast nation. Beijing completes our Asia/Pacific network, already among the most extensive of any U.S. bank. You'll find other First Interstate Bank offices in Bangkok, Hong Kong, Jakarta, Manila, Seoul, Singapore, Sydney, Taipei and Tokyo. In conjunction with the opening of our Beijing office, our First Interstate Trading Company has reached separate agreements with two trade organizations, Bank of China Trust and Consultancy Company in Beijing and Shanghai Foreign Trade Consulting Corporation, to promote a wide range of trade and trade-related services between the U.S. and China. So if you want to develop business or trade with China — for anything from textiles to natural resources development — call First Interstate Bank. Or as we're known in China, "Di Yi Lian Mei Yin Hang."

First Interstate Bank Member FDIC

To announce the opening of the Beijing office in 1983, a full-page advertisement ran in various Asian-Pacific newspapers

China International Non-Ferrous Metals Leasing Company, Ltd

In December 1984, First Interstate's involvement in China business took a further step with the establishment of China International Non-Ferrous Metals Leasing Co Ltd, a joint-venture leasing entity consisting of five partners: First Interstate Bank, Banque Nationale de Paris, Bank of China Trust and Consultancy Company, Industrial and Commercial Bank of China, and China

Non-Ferrous Metals Industries Corporation. First Interstate thereby became the first US commercial bank to have either a wholly-owned or jointly-held booking unit in China.

This entity will concentrate on providing long-term instalment finance for plant and equipment to Chinese organisations and joint ventures involved in developing the country's non-ferrous metals industries, a sector currently targeted by the government of the People's Republic of China for development for the remainder of the century and beyond the year 2000. Besides the immediate opportunity for providing equipment lease finance in China, First Interstate also sees the potential for capital equipment trading and export finance opportunities in the United States and elsewhere resulting from this venture.

On 9 July 1985, First Interstate Bank, Ltd and the Industrial and Commercial Bank of China signed a business cooperation agreement. This agreement, which specifically calls for the establishment of correspondent bank relationships, is the first signed by Industrial and Commerical Bank of China with a foreign bank.

Avenues of development

In addition to the non-ferrous metals-related business opportunities and correspondent banking business, First Interstate will concentrate on developing trade and project finance and capital market services from the following:
– major US and foreign firms trading with China or setting up joint-venture or other types of manufacturing or service operations in China;
– middle market customers primarily in the western United States selling to or buying from China;
– major Chinese organisations in and outside China.

With its broad geographic coverage in the United States, a large number of international banking offices covering both sides of the Pacific Rim, and a major representative office and leasing affiliate in China, First Interstate Bank, Ltd is positioned to benefit from expected continued trade and investment flows between China and the rest of the world.

Conclusion

First Interstate Bank, Ltd was formed to consolidate and refocus wholesale banking activities of the First Interstate system. It is now poised to assume a major role in providing a variety of financial services to worldwide financial institutions and corporations.

The three major categories of services are trade finance, corporate finance products and services, and correspondent banking.

China's renowned 'Red Flag' being assembled in Shanghai

Accounting in China: the Peat Marwick experience

China's continuing open door policy and its large potential market are attracting ever-increasing numbers of foreign investors in all types of businesses to establish operations within the country. Because of its unique position, Hong Kong is, naturally, often used as a base from which contacts can be developed.

Foreign corporations in the China market have traditionally been faced with difficulties concerning how and when they should make approaches, and to whom. The 'red tape' factor can appear a discouraging barrier to potential investors, unless the correct approaches are known and followed. Providing advice and assistance to foreign investors on such matters has become a more and more significant part of business for accounting firms in Hong Kong.

A foothold into the market

Peat Marwick were among the earliest accounting firms to become involved in the China market when, in 1978, they formed a China Committee to monitor the country's commercial and legal developments and clients' activities within the country. Contact between Chinese authorities and Peat Marwick strengthened quickly, with several of the senior partners participating in various government and trade delegation visits to China, and Peat Marwick offices in several countries around the world playing host to Chinese delegations.

A significant step forward in the relationship took place in late 1979, when a delegation from China's State Economic Commission, the organisation responsible for developing China's annual production plan, visited Peat Marwick's San Francisco office. To reciprocate, the Commission invited Peat Marwick to send a delegation to China to present a series of seminars in Beijing and in Shanghai.

The first official Peat Marwick delegation which was led by the then Chairman of Peat Marwick International, W. E. Hanson, was a great success. Peat Marwick made a series of presentations to various Chinese Government and business organisations in Beijing and Shanghai.

The seminars covered such topics as management information systems, production organisation, management and control and comparative studies on management methods adopted by West German, US and Japanese companies. Discussions also took place with several senior government officials and executives from banks, law firms and other multinational corporations.

The in-depth knowledge which Peat Marwick gained

D. W. Gairns, Senior Partner of Peat, Marwick, Mitchell & Co, Hong Kong

from this trip reinforced the belief that China is committed to accept foreign assistance in its plan to achieve a fundamental restructuring of its economy to improve the living standards of its huge population. This therefore confirmed Peat Marwick's intention to establish a presence in China to fulfil a dual purpose. Initially, they hoped to assist the increasing number of their clients who were seeking to do business with China, by introducing them to China and assisting them and the Chinese authorities in evaluating potential business opportunities. Peat Marwick also hoped that while learning about Chinese industrial management and practices on the one hand, they could also play a role in training Chinese management personnel.

Since then, Peat Marwick have presented seminars to various Chinese government ministries and corporations, including the National Centre for Industrial Science and Technology Management in Dalian, the China National Offshore Oil Company, the Beijing Economic Development Corporation and the Law Office of Tianjin. They have also developed a secondment programme under which senior accountants from such Chinese organisations as the China National Offshore Oil Company, the Ministry of Finance and the Ministry of Foreign Economic Relations and Trade have spent a training period in Peat Marwick offices around the world.

Through all this contact with Chinese business, it soon became obvious that all the country's professional people fall into one of two categories: they are either in their early 20s with limited experience, or in their 40s and 50s with a wealth of experience. The country has few professionals in the 30 to 40 age group – a direct result of the disruption of tertiary and professional education during the Cultural Revolution. In order to rectify the shortage, China has had to place great emphasis on training an increasing number of people in a short period of time.

The accounting profession in China

The contact with Chinese authorities and organisations has given Peat Marwick extensive knowledge and understanding of the accounting and auditing profession in China. Although bookkeeping has a long history in China, accounting as a profession came into being only a few years ago, mainly as a result of the country's open door policy and its consequent need to provide such services to foreign enterprises operating in China.

Increased awareness of the importance of accounting as a tool of management has allowed further advances of accountancy as a science, and substantial accomplishments have been achieved in the profession. China has now established a uniform system of accounting, and accounting information and administrative systems with nationwide control have been set up.

The Accounting Administration Department, under the Ministry of Finance, is responsible for the administration of accounting work throughout China, while the financial departments of local government at various levels supervise accounting practices in their areas. The Accounting Society of China was formed in 1980, and has since made contracts and arranged exchange visits with foreign accounting societies and international accounting firms, including Peat Marwick.

The State Auditing Administration, a national ministry under the State Council, was formed in mid-1983 to enforce state law and regulations on finance, promote economic effectiveness and ensure the smooth progress of economic reconstruction. Its supervision, however, covers only government departments and state-owned enterprises.

As far as foreign enterprises operating in China are

Peat Marwick's Beijing office in the CITIC building – the first office building for foreign business tenants in Beijing

concerned, both the Joint Venture Income Tax Law and the Foreign Enterprise Income Tax Law contain provisions for the audit of financial statements by Chinese Certified Public Accountants, with annual tax returns, financial statements and audit reports required to be submitted to the local tax bureau.

The emergence of Chinese Certified Public Accounting firms also came about as a result of the open door policy. At present, there are 54 Chinese CPA firms supported by some 1,000 professional accountants. This number is expected to be increased to 10,000 qualified accountants within the next five years. As yet, however, the country has no professional examination system in force, and applicants are assessed individually on their academic backgrounds and working experience by the Society of Public Finance.

In recent years, Peat Marwick have worked with several Chinese Certified Public Accounting firms in both auditing and consultancy work, and have developed good relationships with them. Through this close cooperation Peat Marwick have been able to develop an exchange programme which has allowed them to learn how best to service their clients' needs in the ever-expanding China market.

Services provided to foreign investors in China

In 1983, Peat Marwick formally established an office in Beijing. This office coordinates closely with their Hong Kong office, as experience indicates that much of the foreign investment into China is in one way or another connected with Hong Kong, because of its close proximity to China and its role as a recognised international trading and financial centre. To date, Peat Marwick have been involved in many Chinese-foreign joint ventures which are negotiated in Hong Kong, project packaged and funded from Hong Kong, or whose management personnel are recruited from Hong Kong.

Peat Marwick have also provided their international clients with a wide range of services within China. These fall into the following four major categories:
– advice and assistance on tax and tax-related matters;
– advice on auditing and accounting matters;
– financial advisory services; and
– assisting companies to set up operations in China.

Peat Marwick staff have travelled to China to assist clients in negotiating joint ventures, they have acted at various levels as financial advisors and interpreters, have provided assistance in establishing internal reporting and control systems for factories and have performed feasibility studies and market evaluations.

The following three case studies briefly illustrate some of the range of projects Peat Marwick have handled to date, the problems which have arisen and the solutions which were reached.

Establishment of joint venture

One of the earliest projects, in 1980, was to assist a multinational company to set up a light industrial consumer product manufacturing operation in China, as a joint venture with a Chinese partner. This was still very early days for foreign investment in the country, and there were few regulations or laws pertaining to such ventures. It is therefore not surprising that much of the negotiation started with the basics.

Peat Marwick staff were a part of a team of 15 executives to be responsible for the project. The first visit to China took place to gather background information, meet with the Chinese parties involved in the project and agree on a work programme and schedule. As an example of the basic level at which many of the negotiations were carried out, the Bank of China had to be visited to discuss how a foreign enterprise should hold a bank account in China.

Areas which were looked at in detail included the market interest and potential, export infrastructure, accounting and tax laws, provisions for the transfer of funds, possibility of bank loans, export collateral requirements, insurance, accounting standards, tax filing requirements and tax rates, staff training, and so on. Studies were also made of the existing factory facilities.

The team's second visit to China for the project was for the commissioning of the joint-venture operations and the allocation of manpower, including expatriate staff. This visit also served to finalise many arrangements such as personnel, salary packages for senior staff, accounting methods and reporting format, and royalties. An audit was also carried out to verify the Chinese party's fixed assets contribution. Subsequent visits saw the implementation of the accounting system and training of accounting staff.

Because foreign investment in China was a new phenomenon and there were no precedents to provide guidelines, the project was also a learning experience for the Chinese authorities and many of the agreements reached on our client's behalf were the result of protracted negotiations.

Peat Marwick's involvement in this project lasted for over two years. By the time they had completed the assignment, the Chinese authorities had, by necessity, become more familiar with the idea of foreign investment in the country, and guidelines had been laid down in specific areas, although this was only the start of a long road ahead.

Receivership

In 1983, a local Hong Kong manufacturing and marketing corporation went into receivership. Peat Marwick were appointed by the bank as receiver for one of the corporation's subsidiary companies, which had little involvement in Hong Kong, but whose main asset was a processing plant located in Shenzhen, China.

The immediate problem which arose was that, because the property was situated in China, it officially came under the jurisdiction of Chinese law, and by the nature of the political systems in China the role of a receiver was not recognised. The initial difficult situation was made to appear much worse when the Hong Kong media decided to report that the Chinese authorities were 'refusing' to hand over the property.

In fact, when Peat Marwick approached the Shenzhen authorities and discussed the situation with them, they were most cooperative and appreciative of Peat Marwick's role as receiver – if not officially recognising it. Understandably, the authorities were also concerned to ensure that any Chinese organisations who were creditors of the bankrupt company would be repaid. After

A group discussion session during a Peat Marwick seminar in China

initial discussions with the Shenzhen authorities, Peat Marwick were permitted to carry out an evaluation of the property and eventually to sell it – on the condition that all debts to Chinese companies were repaid.

The early difficulties on this project arose because there had been no precedent and China did not have any legislation on receivership, although it is thought such rules are currently being drafted by the Chinese legislative bodies. The successful solution to the problems and completion of the project can, in no small way, be attributed to the friendly and trusting negotiations between the parties concerned.

Loan guarantee

One of Peat Marwick's most recent projects in China is a feasibility study for a joint-venture hotel to be constructed in the country. Peat Marwick were appointed by a syndication of banks to review the project, and subsequently, to advise on the taxation and accounting matters relating to the implementation of this project.

The hotel is being built as a cooperative joint venture – the foreign (in this case, Hong Kong) partner arranging the finance and the Chinese partner providing the land. As in almost all cases where banks are involved, they require positive assurances from the joint venture and the shareholders that they can service and repay the debt in good time.

However, as China's laws relating to cooperative joint-venture enterprises are still being drafted at pre-

sent, many aspects of the funding, laws and regulations are open to interpretation and thus require detailed negotiation with the Chinese authorities. Peat Marwick have to work closely with the project's legal advisors, both in Hong Kong and China, the joint-venture partners, the banks, the Chinese tax authorities and Chinese CPA firm, etc. to agree on such aspects as accounting requirements, tax concessions, tax holidays and other financial matters. In certain cases, written rulings on such matters have to be obtained from the appropriate Chinese authority. The project is progressing very well.

Conclusion

It has been only a matter of five years since foreign investment has been permitted in China. This is not a long time for the internal situation to change in terms of developing an infrastructure, services, laws and regulations pertaining particularly to foreign enterprises.

In certain specific cases, such as the petroleum industry, the Chinese authorities have had more opportunities to develop regulations, and the situation is more advanced. In other industries there is still a considerable way to go to clarify all the confusing interpretations of the regulations. The authorities, however, have come to terms with the task which is before them and have made laudable headway – much credit is due to the close cooperation between Chinese and foreign parties in recent cases such as those highlighted above.

瑞士銀行

Swiss Bank Corporation: your key to China

When foreign businessmen are considering business with China they want to know the precise rules on how to approach their Chinese partners. However, there are no precise rules, only basic guidelines and the lessons of experience.

An experienced partner helps

In Hong Kong, we have a special China Desk with staff fluent in both Cantonese and Mandarin.

Founded more than a century ago, Swiss Bank Corporation today maintains the largest international network of all the Swiss banks and has enjoyed active relations with the People's Republic of China for decades in a broad variety of fields.

Recent milestones in this growing relationship include Swiss Bank Corporation's lead manager role in the Sfr80 million mixed credit facility arranged by the big Swiss banks in August 1984 with Bank of China.

Moreover, Swiss Bank Corporation's Euromarket arm in London, Swiss Bank Corporation International, was the only Swiss financial institution to participate as comanager in the DM150 million 7 per cent 1985-92 bond issue for the People's Republic of China.

Long-standing and smoothly functioning arrangements with the Bank of China and its sister institutions allow prompt and efficient handling of all kinds of banking operations in Swiss francs, renminbi (yuan) and other currencies, particularly financial transactions and facilities connected with the import and export of both capital goods and consumer goods and the exchange of services.

Financing: credits
- Financing facilities in favour of suppliers, from the date of placing an order up to delivery, or up to commissioning of the project in China.
- Financing of importers, foreign trade organisations, or the importer's bank for imports of goods and services into China.
- Financing of the down payment (normally 15 per cent) on capital goods and projects, as well as additional local costs.
- Allocation of financing packages for the delivery of capital goods from different countries, made available by Swiss Bank Corporation (Swiss and/or foreign

---

Swiss Bank Corporation, the only leading Swiss Bank with headquarters in Basle, Switzerland

branches) and/or other banks or bank groups (multi-source financing).
- Financing of imports of Chinese goods and services (fixed advances, current account, and/or discount facilities in favour of buyers or agents in or outside Switzerland).
- Intermediate financing of trade companies (fixed advances, current account, and/or discount facilities).
- Assistance for joint ventures with Chinese partners.
- Assistance for projects in third countries with participation of Chinese and Swiss entrepreneurs or sponsors.
- Granting of facilities with fixed interest rates for up to 10 years for Swiss francs and within the refinancing possibilities for other currencies.
- Granting of credits in Swiss francs or other convertible currencies on a rollover basis.
- Financing in the form of book credits or discount of bills of exchange with or without recourse to the seller of the bills.
- Swap agreements for currencies and/or interest rates tied to large export financings.
- Bid bonds, advance payment guarantees, and performance bonds for suppliers or trade companies.
- Guarantees for other services in favour of importers, exporters and trade companies.

Capital markets
Swiss Bank Corporation is one of the leading and most innovative banks in the Swiss capital market as a manager of domestic and foreign public bond issues, private placements and syndicated loans as well as share issues.

The bank has also been very successful in introducing a variety of foreign shares on the Swiss stock exchanges. In the foreign Swiss franc capital market, Swiss Bank Corporation (SBC) has continuously pursued its objective of being a major investment banker for Asian borrowers. In the Euromarkets, the investment banking subsidiary in London, Swiss Bank Corporation International (SBCI), holds a pre-eminent position as manager and comanager of Eurobond issues.

In 1984 SBC and SBCI together topped the list of bookrunners in the foreign sector of the Swiss capital market and counted as number one underwriters in the international market.

Payments: documentary transactions and money transfers
- Advising or confirming of letters of credit (including

transferable letters of credit or back-to-back letters of credit) in favour of suppliers of goods and services to China.
– Opening of letters of credit in favour of suppliers in China for deliveries to Switzerland or other countries.
– Collection of shipping or other documents, bills of exchange, cheques, and payment orders (with or without discount of the collection proceeds, etc.).
– Money transfers in Swiss francs and foreign currencies including eligible renminbi.

Foreign exchange: foreign currencies, banknotes and precious metals
– Purchase and sale of foreign currencies, cash and forward: in round or odd sums; one or more full months or years forward for value on a fixed date; with a fixed or flexible settlement date.
– Purchase and sale of banknotes.
– Sale and acceptance of traveller's cheques.
– Trading in foreign exchange and gold options.
– Purchase and sale of precious metals, cash and forward.

Other services: information, studies, counselling and reports
As a universal bank, Swiss Bank Corporation offers a comprehensive range of financial services including forfaiting, trade information, property management, and more. In many fields SBC publications provide up-to-date information on economic, monetary and commercial topics. A firm seeking commercial relations with China might be interested in the following:
– Credit and commercial information – worldwide.
– Written material on the economic development of the People's Republic of China or any other country.
– Information on projects, economic plans, and priorities in the People's Republic of China.

– Customs regulations on import and export of goods and services from and to the People's Republic of China.

Key facts and figures on the Chinese economy
Since December 1978, when China embarked on a policy of economic modernisation, the Chinese economy has undergone a major readjustment.

In a bid to attract foreign investment, China first (1979) opened four Special Economic Zones and later (1984) designated 14 coastal cities where foreign investors can form joint ventures, cooperative firms or wholly-owned enterprises. The creation of the Special Economic Zones also served to test the new and more liberal economic pattern. In the foreign trade sector, China's imports and exports have expanded rapidly. Between 1980 and 1984 exports increased at an average annual rate of 23 per cent and imports at a rate of about 21 per cent.

In spite of this impressive economic performance and the enthusiasm with which the Chinese are implementing their open door policies, it is important for foreign investors and trade partners to be well aware of the fact that business relations with China have to be developed on a gradual and progressive basis.

As is well known, in order to achieve its ambitious development targets, China has to overcome its short-comings in energy, transportation and communications. Since it cannot do this without overseas technology and know-how, foreign business opportunities will mainly arise in these three fields. Apart from this, the Chinese export industries require modernisation if they are to become competitive on international markets. In particular the quality, design and packaging of Chinese exports must improve over time. Since the biggest advantage China has on the export market is in labour-intensive

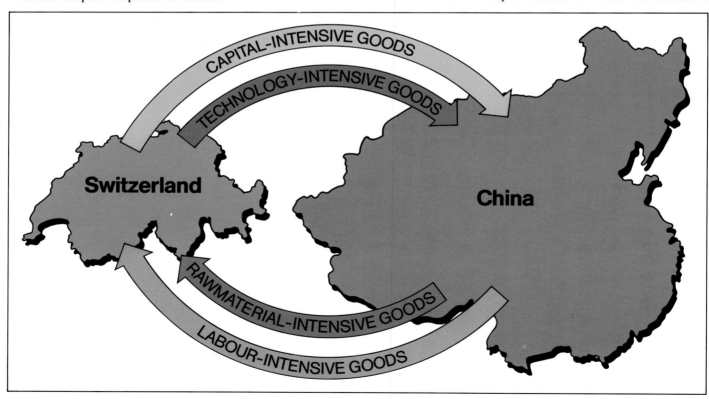

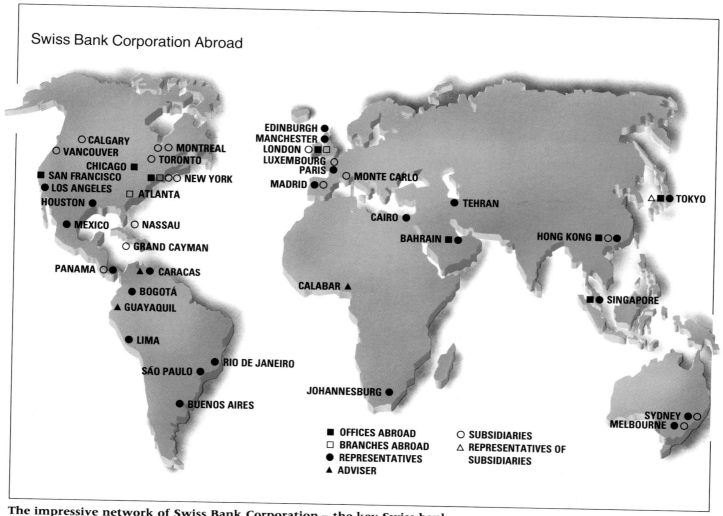

Swiss Bank Corporation Abroad

CALGARY ○
VANCOUVER ○
CHICAGO ■
SAN FRANCISCO ■
LOS ANGELES ●
HOUSTON ●
MEXICO ●
MONTREAL ○○
TORONTO ○
NEW YORK ■□○○
ATLANTA □
NASSAU ○
GRAND CAYMAN ○
PANAMA ○○
CARACAS ▲●
BOGOTÁ ●
GUAYAQUIL ▲
LIMA ●
SÃO PAULO ●
RIO DE JANEIRO ●
BUENOS AIRES ●

EDINBURGH ●
MANCHESTER ●
LONDON ○■□
LUXEMBOURG ○
PARIS ●
MADRID ●●
MONTE CARLO ●
CAIRO ●
TEHRAN ●
BAHRAIN ■●
CALABAR ▲
JOHANNESBURG ●

TOKYO △■●
HONG KONG ■○●
SINGAPORE ■●
SYDNEY ●○
MELBOURNE ●○

■ OFFICES ABROAD
□ BRANCHES ABROAD
● REPRESENTATIVES
▲ ADVISER
○ SUBSIDIARIES
△ REPRESENTATIVES OF SUBSIDIARIES

The impressive network of Swiss Bank Corporation – the key Swiss bank

products, the opportunities for overseas businesses are mainly in terms of supplying equipment and entrepreneurial management, and in possible joint ventures.

The composition of bilateral trade between Switzerland and China (see Exhibit 1) is remarkable for the absence of any significant exports of Swiss consumer goods. The dominant single export item is machinery (non-electrical and electrical), roughly constant (45 per cent) between 1979 and 1983. The Swiss chemical industry holds a fair export share of about 15 to 20 per cent. However, more recently (in 1983) exports of chemicals increased to 28 per cent. As for Swiss imports from China, the major product groups are textiles and clothing (around 50 per cent) and agricultural products (between 20 and 25 per cent). The composition of bilateral trade reflects the comparative advantages of the two countries. This pattern should continue to provide the basis for a mutually beneficial exchange of goods between Switzerland and China for a considerable time to come.

Exhibit 1 Breakdown of Swiss-Chinese trade by commodity groups

	1979		1983	
	US$m	% of total	US$m	% of total
Swiss exports to China	118.7		123.8	
Machinery		75.4		68.1
of which: Non-electrical machines		41.8		52.9
Electrical machines		16.2		14.4
Optical equipment and precision instruments		17.4		10.3
Watches		21.0		19.4
Other		3.6		3.0
Chemical industry		20.6		28.3
of which: Organic products		23.6		37.7
Dyes		73.9		16.2
Swiss imports from China	54.5		75.0	
Agricultural products		26.5		21.5
Textiles and clothing		48.6		50.2
Other		24.9		28.3

Sources: Schweizerische Aussenhandelsstatistik, Jahresbericht: Bezugs- und Absatzländer, Erster Teil 1983; own calculations.

Talk to the key Swiss bank – it helps to have an experienced banker on your side

Consult Swiss Bank Corporation, not only for advice on the mechanics of the transaction, but to work out creative overall solutions to complex problems. With our international tradition and our home base in multilingual Switzerland, we have helped put the finishing touches on a lot of trade packages over the years. All our clients can benefit from the experience and skills of our specialists, regardless of where their SBC branch is located. As you know, our special China Desk in Hong Kong has staff fluent in Cantonese and Mandarin.

Westpac's links with China

Westpac Banking Corporation is Australia's largest financial intermediator, conducting around 15 per cent of the total intermediation. It is the second largest bank in New Zealand, and also has substantial retail banking operations in Papua New Guinea and Fiji.

It has a significant network of representation in Asia, with offices in China, Hong Kong, Indonesia, Japan, Korea, Malaysia, the Philippines and Singapore. These offices promote and facilitate trade and business opportunities with the bank's South Pacific, European and American offices. In 1984 Westpac was the 75th largest bank in the world ranked by total assets, 48th by shareholders' equity, and 28th by profits.

Westpac's links with China trade date back to the late 19th century. However, the volume of trade between China and Australia up to 1945 was spasmodic, with total bilateral trade peaking at about US$21 million in the early 1930s.

The upturn in trade

It was not until the 1960s that Australia saw a major increase in trade with the People's Republic of China, spearheaded by long-term wheat sale contracts. Westpac recognised the importance of the People's Republic of China market from the outset of China's open door policy in 1972, and the implementation of its four modernisation programmes in 1979 brought further awareness of the opportunities to foster growth of business between China and the South-West Pacific. Westpac's involvement in providing financing for pre- and post-shipment trade and capital goods for its export customers to China, and financing their imports, has increased steadily in direct relationship to China's bilateral trade growth.

Westpac has had strong and mutually beneficial correspondent banking links with Bank of China for over 30 years. This strong association culminated in Westpac opening a representative office in Beijing in the summer of 1982 as an integral part of its Asian strategy plans.

The representative office has acted as a bridge between the bank's customer base and their Chinese counterparts in identifying the needs of each and then working towards their fulfilment.

Role of the Beijing office

In more specific terms the role of the office is to liaise with Chinese banking and financial institutions, selected government ministries, state, provincial and municipal authorities with the exchange of international financial and economic data, identifying foreign sources of supply

Westpac Banking Corporation head office, 60 Martin Place, Sydney

for strategic materials and partners for joint ventures, conducting business development activities with Chinese commercial and trade organisations and last, but not least, advising and assisting Westpac's customer base in doing business in China.

These activities are carried out nationwide with special attention given to Shanghai, Tianjin, Guangzhou, the four Special Economic Zones and a selected number of the 14 open port cities. These areas, the bank believes, show the greatest potential for trade and investment development for the immediate future.

While Westpac's financing to date has been predominantly in the field of trade, it also provides financial support to Australian and other foreign companies who have involved themselves in the China market by way of joint ventures and coproduction operations. In many ways Westpac and other Australian banks have complemented the activities of the Australian Trade Commissioner Service, particularly in identifying potential

Philip W. Deer, General Manager, Asian Division, Westpac Banking Corporation

opportunities for trade and investment. This is appropriate, if a coordinated Australian image is to be presented to the highly competitive Chinese market.

The bank's Beijing representative office is staffed by an expatriate Senior Manager with wide overseas experience in the corporate and international banking field, together with three local Chinese personnel allocated from the Foreign Enterprises Service Corporation. Additional technical and administrative support is supplied by the bank's Asian Division headquarters in Hong Kong.

Westpac is under no illusion about profit making in China. China remains sensitive to incurring foreign debt and will for some time to come continue to give priority to sourcing its borrowings from:
– World Bank and IMF bank loans and credits;
– foreign government grants and low interest loans and credits;
– commercial loans and credits at preferential rates and conditions.

International bankers are now negotiating with a comparatively small, but highly astute, conscientious and worldly-wise Chinese management. Increasingly, China looks to involve its own banks in projects requiring substantial financing.

Areas of expansion

However, there are still a number of areas where the Chinese banks seek assistance, particularly in the areas of:
– infrastructure project feasibility studies; and
– project financing, leasing and foreign exchange risk management.

These needs are being met by the foreign banking community in China, either individually or on a joint-venture banking/leasing basis.

Westpac Banking Corporation's physical presence in China is indicative of its firm belief that China will remain open to foreign investment. This belief is founded on the Chinese government's commitment to the development of the country's infrastructure, energy, communication and transport needs in addition to the modernisation of its manufacturing and industrial plants. This cannot all be achieved with self reliance or 'soft' loans, and China will eventually need to employ increased commercially orientated funding lines.

Westpac is in the People's Republic of China to participate in meeting these huge and diversified market needs over many years to come. An increased presence in China is under active consideration. Meanwhile, Westpac continues to promote and encourage growth of business through its substantial network utilising the experience and knowledge that has been developed to contribute to the emergence of China in the world's markets.

The authors

Robert Delfs

Robert Delfs joined the *Far Eastern Economic Review* as China Business Correspondent in 1981. He has also contributed articles to other publications including the London *Times* and the *China Business Review*. Based in Hong Kong, Delfs travels frequently in China and the Asian region. He has previously worked for the Washington-based National Council for US-China Trade, the Film Fund in New York and the Chinese Culture Center of San Francisco. A graduate of Stanford University, he attended Princeton University as a graduate student in Chinese history and studied Chinese and Japanese in Taipei and Tokyo.

Ronald J. Field

Ronald J. Field is Director of Public Relations, R. J. Reynolds Tobacco International Inc, a subsidiary of R. J. Reynolds Industries Inc, a diversified international corporation with major interests in a wide range of consumer products.

Robert Henriques Girling

Robert Henriques Girling is a Professor in the School of Business and Economics at California State University, Sonoma. He is Associate Director of the Institute for Public Management in Berkeley and a consultant to the World Bank and other international organisations. His book *Multinational Institutions and the Third World* (New York: Prager, 1985) deals with debt, trade and counter-trade.

Thomas D. Gorman

A graduate of Princeton University's East Asian Studies Department, Thomas D. Gorman is President and Publisher, China Consultants International (Hong Kong) Ltd. He has been a Hong Kong resident since 1974, and began travelling in the People's Republic of China in 1975 on behalf of China Consultants International.

He has written and spoken extensively on doing business with China, and has been Chairman, China Commercial Relations Committee, American Chamber of Commerce in Hong Kong (1979), Vice President, American Chamber of Commerce in Hong Kong (1983) and a member of the Executive Committee of the Society of Hong Kong Publishers (1983-84).

Owen D. Nee, Jr

Owen D. Nee, Jr is a partner of the international law firm Coudert Brothers, and is in charge of the firm's China practice. He is a graduate of Princeton University and Columbia University Law School, where he was a member of the Board of Editors of the *Law Review*. Nee first studied Chinese in the 1960s at the Chinese University of Hong Kong while serving as a Princeton-in-Asia Fellow at the University.

He first visited China in the early 1970s and over the past six years has commuted regularly between the firm's offices in Hong Kong and Beijing.

Leo G. B. Welt

A graduate of Princeton University, Leo G. B. Welt is President of Welt International Corporation, a Washington-based export trading company that assists and represents companies in their international business. He is also advisor to financial institutions and industrial corporations on barter and countertrade, and on establishing export trading companies.

Michael B. Yahuda

Michael B. Yahuda is Visiting Professor at the University of Michigan Political Science Department and Center for Chinese Studies. He is on special leave of absence from his position as Senior Lecturer at the London School of Economics. From 1982 to 1984 he was Professor of East Asian Studies at the University of Adelaide.

He is the author of numerous articles on Chinese politics and foreign relations in scholarly journals and has broadcast on such matters for the BBC. He is the author of *Towards the End of Isolationism, China's Policy after Mao* (London: Macmillan, 1983).

Acknowledgments

Many of the photographs in this book were provided by the individuals depicted or by their organisations. Other credits are to the Robert Harding Picture Library (the illustrations in the chart on pp. 14/15, and on pp. 34, 41, 58, 72, 87), the John Hillelson Agency (pp. 37, 51, 67, 68, 82, 179), the Camerapix Hutchinson Library (pp. 46, 75), Philip Sayer (pp. 6/7, 60, 163, 190) and the Xinhua News Agency (p. 68). The maps and charts were drawn by Richard Natkiel Associates. The book was designed by John White.